19 Castle Grove,
Kendal.

Dear Betty,

I _must_ write. An eternity has passed sinc...

Saturday ... It r...
time, but I hardly ... arag...
it began to suit m... d for...
I walked the stree... u, a...
you would not be ... ts of...
looking for you, a... d not...
went on to Lowetu... than...
you had once been there. I walked by the lake...
not a soul about. I stood under a tree and li...
rain on the leaves above. I was wretched. For...
I was not merely alone, but lonely. desperately...
folly, to have ... ch distance between us ...
instinct urge... ! I wanted...
you. I thou...

---

ch is not clear, you p...
your communications.
rences, sometimes vagu...
ncerning my past inter...
entirely unwarranted.
it would appear, the s...
of furtive downward gl...
willing prey to morbid...
e of sinister nocturnal...
never knew the real A...
y tendencies I have she...
They were quite superfi...
about 'hillocks' and 'v...
talise me, arouse no fe...
lky bosoms interest me...
pple curve it is with t...
... at the...

Dear Mr Vipond,

Your kind letter of 5th November h...
Gazette office.

Yes, you are right to criticise th...
drawing numbered 50. I was in the greatest o...
use it and did so only because I could not t...
now the place well, and have always come ac...
oardale, as many people will have (unless a...
ombustion engine, to quote your description...
eople, runs higher into the hills from the...
he drawing is a sort of no-man's-land, neit...
erhaps your suggestion of 'Howe Grain' migh...

I share your great regard for thi...
weekends, the motorists seem to have disc...
cnic. Which it is, but I wish they could...
r those who get there on foot. I remember...
d tranquillity, a very lovely backwat...

In fact, present...
ple...

---

38 Kendal Green,
KENDAL, Cumbria,
3rd September 1980

Dear Mr Scholes,

I am writing to inform you that I
have booked the Kirkland Hall in Kendal
for your talk on the Cumbria...
Thursday eve...

I a...
which was fo...
understand th...
recently been...
80 to 100 pe...
in Kendal oft...

I pr...
for sale in a...
for admission...

I wi...
date to see i...
making. I ass...
accommod...
being on...
in Wensl...
to have...

---

38 Kendal green, Kendal
2nd December 1985

dal's postmaster did what he was...
do, and it was an unexpected...
receive and read your letter and...

Through the mists of time I...
your handwriting on the envelope.
annot match your activities durin...
hat have passed. Foreign travel,...
ning mean nothing to me. You...
derful experiences to ...
ife has been unexciting...
ver been out of the...
Lancashire except for...
es. The highlands a...
have been my favourit...
ast 40 years and I ha...
the north of England,...

---

38 Kendal green. KENDAL

Dear Mr Davies.

It's a pleasure.
But why a London address
when Lakeland is at its enchanting
best?

Sincerely
awainwright

---

40 Westmorland Gazette.
Kendal

3rd December 1985

Dear Mr Wilkinson,

Thank you for your kin...
letter and enclosure. Yes...
I remember your earlier lett...
about the Howgills — still a...
very favourite area for me...
I often return to them.

You ought to be asham...
to assoc... your name we...

... C. How are the...
... llen? Their declin...
... ast ten years ha...
... ing. Perhaps...
... Rovers will take...
I still watch...
... vice a year.
... is not as...

A passion for the Lake District
and a passion for letter writing.
I guess this addresses two areas
of parental failure!

Andy & Becca, wishing you
a very happy Christmas 2011, and
all the best for 2012

Wendy & Simon

THE WAINWRIGHT LETTERS

The WAINWRIGHT LETTERS

Edited by Hunter Davies

F

FRANCES LINCOLN LIMITED

PUBLISHERS

Frances Lincoln Limited
4 Torriano Mews
Torriano Avenue
London NW5 2RZ
www.franceslincoln.com

A catalogue record for this book is available
from the British Library

ISBN 978-0-7112-3133-7

Printed and bound in China

9 8 7 6 5 4 3 2 1

Contents

Introduction

How many letters did Wainwright write? Who knows? In his book *Fellwanderer*, published in 1966, he wrote that he had had a 'constant stream of appreciative letters from all manners of folk and all sorts of unlikely places. Some were straight forward about accommodation and itineraries and mountain campsites and the like, and some simply recounted personal experiences and adventures. But a thousand I have kept, and I count them as treasures.'

So if he had at least 1,000 letters by 1966, after only ten years as a published author, then in the next twenty-five years of his writing life, by which time he had published another fifty-odd books, which had sold in all about 2 million copies, and he had also suddenly and surprisingly turned into a TV star, then his total output of letters in his writing life, counting in all the letters he wrote before he became well known, must surely, possibly, have reached 5,000. Maybe even 10,000 – which would still amount to writing only one letter most days for around thirty years.

AW – as we shall mainly call him from now on – lived and was brought up in a time of letter writing, when people wrote to each other all the time, before phones were common, and was employed in the sort of bureaucratic office during his working life where producing endless acres of words and figures was commonplace.

Right until almost the last few months of his life, he did answer all his letters, on his own, without any secretarial help, in either handwriting or typing. His method of replying was to let them build up like a cairn on his desk, then when it collapsed, start writing replies, hoping to get the cairn down.

While he did not care to meet strangers in the flesh, and always dreaded anyone coming to his front door, he was friendly and affable, personal and sometimes quite revealing in his letters. He clearly preferred having chums on paper rather than in person.

Perhaps the most interesting aspect of his letter writing was that even from the beginning, when he was unknown to the outside world, people treasured and retained his letters. Yet it was not as if he was doing a glamorous or important job, mixing with society, people in the arts or politics, or even in a position to give insight into local events. He was basically a clerk, then a trainee accountant, a functionary sitting in the corner of a dusty municipal office, but his fellow toilers, in their stiff collars, always kept his little letters, his drawings, his notes, his home made magazines, written just to amuse himself and his friends.

He had a good hand, so that was one reason. His writing looked attractive, was pretty to have and to hold, but the contents also gave pleasure, being amusing, informative, saucy, reflective. It also seems evident that his friends and colleagues did see something in him, something out of the ordinary, despite the fact that he had done nothing unordinary in his life, hence they found themselves retaining scraps, cartoons and any personal notes that he had done.

When he became relatively well known, it is then less surprising that people kept any letter from him. They knew him from his books, knew how attractive and unusual they were, so anything from him in his own hand was seen as a unique little bit of artwork, personal to the person who had received it. Most people also kept the envelope in which their letter had come. AW's handwriting, even of an address, had his personal, distinctive touch.

How many exist today? Again, one can only guess at a number. Some must have got lost, been destroyed. People have moved, died, their relations done clear-outs. Any from the early 1930s are hard to find – and I still have seen none from his childhood and youth in the 1920s. Perhaps he had no need to write letters at that stage, or no money for postage.

However, there is now a thriving market in his letters, and about six or so dealers and auction houses regularly have AW letters for sale (from about £50 to £500, depending on content) plus they pop up on eBay, but a great many people who personally received them have safely put them away, wanting them to be kept by their family, for ever, and have no desire to sell or offer them to the public.

I have been collecting and tracking down AW letters since 1994, which is the year I started working on his official biography. His widow Betty gave me full access to all his archives and documents – but of course they did not contain letters he had sent to other people. Fortunately, AW kept copies of all his own letters he thought vaguely important or interesting – either by writing out an exact copy or making a carbon copy, if he was typing, which he kept in his files, as a good accountant should. I never quite knew, of course, if the letter he actually sent was the same as the one he had kept, or if he had ever posted it, but Betty assured me his practice was to keep copies of letters sent. (As we shall see, there is one interesting example of answers to a Q. and A. which in fact he typed out but never sent.)

In the loft, stashed away, when I eventually went up there with Betty, we found a dozen or so boxes containing letters sent to AW over the decades. I looked for those who appeared to be the most regular correspondents, took down their addresses, and tried to contact them, asking for copies of letters AW had sent, and any memories or opinions of AW. Almost all of them had never met him, despite being apparently bosom penpals for years.

I also contacted many old colleagues who had known him or worked with him, in Blackburn and Kendal, including several elderly gentlemen then in their eighties, long retired who were still 'hammering the pension fund', so they told me with glee. This was how I came to see copies of his little office home-made booklets, done for amusement in the 1920s, which they had lovingly kept safe.

In the last couple of years, while editing this book, I did try to contact them again, in case I had missed any letters first time round, but alas I was mostly too late. They had died and often I failed to find out who had inherited their Wainwright material – but I think I had made copies of all their best letters.

When the biography first came out in 1995, lots of people wrote to me telling me they had AW letters. I asked them for photocopies, which they were all pleased to send, though at the time I did not know if or when I would ever edit the Wainwright Letters. Over these last sixteen years, I have also bought quite a few AW letters myself, or got copies from other collectors. Two years ago, when I started properly on the job of editing them, I also advertised, put the words around, asking people to contact me.

I have also been able to use letters belonging to the Wainwright Estate (which means Anne and Jane, the daughters of his widow Betty). I am grateful to all who have let me use their precious AW material.

From all these sources, I ended up with around 350 letters – not every one has been included here, as some were too short or repeated what was in other letters. I tried where possible to track down the recipient, find out who they were, why they had written to AW, but of course as time has gone on, this has become harder and harder.

Since the biography came out in 1995, interest in AW has grown greater. We now have the thriving Wainwright Society, founded on 9 November 2002, fifty years to the day when AW penned the first page of his first Pictorial Guide, with almost two thousand members. Programmes about Wainwright and his walks are regularly on radio and TV.

There was a bit of a lull in the book sales for a year or two after he died, though it still does not explain why Michael Joseph, in their wisdom, decided to stop publishing them. Fortunately, the rights were bought by Frances Lincoln in 2003, who now publish all the Pictorial Guides (updated by Chris Jesty) and other related AW books. Sales are now as healthy as they first were, back in the 1950s and 1960s. There seems no reason why the cult of Wainwright – which is what it has become – will not go on for ever.

Each year, more people achieve their ambition to climb all the 214 Wainwright Fells – while those newcomers to Lakeland, who don't realise they are on a so-called Wainwright fell, usually find out later, then rush to buy all the books, marvelling at those little works of art, wondering how on earth he did it, falling in love with the whole notion of Wainwright.

AW fans do tend to be very devoted – and very knowledgeable. Those who don't know him don't know him. Obviously. I mean by that that you do often have to explain to people unaware of the cult exactly who he was, what he did – and usually they shake their heads, disbelieving. You mean someone I haven't heard of has sold millions? You have to climb the fells, hold the guides, before true understanding and love set in. The Lakeland fells will be there for ever. We hope. So, undoubtedly, will AW fans.

In editing the letters, I had in mind that most readers will probably know something of his life, and his works, but some will not, so I had to try and make things as understandable as possible. I aimed to build up his life story, keep a narrative going, not jumping ahead of his letters by revealing events which have not yet happened.

In many edited books of Someone Quite Well Known's Letters, or even those of Someone Dead Famous, very often the letters get slapped down in pure chronological order, with minimal explanation, leaving the reader to work out what was going on, assuming they already know most of the highlights of his or her life.

The more academic volumes of letters offer masses of explanatory footnotes, either with astericks or numbers attached like sticky buds to each letter, sometimes each sentence, leading you to the bottom of the page, the end of the chapter or the end of the book. I always find this distracting, having to jump back and forward, ruining the flow. Often the footnote is fascinating in itself, if not always directly relevant, but you end up having forgotten where you were in the actual letter.

I had a big decision to make – totally self-created of course. I wanted to do notes – but do I offer the notes *before* or *after* the letter in question?

Adding notes after a letter is perhaps the more normal way. I did try it for the first twenty or so letters then decided that too often I was directing the reader back to the letter just read, thus slowing down the pleasure and flow of the letters themselves. I plumped instead for setting the scene before a letter or series of letters, explaining in advance any references, new names, coming up which might not otherwise be quite clear to all readers.

This does have the danger of giving away something interesting in a letter before you have come to it, and possible repetitions, but I reckoned it made for a smoother read, without recourse to going back, jumping around.

So, please note well – the editorial notes almost always come *before* the letter or letters you are about to read. Now and again, particularly at the end of a Part, I might have a note after a letter or letters, but this is just to sum up, tie up that Part. Well, I made these rules. I can break them.

I have arranged the letters into Parts, as opposed to Chapters, as this is not a biography or a novel. Roughly, each Part has a theme or connection, or the letters in that Part are all to the same person.

In real life, all of us have different things going on at the same time, separate problems and dramas, irritations and pleasures, work and leisure, all running concurrently – but in a book, even one comprised of letters, I felt it made it easier to understand and appreciate if somehow main events and major players are served up roughly on different plates, in separate takes.

In presenting the letters, I have stuck almost always to the true chronology, laying out the letters in each Part in the order of the dates they were written, but for the sake of collecting a topic or a person together, some letters in one Part often overlap with the Part which has come before or after. Not all Parts do have a clear theme or topic, being simply assorted letters to assorted people during the years in question, but that was my aim – to give some shape to the story, see his character and people developing.

I have given his full address in the early letters, where he included it, as it is interesting to see where he was and what notepaper he was using. Once the letters progress, and he is settled in his life and habits, he mainly uses two addresses – either c/o Westmorland Gazette, Kendal or 38 Kendal Green, Kendal, which was his home, and only the favoured few had that revealed. Now and again I have deleted paragraphs in certain letters if he is repeating things he has said elsewhere. I have left unchanged Wainwright's spelling, grammar and underlinings, but now and again have rationalised his punctuation, to make things flow.

He was almost always punctilious in giving the exact date, but now and again, when he didn't, I have had to guess from internal or other evidence and have put a question mark after the date given.

If my estimate is correct, that in fact he wrote up to 10,000 letters, then there are loads still out there, waiting to tracked down, collected, copied and then, you never know, edited into another fascinating, amusing, informative, excellent read for all AW lovers, everywhere . . .

Brief Early Biography

The letters begin in 1932, when he is aged twenty-five, and after that, the editorial notes fill in the main biographical events in his life as it unfolds, but it is perhaps useful to give some details about what had happened beforehand. (As for the books he went on to write, a full list of all those he eventually published, with dates, is given at the end of this book, for those who might wish to refer to them while reading the letters.)

Alfred Wainwright was born on 17 January 1907 in Blackburn, Lancashire, the youngest of four children. He had two sisters, Alice (born 1894) and Annie (born 1900) and a brother Frank (born 1896).

His father Albert was a stonemason, originally from Penistone in Yorkshire. He travelled around for his work, in Yorkshire and Lancashire, was unemployed for long periods and also drunk, often for equally long periods. His mother Emily, née Woodcock, was hard working and god fearing and brought up her family in clean if impoverished respectability. Emily had several sisters one of whom, Annie, they remained in close touch with and AW was friendly with his cousin Eric, son of Annie, who lived in Penistone.

Their rented family house, where AW grew up, at 331 Audley Range, Blackburn, was two up, two down, with no inside bathroom or lavatory, surrounded by cottons mills. AW went to the local council school, Accrington Road Elementary, then on to what was called a Higher Elementary, Blakey Moor School.

AW was tall and thin and had bright red hair and while at school had to put up with shouts and taunts of 'Carrots'. He was good at maths, English and drawing, but left school at thirteen, as did most children of his age and class. He secured what was seen as a most enviable job, for a boy of his background and education, as an office boy in the Borough Engineers' Department, working at Blackburn Town Hall.

After three years, he moved to the Treasurer's Department, where the chance of advancement was considered much better. To catch up with his colleagues in the new office, most of whom had come from a grammar school, he had to pass various examinations for which he studied at night school. Having done that, he then began the long slog of qualifying as a municipal accountant, which took many years and was done mainly by correspondence. In the office, to amuse his fellow trainee accountants, he wrote and illustrated little booklets called *The Pictorial Gazette*, in which he mocked superiors and poked fun at his colleagues. His fellow trainees were men but there were girls in the outer office, typists or secretaries, whom the young men spent a lot of time discussing.

AW's first visit to the Lake District came in 1930 when he went on a holiday with his cousin Eric now working as a clerk on Penistone Council.

AW said that this first trip to the Lakes changed his life for ever. He planned to go again, the following year, 1931 and became determined somehow, some day, to live and work in Lakeland rather than amongst the dirt and squalour of urban Lancashire, without knowing how and when he would ever achieve this ambition.

Part 1
Letters to Eric Walter Maudsley, 1932–41

On Christmas Eve, 1931, Wainwright, aged twenty-four, got married to Ruth Holden, aged twenty-one, his first ever girlfriend. She was a mill girl who lived locally and attended the same church as AW: Furthergate Congregational. Both her parents had died and she lived with her sister Dora in Artillery Street, Blackburn. After their marriage, AW moved in with Ruth and her sister and lived there for two or three months, before they acquired their own house.

On the wedding certificate, AW's job was given as clerk in the Borough Treasurer's Office. He was still studying, mainly by correspondence, to become a qualified municipal accountant. He had passed the intermediate part of his exams, though it was another two years, after several attempts, before he passed his final exams.

Eric Walter Maudsley – sometimes addressed as Walt or Walter but later more usually as Eric – was born in 1910 and had worked with AW in the Treasurer's office in Blackburn as a fellow trainee accountant. AW and Maudsley, along with two other office friends (Jim Sharples and Harry Driver) had spent the Whitsuntide holidays of 1931 in the Lake District. AW had planned the holiday meticulously, promising them that in one week they would see every lake, every mountain, every valley. AW had been over ambitious and they never covered as much as he had hoped. But they had a good time, chaps together from the office, out on the fells. In 1932, Maudsley had moved from the Blackburn office to Carlisle.

LETTER I: TO ERIC WALTER MAUDSLEY, 1932?

The Love Nest,
Artillery St.
Blackburn.

Dear Walt,

What poignant (pron. 'pwannant') memories did my old familiar writing on the label bestir? None, probably. Remember that poignant moment at Watendlath when we parted company? – that poignant night at Rosthwaite when we sunk so low as to use the utensil 'neath our bed?

Annexed please find text-books as requested. I have not yet re-commenced the stud.

Well, sonny. I have been thinking a lot about the Lakes of late – Striding Edge, that view of Gable from Kirk Fell, the solitude of Burnmoor Farm, Dale Head, Ill Bell, and a host of other memories give me little rest, and I shall shortly be in the throes of another Gigantic Walking Tour Programme for Whitsun, 1932, but my companion this time will be the wife. Poignant memories!

Let me know sometime how you are getting along.

Alf

AW never did go on that trip to the Lakes with his wife Ruth – in fact there is no record of him ever going on any sort of walk with her. Just over a year later, something clearly was beginning to go wrong with the marriage – judging by his next letter, paragraph numbered 5 and headed Married Life – which he left totally blank.

The other news in this March 1933 letter (having been prompted to write it by Bob Alker, another office colleague) included the birth of AW's son, Peter, and the fact that, along with others in his office, he had failed the latest part of his exams.

The letter contains the latest news and gossip from the Blackburn office. Paragraph 9, 're Cut Shop', could possibly refer to Betty Ditchfield, assistant secretary to the Borough Treasurer, after whom AW, along with most of the other young men in the office, lusted, but without any success or even encouragement.

AW and Ruth and their baby Peter moved into a two-bedroom semi-detached house at 90 Shadsworth Road, Blackburn, in 1934, a more desirable residence, befitting a newly qualified municipal accountant. During the next six years, he went off on lots of walks – locally with groups from the office, to Yorkshire, the Pennines, Scotland and the Lakes.

In 1939, along with some of his office friends, he founded the Blackburn Rovers Supporters' Club. Ruth took no part in the club, nor in the walks, and it could be that one of the attractions of these two activities was getting out of the house, escaping from Ruth and whatever was going wrong in their marriage. Maudsley meanwhile had moved in 1939 from Carlisle to a post in Hertford, where he stayed until 1942 when he was called up for the army and sent to Burma. AW had not been called up. His job was looked upon as vital to the war effort and his call up papers had for the moment been deferred. In late 1940, or perhaps early 1941, for the letter is not dated, he wrote to Maudsley in Hertford, describing a trip to the Lakes he had done with his son Peter, now aged eight. The reference to 'Methods of Blocking the Female Form' might possibly be about some nude magazine he had sent Maudsley – or just some joke. The letter is on Blackburn Rovers Suporters' Club headed notepaper – showing that AW was Treasurer and Acting Secretary. Perhaps a bit of boasting, showing Maudsley the good times he and the rest of the chaps were still having in Blackburn.

LETTER 2: TO ERIC WALTER MAUDSLEY, 19 MARCH 1933

Blackburn
19th March 1933

Dear Walt

Mr Acker told me that you have told him that you would like to hear from me, so I have pleasure in submitting the following information which may be of interest.

1 <u>re Students Society</u>
I have been appointed convener for this area, and am pleased to note your appointment to your local committee

2 <u>re Rev Townson, of Great Harwood</u>
He's left

3 <u>re I.M.T.A Exams, Jan 1933</u>
<u>RESULTS</u>

COMPTON	INTER.	FAILED
PANTER	PART 1.	FAILED
WAINWRIGHT	"	FAILED
ALKER	PART 2.	FAILED
SELLERS	"	FAILED
WOLSTENCROFT	"	FAILED

What's the B.C.A motto?

4 <u>re Film Service</u>
Now a highly efficient machine. Files remain in the hands of Mr Haworth, who has now less time for municipal accountancy. Mr Sye now

rings 'too long' before he decides which pictures to visit. If you have visited the Karlisle Kinemas recently, I should be pleased to have reports on what you have seen (on the screen, not the back row).

5 <u>re Married Life</u>

6 <u>re Parenthood</u>
On the 15th Feb 1933, at Parkside Maternity Home, Queens Road, to Mr & Mrs. A Wainwright (nee Ruth Holden) a son – vide 'Northern Daily Telegraph'

7 <u>re Furthergate Branch, Yorkshire Penny Bank</u>
Little activity. Present pen-nib has been in use over 3 years.

8 <u>Furthergate Church</u>
Now an exceedingly prominent member. Pleased to hear of your call to office in the service.

9 <u>re Cut Shop</u>
Frequent visits continue to be made by the top desk junior. Demands for 'new thrills' are made daily, but are seldom satisfied.

10 <u>re Lake District</u>
Spent a glorious week in June last. Sharples is now preparing plans for a 'sleeping bag' holiday, ie. Taking sleeping bag (weight 1lb) and blanket and sleeping out. Entertainment? Please let me have details of any excursions you may have made.

11 <u>re Ault Lang Syne</u>
You are forgotten at Blackburn, just as I told you. You are never mentioned – nobody cares a hang what is happening to you. Remember our talks on this subject?

12 <u>re Making Water</u>
Do you recall that night in bed at Rosthwaite when you wanted to use the po chamber, but modestly forbade? And your immortal words: 'Well I might as well – it's what it's there for' ha, ha!

AW

LETTER 3: TO ERIC WALTER MAUDSLEY: 1940?

BLACKBURN ROVERS SUPPORTERS' CLUB

Chairman: F.P HASLAM, Esq.

President: W.H DUCKWORTH, Esq.

Hon Secretary: J.L.CROOK, Esq. (With H.M Forces)

Vice Chairman: N McLEOD, Esq.

Hon. Treasurer & Acting Secretary: A. Wainwright, Esq.,

90 Shadsworth Road,
Blackburn
Wednesday night.

Dear Walter,

I have just received your urgent letter of the 11th.

Your briefly-mentioned plans for you holiday fill me with envy. I am just back from a week at Keswick, where I have been fulfilling the pleasant and long-awaited task of introducing my infant son to the Loveliness of Lakeland. Keswick is crowded at present with a well-to-do set who have made it their home for the duration (how your Socialistic soul will writhe at the sight of them!) and there are a great many London evacuees. The food problem is rather acute, and we had to manage as best we could with bed and breakfast, which is all that most places will provide. But around Keswick there are the same hills, the everlasting hills, always changing and yet never-changing. On these hills you will meet just a few happy youths and maidens. The ridges we tramped in days of yore are still there as wild and lonely as ever, and you will find that their appeal is as insistent as ever before. So I envy you, for I fear I shall not be in their company again this year.

Your time is almost too short to expect a reply from Wasdale before the 21st, and I think that at this time of the year, with the school holidays finished, you could almost risk going over to Wasdale on the chance of getting accommodation. However, the address of the Place Perfect is Mrs M.E. Ullock, Wasdale Head Hall, Gosforth, Cumberland. The Hall, now a farm, is on the shore of the lake, just below the Burnmoor track (where we once flogged weary feet on a day notable for W.E.M's reticence to pee in a pot), two miles from the inn. Failing this, there is Mrs Wilson at Burnthwaite Farm, which is not quite the place it was, a cottage at Row Head, by the inn, and of course the inn itself. As a last resort, you could spend a night in the church. I should be very interested to know how you fare.

As a foretaste of things to come I enclose a card I bought in Keswick, intending to send it to you, but due to the constant attentions of my offspring it so happened that I had no time for card – and letter – writing.

I presume you received the weighty tome on Methods of Blocking the Female Form; again I intended to follow this with a letter, but didn't. The road to Hell is paved with good intentions, and alas, I am well on my way there. Damn those snails: I can't forget them. I shall be very pleased to see you on your way to the Lakes; if you are staying overnight in Blackburn, or for a day or two, we might be able to have an hour or two together, or maybe half a day.

We are winning the war.

Yours sincerely

AW

Again he writes on the Supporters' Club notepaper a very cheerful letter, about all the new people he is meeting. Once the war began, lots of men in the office did go off, and their places were often taken by women – younger, rather attractive single women, which was a moral booster for those left behind, doing vital work.

'Pennine Campaign' was an illustrated journal he had written during and after his two-week solo walk across the Pennines two years previously in 1938 – his first attempt at a walking book. He even produced a pretend report of it, as if written by a publisher's reader, and a booklet announcing its publication. It is not known if he sent it to any real publishers, but it was a serious attempt at a book and he let many of his friends read it, wanting their opinion and suggestions about getting it published. But now the war was on, with paper and other restrictions, there was even less chance of any publisher taking it.

LETTER 4: TO MAUDSELY, 2 FEBRUARY 1941

BLACKBURN ROVERS SUPPORTERS' CLUB

Chairman: F.P HASLAM, Esq.   President: W.H DUCKWORTH, Esq.

Hon Secretary: J.L.CROOK, Esq. (With H.M Forces)   Vice Chairman: N McLEOD, Esq.

Hon. Treasurer & Acting Secretary: A. Wainwright, Esq.,

90 Shadsworth Road,
Blackburn
Feb. 2nd 1941

Dear Walt,

It is the Sabbath day. This morning I climbed the hill to Belthorn to worship in the little chapel there, and returned feeling well rewarded: the trudge through the snow was really invigorating, the service was good, but best of all were the magnificent views from the top of the hill. The panorama ranged from Darwen Moors to Pendle, and there was a glimpse of snowclad hills far beyond in the north. High in the blue sky glinted a silvery cluster of barrage balloons over Clayton – a recent innovation this. It was a brilliant morning, and for the first time this year there was warmth in the sun.

I thought of holidays. I thought of winding tracks midst purple heather, of streams tumbling down the mountain-side, of the wind high up on the ridge, of the summit cairn. I thought of beer and strange beds. Son, I fretted for the hills.

I feel that my days of solitary wandering are drawing to a close. I find myself in demand by others who would fain share the blissful secrets I have found in lonely places, and, frankly, I feel the prospect of tutoring them quite pleasing to contemplate. I shall never lose the urge to be off on my lonesome, but there is much to be said, too, for good company.

So I have been making half-promises these past few weeks. I have requests for walking-tours from my son, from a man of 36 and from a boy of 16, whilst a new addition to our staff, a blonde of 27, is making the most alarming hints. The man of 36 will have to wait for another year, and the blonde of 27 will have to wait for ever. She has, however, a passionate regard the Lake District akin to my own, and, although she has been with us only a fortnight, we get along extremely well. Her home is called 'Blencathra'; she is married, not happily I suspect. As for the boy of 16, he is the son of a woman with whom I am at present on most intimate terms, and the happiest and jolliest lad I've ever come across. He'd enjoy himself immensely, and so would I, and I certainly intend to arrange a week with him during the summer. He'll have the time of his life.

At present I seem to have more friends than I've ever had. Until a couple of years ago, I had none. I used to call Lawrence Wolst and Jim Sharples my friends, and still do, of course, but I never sought their company after office hours. I knew nothing of the pleasures of entertaining companions. That's all changed now. The most profitable evening I ever spent was the night when the Supporters' Club was formed. I was elected to office, and put my whole heart into making it a success. I've been rewarded a thousand times. The committee meetings became a joy to my starved soul: there I found bright talk and laughter and beer, and it suited. I made friends, easy-going friends but the best in the world. Better still, with their help I rid myself of an accursed complex: it became easier to meet other people, and to be friendly with them, too. I have become a favourite with the ladies! And I like them a lot. Nowadays I never need to spend a night moping and sighing: the trouble is to resist all the invitations I get for a night out.

Which all fits in with one of your pet theories, doesn't it? How are all your romances faring? You're growing to be an old buggar now, you know; it's high time you were making a move. Don't be too careful in your choice; whoever you select, you'll be disappointed, but safe, at least, from the succession of disappointments that have marked your erratic career so far.

I am looking forward to meeting you at the Green Man, Ashbourne, at Easter. I don't know yet what holidays will be granted, but assume we shall have a decent weekend. I have arranged to travel south with Irene Wyatt, en route to visit her solider husband, and to pick her up on the return journey.

Please let me have 'Pennine Campaign' at an early date. Every day the afore-mentioned blonde comes round to my desk and pushes her soft breasts into me and whispers 'Have you got it back yet?'. I am anxious that she should have it, even though that may mean that she will no longer push her soft breasts into me, which same operation, by the way, I could endure until Judgment Day.

With best wishes.

AlfW

Not content with the Supporters' Club, AW then helped to begin the Pendle Club – named after Pendle Hill, a local beauty spot near Blackburn. Many of his office friends joined in, along with their wives, but there is no sign of Ruth in all this jollity.

Over the next six months, he continues to have good times with his clubs. He makes several Lakeland visits, spends time walking with Maudsley in Derbyshire and gets a pay rise at work.

LETTER 5: TO ERIC WALTER MAUDSLEY, 21 FEBRUARY 1941

BLACKBURN ROVERS SUPPORTERS' CLUB

Chairman: F.P HASLAM, Esq.   President: W.H DUCKWORTH, Esq.

Hon Secretary: J.L.CROOK, Esq. (With H.M Forces) Vice Chairman: N McLEOD, Esq.

Hon. Treasurer & Acting Secretary: A. Wainwright, Esq.,

90 Shadsworth Road,
Blackburn
21st February 1941

Dear Walt,

Forgive my neglect to reply promptly to your welcome letter, but this has been my first evening at home for some time. Not that I've been particularly busy at work, no it isn't that; it's this blessed circle of friends I mentioned before who seem to have set their hearts on establishing me as a social lion, and whose blandishments and entreaties I find hard to refuse, the one unfortunate aspect being that I come crawling home in the small hours, somewhat shamefacedly and in no condition to perform my normal functions as a husband and sadly conscious that I am an erring father.

Tonight I have an opportunity to reflect, for the first time in weeks, on the progress I have made in certain spheres, and my meditations are certainly sobering. I am spending pounds as easily as I used to spend shillings; I am carrying on affairs with half-a-dozen women, all of whom are ready to lie down with me when I give the word; I am consorting with fellows whose incomes run into thousands; I am shifting shandies at an alarming rate, and even whisky has passed my lips of late. What am I to do? I cannot withdraw from these new commitments, I am being carried along willy-nilly, with no hope of escape: I am heading for ruination. I recite to myself at frequent intervals 'C'est la guerre' and this soothes my conscience a little.

I am being persistently urged by the girls in the office to form a rambling club, and this appeals to me hugely, for it is an idea I have secretly nursed in my skinny bosom for many years only to postpone it after a review of the meager female company available.

But now things are different: the office is crammed with plump juicy specimens who are itching for excitement. So I am contemplating forming THE PENDLE CLUB, an association for cultured young men and women interested in walking. The blonde I told you about is as keen as mustard. Perhaps you better send me that Manual of Sexual Methods; I'd like to read it, in case the Pendle Club has a wet day, and I fancy the blonde would take to Method 34 like a duck to water. Send it, will you, please?

I felt flattered at your references to the success my book is having in Hertford, but tell my readers to be bloody handy, will you? – I want it back quick.

I'll see you at the Green Man on Easter Saturday, and if you want to bring 2 women it's okay by me. Don't think I've gone altogether depraved – I've started smoking a pipe which is an infallible indication of inherent decency. N'est pas?

AlfW

LETTER 6: TO ERIC WALTER MAUDSLEY, 1941?

The Pendle Club

Chairman: L Wolstenholme, Esq.   Vice Chairman: A. Wainwright, Esq.

Hon Treasurer: R. Alker, Esq.   Hon Secretary: Mrs Dorothy Coleman

Blencathra, West Leigh Road, Blackburn

Sunday,

Dear Eric,

At last I have a letter from you! Every day these past months has dawned with a promise of news from Hertford – and closed with bitter disappointment. No word! I was forgotten, forsaken, I told myself. My heart grew cold and hard towards you.

Then, last week, came a note in familiar writing, and out of the very winter of discontent was born new hope; as I read, the winding tracks amongst the heather seemed to be very near again. Holidays again! How I yearn for a few days release from the bondage!

I have yet no official news of the Easter vacation, and base the following remarks on the assumption that I must return on the Sunday evening. I shall travel south on Friday morning and arrive Derby in the early afternoon and be in Ashbourne at teatime. So please book a room for me at the Green Man, and we will spend the evening visiting the flicks and consuming mineral waters.

You will observe with your customary shrewdness that the Pendle

Club has come into being, but alas, far from being a rambling club, it is already developing into an association of Mature Men and Young Ladies Who Have No Dread Of Pregnancy. The idea was originally good and completely moral, but so far the primitive urge to sit in a dark cinema and play with the genital organs of a member of the opposite sex has been paramount in our thoughts, and there has been very little walking done. Hence our practice to date has been to clear off to a strange town (Clitheroe, usually), have tea, and then do a bit of groping on the back row of the local picturedome.

Your Manual of Sexual Methods has not yet arrived, in spite of your assurances; I am anxious to discover whether certain of my own devices have been publicly recognized; if not, I shall be able to affix an allonge for the benefit of subsequent readers.

What I'm much more concerned about is the fate of my Pennine Campaign. WHERE THE HELL IS IT? There are several people here panting to read it; must I forever put them off with feeble excuses? Get it back TODAY and send it on to me TONIGHT. The Hon. Secretary of the Pendle Club has promised that I can so-and-so her when I produce it, but not before, and I should like to get this done on Thursday night before joining you the day after, as it appears from your letter that I must be continent during the weekend.

So you'll book the Green Man for Friday and get there yourself for teatime if possible. BRING PLENTY OF CIGARETTES; they are unobtainable in Blackburn. I'll bring some matches.

AW

LETTER 7: TO ERIC WALTER MAUDSLEY, 9 APRIL 1941

> 90 Shadsworth Road
> Blackburn
> 9th April 1941

Dear Eric,

Your latest letter has caused a quiver of apprehension – it appears we shall have difficulty in getting beds, never mind bedmates.

I shall proceed to Ashbourne as early as possible on Friday, and shall be standing on the pavement outside the Green Man, clothed in rags at one of the following times

2pm	exactly
4pm	do
6pm	do
8pm	do

If possible, I shall be there when the clock strikes two. If I am, and you are not, I shall walk away and return at four. And so on, at two hour intervals until you appear. Do you the same.

I should most urgently counsel you to get an extra gallon of petrol and bring the car into Ashbourne with you, so that if accommodation is unobtainable, we could as a last resort push the car into a woodland glade and sleep in it.

Should we both arrive early we could of course be away from Ashbourne and stuck well into Dovedale by nightfall.

I shall return home on Sunday evening. You'll have had enough of my coarse humour by then. Bring a camera and plenty of cigarettes.

'Manual of Sexual Knowledge' has arrived safely, thanks. Have you dispatched 'Pennine Campaign'?

See you Friday, son.

I'm looking forward to it.

Alf

LETTER 8: TO ERIC WALTER MAUDSLEY, 17 APRIL 1941

> 90 Shadsworth Road
> Blackburn
> 17th April 1941.

Dear Eric,

I last saw you, a lonely disgruntled figure, on the Black Rocks at Cromford, and this is what happened to me afterwards: I went down the hill into Cromford and proceeded at a good pace northwards to Matlock, arriving there at 2.15 to discover to my chagrin that there was no train til 5.36. Matlock's shops were all closed, and the whole place was enveloped in a familiar Sabbath atmosphere, so I retraced my steps to Matlock Bath, where, by comparison, there was lots of life and plenty of opportunities to spend money. I had a 3s 3d tea, and, after passing the shop several times, finally expended a shilling on the current 'Sun Bathing Review', this purchase being effected without a blush. A disappointing book, though – no hairs on. Arrived at Manchester at 7 to find there was no train til 9.40, so went across to the bus station and returned by bus, getting home at 9.30. The later stages of the journey were made miserable by an acute shortage of smoking material. I had conserved the five cigs as far as possible, but the last one turned into ashes in Manchester, and as I had already scraped out the corners of my pouch, I was left completely destitute all the evening, and was not able to satisfy the craving until Monday noon.

And now I am back to the familiar life, women fore and aft and right and left, and find myself besieged with invitations. Absence, it seems, had made their joint and several hearts grow even fonder. Dorothy is treasuring her letter, 'the loveliest I ever received' she says. Doris thought hers was 'beautiful' and has returned it for me to preserve for her out of her hubby's reach. Both wanted me to take them for a walk last night (after much indecision, I chose Doris). If ever they meet and swop confidences I shall have to flee the town: could you then find me a job? Anyway, I have made them both wonderfully happy: what does it matter that I have sacrificed honour? I told them about your disturbed first night and confided that I must have been dreaming about them, and this pleased them greatly. Are these white lies? I think they are.

What of you? The gloom of Wirksworth was biting deep into your soul when I departed from you: the holiday was a disappointment to you, n'est ce pas? The time at our disposal was too short for a proper expedition to be planned, and the weather was lousy, but I thoroughly enjoyed it: I found your blasé sophistication and naïve innocence stimulating.

Yet I sensed that you are not a happy man, or only superficially so. There's something missing in your life, Maudsley lad, and it will still be missing when your salary runs into four figures. I told you what it was and I tell you again: go and find a little hole to put your old man in. Remember the snails, and go and do likewise.

I have just written to Wasdale Head for accommodation for Whitsun for Doris and myself and her husband and son. Later in the year Dorothy and I are going hiking in the Lakes; this might develop into an organized holiday of the Pendle Club, and if so, there will be a sincere invitation for you to come: imagine us all strewn in couples along Langstrath after the fashion of the Dovedale snails!

I should be interested to know how you fared on the return journey, and if and when and how the black mood passed, and I should be positively delighted to receive 'Pennine Campaign' by return of post. Blessed if I can get that book of yours back from Billy Ashton yet; I think he must be making a copy of it!

AlfW

LETTER 9: TO ERIC WALTER MAUDSLEY, 28 APRIL 1941

90 Shadsworth road
Blackburn
28th April 1941

URGENT

Dear Eric,

Doris has had a breakdown in health, and is going to the seaside on Thursday to rest for a few days.

It is my earnest desire that she should have 'Pennine Campaign' to read during this Period.

The matter is particularly urgent. Will you please recover the book and send it on immediately? If you will I will return it afterwards.

AW

URGENT

LETTER 10: TO ERIC WALTER MAUDSLEY, 4 JULY 1941

90 Shadsworth
Blackburn
4th July 1941

Dear Eric,

Glad to hear from you again, sonny, and to note from your letter evidence of a return to better humour after your harrowing experience at Wirksworth.

Yes 'Pennine Campaign' came back quite safely, thank you, but I believe you have somewhere two other publications of the Shad Press, viz

1. 'Alpine Adventure', 1939
2. 'British Lakeland Climbing Expedition 1940', complete with graphs etc.

I still peep furtively at times at your Manual of Sex, and can say definitely that the Posterior Seated Position has nothing to commend it. I'll let you have the book back shortly.

I was at Keswick for Whitsuntide: couldn't get a bed so went up Skiddaw and watched the sun rise from the top: a wonderful experience. Food was scarce, breakfast being the only meal obtainable and there was a queue a mile long outside the chip shop.

In these circumstances I felt myself quite unable to recommend an organized expedition, for I hear that every place in the Lakes is the same and hundreds are sleeping under the hedges at night. So this summer it's every man for himself. Next year the war will be over and things will be back to normal, and then the Pendle Club will venture forth en masse.

I am, however, going to Keswick for the week July 26 to August 2nd, having booked a bed, but as I shall be taking my infant son, activity will be restricted and I don't think you'd like to join us even if you could get a room and food.

Possibly I shall go north again in September – if so, I'll let you know. Best wishes to you and the snails.

AW

LETTER 11: TO ERIC WALTER MAUDSLEY, 5 SEPTEMBER 1941

90 Shadsworth road
Blackburn
5th September 1941.

Dear Eric.

I received my Baddeley and map safely, thank you, but was considerably surprised, almost alarmed, to get them so early. You must have dispatched them on the Saturday, yet I thought your stay was to extend until the following Tuesday, and you are not usually so prompt in returned other people's possessions. Did anything go wrong? Did vile weather send you scampering off back home, prematurely, away from a storm-wracked Wasdale? Surely not! Armed and fortified with Dunn's Supreme Headgear the weather would have no terrors for you. What else then could have happened? Was not one of the horde of females rapeable? Nor Hazel? Or perhaps you found after all that the solitude had no longer any appeal and hankered for the bright lights and jolly company of the drink-loving mob in Hertford. Fie on you!

I am most anxious to have the details of your holiday. Did you have a squint at Broad Stand, go up Lord's Rake? How did you like Wasdale head Hall?

If you returned before the Tuesday you would not receive the letter I posted to you at the week-end, although possibly Mrs Ullock has sent it on. In that letter I asked if you would kindly forward me a big consignment of Three Nuns Baccy when conditions were favourable. Will you, please, when they are?

My love to Longland. I shall never forget the noble manner in which he brought the Sherpas safely down to the North Col.

LETTER 12: TO ERIC WALTER MAUDSLEY, SEPTEMBER 1941

Dearest Eric, or Little by Little;

Many thanks for the card received this morning; as it does not depict a human being adhering impossibly to a rocky bastion I confidently await a second one.

The weather ere has verged on the putrid all week, with high winds and rain; often I have thought of you tirelessly pacing the hills, pondering deeply on your New Order, shielded from the downpour by Dunn's Latest and Greatest Creation. I cannot join you, alas, despite the added incentive of a horde of blockable women. Go to it, son. I recommend Method 7b. I have today celebrated an increase of salary by sending 2-14-0 to the publishers of Smythe's PEAKS AND VALLEYS, A CAMERA IN THE HILLS, MY ALPINE ALBUM and THE MOUNTAIN SCENE for a copy of each: these are magnificent books and I advise you to follow suit.

Well, how is the gradient on Brown Tongue; any easier than of yore? What of the merciless scree in Hollow Stones? Had a look at Broad Stand yet? Got lost on Lord's Rake? Oh boy, the mere mention of the names tears my heart out. How I would like to be there!

Remember me to Mrs Ullock, please. Last time I was there she was seriously considering an assault on Scafell; has she tackled it yet? I'll bet she hasn't.

Good hunting during the few hours that remain to you.

AW

AFTERTHOUGHT: when returning Baddeley will you please send also a consignment of 3 nuns, if possible?

On 8 October 1941 AW had some big news to tell Maudsley. In September, Bob Alker, one of his colleagues in the office, had spotted an advertisment for a job. It was the last day for application, but AW decided to apply all the same. He got a good reference from Blackburn's Borough Treasurer R.G. Pye, who mentioned an accountancy prize that AW had won, albeit ten years previously. In October, AW heard that his application had been successful.

LETTER 13: TO ERIC WALTER MAUDSLEY, 8 OCTOBER 1941

90 Shadsworth Road
Blackburn
8th October 1941

My dear Eric,

Yes, it's true. The old stick-in-the-mud has bestirred himself, renounced fame and fortune, and committed himself and his family to a way of life which must now always lack the pleasures that a little surplus money can bring. Such action, to your ambitious mind, must seem abhorrent, crazy. Once upon a time you might have been inclined to approve. In those happy days of youth, when nothing seemed better to you that to be amongst the hills with a carefree crowd, before the bewitching dream of monetary gain got you in its foul clutch, I fancy you would have understood. Now, of course, you won't. your spirit has grown flabby: never again shall I hear your inspiring cry 'En Avant!' resounding amongst the crags. Your aim in life, and mine, lie along very different paths.

It's the simple life for me henceforth, to be lived in the surroundings I should choose more than any other.

I cannot believe I have made a wrong choice.

Here's 7/4 for the baccy; thanks very much.

Will write more fully later.

AlfW

Part 2
Letters to Lawrence Wolstenholme, 1941-2

AW's new job was in Kendal, a move he had been contemplating and then dreaming about for some time. He had decided that Lakeland, or as near as possible, was where he really wanted to live, in striking distance of the fells and lakes. He wanted to be out walking on the high stuff as often as possible and not, perhaps, thinking so much about his unhappy marriage or girls who might have been. Or were – it is hard to know if some of his suggestive remarks about his 'girlfriends' in Blackburn were fantasy or reality.

He was willing to move, even though it might mean a drop in pay and status. In the Blackburn Borough Treasury department he was on £350 a year. In his new job in Kendal, a much smaller Borough, as an accountancy assistant, he started on only £275.

He was by now coming up to his thirty-fifth birthday and had spent twenty-one years in the Blackburn office. Over half his working life was over, if being a municipal accountant was going to be all of his working. He had become part of the fixtures and furniture of the Blackburn office, had a close set of friends, lots of outside interests, usually involving the same set of friends. His wife Ruth was not quite so keen on Kendal and didn't want to leave her own friends and relations.

AW arrived in Kendal on his own, moving into digs in Burneside Road, Kendal at the end of November 1941, waiting for accommodation where his wife and son could join him. He had been promised a council-owned property.

His position – as accountancy assistant – sounds quite humble, but he was in fact third in the hierachy. At the Blackburn office, he knew there were many people ahead, so it would have taken a long time and slog to rise nearer the top. Several at his own level had already left, such as Maudsley, looking for experience and advancement elsewhere.

One of the people who remained in Blackburn was his good friend Lawrence Wolstenholme, a fellow walker whose wife Marjory did join them on local outings, unlike poor old Ruth. He eventually became the Borough Treasurer.

*AW sat down at his typewriter to write to Lawrence on 4 December 1941,
a few days after he had arrived in Kendal. He numbered the letter in the top
left hand corner 'LW 1', indicating that he expected this to be beginning of a
regular correspondence – and also indicating that he had been a well brought
up, well trained accountant.*

LETTER 14: TO LAWRENCE WOLSTENHOLME, 4 DECEMBER 1941

'Stanegarth'
Burneside Road
Kendal
Thursday evening,
December 4 1941.

Dear Lawrence,

Fancy sitting down to write to you, old friend, and not knowing what
to say!

What would you like me to talk about? What do you want to hear?

Shall I tell you how, when I set out for the office this morning, there
was white mist surrounding the valley, softening the lines of the old grey
buildings I am learning to know well, making mysterious a scene that
is fast becoming familiar? And how, up on the nearby hillsides, the tops
of the trees showed faintly through the haze as though they were afloat,
suspended, belonging neither to earth nor sky? Shall I tell you how, as I
sit at my desk, I can hear the seagulls screaming on the river? Or try to
describe the cleanness and freshness of the morning air as I walk along
to the town, the strange stillness of the atmosphere, the quietness: those
indefinable charms which no visitor to the Lake District ever forgets?

But need I speak of these delights? You know them so well. Already
I am under the spell. This is different, vastly different. It matters not a
scrap that nobody here cares tuppence about me, or wonders who I am
and whence I came. I am a lover come back to his first and best love, and
come to stay. I have cast away, without regrets, the black boots of my
profession, and put on joyfully, with relief, the comfy slippers of semi-
retirement. Now I am content. Now for half a lifetime of doing what I
want to do! Now watch me go rustier and rustier and enjoy the process
of disintegration. When my mind itself is corroded and worn out, I shall
die. Then I will go to heaven, and not know the difference. Yes, Lawrence,
the prospect pleases.

Nobody here knows me, yet I am surrounded by friends: the tall trees by the river, the enchanting path over by the castle, the birds and the squirrels in the wood; and all around me, most faithful and constant of all, the unchanging hills. Soon I shall have other acquaintances: people will come to know me, smile at me, whistle after me as I walk along. Time will bring them. If I could only hope for a small part of the affection which people in Blackburn have shown me I should be quite happy.

This morning as I turned the corner of the road, a street-sweeper called out a cheerfully 'Good morning' and bestowed on me a most engaging smile. In less than a week I have gained a brand-new acquaintance!

I shall look out for him tomorrow. There, you see, Lawrence, is the way life must start again for your old pal

AlfW

LETTER 15: TO LAWRENCE WOLSTENHOLME, 12 DECEMBER 1941

'Stanegarth'
Burneside Road
Kendal
Friday evening
December 12 1941

Dear Lawrence,

There's snow on the hills Lawrence! Wetherlam and Coniston Old Man are white from the cairns on their summits down to the valleys beneath, but the clouds which brought the snow got no further, for across Little Langdale the Pikes and Bowfell are still draped in robes of gold and purple where the bracken lies dying.

Every day I walk to the office with my eyes to the north, where Red Screes and Fairfield and Ill Bell and Harter Fell soar up into the sky. Some mornings they have a very grim forbidding aspect, and, possessed as I am with vivid memories of wild wet days spend athwart their broad shoulders, I can easily imagine the conditions up there in these days of mid-winter: I shudder, but cannot avert my gaze. Sometimes, too, they are lost to sight behind a vaporous mass of dark clouds. But on other mornings when the sun is peeping over the horizon their tops are aflame, and then I sigh for blessed days of freedom again.

Kendal is delightful. So is life in Kendal. So is work in Kendal. After the clatter and clamour of the Borough Treasurer's office at Blackburn, I am, by comparison, encompassed by a deathly calm. Everything here is on so tiny a scale that I feel like a giant playing with a child's toys. Cashbooks are written up once a month, in five minutes, and reconciled every six months. Some of the ledgers are posted twice a year; the others (including Education) not until the end of the year, so that there is some resemblance to the old bookkeeping questions we used to get in the R.S.A. Examinations: given a trial balance, prepare the ledger accounts and Balance Sheet (40 marks). And certainly I am not harassed by dam-silly Reports on Progress, etc. 'Have reminders been sent re unpresented cheques?'. I pause to smile.

Unquestionably I am the best writer in Kendal. Having lots of time to spare and no interruptions and no questions asked I go about leaving a trail of artistic efforts in various books which evoke excited comment from the staff, much to my gratification.

Before I forget! Tomorrow I move into my first Lakeland home, so please note the address: 19 CASTLE GROVE, KENDAL.

Your letter was very welcome. (So will Jim's be when he is finally moved to reply.)

More dreamy and soulful than ever, am I? Perhaps you're right. Maybe I am drifting into a state of coma again. I want to, because I work better when I am torpid. The mood will burst with a loud bang, however, when its purpose is served, and then, out of its agony, will be delivered Wainwright's First Lakeland Classic.

With regard to your other principal point, I refuse to be inveigled into a discussion of the female sex in this correspondence. That can wait until we are face to face once more.

'Mountain Vision' by Smythe hit me between the eyes as I was idly scanning a bookstall a few days before your letter arrived. A day earlier I had bought 'Snowdonia through the Lens' (18/-), so that I gazed upon 'Mountain Vision' long and earnestly, jangling my money the while, but finally moved away in meditative mood without having effected a purchase. Your proposal, therefore, I greet with acclaim.

Your letter contains no invitation to me to join Marjorie and yourself at tea or supper on some occasion during Christmastide. I am a little pained. Would you have me go to the British Restaurant when I visit Blackburn?

Alf

His third letter to Lawrence is in handwriting. He did not add the date, but it would appear to be later in December 1941, judging but the reference to a Christmas card, and the mention of a 2d stamp. Basic postage was still 2d in 1941 – rising to 2½d in 1942.

Dorothy (Coleman) was a married blonde in the office, who had been made Honorary Secretary of the Pendle Club. Miss D, of course, was Betty Ditchfield, the one in the office whom AW really fancied . . .

LETTER 16: TO LAWRENCE WOLSTENHOLME, DECEMBER 1941?

Kendal, Saturday

Dear Lawrence,

There was a time, I agree, when I would have been deeply hurt, and not a little chagrined, to hear myself described as 'benign'. But long years of service devoted to the public weal have finally effaced the rebellious, contrary spirit of the old showman. Benign is the right word, now.

The role I am assiduously fostering now, with some success, is that of 'Patriarch of the Fells'. A fine upstanding figure of a man, no longer young, with white locks flowing behind him as he faces the wind in the high places, a tireless and appreciative walker on the hills, with a kindly (yet a little sad) smile and a warm greeting and helpful advice for those he meets on his wanderings. On the hills I am as a king in his kingdom, with a friendly blessing for all my admiring subjects. I have even been known to pat the heads of youthful fellow travellers. That's AW, now.

Perhaps the turn-about is best illustrated by the fact that I am no longer a borrower of half-crowns till monthend, but a cheerful and accommodating lender of same. Since I have no evidence that a similar transformation has taken place in your own life, there is nothing I can say about Dorothy that would not be misunderstood.

To have a twopenny stamp (blooming expensive, being benign!) I send you Helen's Christmas card herewith. You must send her up here when she is old enough to be really interesting, and let me introduce her to the hills, inter alia.

I only want to be remembered to miss D, nobody else.

AW
Best writer in Kendal

LETTER 17: TO LAWRENCE WOLSTENHOLME, 10 FEBRUARY 1941

Tuesday evening,   19 Castle Grove
February 10 1942   Kendal

Dear Lawrence,

For some reason which is not clear, you persist in harping about ladies in your communications. From time to time you make references, sometimes vague but more often pointed, concerning my past interest in the other sex which are entirely unwarranted.

You remember best, it would appear, the sham A.W., the poseur; the man of furtive downward glance and lascivious habit, the willing prey to morbid phobias, the evil creature of sinister nocturnal missions. Apparently you never knew the real A.W.

All those unhealthy tendencies I have shed as easily as a garment. They were quite superficial. Believe me, your remarks about 'hillocks' and 'valleys' doubtless intended to tantalize me, arouse no feeling whatever. Blue-veined milky bosoms interest me not at all. If I admire a supple curve it is with the eyes of an artist.

Lawrence, I once sat on a boulder at the foot of Sty Head Pass and gazed up at the Napes Ridges for two hours without blinking. Fifty yards away, at Burnthwaite, there was a huge feed awaiting me: I was both tired and hungry after a hard day. Yet I could not take my gaze away from the rocky pinnacles above me, and not until the setting sun drew his concealing shadow across the scene did the fascination depart. . . . Now I submit seriously that no woman, however shameless her antics, could compel my attention to such a pitch of absorption. Let her reveal herself to the uttermost whisker, and let sweet seductiveness do its darnedest – and still I would greatly prefer to sit on a stone with an empty belly and aching limbs and look at a naked mountain.

No, Lozenge, you have got my heart's desire all wrong. I left Blackburn not merely satiated with women, but gorged. There were no lofty peaks there for me to regard, and willy-nilly I found certain passing interests in the depths. When the chance came for me to cast these petty charmers aside in favour of holier joys I was off like a shot, with heart triumphant. Was it not so?

On Saturday afternoon I climbed the Helm, a strange isolated hill two miles out of the town, which sticks up above the countryside like a stranded ship with keel upturned. Snow-covered and detached, it looked as if terrific winds had piled up a mammoth drift, for the gorse and bracken on its steep sides were deeply covered beneath the glittering whiteness.

I made my way slowly to the top, ploughing through snow that was pure and virgin (dam the word!). The panorama was indescribably beautiful. Morecambe Bay, Arnside, Grange, the great wall of Lake mountains, Shap Fells, the Sedbergh Hills, the Pennines: there were the boundaries of my vision, and within the circle were five hundred miles of country wondrous fair to look upon. I was uplifted and enriched by the scene. These are the conquests I seek, the objects of my endeavour, the virgins I prefer to grind beneath me.

Yes, I was in Blackburn on the 31st ultimo, but why the croak of triumph? I came, not to bury Ceaser, but to complete the BRSC accounts for 1941. I shall be there again on the 21st instant, for another dib in the fleshpots. How is sweet Nell of Old Witton? Why doesn't she write?

I duly cashed your Money Order at the Post Office, a la Billy Bunter, and forthwith made my way to the tuckshop, where I bought a lovely book called 'Mountains in Flower', a collection of photographs of alpine plants in their natural surroundings. Note that I could have bought a dozen French-lettres with the money. Sorry to confound your theories still further!

I have found a kindred soul here in the person of an adorable young lady who answers to Marjorie. She is a typist at the Health Office next door. We talk wistfully of Wharfedale and Malham and Dent, and of Teesdale and Muker and the Lakes, and together we sigh and yearn for the sunny weekends to come. She's a sweet child. And a healthy one: I have checked her particulars from her medical report for superannuation. She's 26, weighs 100 pounds, stands 5' 2", is sound in wind and limb, and the condition of her urine is satisfactory.

So roll on, ye sunny weekends!

Alf

This is a nasty letter.
Don't mention 'em again.

After three months in Kendal, AW is beginning to feel slightly nostalgic about Blackburn, the folks he left behind and visits to Ewood Park, the home of Blackburn Rovers. He still has a soft spot for Nellie, a girl in the office, née Lynch, whose husband had died.

In Keswick, with the money he receives as a leaving present from the Blackburn office, he buys a photograph from the Abrahams brothers, the famous Lakeland photographers who specialised in mountain scenery. Teresa is Lawrence and his wife's first child.

LETTER 18: TO LAWRENCE WOLSTENHOLME, 4 MARCH 1942

Wednesday evening,   19 Castle Grove
March 4 1942.   Kendal

Dear Lawrence,

When I closed my books at midday last Saturday and came out into the street I had completed a quarter of a year's service with Kendal Borough Council. A quarter of a year! It's been a long time, and in many ways a lonely time; yet the incidents of my last few days in Blackburn are so vividly engraved in my memory that I find myself still able to live them over again in detail – and often do, for my idle thoughts are all of Blackburn folk: there is, as yet, nobody to occupy my attention out of office hours.

I recall my last visit to Ewood: how carefully I deliberated which way I should go to the ground on this final occasion, for there were many familiar and oft-tramped alternatives, all dear to me, before deciding at length to follow the route of my earliest pilgrimages twenty years before, by way of Old Bank Lane and Longshaw. I proceeded very sedately and soberly, like a man going to a funeral. And you may be sure I lingered long after the players had left the field, surveying this scene of past glories from a favourite position by the scoreboard ere I turned sadly away . . . I think often of my social visit to the palatial home of James Ashworth during those closing days; of my farewell call on Owen Whitfield Hives; of my last walk down Shadsworth Road to the tram at Intack . . . I recall every detail of the B.R.S.C Party on the Friday night before I departed, and of my last hours at the Snapes' house, when I sat and watched the clock.

Most of all, perhaps, my thoughts revert to that Saturday morning which brought to an end my long and revered association with you all. I had worked hard for some weeks in an attempt to get everything straight and about eleven o'clock I suddenly realized that all was completed; there was nothing else for me to do.

From that moment I was no longer part of the office. I had but to wait until twelve o'clock, and then put on my hat and walk out for ever. One by one my old friends came to say a hearty goodbye, or to whisper farewell, and gradually the room emptied. You were there, head down over your books, as ever; Miss D was talking to me by the safe; nobody else remained. How unreal the scene; how well I remember!

Then Miss D slipped away, I was ready to go, and you came across to wish me godspeed. You did not see how earnestly I gazed across the room before I closed the door, at the old desk and rickety chair which would know me no more. I have seen Darwen Tower again. I have walked once more the long mile of Audley Range, along the old familiar pavement where every crack in the flags is remembered well. I have seen again, from a distance, 90 Shadsworth Road.

I have walked along the new road and studied intently the actual extensions to the Whitebirk Generating Station. (Of the hypothetical extensions there was no sign). I have gazed at the barrage balloons with a new interest. I was minded to call on you during this last brief visit, to inspect at close quarters the collapsible knee and more particularly the flat bottom mentioned in your letter. (I always had a partiality for bottoms). However, I learned that you had then been back at work for a week, and so let the opportunity pass.

About half of my presentation money has been spent in the purchase of pictures. One especially, my main purchase, I am pleased to have acquired, because I have long coveted it; every time I have been in Keswick in recent years I have gone round to Abrahams' to look at it. Now old Abrahams has sold it to me, and it is mine. I lift my eyes, and I can see it now. 'Buttermere and High Crag' – a well-loved scene. The other half of my present has been expended in tobacco and razor-blades and liquorice-all-sorts and other sundries. When next I go to Keswick I shall, however, atone by spending the monetary equivalent on the purchase of further photographic gems of Lakeland.

Last Sunday I went to Skelwith Force and Elterwater, returning by Red Bank and Loughrigg Terrace and Rydal. The days of prodigious effort are gone; now I can stroll as slowly as I please, and sit on a wall for a smoke. Time doesn't matter any more. I have no programmes to rush through, and no burdens to carry. There is no longer any need for desperate hurry. The Brathay Valley, awakening to springtime beneath the snowy domes of Wetherlam and the Pikes, was really beautiful, while the view across Grasmere from the Terrace was never more entrancing . . . Then home for a smashing tea, and an evening spent sleepily gazing into the fire and thinking of absent friends. It's a nice way to spend a day, Lawrence!

Alf

Please remember me (in a gentle undertone) to Miss Ditchfield and to the infant Teresa. AW

LETTER 19: TO LAWRENCE WOLSTENHOLME, 8 APRIL 1942

Wednesday evening,
April 8 1942

19 Castle Grove,
Kendal

Dear Lawrence,

Many thanks for a very welcome and 'newsy' letter. You little pen-picture of the infant Teresa was delightfully expressed, and I am pleased to learn that you have succeeded in winning the affections of this winsome maid – such a faith cannot do other than keep your heart and mind clean, and inspire you to the gallantry of a Galahad. And Nellie starts afresh at Whitsun! This was good news, and here's my 3/6 for the subscription list. This marriage will be a success, and blessed with much issue (for she is remarkably fertile). We do not correspond, bad cess to her; so would you please remind her that she owes me two shirts? As for Dorothy's chances of happiness anew, I ha' ma doots, and I suppose you have, too.

Now I must take you to task. I cannot understand your vehement objection to my 'hugging the past' as you wrongly term it. I don't hug it at all, and certainly nothing would every induce me to return to the old scenes. But remember that Blackburn has 35 years of memories for me; and pleasant reminiscences are as much a delight, and a wholesome a joy, as a good meal or a classical concert or a tramp over the hills. What do you do when you listen to Mozart and Offenbach and all the other ancients but hug the past and find a present delight in doing so? There's absolutely no difference. And would you have me forget Jim and yourself – and my mother? My roots in Blackburn went pretty deep, son!

But, if you are in any doubt, let me assure you that the transplanting has been a complete, overwhelming success. I am a thousand-a-year man in everything but cash. I am an outrageous success at work, and am happier than ever I was. I can step out of the office on to a passing bus and in a few minutes be on Orrest Head, or in an hour on Loughrigg Terrace – and how fearfully shabby Revidge and Ramsgreave and Shadsworth are by comparism! I can stroll through the fields behind the house after tea, and in five minutes reach a little stile whereon I habitually recline, for before me in splendid array I see the Crinkles and Bowfell, the gap of Mickledore, Gable in magnificent isolation, the Pikes, Fairfield – and not yet has the scene failed to send a quiver through me. No, if you mistake reminiscence for regret you are hopelessly wrong. My only regret is that you and a few others are not here to share the good things with me.

Plans for the future, which you assume to be non-existent, are going on apace. The new bungalow is planned down to the last detail: 'twill be built of the familiar grey-green stone and slate familiar to these parts, and will be dry-walled so that the wisteria and clemati can grip; it will stand high on a hillside, by a wood, with the open fell behind. It will merge harmoniously into the landscape. The view from the big windows at the front will comprise many miles of the loveliest country God ever made, a park where I may wander at will, and from my seat by the ingle I shall see this view as a picture, ever-changing, set in the frame of the window. I might, even then, think occasionally of Audley Range and Shad, but do you imagine that I shall be 'hugging the past' and wanting to return? Not on your bloody life, you silly old buggar. Only the name of this desirable residence remains to be chosen, and at present I am licking my lips over LINGMOOR, GARTH and WANSFELL. Names like these would be inane in Lammack Road, but up here, where they belong, they sound grand and sane and in tune with the surroundings.

I saw you on Easter Sunday, in the evening. You passed the Snapes' at a great pace, heading westwards, following by a fleeting shadow which, knowing you, I fancied would be Marjorie. You would have been pleased to listen to some of the new record the Snapes have recently acquired, just the stuff you like: Offenbach, Lizst, Tchaikovsky, Elgar. It thrilled a poor infidel like me to hear them. 'Concerto for Two', is grand, is it not?

The Wainwrights made their first major ascent last Sunday week, having a great time on Red Screes, in snow still waist-deep. This, by the way, is the first recorded ascent of this peak in 1942.

Will you kindly let Jim have the enclosed card: it contains a business query which I am anxious to have settled. At five o'clock you might ask him if he has replied.

Kindest regards to Marjorie and yourself. I hope to be able to answer definitely your other cheeky query in my next letter. From the few potent signs around me I should hazard a guess at mid-September!

Alf

The final reference to a 'few potent signs' and a 'guess at mid September' – could possibly suggest that his wife Ruth is pregnant, but it never gets mentioned again. Ruth and AW do not have another child. A reference to the 'Wainrights' making their first major ascent suggest that Ruth and Peter had gone with AW on at least one walk, so the marriage was perhaps going through a slightly better spell.

He also appears to have new fantasies, which presumably his old office friends had known about for some time, about what he really intended to do in life . . .

LETTER 20: TO LAWRENCE WOLSTENHOLME, 2 JUNE 1942

Tuesday evening,
June 2 1942.

19 Castle Grove
Kendal.

Dear Lawrence,

I am indebted to you for another very interesting letter. Gossip and intimate gleanings of the staff are very welcome, although, perhaps, I do not 'lap it up' quite as thirstily these days. Six months' absence has rather clouded the general picture of Blackburn; my thoughts nowadays are much more of Kendal than of Blackburn, of the next 35 years rather than the past 35 years. Nevertheless, it is surprising how retentive the mind can be.

I wager that I could come back to you tomorrow and carry on where I left off and never need to ask a question; my duties there are as fresh in mind as if I had left them only at 5.30 this evening.

I have, in fact, been most absorbed during my sojourn here in studying the effects of absence upon memory, for I always used to wonder when other members of the staff went away how long it would before routine details slipped out of mind, what effect new faces and new scenes would have in effacing the old. Possibly you have speculated similarly. So, at random moments, I have tested myself.

I have, for example, recalled the headings in the Bank Transfer Book (the 'tick' columns still raise a crooked smirk) or in the Out-relief Lists and other familiar journals, followed through the Friday wages routine from 9 a.m to 5.30, recalled the names and addresses of the worst housing arrears cases, and so on.

I find that I can bring these back to mind without the slightest effort; I have forgotten nothing. Surprisingly, though, it is the little unimportant things, the details, which remain evergreen, which flash most often across that inward eye when oft in pensive mood I lie: for example, I remember Doris R's passion for wimberry pie, Alf Shaw's cuckoo photos, Miss Stairmand's Aston Villa jersey, Coggins' sonorous laugh, Gregson

Heyes and his bull stories, the erratic but energetic ascent of steps by Miss Graham. These things don't matter, but they're the things I can't forget!

And I certainly haven't forgotten the wild despairing rush of events at Blackburn at year end! You may be sure you have been often in my thoughts these past few weeks. We always suspected that there was something radically wrong in the office somewhere.

Looking back on the maelstrom now, it is perfectly clear that it's the much-vaunted organization (a word I haven't heard since I left) that itself wants organizing. You will never prepare your accounts in good conditions until the accountancy staff and the general staff are separated.

As far as my own work is concerned, I have finished the Rating, Superannuation and Education Accounts, am now stuck into Gas and Water, and will complete Housing and Electricity by the end of the month. Conditions here are ideal, too good to be true. I work unhurriedly, for there is no timetable and nobody wants to know how I'm getting along; I have morning coffee, and am free to smoke and sing 'Deep in the Heart of Texas' if I want to. It matters not if I absent myself from the office for a few hours; I don't have to chalk up my destination.

Tomorrow I am going over to Beetham Chruch (you remember Beetham, with its river and deer-park, where the journey north first becomes exciting?) to investigate a query arising out of tithe rentcharge. In a day or two the Electrical Engineer (a lad like myself) and I are having a day at Carlisle, whence he came, to have a look round their Electricity Department. In short, work is a damn pleasure. So, like Fred Smith but with a different motive I seriously counsel you to sling your hook from Blackburn; I never dreamed that I would have so few regrets and be so much happier away from it. Now let's have a look at your letter.

My terse communiqué to the effect that I was joining H.M Forces, you say, left everyone impatient for more detail. Nobody turned a hair, I'll bet. That's five weeks ago; any of you could have settled his impatience' at the cost of a 2 and a half d stamp. I used to think when I worked there that the staff of the B.T., myself excluded, were the most bovine unemotional selfish crew I ever struck, and I see no reason to change my opinion. Only yesterday Tennant wrote to me, and mentioned that, my letters apart, he has not had even a word from any member of the office since he joined the Forces. It's bloody rotten, you know!

Anyway, what happened in my case is this. The day before I wrote Jim from Patterdale (where, by the way, I had a perfect cameo of a holiday all in a weekend) the Kendal Council were informed that my deferment expired on the 30th inst. And thereafter I would be liable for military service. I lost no sleep as a result of this harsh decision, but it proved so repugnant to the Treasurer that he called a meeting of the Finance Committee forthwith and two members were deputed to go to London to make a spirited protest.

They went a fortnight ago, innocents abroad, had a most cordial interview and returned with news that it had been agreed that I should be deferred indefinitely (the terms, I suppose, being similar to yours). No written confirmation has yet arrived.

I was surprised to learn that you did not know of Crook's pending marriage. I had some wedding cake from him, and he spared a moment from the frothy expulsions of his honeymoon to send me a card from Abinger, the place chosen for purity to go pop.

I was in the company of Fred Percy Haslam during Whitsuntide. On the Saturday I was sorely tempted to ask him if Nellie was being married that day, as I suspected she was from an earlier letter of yours. But no, I could not venture the question; I dare not retire to a lonely bed with the knowledge that she was at that moment being well and truly blocked while my own much-more-deserving organ lay adroop for want of company. I had the news next day. Strangely I saw a girl that day, at Giggleswick, who reminded me very much of her; and another at Grasmere on the Tuesday who was her spit an' image, even to the kiss-curls on her cheek. But these were mirages. Then, at work on Friday afternoon, I happened to be walking through the General Office and glanced casually through the open door. And there, gesturing wildly to attrace my attention, was Nellie Myerscough, alias Morrison, alias Lynch. No doubt about it, 'twas she, and looking lovelier that any human being has a right to look. My brain did a little somersault; it seemed so <u>odd</u> that she should be there, in the Borough Treasurer's office at Kendal. I was introduced to her new husband, a pleasant but unimpressive youth almost lost to me in the glow of his wife's radiant personality. I thought their gesture in calling at Kendal to see me was extremely nice; we camped for half an hour and I did no more work that day.

Funny how things work out, isn't it? To my dying day I shall be convinced that N would rather have it from me than Frank or anybody else.

Your scanty note that you are visiting Lakeland in June pleased me as much as anything in your letter. Why didn't you give me the date? And am I correct in presuming that you will again stay with Mrs Postle? If you are traveling by bus you will have to change at Kendal (remember how the Town Hall bells used to play a tune when we changed buses in the years that are gone?), and I could be there to see you safely on the last stage of your journey. Note that the difficulties of travel by bus are nowadays extremely acute, especially at weekend, and you must be prepared for a wild scramble and possible disappointment at both Preston and Kendal.

I shall be taking a few days holiday during the week June 13–20, when my cousin is bringing his family over from Penistone to stay with us for the week, and quite probably we shall be awalking in the Lake District and mayhap will drop upon you if this is also your week, but not on a mountain-top, I'll bet. Do you realize that you haven't set foot on a summit since Bowfell in August 1935?

When we have stayed at boarding-houses in the past we have often espied a mild insignificant man pottering about the kitchen while all our contacts have been with the lady of the house. That meek quiet creature is the husband, and gradually I am assuming a similar position. We have already had a great many visitors at Castle Grove, but until Whitsuntide they have come only for a few days, and never more than two at a time. But now the relatives are upon us with a vengeance. We had three all Whitweek, and there is one next week, and then we are continuously booked up for bed and full board until August with never a respite. Sleeping three or four in a bed could be quite jolly if there was a preponderance of young and healthy females but I don't relish the idea of being sandwiched between uncle and brother-in-law. There is ample room in the house to sleep a dozen; it's beds we're short of; we've only two, and they both rattle like hell. We mustn't have any honeymoon couples here!

Sorry to hear of Jim's indisposition!

Can I visualize the time when I walk in the B.T's Office Blackburn and the majority of the staff whisper 'Who's that?' I can visualize the time when I enter that same office and everybody falls flat at my feet in reverent awe, for already I am well on the way to being as great a CELEBRITY as Wordsworth was. As yet, I cannot give details, but ere long it's going to be your greatest claim to notoriety that you knew Alf Wainwright. So when I am a great man I will patronize your office with my presence, and to show that I have lost nothing of my humility I will bring my photographer to take my picture sitting at the old desk. Besides, if I called now I might be offered a cheque for the 35 pounds owing to me for work done on the Generating Extensions, and it would hurt me to have to accept it after all these months.

Best wishes for a really happy holiday

Alf

Part 3:
Letters to Maudsley and Wolstenholme, 1942-3

LETTER 21: TO ERIC WALTER MAUDSLEY, 13 MAY 1942

Wednesday evening
May 13 1942

19 Castle Grove
Kendal.

Dear Walter,

Talk about the long arm of coincidence!

For a week the address '8 Sandy Close, Hertford' has been in my thoughts insistently, and I had decided that tonight I would write to the house to see if an old pal of mine was still in residence there. Honest! I should have written long ago. Will you believe me if I say I haven't had time?

You see, my first few weeks here were spent exclusively in writing to about a dozen people I knew in Blackburn, people with whom severance was rather painful. In those early days I found a particular pleasure in coming home when the day's work was done and spending the evening in Blackburn, as it were, chatting to familiar folk, talking about familiar places. By doing this I passed very smoothly through a period which must otherwise have been lonely. But I released a boomerang. Replies poured in, a fistful at a time, demanding further letters. Further letters were sent, further replies received. I don't suppose any exile ever wrote more letters than I did during the winter. And, as you know, I never scribble hasty letters; if one is to be written I like to spend an evening on it.

Not until last week were my arrears of correspondence cleared, and then it was I began to think of the lost legion I had neglected – my cousin at Penistone, you, Jack Jones at Ardrossan, Mr Ashton. So it happened that tonight was set apart for a Maudsley Missive. And damme if I don't get a letter from you this afternoon.

Let me hasten to assure you that I have often found myself thinking of you, at odd moments, since coming to Kendal; and not merely during the past week. Always my thoughts have ended on the same note of perplexity: what on earth persuaded you to leave this fairest spot of England for life on a miserable plain? Money, was it? The Royal Mint itself wouldn't induce me away! Now, more than ever before, flat country gives me the pip. A flat landscape is a picture only half-finished; it contains nothing to arrest the attention; there is no satisfactory horizon; the gaze wanders aimlessly over the scene and trails away to nothing; there is no background, no climax. It's like a story without a plot.

Listen to this saga of my life in Kendal. Every day starts with an awakening, and when my eyes pop open I habitually emit a great (silent) whoop of ecstatic joy. I am immediately in a frenzy of frantic delight. Another day in Lakeland! Another day of life at its best! By my side is the recumbent form of a female, but it is not on she that I feast my eyes, it is the square of the window. That frames a picture which lifts my heart. There is the old castle, perched on its hill and surrounded by lofty trees, set against a wide sky of Mediterranean blue or of massed clouds; around the edge of the frame hang golden tresses of the jasmine that climbs up the outer walls of the house; I can see the slender branches and fresh green leaves of the silver birches in the road below. Oceans of fresh air are pouring into the room through the open casement, the same tonic stimulant which has greeted us so often o' mornings at Rosthwaite and Wasdale and other beloved places. Stuff of this rare vintage won't permit lying in bed; there's no turning over for five minutes, not any desire to; it says, bluntly 'Up, devil, get your pants on; you're in Lakeland, and a new day is here!' I still look out of the window with the same eagerness as of yore, when Lakeland mornings were few and precious. Not always, of course, do I see bright sunlight; sometimes, not often, the castle is hidden in a flurry of driving rain, and for a month it lay like a ghostly shadow in a snowy covering. But the gloriously clean air never has a day off. It's there every minute of every hour – and it makes me feel good and fit and glad to be alive.

I go out into it after breakfast, hatless and coatless, wearing old flannels which weren't suitable for the Blackburn office (anything which serves to conceal nakedness is appropriate here; it's a town of odd attires). I cross the road to a stile (fancy climbing stiles going to work!) and go up the springy turf to the castle. I am always first up there in a morning, always first to disturb the sheep from their slumbers in the dry moat. It is from the hilltop, by the crumbling ruins, that the view of the mountains suddenly smites me between the eyes, and you can bet I go on and down the others side without watching where I put my feet. I always try to discern the cairn on Thornthwaite Crag, and usually on these clear mornings can do so without difficulty . . . I go on my way, a happy man, down by a wood, across the river, and so to the office.

At the office I do the work allotted to me, and I do it extremely well. Two or three times a day the Treasurer (a grand fellow) comes in and sprawls across my desk for a camp and a smoke. He likes me immensely; his early regard has turned to awe, for I have simply staggered him and the staff with my superb competence. Every job I touch is polished perfect, flawless. The work itself is varied and interesting, and very simple – it's like learning the A.B.C all over again. I am allowed to smoke at my desk, itself a boon and a blessing. The Mayor Aldermen and Burgesses are all as nice as ninepence; I get along extremely well with all of them, and am treated with deference and respect by the chief officials, who are, uniformly, gentlemen who wear cloth caps. There is complete freedom from restrictions and interference. Believe me, working here is a positive delight!

The atmosphere of Kendal is soaking thoroughly into me, but I have not yet lost the feeling that I am on holiday. It's a grand old town. I browse around the shops and quaint old inns and alleyways with undiminished interest. A few people now, not many, greet me with a nod and a smile as I pass along the streets. And I see walkers, heavily laden, on their way to the hills, any my silent blessing goes with them; I see them return, brown as berries, and feel sad that they must return to the towns where there are no hills. Sometimes I look in the excellent Public Library, a treasury of Lakeland lore, and bring home the books I love best to read. If the evening is mild I climb up to the castle to watch the day depart, but more often I go across the fell to Scout Scar, eight hundred feet above the Lyth Valley, and lie down on the brink of the cliff. From this exalted viewpoint my gaze roams at will over the assembly of mountain peaks before me. They are all there, all the old friends – Bowfell, Scafell, Gable, the Pikes, Fairfield and High Street. Ah yes, I have smoked many pipes of utter contentment on Scout Scar! When the sun gets low and the valleys fill with white mist, I come back at a swinging pace, calling at a little inn on the edge of the fell, an so home for a mammoth supper. It's a grand life, mon ami!

I am in excellent, robust health. Every weekend finds me amongst the hills, knocking lumps off Baddeley's regulation times. There's nothing to beat mountaineering. It keeps a man sane, stimulates his spirit. It's what you lack, son, and precisely what you need. You were never so happy as at Carlisle, with the hills so near that you could spend your weekends amongst them. I well remember your stirring call 'En avant' during our Whitsuntide 1931 holiday. You were happy then. Your wants were simple. There was no vain chasing of phantoms in those days, no bitter disappointments, no disillusionment. A simple life is a happy one. The thing most worth seeking in life, Eric, is beauty. Make no mistake about that. I couldn't be persuaded to swop this existence for any other. I have reached the foot of the rainbow, and here, sure enough, is the pot of gold I have been seeking – beauty so exquisite that it makes the heart leap with exultation, loveliness so enchanting that it brings tears to the eyes. This is wealth, real wealth; it is free of tax, and it is mine forever.

– – –

That's the letter I was going to send you. Now I have yours, which calls for attention also. I have not forgotten Blackburn, nor ever will. But surprisingly it has not the grip I feared it would have. Already it is fast receding from my thoughts. I have made a few brief visits, staying with the golden-voiced singer you mention, but I have not been in the old office. Frankly, the old town seems a hell-hole after Kendal, and it is with relief that I come again within sight of the hills on my return. I find that many of the delights (pursuits may be a better word) I enjoyed there were shallow and superficial, after all. Not one of them gave me such keen pleasure as the view I had of Ullswater from St Sunday Crag last Saturday evening: the latter experience seemed to me one of the intimate joys of existence. I must be a very simple soul!

You tell me you are still as miserably dissatisfied as ever. No wonder. All your pet theories have crumbled before your eyes. Your philosophies have had no root; how could they survive? You need a foundation to build on, a firm belief, a simple faith; then all else falls naturally into place. Get a month's leave of absence, stay at Burnthwaite, climb Gable every day, attend the services at Wasdale Church every Sunday. If this doesn't cure you, nothing will. I think it will. Avoid marriage. You'd be a wife-beater. A child of your own would help to restore balance considerably, but in your case it's too big a risk. Continue with your married friend, by all means. A widow would be better, if you could find one young and attractive. Either class is far preferable to a spinster; they are easy to get on with, not prudish, ready and eager to lie down and play snails.

I agree with you remarks re Wainwright letters. They are good, unquestionably. Actually, you know, I came here to write and draw. Wordsworth and Wainwright, these two! Here are some of the prospective titles chosen for my books:

MEN AND MOUNTAINS, by Alf Wainwright.
ONCE I CLIMBED A HILL, by Alf Wainwright.
HERITAGE OF THE HEATHER, by Alf Wainwright.
MOUNTAIN MEMORIES, by Alf Wainwright.

Demy 8vo, profusely illustrated, 10/6 each. The real classic, however, will not be published until about 1960. My life's blood will be in it: it will be my memorial. This of course, will be WAINWRIGHT'S GUIDE TO THE LAKELAND HILLS. Look out for these publications on the bookstalls, in vivid yellow jackets. And please buy a copy, for auld lang syne!

You want PENNINE CAMPAIGN again. Such a fag having to find brown paper and parcel it up and send it! I intended to make minor corrections, and amend the title to PENNINE JOURNEY, but the months have sped by and nothing has been done. Who wants it this time? Anybody with 'fluence? Longland, for instance? I'd like to see it published, and anybody can have the copyright for fifty pounds: a rare opportunity for someone with business acumen, for royalties will roll in! I'll send it, if you really want to have it. But it's in tatters now. See that it doesn't get amongst the salvage.

I mustn't forget to tell you that my deferment expires on June 30th. The Council have lodged a spirited appeal against this decision.

When shall I see you again? When shall we sup together once more? In Munich, Vienna, Belgrade and Athens after the war? Or in England before this?

I remember an occasion when you were too shy to urinate in a chamber at Rosthwaite.

It's ten years ago.

You were happy in those days, son.

Your old pal

Alf

LETTER 22: TO ERIC WALTER MAUDSLEY, 11 JUNE 1942

Thursday evening,   19 Castle Grove
June 11 1942   Kendal.

Dear Walter,

I can do no other than send the blessed book forthwith. Here it is. Bessie seems a grand girl! Your brief but eloquent description of her early-morning salute made the red blood pulsate a trifle more rapidly in certain of my veins. Caresses 'long, luscious, and sweet as nectar' – this reads like poetry from one I always considered prosaic! I envy you. Nectar I never tasted; my dictionary tells me it is the fabled drink of the gods, the honey of flowers. I can well imagine that your treasured privilege of sipping daily at so delicious a fountain, of submitting gladly and eagerly to the ministrations of such a charmer, is one not conducive to earnest application to your duties until long after the spell is broken. Indeed, it is by no means difficult for me to visualize the Scene of Shame: I see her jolly entry into your sanctum at the appointed moment, the beads of dishonest sweat on your brow as you tremble at her approach, the soft brushing of her hair across your ageing jowls, the gentle pressure of the soft young body against the matured, the sucking lips, the intoxications of her nearness; then she is gone. I see your lank frame sink into the chair, morally softened and organically stiffened by the incident, a prey to uncontrollable fits of shuddering until the state of ecstatic prostration is again dormant. Very gradually Hyde merges into Jekyll, a ray of clear light shines through the writhing tumult of your thoughts, then another, and ultimately your gaze fixes on the papers on your desk.

As I say, I envy you. She must be wonderful. Are you sure she is not the one you seek? Cannot you imagine yourself undergoing the frothy expulsions of an enchanting honeymoon with her? Dammit, I'm getting worked up about her myself! Ask her to write to me when she has read the book.

Otherwise, your letter is again a Lament. Life has no meaning. There is no lasting pleasure, no true rapture. You drift aimlessly on through the years, going this way and that and always coming back to the crossroads. Have a care, man! The clock is ticking your life away.

Whitsuntide I spend at Giggleswick, near Settle, in the company of some Blackburn friends (including the aforementioned golden-voiced operatic star). So far as the weather could disrupt the proceedings, it did so. It was wet, it was wild, it was windy, it was wintry. I fled the place on the Monday, and came over to lovely Grasmere, where I sat on a boulder by Easedale Tarn and witnessed a thunderstorm stalking across the mountains. This, I thought, was better far.

This weekend I am taking a short holiday with my cousin, who is bringing his family over for the week. Probably we shall get over into Borrowdale for a night or two: we may even realize an old ambition of mine and watch the sun rise from Gable's grim turret. We shall sojourn at Rosthwaite, so that it is quite on the cards that the House of the Spurned Utensil will again harbour me. If so, you may be sure there will be chamber music before retiring, and I promise to spare a thought, whilst in the act, for the maidenly youth who could not and would not in an age long past. 19 Castle Grove is being deluged with relatives at present. They have been coming since Christmas, but only for week-ends; now however they are coming for weeks on end; sisters, brothers-in-laws, aunts, hordes of nieces and nephews. We are completely booked up, and sleeping three or four in a bed, until mid-August. They leave very reluctantly, too, vowing to return here to live after the war, so I can see myself being installed as the first President of a local Blackburnians Assocn ere long. No doubt about it, Kendal's a grand place!

News of minor interest to you may be the second marriage of your old Technical College fellow-student, Nellie Myerscough, alias Morrison, alias Lynch. She honeymooned at Arnside, and came over one day to pay me a call at the office. Thus another chapter comes to a close. Look out for a special chapter devoted to her in my Published Memoirs under the title 'ONCE I CLIMBED NELLIE'. Ah, me!

I was very pleased to learn that the Call of the North was again tugging. Your description of pastoral Herts did not convince me. Tree-studded backsides! Where, in Herts, is there a Mickledore, a Black Sail, a Stonethwaite, a Buttermere? There's hope for you still if the yearning for Lakeland is not dead, and I was interested to find hat names such as Broad Stand and Lord's Rake still flow easily from your typewriter apparently without too great a strain on distant memory.

Broad Stand – how often have I squeezed through the narrow cleft of Fat Man's Agony and lovingly stroked its grim walls; how often have I turned sorrowfully away without attempting the climb! Other people's lives hold regrets as well as your own, and Broad Stand is prominent amongst mine. Lord's Rake, of course, I have flogged underfoot often.

Let me know when the date of your visit is certain, for I would like a rendezvous with you, if only for an hour. I am anxious for more details about Bessie!

I must close this letter here and now. If I don't I shall have to blackout, and I resent having to do that; it reminds me there's a war on.

So be strong, of good courage and stout heart. There's always tomorrow, and Bessie will not fail.

Your old pal,

Alf

LETTER 23: TO ERIC WALTER MAUDSLEY, 21 JULY 1942

Tuesday evening,   19 Castle Grove
July 21 1942   Kendal.

Dear Walter,

Your letter of the 17th, reeking with pungent wit, is before me.

I enjoyed every word of it.

Tonight, unfortunately, I have not time to reply at length, but write tonight I must if you are to receive my letter before you set your face to the frozen north. Only the scurvy machinations of unkind fate prevent me from shouting 'Yoicks!' in a loud voice and rushing to join you at an appointed rendevous. Yet I cannot, and I deeply regret the circumstance. The fact is that at present Wainwright no longer stands majestically aloof from his fellows, but forms the geometric centre of a turmoil of frantic humans who descend upon him singly and in droves. This Queen Bee with a myriad workers is the Secretary of Kendal's Stay-at-Home Holiday Week (August 3rd–8th). In a way, the work is decidedly enjoyable, as it is permissible to stroke my female assistants at odd moments during the preparation of the programme, and it adds to a man's stature to have his telephone ringing all day, and have a stream of callers and a fan-mail like a film-star. It would be a reasonable assessment of the present position to say that as a result of my efforts these past few weeks the arrangements have been methodically reduced to chaos. So I'm sorry, but you are not to know the intimacy of my brace of bony knees this time. A pity! I would have loved to be awaiting you on Mickledore as you came toiling up Hollow Stones at noon on the 30th. Then we could have shoved each other up Broad Stand and rushed down to Wasdale to celebrate our triumph in a succession of foaming flagons. And later, beneath the coverlet, I should have heard from your drooling lips the Story of Bess, told with maudlin simplicity and punctuated with intervals of noisy urination. Alas, these things cannot come to pass this year! Thanks for the invitation. I shall reply more fully to your letter in a week or two, and I must thank The Girl for her criticism of my book.

I would appreciate a card from Wasdale, if you get there – a picture of jagged mountain-tops, please.

Have a good holiday, son.

Alf
for x Bess

AW, writing this next letter to Lawrence in Blackburn, also tells him about the great success he has made of Kendal's Holiday Week. This was a Government-inspired scheme to encourage people to have holidays at home, as there was a war on, and stop them from travelling. AW was made Secretary of the Kendal Holidays at Home Week, 3–8 August 1942, and was given a free hand to organise dances, concerts, sports events, competitions to amuse and attract the locals. AW himself did the illustration for the front of Holiday Week Programme. It did him a lot of good, socially, and also workwise, increasing his status in the office and in the town.

LETTER 24: TO ERIC WALTER MAUDSLEY, 12 AUGUST 1942

Wednesday evening   19 Castle Grove
August 12 1942   Kendal

Dear Lawrence,

Kendal's Holiday Week is over.

It's been an outrageous success, of course. It couldn't have been otherwise, with me bossing the show. Talk about superb efficiency! Everything went like clockwork, and the sun appeared whenever he was wanted. The arrangements, planned to the last detail, worked so smoothly that I was left with nothing to do during the week but watch the events and eat ice-cream. Aldermen and Councillors were my errand-boys. The Mayor came at a whistle. . . . A Wainwright Production!

It's all been very enjoyable, and there's no doubt the experience has been a profitable one for me. You will have realized that I have at last decided to pull my light from under the bushel, the result being that I have been acclaimed on all sides as an artist of outstanding ability. I have had commissions to draw landscapes, which for the moment I have declined; I have other plans, big plans. My next job is to design a new cover for the Kendal Parish Church monthly magazine, at the request of the Vicar; then I shall start on the biggest and loveliest job I ever undertook, that of putting Kendal right on the map. It's a grand grand place, Lawrence. I intend to do a series of sketches of the town and neighbourhood, accompany then with a narrative, and offer the lot to the Council as the Official Handbook for the years of peace when the holiday crowds return. This isn't something you'll get by enclosing a stamp; it will have to be paid for, but, believe me, what a success it will be! Out of the immaturity of countless expedition handbooks will come the Super Guide-book, and I shall love preparing it, for Kendal was just built to be drawn and written about. It will be my book, all of it; written, illustrated and designed Wainwright – and I have found just the printer who will make a really high-class job of it.

So I'm a big noise here now. I'm in a town where ability is appreciated, and civic pride counts a lot. There'll be a statue to me before I'm through.

Now that the Stay-at-Home week is ended, I am stealing away-from-home for a holiday. On the 15th instant I am coming to Blackburn for a few days. I shall be Jekyll by day, Hyde by night. Then I shall wash my hands and return to Kendal the well-beloved and a rosy future. The last thing I am likely to do whilst in B. is to call at the old office. The thought appals! Life only started for me when I fled the place. I should not, however, want to deprive you of the opportunity of basking in the radiance of my company, and if anything goes awry with my arrangements re the womenfolk I will invite you and Jim to quaff vimto with me in some suburban inn. You will understand, of course, that I shall have to depart when darkness cloaks the earth.

I saw Jimbo the other Saturday afternoon and we spend an idle hour lying on our backs on a warm hillside overlooking the town, talking of old times. 'Twas a bleasant meeting. Tell him, will you please, that I've asked Dot to write to him.

I was interested to learn of your holiday in Keswick and endorse our remarks anent the beauty of the hills: my eyes still turn to them as I walk about Kendal, and no view containing hills ever disappointed me. I am well qualified to extend sympathy regarding your train journey, for I too have had to stand in corridors with the window at elbow-level. Pity you didn't see Shap: it's grand wild country.

Maudsley was over in Wasdale last week. He wanted me to join him there, but I wasn't able to, unfortunately being submerged just then in the Holiday Week. Dorothy, too, was in Keswick again, and tells me she climbed Scawfell (I wonder!).

As you managed Esk Hause, and enjoyed it, I assume there must even yet be a spark lingering in your atrophied spirit. Tell me frankly: wasn't it your best day for many a year?

See you soon

Alf

LETTER 25: TO ERIC WALTER MAUDSLEY, 24 AUGUST 1942

Monday evening   19 Castle Grove
August 24 1942   Kendal

Dear Walter,

I have just returned from a week's stay at Blackburn. It has not been a successful holiday. I've lived like a lord, with a golden-voiced operatic star bringing lovely meals to me in bed; and I've enjoyed every comfort in palatial surroundings; I've listened over and over again to my favourite musical classics, and feasted on good literature; I've met and wined with old friends from the office and been driven about in a car. I've had a really lazy time, and that's just why the holiday failed. It's been a week of lounging about in slippers; better far I had put on my walking shoes and gone over the hills and far away!

Blackburn is no place to spend a holiday. By the end of the third day I was pining for the hills and the woods and the racing rivers, and ready to return to my beloved Kendal. Blackburn, with its endless rows of grimy brick houses, its chimney-stacks and monstrous factories, its smells and filth, its black henpens and rubbish tips – ugh! There is no glory and no glamour about Blackburn. Life only started for me when I fled the place. Affection for the old town is not dead, but I fear it is growing very dim. The expectant delights of the sentimentalist, the sight of the scenes of boyhood, the joy of meeting former friends: these are proved spurious when the reality is at hand. I visited the old familiar places, I walked the old streets where every crack in the pavements is remembered, I saw people I once knew well – and I gazed dispassionately; there was no thrill in renewing acquaintance. Instead, the bleak poverty of the town, the ugliness and meanness, got me by the throat; I had a feeling of depression during the whole of my stay which was not banished until Lancaster was behind me on the return journey and, with nose flattened against the carriage-window, I could discern a long rugged skyline to the north.

So now I am back here in Kendal, where I long to be, and where, in 1987, I shall die.

The Kendal Holiday Week was a great success, thanks largely to the superb control exercised by an efficient organizing secretary. It proved a profitable experience for me, too, for I was finally persuaded to bring my light from under the bushel and have been acclaimed as an artist of outstanding merit. So much so that I have received commissions for further drawings (chiefly of landscapes), and my future as Lakeland's Greatest Artist is assured. The cover design on the enclosed Programme is by Wainwright. Before I go on to a series of drawings of the Lakes, however, I am determined to put Kendal right on the map. I intend to spend the next two years in sketching the town; these drawings, with a narrative written by self in self's inimitable style, will then be published by the Council as the official handbook to the town. It's going to be a lovely job, for Kendal was simply built to be drawn. So out of the immaturity of countless expedition itineraries will be born the Super Guide Book, and it will be a huge success. You won't get a copy by enclosing a stamp; you'll have to dig in your pocket, but it will be a bargain at any price. Watch for the advertisement in all the national newspapers in the first summer of peace!

Now what of your visit to Wasdale? Lawrence told me of the embarrassment of your return journey to Carlisle, but he had nothing to tell of your grim vigil amongst the rocky ramparts of Scawfell. He had some vague story of your mounting three free Frenchwomen in rapid succession, but I am more anxious to have the exclusive details of your mounting of Broad Stand, of your privations in the gloomy chasm of Fat Man's Agony, of the musical tinkle of falling urine in the darkness of your room. How is Wasdale Head, and Burnthwaite and the glorious Sty? The details, please! Two years have gone by since I sojourned there; two long years. Soon I must go again.

And on your return to pastoral Herts what had the fair Bess to offer you in welcome? I wonder! Now I must thank the dear child for her review of my book. So for the present I take my leave of you

Your old pal

AlfW

LETTER 26: TO ERIC WALTER MAUDSLEY, 21 SEPTEMBER 1942

Monday evening,
September 21 1942

19 Castle Grove
Kendal

Dear Walt,

The days go by, and I wait in vain for the sordid details of your Lakeland trek. Silence envelops Hertfordshire. I am sending herewith a handsome present: a print of my first drawing. My first has since been succeeded by my second and my third, in that order, and they are evoking prodigal encouragement in this grey old town of my adoption; so much so that I am now convinced that a lucrative additional source of revenue awaits my clutch. Since this is the first, however, I have had a few copies made for my friends, regardless of cost, and here is yours. It is eminently suitable, I claim, for tacking up in the lavatory and surveying moodily when in he throes of excretion.

Gable I see most evenings from fields behind my home: has Hertford anything as fair to show? Gable will have charms when Bess is gone and forgotten.

This isn't a letter.

It's your turn to write. When you do, please use the same envelope so that I can use it again. They're 2d each!

Alf

AW was full of plans for books, but it's not clear if at this stage he ever got round to much more than thinking about them, boasting about them, but he does seem to have had printed, at his own expense, quite a few copies of some of his Kendal drawings. One of several AW drawings from the 1942 period which has survived is the cover of the Holiday Week brochure.

LETTER 27: TO LAWRENCE WOLSTENHOLME, 2 OCTOBER 1942

Friday evening
October 2 1942

19 Castle Grove
Kendal

Dear Lollipop,

I've had <u>one</u> letter from you in the past <u>four months</u>.

Shame on you!

Bob will have given you, or will be giving you, a print of my 'Blea Tarn, Langdale'. This isn't my latest drawing, and it isn't my best; it's my first, and because it is the first, the prelude to many, I have had thirty copies made, regardless of cost, for my new friends and for those whose encouragement in the past I have not forgotten. I could have sold these thirty copies in five minutes, and wallowed in wealth for a few days, but that would spoil the idea. I hope you like the picture. I claim that it is eminently suitable for tacking up in the lavatory and surveying moodily during the throes of excretion, or in intervals of noisy urination.

I have set aside five more copies for others there who may like to have them. I thought originally of sending these to you to distribute as you thought best, but on reflection I think it wiser to let those who are genuinely interested ask for a copy. You might see if Jim Ashworth would like one, and N.W.E. Hamm. Alf Shaw might; Wilbur probably wouldn't. FRED Sellers is a possibility. Perhaps you won't have a single request! However, see.

In a few days I am setting off for wildest Lakeland for a strenuous holiday. I have developed such a belly on me these past few weeks that I can't button my flies, so I'm planning to shake it off over Wasdale way.

The weather at present is delightfully mild and sunny, and the hills were never more colourful and attractive. But the leaves are falling from the trees – winter will soon be here.

Did you guess, by the way, where I had supper last Saturday evening.

Best wishes to the whole bloody lot of you.

Alf

LETTER 28: TO ERIC WALTER MAUDSLEY, 6 OCTOBER 1942

Tuesday evening   19 Castle Grove
October 6 1942   Kendal

Dear Wal.

The morning of Monday, October 5th, was murky, cold and damp. I went to work in the gloom, watching a blustery wind whirling the leaves from the trees. I shivered as I walked. Winter had come.

But at the office I was to experience a shining ray of bright light that cut through the gloom of the morning and quite dispelled it. I was hardly seated at my desk before Dorothy brought me your letter of the 23rd

Sept. et seq. I opened it, and commenced to read. It was truly magnificent. Your description of your first ascent of Scafell held me enthralled. It took me right out of my surroundings; I climbed Scafell with you. Together we strode along Eskdale, loveliest of valleys; we stood admiring the white lace curtain of Cam Spout, and later idled by its brink; we toiled side by side to the rocky ramparts of Mickledore; agreed that Broad Stand had better be left until the next time; made our way beneath the cliffs to Lord's Rake; palpitated on the West Wall Traverse; and finally emerged, sweating and triumphant, from the steep funnel of Deep Ghyll to claim our reward. I know the spot well where you sat and gazed at the scene of grandeur that encompassed you. It hasn't an equal in Lakeland. The Napes Ridges are fine, and so is Pillar Rock, but there isn't a rival to Scafell Pinnacle and its Pisgah. Here you are right on top of the world; you look down on it as its Creator looks down on it, with utter satisfaction; you are conscious of nothing but tranquility so profound that it is almost a pain; would you could take the image away in your mind and never lose it, never let it be dimmed or put aside by material considerations! A few hours spent in contemplation and meditation above the cliffs of Scafell, in silent worship at the cathedral of the Pinnacle, does more for a man's soul than a thousand sermons. Could you sit there and call yourself an atheist, an unbeliever? I do not think so for a moment; your doubts must surely have been lost in the gulf of Mickldore, swept away by the clean winds.

Once I sat where you sat and lost count of time as you did. Not until darkness had hidden Hollow Stones below me, and only the neighbouring peaks retained the rosy flush of the departed sun, could I tear myself away from the majestic, awe-inspiring scene. My long-delayed communion with the spirits of the mountain cost me dear then: in the gathering dusk I could not find the top of Lord's Rake, and essayed a descent by a wide gully I subsequently found to be Red Ghyll, not without mishaps; when I reached the comforting turf of Brown Tongue I was both bloody and bowed. But I remember how long and earnestly I looked upwards at the jagged black rock-towers above me before limping down to Wasdale ... the spell of that day's glories is with me yet.

It is a regret to me that I put off the ascent of Scafell by Cam Spout until late years. Thoughts of the weary grind so-called in the guidebooks, up the screes to Mickledore caused me to postpone it time after time. When I finally made the attempt I found it so easy and enjoyable that I wept with chagrin at the lost opportunities. I too was staying at Boot, and walked along Eskdale while the dew was still on the ground; I too thought it sublimely beautiful. Cam Spout looked stiff, but proved an easy staircase, with the added attraction of a supremely lovely series of cascades to delight me. Up above, I squeezed into Fat Man's Agony, and lingered a long time on the rock platform at the foot of Broad Stand, intently studying the ample footholds that climbed the corner and disappeared aloft. I was sick with desire, palsied with fear . . . I too turned reluctantly away. Someday we must do it together.

You didn't climb Deep Ghyll, and shouldn't claim credit for it. That passage, inherently false, rather mars your masterly narrative. What you did was to ascend Lord's Rake <u>beyond</u> the entrance to Deep Ghyll and made your way into its upper reaches, above its two pitches, by the West Wall Traverse. If Broad Stand turned you away, you certainly would not have attempted the cavern which forms the first pitch of the Ghyll. Unroped and alone you just couldn't have climbed it.

And Scafell is the King, not the Queen, of the Lakeland mountains. Helvellyn is the Queen, and Skiddaw the Prince. You enjoyed relating the details of your day on Scafell, didn't you? That much is clear from your description of it. And I revelled in reading it. I simply devoured it, wallowed in it. When I finally put it away in my pocket, and looked up, lo! The sun was shining, the sky serene. I am sending it along to Lawrence to leaven the weary barm of his existence for a few minutes; my heart is still heavy with compassion for those I left behind me in that soul-destroying hellhole at Blackburn.

On October 16th I am going into the hills for a few days holiday, my last fling in 1942. I shall have a night at Patterdale and another in Borrowdale; I doubt whether I shall risk dropping down into Wasdale, having regard to the lack of accommodation.

Last week I sent Alker a selection of my 1941 collection of photographs of Lakeland peaks. I'll let you have them at an opportune time.

The Holidays Committee treated me nobly after my efforts for them, and my library of mountaineering classics is not augmented by several volumes I have long coveted.

Thanks for your kind remarks anent 'Blea Tarn'.

Now what's this about an operation and service in the Forces? A minor operation, you say. That is a matter of relativity. Having your useless dick cut off would be a minor operation for you, but definitely a major amputation for me.

If you really are joining the Forces I wish you well. But why the Navy? Why not

Blast it

An Alpine Corps?

However, if you entry is imminent, you probably won't have time to write again before you go. But I sincerely hope you will find time occasionally to put aside your sword and take up the pen, and tell me of your feats of derring-do. And if I, in return, can bring a breath of Lakeland air into my replies, and bring back memories of happy days on the hills, I shall be happy. Let me know what happens to you.

Yours sincerely,

Alf

I saw your brother walking along Bolton Road, Blackburn, a week last Saturday.

You'll not forget to return my book, will you, if you have to go?

Remember me to Bess

What will <u>she</u> do, poor thing?

See o'er

[On the back of the letter AW has drawn a map of Scafell entitled 'Scafell from Pikes Crag: Probable Route of W.E. Maudsley 30.7.42'. The drawing is a rough sketch, but reminisecent of sketches and routes to come.]

LETTER 29: TO LAWRENCE WOLSTENHOLME, 20 NOVEMBER 1942

Friday evening
November 20 1942

19 Castle Grove
Kendal

Dear Lawrence,

It was a very great surprise to me to receive your letter the other day. The trees were in new leaf and the birds were mating when last you wrote. It was springtime. Now the trees are bare of leaves and the birds have gone to warmer lands. Spring has passed, and summer, and autumn. It is winter again. In the meantime I have written to you occasionally, sent things I thought you would like to see. They brought no response until this week. It grieved me deeply, angered me almost, to be ignored thus. It is discourteous, to say the least, not to reply to letters received. Good manners demanded that I should have an acknowledgment that my communications had safely arrived. Nothing came, however, and it is now some time since I deleted your name from my list of correspondents and erased you from my mind. One does not write to a man who is dead, nor think of him. Your word, inertia, is not half strong enough. Even with this latest belated effort you made the admission, as though it were a joke, that it would not yet have been written but for your wife's entreaties. You should be grateful to Margery for propping you up thus and reminding you of ordinary moral decencies which should be observed, but this time she was too late. Thoughtlessness has cost you a friend. I will reply to our letter, but I tell you frankly that there are other things I would much rather be doing tonight than writing to you.

In a few days time I shall have been at Kendal a year, and it has been a year of sublime contentment, of progress, of rapid advancement towards the attainment of an ambition that was born early and somehow survived the ghastly, soul-destroying environment of the Blackburn Town Hall. I look back on those years with horror. Coming here was like escaping from a foul pit. There are no days of desolation and gloom, as there were then. There are no days when things go wrong at work, no days of desperate endeavour, no weary nights of overtime, no rush jobs, no office squabbles, no R.G wanting to see me, no interferences, no questions asked, no kow-towing to little Ceasers who ought to be shot.

In twelve months I have earned for myself a classical reputation. My ledgers, illustrated and illuminated, are things of great beauty. There is nothing here to cramp my style, no jealous criticisms and senseless comments, and I have flourished exceedingly. There is positive joy in working in these happy conditions. I am <u>very</u> highly thought of, and the Council's special pet. My flair for the artistic has been quickly recognized, and applauded. Unlike the dullards who govern Blackburn, here are men of breeding and intellect and imagination; men, moreover, to whom civic pride is a religion, not a sham. And with justification, for is this not a lovely old town and are there not centuries of proud history in its mellow grey stones?

So I prosper. Kendal folk have a reputation for clannishness, but I have blasted my way right through the outer shell and find now that every man has a smile and a kind word for me. I was one of the gentlemen of Kendal who took the mayor to Church last Sunday, and am to be found in my place at all civic functions. A wealth of tradition still clings to Kendal, and I find its varied ceremonies of absorbing interest. I keep the Education, Gas, Water, Electricity, Rating, Housing and

Superannuation Accounts of the Council as they have never been kept before, and yet have lots of time to free-lance. Much of my time in future will be spend at the Museum, for the Council have asked me to take it under my control and look after it. Now Kendal Museum is a very remarkable place; I'd as soon drop in there to look round as go to the pictures. It is widely acknowledged as the finest in the North of England; it is not a place of death, as yours is, but a live, exciting place which attracts hordes of visitors. Now it is mine, to display the exhibits, to publicise, to curate and to catalogue. Could there be a more delightful hobby? I have long wanted a collection of birds eggs: now I have ten thousand at one fell swoop, gratis. A public-minded citizen has provided the funds to build an extension: I shall enjoy spending the money.

My work, then, is a joy to me. But it is the hours of leisure which make life in Kendal a delirious delight. At 5.30 I promptly forget about the office (my aggregate hours of overtime since I started here are precisely nil) and continue from the night before my plans, fantastic, exhilarating, wildly exciting, for a future which has bounded much nearer and is now within my grasp. These dreams are no longer transient and far away, but real;

[next page lost]

LETTER 30: TO LAWRENCE WOLSTENHOLME, 25 NOVEMBER 1942

Wednesday evening   19 Castle Grove
November 25 1942   Kendal

My dear Lawrence,

Sorry to butt in on wages, but I must insist that the 'privilege (sic) of having the last word' be mine. So get 'em balanced, in a fashion, and stuck up, and then lend me a cavernous ear.

First let me thank you very sincerely for your condolences and those of the unnamed others in the office.

Then let me say that your letter afforded me acute delight. Listen. When I first knew you, back in the days of silent films, you were a romantic: you had a flashing eye, a fiery tongue, a ready temper. Sadly I have watched the years change the baleful glare into a bovine stare; calm the tempestuous flow of your invective, damp almost to extinction the flame that once burned so brightly within you. You are not as you were, by a long chalk. The Wolst of recent years has been characterized by meekness, timidity, submission – and I exhort you to save these qualities, such as they are, for your old age. When you were a youth you had dreams; now these are gone too. You are growing old too fast, Lawrence, much too fast. I don't like to see you straddled with cobwebs. I preferred you as a man of passion, of action. And now, at last, I have roused you from your torpor. Every word of my harangue was designed with this end in view. Far from being a 'hysterical out-burst' it was written, as you should have guessed, with a placid smirk on my venerable visage. It worked. For the first time you are inspired to send me a letter which is not a doleful diatribe of distress, and not only that but you reply within 48 hours. Furthermore, your reply is couched in the violent language I hoped for. I rejoice. The red blood is flowing again.

Now actually it doesn't matter whether you write me letters or not. A letter received is a letter to be answered (it is with me, anyhow!), and when I tell you that in the past twelve months I have received over 200 (TWO HUNDRED) personal letters from folk who still think a lot of me, you will appreciate that this drain on my leisure time is hindering the fruition of my Major Plans. So you can please your damn self.

No it wasn't your tardy letter-writing that I had a grouse about. What disappointed me was that you failed even to acknowledge my sensational free gift. Then you yap about friendship! If, in your analy-sis of friendship, thanks are never called for, then, sir, you are a pig. In my friendships, courtesy has prominent place. It is your sense of friendship, not mine, that is pathetic. And I repeat (to further revive your drooping ire) that you are a pig. Margery will agree with me; if, that is, she sees this letter, which I doubt.

Your cheap gibe about CEASERS shows that you quite misread my letter. I mentioned <u>little</u> Ceasers. By the way, are we spelling this word right?

The only passage in your letter to which I bow my head and agree is that all have not my ability to wield a facile pen. How I wish they had! Oh, how I wish they had!

I had better mention that I shall be sending you a card at Christmas. I would not like to place you at a further advantage.

Your old pal

AlfW

LETTER 31: TO ERIC WALTER MAUDSLEY, 27 JANUARY 1943

Wednesday evening   19 Castle Grove
January 27 1943   Kendal

Dear Walt

I received your letter with acclamation, but my face grew grave as I learnt of your somber news. Truly, the swing of fortune has brought low the once-exalted bastion and bulwark of Congregationalism, the man Maudsley.

You still do not hint at the nature of your operations in hospital, and in view of this reticence on your part to uncover all I am driven to the surmise that it was on your hind quarters, on that fleshy globule called your bottom, that the knives of your tormentors descended so relentlessly. I admire your phlegm in the matter of the bedpan, but I am of course reminded that ten years ago chasteness would not allow you to regard humbler vessel, a chamber, without searing your soul. You have become worldly since then.

Then, make darker the sky, is your calling-up for military service, which appears to be imminent. Indeed, since it is now some weeks since your letter was penned, it is by no means improbable that you are already engaged in feats of derring-do as a regular soldier, that the Hertfordshire belles are now shaking sad heads over your departure.

But your gravest item of news was the brief mention that relations with Bess have lost their early rapture. Surely not! 'Long, luscious, sweet as nectar' . . . these are your own words. Having regard to the fact that [word blacked out] it was who, more than anyone before [three lines blacked out] will later bring in full measure – having regard to these, I cannot help but feel sad. Then, to crown your woe, you lament bitterly on the dung-coloured, uninspiring countryside in which you have chosen to live. Your happiest days were spent within sight of the hills. After the War you must come back north, for the man who goes to live amongst the pine-trees and cascades and purple heights gains the whole world by so doing. How well I recall your valiant cry, echoing amid the peaks: 'En Avant!'

At the moment I am at rather a low ebb myself. I am typing this letter with the machine half-way up the chimney and a pair or brace of bony knees thrust forward into the smouldering embers of a dying fire. I have, I fear, developed a cold, due primarily to artistic zeal which kept me sat on a boulder up at Sweden Bridge for an hour last Sunday until I was tolerably content with the rough sketch I had made. You may gather from that

that I have at long last, after months of dreaming and planning, rolled up my sleeves and gone to work in earnest. I am engaged in preparing fifty drawings of Lakeland scenes (after the style of Blea Tarn): these I intend to publish on completion in book form under the title of LAKELAND SKETCHBOOK at 12/6 a copy. This will be a venture entirely new, and should bring me fame. And money, for if I sell 5,000 copies, which is my target, I shall profit on the enterprise to the extent of two thousand pounds. My only other piece of Lakeland news since I wrote last is that on Boxing Day morning I was tempted by a blue sky and warm sun to follow the Coniston Foxhounds from Ambleside 'ower top o Kirkstone'. It was a bonny morning, springtime at Christmas; the colouring of the fells was exquisite, with wisps of white mist trailing across the hillsides and adding a peculiar charm to the views.

I was not in Blackburn at Christmas, hence your suggestion as to the reason for the unrelieved gloom of the populace was well-founded. I went over for the New Year, and wallowed in an atmosphere of fish and chip shops, black puddings, tripe, clogs, hen-pens, cloth caps. There is little joy in returning now; I have advanced and matured since those humdrum days of pre-1941. By arrangement, I met Willie Ashton on this trip, and by accident Norman Hamm.

I am not enclosing my Lakeland photographs this time, chiefly because I am using some of them to supply the details for my sketches until I can get out into the district more. And again because you may already have slung your hook from Herts. Later on I'll let you have them, augmented by my 1943 collection.

You must let me know what happens to you in the near future, for I shall always retain a mighty interest in the welfare of one who, though misguided in some respects, always struck me as a being a very likeable cove. Good luck!

Your old pal

Alf

LETTER 32: TO ERIC WALTER MAUDSLEY, 10 APRIL 1943

Saturday evening
April 10 1943

19 Castle Grove
Kendal

Dear Mr Maudsley,
14566772!

What have they done at you, boy? If ever in the past I have thought of you as having a number as a handle to your name it has been when criminal tendencies have oozed through the smooth veneer of your sophistication and the prospect of an ultimate Dartmoor has passed, like a vague shadow, through my mind. Such occasions have been, I admit, infrequent. You were never the type to rob a bank, but sometimes you expressed anti-social views which might have landed you behind bars.

Yet you've got your number, all the same. You are now no longer Muadsley the peerless, nor even Maudsley the elegant. You are no longer Maudsley the one and only but 14566772, one of fourteen million odd.

It isn't good enough, damn me if it is. All these years you've spend in acquiring and fostering distinctive touches so that your personality might be a rare and beautiful thing, and now, overnight, the lot goes to hell, and you with them. Out of the grey dawn emerges 14566772, a miserable and bedraggled creature shorn of his trimmings.

In a way, this experience will do you good, yes. Discipline builds character, physical training builds a fine body. But the main thing is that these attributes are being enforced upon you. You have lost your freedom. You can't do as you please any more. You are a slave. You must be content with lesser joys now for a while. You must learn to find pleasure in grosser company than that to which you have been accustomed, to be ready to guffaw at lewd and unfunny remarks, to appreciate the appeal of cheap and frowsy women, to enjoy raw food served in a dollop on a tin plate, and, above all to squirt in a chamber if need be.

Compare your lot with mine! Inwardly I cannot help but gloat. When am I going to join the Army indeed! Never. In fact, your letter was a jolt; I had well-nigh forgotten there was a war still raging somewhere far from this peaceful Utopia of mine. I am sitting at the foot of the rainbow with my pot of gold, lady, and I am here to stay.

Take last Saturday, for instance, when you were marching and sweating in the barrack-square. I, for my part, was comfortably laid on a fragrant couch in Dora's Field at Rydal, idly watching the blue smoke from my pipe curling upwards into the sunny sky. I was a man at peace with the world and with himself, a man inexpressibly happy and utterly content. The tree in whose shade I lay was in blossom: I could see the delicate tracery of the petals against the brightness of the sky. Around me were daffodils in profusion, a golden carpet of bloom. Life was very very sweet . . .

In due course I sauntered along to the Glen Rothay Hotel for tea, and subsequently made my way beneath the dark pines and the vivid-green larches by the edge of the quiet lake, and so, at length through the bracken on to Loughrigg. And there was the vast pageant of hills, sleepy in the sunshine: Bowfell the beloved, Gable, the Langdales, Fairfield. Oh, how grand to be in Lakeland, to be rid of things earthy, to dwell amidst eternal beauty!

The following day I spend in the Lyth Valley, amongst the lambs and the nesting birds, following winding paths beneath trees loaded with sweet blossom. Pastoral tranquility wheree'er I turned my steps. Again, life was very sweet.

You could have been a happy man, too. But there was the stink of money in your nostrils, and you chose, like a he-dog, to follow its trail. Thou fool!

Future generations, when they think of Wordsworth and Southey and Coleridge and de Quincey, will think of Wainwright also. All my energies are now devoted to this aim. I am engaged on a work which will bring me fame, and enthusiasm for it is running white-hot; life is deliriously exciting. I haven't left myself time to tell you of my plan in detail, but believe me, this is Wainwright attaining a new best. And backing me up are friends with the stuff that counts in an enterprise of this sort. Today my researches took me on a first visit to Shap, where, by the side of the infant Lowther, in a sleepy hollow of the fells, I spent an enjoyable hour amongst the primroses gazing at the ruins of the old Abbey. I wore flannels, not khaki. I listened to the myriad voices of nature, perfectly attuned, not to the raucous call of the sergeant-major.

So leave me here with my dreams and my plans, in the Lakeland I love so passionately. Write to me whenever you wish. And fight my battles for me, that's a good chap.

Tell me when the war's over!

Your old pal,

14566773

Maudsley, in early 1943, having served in the Home Guard for two years, after he had recovered from his minor operation, was called up – but not into the Navy as he had hoped. He found himself in the Royal Signals, en route to Burma. He was in the army till the end of the war in 1945. His relationship with Bessy had finished before he went into the army.

AW remained in Kendal for the rest of the war, still planning the brilliant books with which he was going to astound the world.

Part 4
Letters to Family and Friends, 1942-54

AW's mother Emily died in Blackburn on 13 November 1942, aged sixty-nine. The mention of thanking for condolences in his letter to Lawrence Wolstenholme of 25 November 1942 (Letter 30) refers to her death.

She left furniture – which AW was involved in trying to sell off – and also a bequest which led to many complications. Her father had left her a house – which is presumably the one in which she had lived and brought up her children – but in order that it did not fall into the hands of her drunken husband Albert, he had set up a trust to benefit her children, namely AW and his brother and two sisters.

He writes to his Aunt Nellie – his mother's sister – about her son Oswald, AW's cousin, now going in the services. Peter, AW's son, now aged nine, had been in hospital to have his appendix removed.

He also writes about the problems of the will and the disposal of the grandfather's trust. Uncle Tom is the husband of Emily's sister Annie and AW was not best pleased with his handling of the will as a Trustee, or the behaviour of the solicitors – but was obviously quite pleased with his phrase 'recrudescing in a more violent form' which he uses in both his letter to Uncle Tom and his Aunt Nellie. Alice is AW's sister.

Emily's personal estate came to £182-16-2, which included furniture sold for £17-15-0. The money in trust, from the property, came to £572, shared between the four children. AW's total share came in all to £174. He planned to use it as a deposit on a bungalow and leave his rented council house in Castle Grove, but this was not done for some time.

LETTER 33: TO HELEN (NELLIE) SMITH, 24 NOVEMBER 1942

19 Castle Grove
Kendal
November 24 1942

Dear Auntie Nellie,

Your letter was a very pleasant surprise for me this morning.

So Oswald is to be a pilot in the Fleet Air Arm. Is he? Well, well! Somehow I can only remember Oswald as a small boy with a colourful smile and with hair which, although obviously the subject of much attention, never would just stay as it was put. I did once, I think, see him in long trousers. And now, quite suddenly, he has reached man's estate. A pilot in the Fleet Air Arm! My word, I'll bet he's delighted.

You needn't worry much about him, he'll have a grand time, and take to the strange new life like a duck to water, see if he doesn't. The house will seem strange without him when he goes, and for a long time afterwards; you'll regret the parting naturally, but I rather fancy you'll be a proud mother all the same.

Peter is very much better, thank you; so much better, in fact, that we are to ring up the hospital tomorrow to see if he is ready to come home. He has not worried unduly over his long confinement away from home. Indeed, on the contrary, he has taken very great interest, almost a morbid interest, in the operation and in the treatment to which he has been subjected, and he must certainly now be regarded as a complete authority on matters appertaining to the routine and administration of a hospital. Better still, he's got something to swank about for the rest of his life!

I am glad to have your explanation regarding the price fixed for the bedroom suite, etc. of course I do not think you are interfering! Alice was correct when she told you she was paying 12 pounds for the suite and 4 pounds for the bed, this being the price agreed with mother. It does seem, therefore, that you were misunderstood. Nevertheless, although I shall now offer to reduce the price to 10 pounds, it seemed to me that both Alice and John were perfectly satisfied, and in my opinion they had a good bargain. The only fair price is, of course, the market price ruling at the time they acquired the furniture, and this, of course, is much higher than in normal times. However, I'll see how they feel about it, and in the meantime must thank you for drawing my attention to this matter.

I must thank you, too, for your further invitation to stay with you if I find it necessary to come over to Sheffield. I should be delighted to, so much so that I do hope the necessity will arise, but I hardly think it will. To tell you the truth, Smith Smith and Fielding (now Wake Smith and Co.) are contriving very adroitly to snatch the whole business out of my hands.

When uncle Tom showed me my grandfather's will last week, it seemed to me both then and afterwards on further reflection, that my mother had in fact no power to provide for the disposal of the money bequeathed to her, as grandfather himself had expressly provided that the Trust Fund should be divided equally between her surviving children at the time of her death. Fortunately the terms of my mother's Will were similar, but there is this difference, that it remains the duty of Uncle Tom and Uncle Armitage to convert the investment into cash and themselves distribute the proceeds amongst the children. Smith Wake and Co. have pointed this out to me, and I am compelled to agree with them. The position is further complicated by the fact that payment of the mortgage cannot be enforced, and in any case, there are no funds in the hands of Mr Mellor's Trustees to repay the money. It will be necessary, therefore, for the mortgage to be transferred to a new lender, if possible.

Poor Uncle Tom; he thought last week that his trials and troubles as a Trustee were finally over. I have had to write to him and point out that they are far from finished, that they are, in fact recrudescing in a more violent form after lying dormant all these years. I have explained the position very fully to him, and suggested that he avails himself of Eric's legal mind before Wake Smith and Company descend on him.

I have met many of Kendal's citizens by this time, but not, as yet, a Mr Buckley. If I do, I'll remember Woodhouse to him.

With kindest regards,
Yours sincerely,

LETTER 34: TO TOM BEARDSALL, 24 NOVEMBER 1942

> 19 Castle Grove
> Kendal
> 24th November 1942

Dear Uncle Tom,

I'm bothering you already, you see.

As a matter of fact, your trials and troubles as a Trustee, which you fondly thought were ended last Tuesday, are far from finished. They are, on the other hand, recrudescing in a more violent form after lying dormant all these years.

You will remember that when you showed me my grandfather's Will, I pointed out to you that its terms provided for the distribution of my mother's share equally amongst her surviving children at the time of her death. It seemed to me, both then and afterwards on further reflection, that my mother had in fact no power to dispose of the money bequeathed to her. Fortunately her Will provided as grandfather's Will provided, i.e. that her estate should be divided in equal shares amongst her children: nevertheless the money was not hers to dispose of.

The means nothing prejudicial against anybody – except the poor Trustees. It is still your job to administer grandfather's Will, and you have not done your job until mother's Trust is apportioned for the benefit of her children. In doing this, you will not be carrying out my mother's Will, but my grandfather's as you were appointed to do.

Now let me explain what has happened since I saw you. In the first place I wrote both to Mr Mellor (giving notice for repayment) and to Smith Smith and Fielding (asking if the mortgage was in their keeping). S S and F, now known as Wake Smith and Co. replied to tell me that the mortgage was in their possession, but that payment could not be enforced and in any case there were no funds in the hands of Mr Mellor's Trustees. The only way to get cash would be to transfer the mortgage to another lender, if possible. This I instructed them to do, reluctantly (since it involved legal expenses). Then they come along and report that they have been looking through their books and discover the fact above stated, that is, that it is the duty of the Trustees of R.D. Woodcock to administer my mother's estate (or so much of it as was bequeathed to her). With this I have been compelled to agree, and you may therefore expect a call from a representative of Wake Smith and Co. in the near future. They will request you and Uncle Armitage to sign for the release of the mortgage and you should then, in due course, receive a cheque for 400 hundred pounds less legal charges and disbursements. It is then up to you to comply with the terms of the Will by distributing the proceeds equally between the four children. This could most easily be done, if you are agreeable, by endorsing the cheque in my favour and sending it along to me, for as you know I have other moneys here to distribute and would like to pay out each beneficiary in one amount.

I have a suspicion (born out of other dealings with solicitors) that Wake Smith and Company are out to make something for themselves out of this transaction. They will, I am sure, want you to leave everything in their hands, including payment of death duties and apportionment of the estate to the children. They have asked me for the names and addresses of the children and I have supplied them. Their job, until instructed otherwise, is merely to transfer the mortgage and pay you the net proceeds, not to arrange for payment of death duties and an apportionment between the children.

But this is not all. There is the War Stock to be realized. I have hopefully sent away for a form of repayment. This Stock is also registered in the names of yourself and Uncle Armitage, and your signatures will again be needed before payment can be expected. I have been wondering whether Wake Smith and Co also had a hand in making this investment? This money of course is to be treated precisely as the mortgage for 400 pounds, that is, it is your duty, not mine, to see that it is distributed. I expect complications will arise here too before this is finally settled. When I have a reply from the Bank of England I will write to you again.

I should rather like Eric, blessed as he is with a legal mind, to see this letter before you are swept up in the fell clutch of Wake Smith and Co. I think he'll agree with me.

I return herewith the Will you left with me. Your need of it is greater than mine.

I have left myself little room for social greetings, but I hope you had a pleasant journey home from Blackburn and are keeping in good health.

Yours sincerely,

LETTER 35: TO ALICE FISH, 25 NOVEMBER 1942

> 19 Castle Grove
> Kendal
> November 25 1942

Dear Alice,

Thank you for your letter received today.

You seem to have been quite busy running errands which really the Executors should do! However, you appear to have made good progress with your enquiries, much better, in fact, than I have, for I am already caught up in a mass of complications.

When Uncle Tom showed me my grandfather's Will last Tuesday, it seemed to me then, on reading it, that my mother had in fact no power to say how the money bequeathed to her should be disposed of, since my grandfather himself provided that on her death it should be divided in equal shares amongst her surviving children. I mentioned this to Uncle Tom at the time, but he merely looked blank. Fortunately, my mother's

Will provided in similar terms, but there is this difference, that the money will have to be administered not under the terms of mother's Will, but under grandfather's: that is to say, it is the duty of

Grandfather's Trustees, Uncle Tom and Uncle Armitage, to attend to the settlement. Their solicitors have now pointed this out to me, and I have been compelled to agree. Furthermore, I find that repayment of the mortgage cannot be enforced, and that in any case. Mr Mellor's Trustees have no funds available for repaying the money owing. I have therefore had to instruct the solicitors to transfer the mortgage to another lender, if possible; and I have to tell Uncle Tom that his troubles as a Trustee are by no means ended.

Auntie Nellie wrote yesterday to say that perhaps my mother had misunderstood her about the price of the bedroom suite. The price she mentioned was 16 pounds new, 10 pounds now. My own view is that the furniture is worth the price you agreed to pay, but if you feel at all dissatisfied I will substitute the lower figure. Have you arranged to dispose of the other articles yet?

I enclose a form of authority for you to take to the Co-op. Frank should sign it also.

Please keep a note of all that is happening and don't send any money by post. I will be over soon, probably on the morning of December 5th

I'll leave Ruth to tell you the news.

On 1 August 1948, AW became Borough Treasurer of Kendal, on the death of the previous Treasurer. He was aged forty-one, relatively young for such a position – his friend Lawrence did not make the position for another five years, but then Kendal was not as big as Blackburn. His pay rose to £900 a year and he at last decided it was time to give up his council house. He bought a plot of land at Kendal Green, on the edge of the town, and worked with the architect on the design for the house he wanted built and also on a five-year plan to create a garden, with paths, trees and cairns, which he was going to do himself.

He was still walking on the fells at every opportunity, mainly alone, sometimes sleeping out overnight, and doing drawings of local buildings and churches in Kendal and of well known Lake District scenes, while still nursing an ambition to create a greater Lakeland project.

– – –

LETTER 36: TO LAWRENCE WOLSTENHOME, 13 JULY 1949

13 July 1949   Kendal

Dear Lawrence,

Delay in replying to your letter has been caused by a severe bout of overtime: I've been earning emoluments for myself as the offices designated to prepare the next electors list. That task is now completed, and the next is to select and send two pictures to decorate the walls of your sanctum at the Town Hall. (Presumably this is the room I remember best as the Rate Enquiry Office, subsequently tenanted by Mr Bennett?)

You ask for 'soft beauty', whereas my preference would be for 'rugged grandeur' in the shape of rocks, scree and snow. As this exhibition is, in a way, my memorial, I feel tempted to offer you PILLAR ROCK and SCAFELL CRAG. On the other hand, you have to live with the pictures, and your wishes must be observed. Here, then, with my compliments, are ASHNESS BRIDGE, WRAY BAY and CALF CLOSE BAY – three of them. You are entitled to two, the third being added to give you a choice. I feel sure you will pounce on ASHNESS BRIDGE, which is always a safe bet, and that your second choice will be CALF CLOSE BAY. Both are 'pretty' pictures, but not good drawings – they represent a style I abandoned some years ago, before I had confidence enough to draw firm lines and splash the ink on. Nowadays I would do these scenes in half the time, use only one-tenth of the lines, and feel much more satisfied with the results. Of the three submitted, my choice would be WRAY BAY first and ASHNESS BRIDGE second. Please return the one you reject. When having the pictures framed, note that a white mount 3" wide and a narrow black frame would give the best effect. I'll not be there for the unveiling.

Quite the biggest thing that's happened to me lately is my conversion to colour photography. I switched to colour a couple of months ago – after spending an afternoon, feeling that my poor talents were quite inarticulate, on a hillside carpeted with bluebells, and bracken that was bronze and gold, with Grasmere's blue lake and green woods in the distance, and white galleons of cloud above. Something had to be done about it, and a day or two later I returned to the scene with a colour film in my camera. The pictures I obtained, after a week's anxious waiting, were just too beautiful for words. I developed an insatiable appetite for more. It has been a great and thrilling experience this summer to walk along familiar valleys and over well-loved hills as if seeing them for the first time – looking now not for contrasts of light and shade, as before, but for colour. Already I have an album of a hundred lovely pictures: not only of bluebells at Grasmere, but of wild roses in Langdale and foxgloves by Ullswater, of water-lilies on Easedale Tarn, of hawthorn-blossom at Elterwater. And not only of flowers: the hills come first in my favour, as always, and now I have captured for the winter evenings the lichen and moss of Scafell Crag, the red screes of Gable, the grey rocks and brown tarns of Bowfell and Crinkle Crags. I have pictures of views from mountain-tops, many taken just after sunrise, that I could (and will!) gaze at for hours.

The crazy season is in full swing – that of spending nights alone on the mountains. The weather has aided and abetted wonderfully this summer, and the exciting memories I have hoarded up for old age (which seems as far off as ever!) are pearls beyond price. Best of all, per-haps, was a glorious red sunrise seen from Harrison Stickle in a purple sky, while Langdale below was choked with cotton-wool clouds and seemed like a huge curving glacier, from the sheepfold below Rossett to Loughrigg, where it was joined by another glacier coming down from Grasmere. Out of this sea of white cloud rose all the familiar peaks of Lakeland, curiously detached, but warm and rosy and friendly in the early sunlight. Another lovely dawn was witnessed from Scafell Pike: at 3a.m I could see quite clearly the outline of the Isle of Man, and its winking lighthouses, and the Scottish hills were so distinct that they seemed on the fringe of the Lake District. The sun came up like a ball of fire, immediately touching the stones of the summit with a warm, ruddy glow where before they had been ashen-grey: and it was unearthly to watch Gable and Bowfell and Pillar and the rest of them all light up, one after another. Below, the valleys were filled with white mist . . . another time, last month, I was most luxuriantly sunbathing on Bowfell at 5am and watching shadowy Langdale slowly coming to life. Experiences like this have a heavenly beauty about them that sort of gets me in a soft spot. I hunger for more. I really must get my Lakeland book written. I shall have to do it finally in self-defence! There's an article in tonight's Lancashire Daily Post (north edition) about austere borough treasur-ers, and a recital of the weird habits of Kendal's b.t, who spends his Saturday nights sleeping (sic) on hill-tops. This will take some living-down: as ever, I have many critics of my conduct, but a perfectly serene and untroubled mind sends me about my daily affairs with a happy smile for everyone. Water off a duck's back, that's me!

I may have missed the announcement of the advent of your daughter, for a morbid curiosity attracts me only to the 'Deaths' column in the

Times. Or it may not have happened yet. Either way. I hope everything is O.K. you'll see, it'll be like starting your life all over again. You're going to enjoy these next few years as never before.

AW

At the beginning of October 1949, the death occurred of Tom Snape, one of AW's oldest Blackburn friends. Along with Tom's wife Doris, they had been founder members of the Blackburn Rovers Supporters Club and had also been on holidays together to the Lake District. AW and Doris were very close friends – it is not clear how close but in her diaries she referred to him as 'my old playmate' and mentions secret rendezvous, while AW boasted in letters to his male friends that she was one of his girl friends.

Tom had been ill and in poor health for some years. AW wrote a long letter to Doris two weeks after Tom died. From then on, AW always used to visit her, staying with her at her house, when he visited Blackburn.

LETTER 37: TO DORIS SNAPE, 21 OCTOBER 1949

> 19 Castle Grove
> Kendal
> 21 Oct 1949

Dear Doris,

I wonder how you are feeling now, a fortnight after? I have often wondered during these past days. More and more I am coming to think that your attitude is right: that we must regard Tom's passing not as a tragedy but, in many ways as a blessing. When I think back over the years I have known him, I feel that I never fully understood what his sufferings must have been. I never understood (nor did others who knew him) because he took such good care to show always a bright and cheerful face. The last thing he sought was sympathy – it suited him far better to double everyone up with laughter. He was the funniest man I ever met: with all respect to him, he was a wonderful clown. I could never tire of hearing Tom tell a story, or recount some of his experiences – it was always a joy to me to be his listener. But because he was such jolly company, I never quite appreciated the effort it must have cost him sometimes. How often he must have dearly wished (inwardly) that he could have been fit and well like those he entertained, that he could have enjoyed, too, many experiences which were denied him by his poor health. He must have realized keenly that many simple pleasures which others enjoyed as a matter of course, would never be his, not in this life.

He must have had many regrets, and they must have been in his mind continuously, but never once did I hear him mention them. He never complained, never. A stranger would have thought he was the happiest jolliest fellow in the world, without a care or worry of any sort. We who knew him better knew different, but he never allowed us to dwell on his misfortunes. His physical failings he couldn't hide from us, but he refused to let us reflect that he must have mental sufferings, too. But of course he must often have wondered to himself why he was called upon to bear, such a cross, and for so long. The burden was with him all the time, and it grew heavier, not lighter. He must have realized long ago that his health was worsening and that there was no hope of any permanent improvement, but his smile continued as broad as ever, and no one was allowed to suspect his real feelings. The future for him was as bleak as it could be, and what a consolation it must have been to him to know that he could depend absolutely on the unfailing love of his wife and son! At the same time, how bitterly he must have regretted that his misfortunes should be such a source of concern and worry to those two he loved best, and how he must have wished he could spare them their anxiety!

Now he is at rest, as you said, and in such peace that he would never have known in his life. But you will be finding that his presence in your home seems no less real, that he lives on without pain. How could it be otherwise? Every corner of the house has its own special memories of him: you must be feeling constantly that he is still there, watching you as you lay the table, as you sit by the fire, as you walk in the garden. And watching not sadly, but with a happy twinkle in his eye, and a ready chuckle. He will be especially watching you in the kitchen, and longing to put on his pinny and take over the cooking from you! Yes the new arrangement of things is rather nice don't you think? The initial shock was awful, but that is over, now – and you find that Tom hasn't gone at all. He's still there, about the house, and as real as ever – and, best of all, not now suffering, but happy with a new happiness. Happy because his suffering is over, happy because he has been able to ease your burden at last. He will be happiest of all when he sees you are happy again, when he can hear you singing again.

He'd like you now to enjoy some of the pleasures you denied yourself to attend to him. He'd like you to take a little holiday now and then, and go to theatres and shows, and have the folk he liked best to come and share your fireside sometimes.

So try to go on pleasing him, as you have done for so long!

I do hope you are feeling better now, and finding that the 'new arrangement' (as I call it) has its own quiet joys that you would never have suspected before. If you don't agree with me now, I'm sure you will before long! Take good care of yourself, and look after Derrick – by which I mean send him out in the evenings to find his own friends. (then you can share your fireside with Tom alone, and play some nice records for him, eh?)

Don't forget, too, that Eddie is eager to be of service. He's your best friend, remember (you knew that, didn't you?). find him an odd job to do about the house, now and then – he'll be happy to help.

And then there's me, too – a world away. Don't forget me, either: I'm anxious to be hearing from you.

Funny thing, I feel ever so much better inside after writing this letter. I've convinced myself that Tom is happy, and I only wait now to hear from you that you are happy, too. Tell me so, please!

With love,

Alf

p.s I haven't forgotten about Derrick's new book keeping system!

p.p.s have you go a copy of the current issue of 'OUT OF DOORS'?

LETTER 38: TO LAWRENCE WOLSTENHOME, 17 NOVEMBER 1950

KENDAL   FRIDAY   17th NOVEMBER 1950

Dear Lawrence,

I am writing this letter in manuscript, as a special treat for you. It hadn't occurred to me earlier what a rare pleasure it must be to you to see handwriting like mine, and the steadiness and rhymthic flow thereof will serve further to demonstrate that I am not merely 'hale and hearty', as you suggest, but quite superbly magnificent.

Thank you for the book, now returned.

Your shame at not having heard about (or forgotten) 'Pennine Campaign' is quite merited, and I am chagrined to learn that this classic means nothing to you. To Miss D, who never seems to forget anything, my message is

> Bless you, for remembering!

Cut along the perforated line.

Enclosed is another shad Production I found when flitting this summer. Do with it what you will: 'tis but a worthless trifle. I send it merely in the hope that it might bring a momentary gleam to your darkness.

In reply to your enquiries:

'PANNUS MIHI PANIS' means 'WOOL IS MY BREAD'

(centuries ago, wool was the main industry here)

the 'bent tin-tacks' are fishhooks (used for weaving in those days)

I never attend Branch meetings (not being interested in the things they talk about)

Reading between the lines of your letter, it is palpably apparent that you are pathetically eager to see me again. When I've saved up enough for a haircut, I'll be paying my annual weekend visit to Blackburn – within the next fortnight or so. I'll ring you on the Saturday morning, and then, if your can tear yourself away from the several arms of your wife and daughter that afternoon, perhaps you'd treat me to the Rovers, or stake me for a walk, or something equally stimulating?

AW

This next letter is from Mr Wainwright, Borough Treasurer. Not many have survived – compared with those to his family and old friends and of course later, as A. Wainwright, author. Presumably people did not treasure letters received from council officials whom they did not know and who meant nothing to them. But a Mr W. Tate was so upset by one letter he got from the Borough Treasurer in May 1954 that he always kept it, containing as it did a suggestion that he, Mr Tate, was somehow attempting to bribe a council official.

LETTER 39: TO MR W. TATE (COUNCIL HOUSE TENANT), 11 MAY 1954

TELEPHONE No 130   **BOROUGH OF KENDAL**   Municipal Offices

A. WAINWRIGHT   Lowther Street

BOROUGH TREASURER   KENDAL 11 MAY, 1954

AND RATING OFFICER

Mr W. Tate
c/o 122, Burneside Road
Kendal

Dear Sir,

I have today received your letter accepting the tenancy of a house on the Hall Garth Estate.

There was a pound note in the envelope containing your letter. I do not understand why this was sent and should be obliged if you would let me know the reason. I will keep it until I have your explanation.

Yours faithfully.

A Wainwright
BOROUGH TREASURER

Bill Tate went along to AW's office, puzzled by the accusation. 'Young man,' AW said to him, 'what's the explantion for the pound in the envelope?' Mr Tate said it was a pure mistake – his wife had put the £1, meant for the coal man, in an envelope so she wouldn't spend it, and he by mistake had used that envelope for his letter. AW accepted his explanation and solemnly from a drawer produced the pound note and gave it back to him.

'Looking back to 40 years ago,' so Mr Tate told me in 1994, 'I should have thought that even then it would have taken more than a pound note to bribe a local government official. I did find Mr Wainwright to be a very courteous man.'

Part 5
Pictorial Guides, Book One: Letters, 1955

By the autumn of 1952, AW, now in his new house at 38 Kendal Green, had knocked his garden into shape, three years ahead of his self-imposed schedule, and on 9 November 1952, he sat down to write the first page of Book One of his Pictorial Guides to the Lakeland Fells. His letters show that for many years he had been thinking of a Lakeland project, but at last he had it all planned out: seven books, covering 214 fells, which would take him thirteen years to complete.

He had finished Book One by the Christmas of 1954 and made plans for publication, deciding he would do it himself, with the help of Henry Marshall, the Kendal Librarian, who agreed to act as the official publisher, with Marshall's name and address going on the books and all the leaflets, as AW did not want to reveal his own address and occupation.

A local jobbing printer in Kendal, Bateson and Hewitson, quoted him a price of £950 for 2,000 copies. AW had only £35 in savings, which seems a small amount, given that he had a quite well paid position, but perhaps he had spent all his savings on his new house and garden. However, the printer agreed that AW need not pay any more money till there was an income coming in from the books – if any.

Despite his aversion to personal publicity, AW realised he would have to make an effort to draw attention to his book, get some promotion for it in order to get it into the shops.

In April 1955, he wrote to the magazine Cumbria to enquire about advertising rates. Cumbria – and its sister magazine The Dalesman – was based in Clapham in North Lancashire, but the magazine was printed in Kendal by the Westmorland Gazette, who were also printing AW's book, it being too big a job for Bateman and Hewitson, even though they were nominally handling it.

AW was pleased to find the rates were only £10 for a page. He asked if there could be some accompanying editorial about the book – which he suggested could be done by Mr Griffin (his friend Harry Griffin, the journalist and author and noted Lakeland walker).

LETTER 40: TO MR HEWKIN, 29 APRIL 1955

Mr Leslie Hewkin
Wykefield Cottage
Ambleside
Westmorland

Municipal Offices
Lowther Street
Kendal
29th April 1955

Dear Mr. Hewkin,

Thank you for your letter – and enclosure, which was just what I wanted.

The advertisement rates for CUMBRIA are actually <u>less</u> than I thought they would be. I must now write to the Advertisement Manager to reserve a full page for the June number, but before doing so wonder whether you would have any objection if I asked for the left-hand page opposite your editorial? I think you usually like to keep this free of advertisement, but my own display (which I now have ready) is quite neat and attractive with a couple of small drawings and would not look out of place in that position.

Please don't go out of your way to see Mr. Scott. The question of the drawings is a small one really and I doubt whether they would reproduce well in any case – they would in half-tones, but this isn't altogether a satisfactory treatment for line drawings.

The book is now being printed. I am terribly anxious to see it finished. As soon as I can get hold of a full set of pages (with or without the binding case) I will send it on to you. Mr Griffin will collaborate in the drafting of the editorial matter if you want any assistance.

Yours sincerely,

LETTER 41: TO THE ADVERTISING DEPARTMENT OF CUMBRIA, 4 MAY 1955

The Advertisement Manager
Dalesman Publishing Co.
Clapham
Via Lancaster

38 Kendal Green
Kendal
4th May 1955

Dear Sir

Please reserve for me a full page in your June issue of CUMBRIA (issued June 1st) for the purpose of advertising a book that is due for publication at Whitsuntide.

If it could possibly be arranged, I should be especially grateful if I could have the left-hand page facing the Editorial comments, which, I understand, will make reference to the book.

The advertising matter will take the form of a display for which a full page block will be supplied direct to the Westmorland Gazette. The block is at present being made, but a proof will be sent to you for approval within a few days.

A cheque for 10 pounds is enclosed.

Yours faithfully

AW

The publisher of Cumbria, Harry Scott, had caught sight of some of AW's hand-drawn, handwritten material from Book One – still not published until June – and wrote to AW to say how impressed he was by it. This was probably AW's first ever fan letter for his Pictorial Guides. Once it was out, readers were even writing to offer him a bed, if he was in their area.

LETTER 42: TO MR SCOTT, 9 MAY 1955

9 May 1955

Dear Mr Scott,

I can't remember ever receiving a kinder and more generous letter than the one I have had from you. It is really extremely nice of you to show such an interest in my book, and I feel greatly encouraged by your remarks.

I welcome your opinion particularly, because it was always in my mind when I was compiling the book that I would take it over to Clapham when it was finished to see if you would publish it! Then, when the job was done, I hesitated. It seemed to me then to be unfair to ask anyone to risk money on something so different – success or failure, and the extent of success or failure, were unpredictable. Finally, I decided to [illegible] the risk myself. I just hadn't the nerve to ask you, or my other publisher, to do something I wasn't prepared to do myself ... that's how it comes about that I now find myself suffering the anxieties (and enjoying the excitements) of putting a new book before the public. At the moment, I feel like a man going to the gallows!

I am grateful for what you are doing, and are prepared to do, to help me, but must not trespass further on your kindness.

You shall have the [illegible] copy!
y/s

AW

LETTER 43: TO MRS CHANDLER, 8 JUNE 1955

Municipal Offices
Lowther Street
Kendal
Westmorland
8 June 1955

Dear Madam,

I don't know whether I should address you as 'Dear Miss Chandler' or 'Dear Mrs Chandler', or which is safest in case of doubt – you don't give me a clue. As for 'Dear Sally' – No, I just couldn't!

Thank you for a wonderfully kind letter. Your extremely generous invitation quite affected me: how <u>can</u> you have such confidence in me, a stranger? But really, I cannot accept. I shall not be back in the Grasmere area until Book Three, that is, not until the winter of 1956. And anyway, I'm much too shy!

One thing you can do for me, though, if you will and are able to, and that is to recommend the book to other kindred souls. I fear the railway strike has sadly upset my publicity arrangements, and sales are too few for my peace of mind.

Do this for me, please, and I promise that when I am back in the Grasmere area, I will venture to peep in at The Wray. Not for a bed, and not for a meal, but just to look upon the gracious woman who went to the trouble of writing so charming a letter and offering such kind hospitality to someone she had never met. Besides, I shall always be a bit curious about the 'Miss' or 'Mrs'. You can't blame me if, in the meantime, I think of you as Sally!

Yours sincerely

Perhaps the early fan letter which gave him most delight was from Walter Poucher (1891–88), a noted Lakeland author and photographer (and also chief perfumer for Yardley), whose books AW himself had greatly enjoyed.

LETTER 44: TO WALTER POUCHER, 8 JUNE 1955

Municipal Offices
Lowther Street
Kendal
Westmorland
8 June 1955

Dear Mr Poucher,

I was delighted to receive your very kind letter. No other I have received, or may receive, could possibly bring me more pleasure.

It gave me quite a thrill even to see your order form when it came in a fortnight ago. I said to myself 'now the boot is on the other foot' because for years I have been an ardent admirer and collector of your wonderful books: indeed, I acknowledge with gratitude the help I have gained from your photographs of the Lakeland fells, especially in cases where my own sketches left me in some doubt about details. Occasionally, in fact, I have been tempted to make my drawings direct from your photographs: this I must never do, but certainly you are entitled to some credit for giving me a fuller appreciation of the importance of choosing the right viewpoint and the skilful use of light and shadow.

Must your last Lakeland book really be your last?

Do please come again!

— — —

Now dare I risk spoiling this reply by asking a favour?

This book is a private venture (a mistake, I am beginning to feel) and unfortunately much excellent publicity has been negatived by the railway strike. Postal enquiries are very few, and I am getting a little anxious. Your letter, indeed, came as a great encouragement when I was feeling a wee bit depressed. I must now rely on personal recommendation, and I wonder if you could, without going to any trouble about it, manage to put in a good word for the book if opportunity offers when you are amongst kindred souls. A word from you here and there would, I am sure, help quite a lot.

This letter does not call for any reply. You have already done much to cheer me up by the kind thought that prompted you to write, and I am really most grateful.

Yours sincerely,

AW sent out flyers announcing Book One, hoping for orders or publicity, to various bodies who might help the book, such as The Sanitarian, the official journal of Municipal Sanitary Inspectors, who kindly gave the book a mention and an address for orders. He also sent the flyer to old friends in the Blackburn office. One of those who replied and bought a copy was Fred Sellers (1906–90), who remained in the Blackburn Treasurers Office all his working life. He had worked beside AW in the 1920s. He was small and thin, as opposed to AW who was tall and thin, and featured in many of the office caricatures which AW drew at the time.

LETTER 45: TO FRED SELLERS, JUNE 1955

Henry Marshall
Low Bridge
Kentmere
Westmorland
Telephone: Kentmere 45

Dear Fred,

I recognized your handwriting on the envelope. It rather pleased me to be able to do this after all these years.

Thank you for your kind letter, for the generous references to myself and for certain nostalgic memories which, in turn, have revived others in my own mind – of the snivvies ('hey, you're going down the wrong one!'); of weary nights of swotting; of munroe's teas (and wasn't there someone called Tina?); of the Pay Office Male Voice Choir – and particularly one I shall never forget, of the time you opened a bottle of red ink.

I thought then that those were happy days, but they weren't; these are the happy days.

It is a pleasure to send you an autographed copy of The Book, and an even greater pleasure to pocket your remittance.

Yours sincerely,

Alf Wainwright

Then the more nit picking letters started to arrive, with readers loving his work but showing off their own knowledge, trying to counter some of his assertions.

LETTER 46: TO MR POLLARD, 8 JUNE 1955

Municipal Offices
Lowther Street
Kendal
Westmorland
8 June 1955

Dear Mr Pollard,

Mr Marshall has passed your letter on to me, and I was delighted to have it. Among the many letters I have received, yours in the only one that goes into any detail, the sort of detail I find so interesting. Quite obviously, a kindred soul!

Yes, fancy calling 'Cofa Pike' 'Cawkhaw Pike'! And 'Ill Bell' 'Hill Bell'! And 'Yoke' 'York'! And still showing what is now a grassgrown track up Langdale as the main road! Yet, with all these criticisms, and many more, of the 2 and a half O.S map, I'd much rather use it than Bartholomew. I'm rather surprised that you, a stickler for detail, don't prefer it too, for Bartholomew is so lacking in information.

I wish I had time to point out some Bartholomew (and Baddeley) routes that you wouldn't find at all reliable! You'd be on hands and knees much of the time:

'Catstycam' I preferred to 'Catchedicam' because it looks so much more pronounceable, and anyway, I thought the second name was a corruption of the first?

I know the spot exactly that you mention in your separate note. The edge of the main path is badly eroded just here and the start of the zig-zag is obscure. Most people, not knowing it, are bound to miss it and continue into Kepplecove.

If there are <u>two</u> cairns, as you say, perhaps we'd better scatter one next time we are up there and make the book up-to-date!

Thanks a lot for writing. I should be delighted to hear from you again if you find any other points worth mentioning.

In the meantime, you could do me a tremendous favour by recommending the book to others interested in the hills. I'm afraid my publicity and distribution arrangements have been badly hit by the strike, and a word from you here and there would help. I should be grateful if you would do this, without, of course, going to any trouble about it.

Yours sincerely

In placing his advertisement with Cumbria, AW had been promised extra editorial coverage and it was agreed that Bill Mitchell, editor of Cumbria, would interview him and write a personal piece. Mitchell saw AW at his office – but got nothing out of him, and produced nothing worth using. AW had suddenly gone all private and uncooperative – for which he apologised to Mr Scott, the publisher.

LETTER 47: TO HARRY SCOTT, 10 JUNE 1955

Harry J Scott, Esq.,
The Dalesman Publishing Co,
Clapham,
Via Lancaster.

Municipal Offices
Lowther Street
Kendal
Westmorland
10 June 1955
Tele. 130 Kendal

Dear Mr Scott,

Thank you for your friendly and helpful letter.

I apologise profoundly for what has clearly been a misunderstanding on my part. When Mr Mitchell came to see me I somehow got the impression that the June Cumbria was already made up and that he was seeking a 'follow-up' for the July issue – and therefore that I had time to give some thought to his questions. However, it is my fault, and my loss; I appreciate your position. I would like you to tell Mr Mitchell, please, how sorry I am that I have muddled the matter.

Your other remarks about distribution are very interesting. I must admit that things are working out very differently from my expectations. The personal invitation by leaflet has proved a flop, and has taught me not to expect people to part with their money for something they have not seen. On the other hand, enquiries from bookshops and libraries are now coming in steadily, and it is unfortunate that for the past fortnight we have not been able to get many books out. So far as I can ascertain, 300 copies have been sold up to now, and I have many more to send out to bookshops when the strike is over, so perhaps things are not going so badly, but as you suggest, it is going to be a longer and slower process than I expected. The book has had excellent reviews, and I have had many contratulatory letters which have done much to encourage me and relieve my anxieties.

I am extremely grateful to you, Mr Scott, for your continued interest and offers of help, and someday, when the thing is on its feet, I will look in at your office, and thank you personally. I shall always remember that you were one of the first to pronounce a blessing on my efforts.

Yours sincerely,

LETTER 48: TO MRS MARY HELPS, 15 JUNE 1955

Henry Marshall, Low Bridge, Kentmere, Westmorland.

Dear Mrs Helps

Mr Marshall has passed your kind and interesting letter on to me: he is out of action at present

I hope you had an enjoyable holiday and collected more precious memories.

Here is the book. I do hope you like it!

Yours sincerely

AWainwright.

In June 1954, John and Mary Helps, who lived near Ilford in Essex, where he worked with his father running a mail order business in flower bulbs, were on their honeymoon in Scotland on the Isle of Skye. Staying by chance in the same bed and breakfast were AW and Henry Marshall. While climbing Sgurr nan Gillean, they came across AW and Marshall struggling to get the top, which they themselves had just done, so they escorted them to the top. Mr Helps took a photo of AW and Marshall, with his wife Mary, beside the cairn. (I used this photo in my biography of AW, purely as evidence that AW and Marshall had once been reasonably close friends, though I did not know at the time identity of the woman in the photograph.)

About a year later, Mrs Helps sent the photo to AW and Marshall and Marshall replied by telling her that he and AW had just published their first book – would she like to buy a copy? She posted the money and AW sent a signed book – which they still have in their Keswick home, which is where they retired to in the 1980s. AW always liked the photograph and kept it carefully.

LETTER 49: TO MR SCOTT, 21 JUNE 1955

Municipal Offices
Lowther Street
Kendal
Westmorland
21 June 1955

Dear Mr Scott,

Your very kind letter about 'The Eastern Fells' really gave me the most warming glow of pleasure!

This is a personal venture I have embarked upon, not without a great deal of anxiety lest it should fail. The expressions of appreciation that are coming in are a comfort to me, and make everything I have done seem well worth while.

I am greatly encouraged by your generous remarks, and thank you for taking the trouble and finding the time to write. It was nice of you to do this.

Yours sincerely

AWainwright

AW then agreed that he would answer by post some questions and answers if Bill Mitchell sent them to him. AW replied to each question – and also scribbled a covering note to Mr Mitchell – but never posted either of them. (I discovered them in 1994 in AW's papers when working on his official biography.)

LETTER 50: TO MR MITCHELL, UNDATED

Dear Mr Mitchell,

As promised, I enclose some notes from which you may be able to put together the article you intended for the July Cumbria. I apologise for the delay, but have had much on my mind since I saw you.

I found your two principal questions ('why did you do it?' And 'why did you do it in this particular way?') not at all easy to answer, but [illegible] my observations. I enclose also Griffin's article from the Lancashire Evening Post which contains certain biographical and other details you were interested in, and which you may care to re-hash in order to form a complete story. I feel myself that the article should be in narrative form, as Griffin's is, rather than in the form of an interview, but please yourself on this point. In fact, I'm ready to agree to anything to get a bit more publicity. One problem has been the rail and postal restrictions which have disrupted deliveries. At least I'm making that the excuse for the negligible response so far.

Only 70 odd replies have been received to the 1400 leaflets sent out. Griffin's excellent article has produced only three enquiries and the June Cumbria only two! All this is a tremendous disappointment. Fortunately, the shops are doing better, but I don't know whether more than 150 copies have been sold as yet. On the brighter side, the reviews of the book have been excellent and I have had an offer (not accepted) from another publisher to publish the six volumes that are still to come. Still optimistic, I believe everything will be OK in due course. We'll see.

y/s

Q: What impelled you to write this book?

Oddly, perhaps this is a question I have never asked myself and I am not sure that I can answer it satisfactorily. Certainly it cannot be answered in a single sentence. Ideas grow, like habits, until they become a way of life. What planted this particular seed in my mind is difficult to say. Perhaps I was born with it. Looking back, I seem always to have had a passion for hill-walking, even when a small boy; other enthusiasms have come and gone, but my love of the fells has been constant. As far back as I can remember, mountain country has attracted me and mountain literature and maps have been my favourite reading. The growing supply of mountaineering books, with their inspiring photographs and diagrams, must have influenced me considerably. It was always an ambition of mine to climb Everest (it used to be my fondest wish to die on the summit, but I've grown up since then!) the Everest books fascinated me and I studied them intently: in my imagination, how often I have toiled upwards towards its summit! Well, I could never go to Everest, but there was Scafell, and Helvellyn, and all the other fells I knew so well. They too had lofty ridges and hidden recesses, and, in winter, snow and ice; away from the paths there were wide areas of lonely territory to explore, places where few walkers go. Gradually the fells have taken the place of Everest in my life; they have provided the outlet for the climbing and exploring urge fostered by the many books of mountain travel. Some years ago I started to put a notebook and a pencil in my rucksack, and to be methodical in my wanderings. Later I started to be methodical in my notes, too. Every fell had to yield the answers to the same questions: the details of its structure, the best routes of ascent, the secrets of its untrodden places, the views from the top. I regarded them all as Himalayan giants, and myself as a lone explorer. The game took a hold on me as nothing else has ever done; it became a completely absorbing pastime, but more a passion that a pastime. For every day I could spend on the fells I had six in which I could do no climbing; these I started to spend carefully putting my notes into more attractive form and planning future expeditions. The map of Lakeland had now become a vast territory for exploration, and I planned my walks as though conducting a military campaign. You remember the war maps, the black arrows of advancing troops, the pincer movements, the mopping-up operations? That's the way I worked, but my thoughts were not of war, but utterly at peace. A tremendous impetus was given to my investigations by the re-publication of the 2 and a half inch Ordnance Survey maps, which, though not up-to-date, contained a wealth of interesting detail and provided a fuller appreciation of the meticulous accuracy of the cartographer's art. With these fine maps as examples, my rough notes would never do for me now: the job I was tackling must be done properly. I must make my own up-to-date maps, my own diagrams, my own drawings, all carefully designed and presented as attractively as I could. Writing is a form of drawing, and it was natural that I should try to describe the fells in words, but only where necessary to supplement the illustrations. I started to put pen to paper in earnest, hesitatingly at first. That was in November 1952 and by Christmas 1954 I had completed the first part of my plan.

Q: Why does the book appear in this particular and unusual fashion, that is, entirely from hand-written manuscript?
Because the book was intended originally only as a personal chronicle of my observations, so that everything in it, the notes as well as the illustrations, was prepared by hand. The thought of publication came much later, when it began to appear to me that my observations would be of interest to others who shared my regard for the fells. So it is that the book that has emerged is nothing more than my own personal notebook, reproduced exactly as I penned it, and embellished with an introduction and a conclusion which serve the purpose of explaining the plan to which I have worked in compiling the information.

Q: Have you had any training in art or book illustration?
No, I have had no training in drawing, but because the fells were never out of my mind, I have for years occupied much leisure time in translating

into pictures the vivid impressions I had of them. At first, I started to do this idly, but it quickly became an absorbing occupation and to me a very satisfying one because I found that by building up a favourite mountain from a blank sheet of paper I could experience the subtle joy of feeling that I was actually engaged upon the ascent physically as the familiar shape came in to being under the pen. To me, this was a discovery of some importance. I could now sit in my chair on a winter's evening and bring Scafell of Gable into the room with me. When I could not go to the hills I could make them come to me.

Q: You must have a remarkable amount of patience?
I don't think patience is the right word. Patience lies in doing a task unwillingly. When a task is done because it is enjoyed, its is enthusiasm.

Q: Have you had any interesting experiences during the making of the book?
If you mean during my walks, yes. Every walk is an interesting experience in itself, doubly interesting because it is walked with a definite purpose. I could not begin to detail my experiences now, although someday I hope to – when the Guide is finished. In general, I would say that the most intense experiences have occurred during nights spent upon the fells. Occasionally (not often, and only in Summer) I have bivouacked alone in high places; these occasions remain vivid in memory! Nobody who has not done it can imagine the splendours of sunset and sunrise from the summits, the eerie stillness of the hours of darkness, the joy of being on the tops at dawn when the larks are rising. I recommend this to every-one who loves the fells, but I recommend company to all but guide-book writers.

Q: Do you always go alone?
Invariably. I prefer to go alone, and must be alone if I am to get any work done. One cannot concentrate and comprehend another's conversation at the same time. Besides, I should be a poor companion, for my walks must often seem to be erratic, leading into unfrequented corners, zig-zagging where there is no need to zig-zag, sometimes returning to the same summit two or three times during the course of a day. In fact, I have often reason to be thankful that my antics are not being observed.

Q: When do you expect to finish Book Two?
All being well, by the autumn of 1956.

Part 6
Fan Letters, 1956–61

Book One, The Eastern Fells, was officially published in May 1955 but because of a rail strike there were few copies around until July. There was no dustjacket on Book One – AW had forgotten to do one – but when the book started selling well, and a second printing was ordered, AW decided to add one.

One of the early fan letters about Book One came from his Aunt Nellie (also known as Helen), his mother's sister, still living in Penistone, Yorkshire, from whence AW's parents, on both sides, had originally come.

LETTER 51: TO HELEN (NELLIE) SMITH, 17 JANUARY 1956

48 Kendal Green
Kendal
17th January 1956

Dear auntie Nellie,

Thank you so much for your very kind letter about 'The Eastern Fells'. It was a great pleasure to hear from you – and not, of course, merely to receive your congratulations and good wishes, but because you are a link with a past that becomes more and more remote and yet which often comes to mind: not always a happy past, perhaps, but rather one with some happy memories. Eric, on his annual visits, serves similarly to remind me of days that are gone, although I never mention this and I'm sure he doesn't realise it. It's strange, really, how well I remember Penistone – a grandfather clock at Grandpa's, auntie Lucy's shop, aunt Grace's little cottage, the viaduct, Percy Snape, Scout Wood – a jumble of memories, still vivid; and yet it is so many years (over thirty, I suppose) since I spent a holiday there. One of these days I really must go again!

The printer is now working on a second impression of Book One, and for this I have designed a paper book-jacket. I must remember to send you one to put round Helen's copy. Every spare moment is spent on Book Two: either working on it or thinking about it. It's more than half-finished but probably won't be published until Easter next year.

I enjoy so much preparing these books that I look for no other reward, yet other rewards there have been in plenty in the form of letters I have received from readers all over the country – wonderfully kind letters, messages even of gratitude from elderly people who used to walk the fells and now can do so no more. Yours I will place with these, and always be grateful for it

Alfred

The following month AW got a letter from Weaver Owen, formerly manager of Lloyds bank in Kendal from 1949–55, now moved to Banbury. He had lived near AW in Kendal, and was also a keen walker. One morning in 1949 they had met at the same bus stop and discovered they were about to go on the same walk. They did several walks together and one hot summer's night they even spent the night together, sleeping on a fell out in the open. (Mr Owen said later he never slept a wink but AW did as his pipe kept the midges away.)

In his reply to Mr Weaver, AW was a trifle pompous, saying he did not care to be addressed by his Christian name – even from somebody with whom he had once slept – but his letter was friendly and chatty, giving him news on Book Two. In a letter a year later, he gave him news of Book Three.

LETTER 52: TO WEAVER OWEN, 7 FEBRUARY 1956

Municipal Offices
Lowther Street
Kendal
7th February 1956

Dear Mr Owen (or Weaver, if you prefer it although personally I don't)

I was delighted to receive your letter with its inspiring enclosure. I had seen the photograph of Swindale Beck in the Lancashire Evening Post some days earlier, but there it was reproduced badly and failed to stir the emotions as the Times picture undoubtedly did. O, to be in

Swindale at this very moment! What am I doing here in a stuffy office surrounded by books?

As your letter was on its way north to me, you were very much in my thoughts, because I was en route to London on business. On a train journey I always like to sit with my nose flattened against the window and a railway map on my knee – and on this occasion I noted keenly all references to Banbury as the train passed through nearby stations, and surveyed the surrounding countryside with interest. Pleasant, yes; beautiful and exciting, no, not for me, I concluded; I'm no sicker after the fleshpots, as JSWOwen obviously is. Our ambitions run in different channels . . . yet perhaps I was too harsh, for the sight of you on hands and knees trying to insert yourself in a tiny shelter on the shores of Small Water remains one of my richest memories.

Life here goes on as smoothly as ever. I miss your cheerful smile, but, to be quite honest, so inflexibly have I set my course that your departure was no more than a ripple on a placid sea.

Nevertheless, I shall be very pleased to see you in April. I am 'engaged' at present on the fells around the head of Longsleddale (Harter Fell and company), having just completed a three-months exploration of the Thornthwaite Crag – Ill Bell Group. My programme tells me that April is scheduled for Branstree and Selside Pike, so that if you were to accompany me on a walk in that month it would probably be from Garnett Bridge, up Longsleddale and over the tops to Swindale (scene of the photograph) and Shap – which means using the bus, not your car.

If this prospect appeals to you, please give me a week's notice if you possibly can. Officially I shall be at work throughout april, but will try to arrange a day off if this can be done.

Book One goes into a second impression at Easter (this time with an attractive 'jacket'). Book Two will be finished on September 30th, but publication will be held over until the following Easter. Thank you for your very generous remarks about my efforts. It pleases me to recall that you were the first person I told about my plans (Grasmere bus stop after a hurried descent from High Raise). Remember?

AW

LETTER 53: TO WEAVER OWEN, 27 MAY 1957

Kendal
27th May 1957

Dear Mr Owen,

Thank you for the note enclosed with your donation. I am glad you like Book Two. I shall always associate those shelters you mention with a certain happy weekend spent in your company. Similarly with Book Three on which I am now feverishly engaged. I am 'doing' High Raise at present and in the process I am constantly reminded of one winters' day in particular which ended in a race against darkness. On the summit your face turned quite a vivid blue, with crimson splotches – a phenomenon *[he spells the previous word wrongly and corrects it]** I had never before witnessed and am not anxious to see again.

Today is gloriously fine, as most days are at present. As I left home this morning, the Ill Bell ridge looked wonderfully inviting. I could clearly see the big cairn on Thornthwaite Crag – and how I wished I was sitting with my back propped up against it! Yesterday, after taking the mayor to church, I caught the 1.30 and rattled up Loughrigg and Silver How.

For a change I am going on a solitary walking tour in Wester Ross and Sutherland next week.

I hope you are now happily settled down in Banbury. I look forward to seeing you again before long.

Yours sincerely

AWainwright

* this word always drives me to a dictionary

In 1958, while working on the early pages of Book Four, The Southern Fells, AW allowed a one-page extract to appear in the magazine Cumbria. Alas, it contained a spelling mistake – one of the very few that AW ever made – or ever admitted to have made. He had spelled the Britannia Inn at Chapel Stile as Brittania.

It was spotted by bright-eyed Jack Thornton, who just happened to be Deputy Director of Education for Cumberland, so was hot on good spelling. He wrote to AW, saying how much he was enjoying his books, then gently pointed out his mistake. AW humbly admitted his mistake – and said he would correct it with a razor blade. (And if you look in Book Four, on the page headed Lingmoor Fell 7, you can see how he craftily he corrected the spelling.)

LETTER 54: TO JACK THORNTON, 23 AUGUST 1958

Henry Marshall,
Low Bridge
Kentmere, Westmorland
Telephone: Kentmere 45
23 August 1958

Dear Mr Thornton

Thank you so much for your exceedingly kind letter. It is always a great pleasure to be told that the work one is doing is being appreciated by others, and although I must maintain that I am compiling my series of books primarily for my own gratification, it is, nevertheless, nice to know that they are proving of interest and use to others who share my affection for Lakeland; and letters such as yours are an encouragement to me to continue.

I hang my head in shame for my unaccountable lapse about the Britannia Inn! I was completely unaware of the mis-spelling (apparently nobody else has noticed it). The funny thing is that the word looks right to me with two Ts and one N, and I had no doubts when penning it, but of course I was wrong. This is the first mistake ever pointed out to me, although I have had several hundred letters from readers, and I am grateful to you for pointing it out, even if you have shaken my confidence a bit! How odd it should happen on the only page printed in advance of publication!

It's too much to ask the inn proprietor to exhibit a new sign with two Ts and one N, but I think I can, with careful manipulation of a razor blade, make the necessary alteration. Look for it when you get your copy of Book Four!

Yours sincerely

AWainwright

AW made a point of replying to every fan letter, grateful to people for having bought his books, and with many of them he got into a long correspondence which lasted some years, without him ever meeting them. He enjoyed their observations about his books and also hearing about people's own experiences of walking in Lakeland, and often encouraged them to write again. Once that started, he often revealed personal things – about what he was doing and feeling.

He wrote six letters to Bert Markland between 1957 and 1961 – all on
Henry Marshal notepaper, thus not giving away his home address – that
were full of information about his walks and books. He also wrote that
at fifty he felt his health was not what it was and his eyes were going. Mr
Markland had remarked on the huge task which AW had set himself, and
worried that he would finish it, but AW reassured him he would. Bert
Markland, born in 1909, lived in Bolton. He had been in the textile trade
till made redundant then worked for Department of Emloyment. He was
married but had no children. He had been a keen Lakeland walker since
his youth and had bought all the AW books from the beginning, as each
appeared, usually asking AW to sign his copy.

LETTER 55: TO BERT MARKLAND, 13 MAY 1957

> Henry Marshall
> Low Bridge
> Kentmere
> Westmorland
> Telephone: Kentmere 45
> 13th May 1957

Dear Mr Markland,

Thank you so much for your exceedingly kind and interesting letter. It was a pleasure to read it. I have noted your observations and suggestions most carefully, and was especially delighted with your account of the chance meeting on Catstycam (or Catchedicam, if you prefer!). It is both gratifying and encouraging to find that my books are proving useful, and little incidents such as that you relate please me a lot.

My own anxiety about keeping to schedule is even greater than yours! <u>My</u> climbing days, too, might be numbered – this nagging fear is beginning to haunt me. I am turned fifty, and simply <u>must</u> manage about seven more years <u>continuous</u> fellwalking without illness or accident. More than that, I cannot take a drink (even after a hard day on the tops) that would unsteady my hand! And I am running a race against deteriorating eyesight. I have no time to lose at all. I am out every weekend and so far am not aware of any physical failings except that I seem to get slower and slower on uphill gradients – but this I ascribe to increasing weight.

I am greatly indebted to you for recommending the books to others, because except for a preliminary announcement in 'Cumbria' we do no advertising. Mr Marshall and I both have our bread and butter professions to follow, and the publishing of the books is therefore more of a spare-time hobby than a business. The books pay their cost without being in any way lucrative, and of course the more we can sell the better is our guarantee against loss on a future volume. However, the immediate sale of Book Two has been so remarkably good that I am sure we need have no anxieties on this score.

I enclose a jacket for Book One (there are more available if you know anybody who wants one), and again thank you for taking the trouble to send me such a welcome letter. If you can find time to write, I would like to have an account in due course of your explorations to the east from Patterdale in June!

Yours sincerely,

AWainwright

LETTER 56: TO BERT MARKLAND, 5 MARCH 1958

Henry Marshall
Low Bridge
Kentmere
Westmorland
Telephone: Kentmere 45
5th March 1958

Dear Mr Markland,

Your very kind letter reached me at a time when I was very busy at work (hence my delay in replying, for which I am sorry). Coming at such a time, it was doubly welcome. For a few refreshing minutes it was really a pleasure to push to one side the uninteresting papers on the desk an read instead about places like Ill Bell and Froswick, Howtown and Fusedale, and so on. I confess to a great fondness for the quiet hills and valleys east of Kirkstone, and feel a little sorry that I shall not be seeing them again for some years.

It seems to matter more that one should have good weather at Patterdale than at other centres such as Borrowdale or Grasmere, and it is a pity that you were unfortunate last year. I agree that Helvellyn (and, I might add, Fairfield) must always be on any programme of walks based on Patterdale, their eastern flanks being infinitely more interesting than the western. The side valleys, too, from Dovedale or Glencoin, are exceptionally attractive (especially the first named). If I were stood on Grisedale Bridge on a bright sunny morning my natural inclination would be to turn up Grisedale rather than cross to the other side of Ullswater, and this would be so nine times out of ten; and perhaps on the tenth occasion I would merely climb Place Fell to study these same hills and valleys from a distance. Perhaps it was to force myself away from the familiar and well-loved walks that I had done dozens of times into quieter and less trodden ways that I started to compile my books! Whether this is so or not, I have most certainly found an equal pleasure in places I should not otherwise have visited, such as, for example, Angletarn Pikes and Hallin Fell, which I had been 'putting off' for years.

Much of the ground in Book Three also was new to me, but here again I found the unfamiliar territory of fascinating interest and returned to it week after week with increasing eagerness. So it goes on. I finished Book Three at the end of January and sadly turned my back on the delightful places I had discovered the following week found me on Lingmoor Fell, in Langdale, making a start on Book Four. I have spent the last four Sundays there in a fever of enthusiasm, and the sadness at forsaking the Central Fells has already passed. All my thoughts now are of the splendid hills running up to Bowfell and the Scafells, and the prospect of getting amongst them week after week makes me feel as excited as a little by with a new toy (and I am 51, which beats you by a couple of years!!) so don't worry about physical limitations – we're good for another 30 years yet, surely!)

I mention all this because of your very generous comments and words of encouragement. It is really most kind of you to take the trouble to write, and I appreciate all you say more than I can express. Of course it is nice to know that the work I am doing is giving pleasure to others, very nice indeed; but, to be perfectly honest, I rely not at all on the encouragement of others but am sufficiently inspired by my own burning desire to carry on with the job! It is actually a purely selfish motive. I do it for my own gratification, and any pleasure others derive is quite incidental. I have had hundreds of contratulatory letters, and am deeply grateful for them, but I would have gone on just the same without them – which sounds unkind, but isn't meant to be! I am just trying to say (and perhaps making a mess of it!) that you need have no qualms about me suddenly getting tired of the job and quitting. Good heavens, no! the only thing worrying me is what I am going to do with my spare time when Book Seven is finished! Life won't be worth living unless I can find something else to do instead . . . of course, there's always the Pennines and Scotland! How I wish we didn't keep on getting older and older!

There's north Wales, too, and the Alps and the Himalayas – work for me for a thousand years, but already life is drawing to a close! It's no joke being 51 when one's allotted span is 70 – time becomes precious.

However, we still have a few years left to us (I'm a bit doubtful about the 30 I mentioned earlier), so let me, in return for your kindness to me, express the hope that you will thoroughly enjoy many more seasons of happy hill-wandering in Lakeland. Book Three will be ready about May 1st. it will be my pleasure to send you an autographed copy as soon as I can.

Yours sincerely

AWainwright

LETTER 57: TO BERT MARKLAND, 23 AUGUST 1958

Henry Marshall
Low Bridge
Kentmere
Westmorland
Telephone: Kentmere 45
23rd August 1958

Dear Mr Markland,

It is always a pleasure to hear from you, and your latest letter is a joy to read. Your comments on Book Three are interesting, and I fully appreciate your feelings during your first ascent of Jack's Rake – I felt precisely the same, and, in fact, broke a rule and took a companion on my first visit, although subsequently I did it again alone. I am very clumsy and apprehensive on steep ground and always feel happier in places where I can stride out. Still, like yourself, I enjoyed Jack's Rake. Last week I discovered a counterpart to it on Dow Crag. Coniston, which I shall be describing in Book Four.

The curious thing about the Harrison Stickle axe 'factory', so the experts tell me, is that it appears to have been a place for <u>working</u> the stone only, not for extracting it. Apparently the chippings found there are from stone brought from Pike O' Stickle and not 'native' to Harrison Stickle.

I hope you have good weather at the Burnmoor Inn in September. I had a week at the Woolpack in May when the weather was very unsettled, but managed to get a lot of work done in Upper Eskdale – which, incidentally, is delightful. Have a look at the Roman Camp on Hardknott, which is undergoing extensive restoration (not sure I agree with it!). I may manage a few days myself at Seathwaite, Duddon Valley, next month.

Thank you for sending me the newspaper cutting, and for all your kind remarks. If you feel like sending me an account of your Eskdale holiday later on I should be interested to have it.

Yours sincerely

AWainwright

LETTER 58: TO BERT MARKLAND, 25 JULY 1959

> Henry Marshall
> Low Bridge
> Kentmere
> Westmorland
> Telephone: Kentmere 45
> 25 July 1959

Dear Mr Markland,

I am sorry to have been such a long time in replying to your welcome and interesting letter. Please do not think, because of this delay, that I am not appreciative or your kindness in writing to me. It is always a pleasure to hear from you.

Book Four is going on very well, thank you, but there is so much to record in this particular area that it has already overflowed into extra pages and will certainly be the biggest of the series. I have been exceptionally favoured by the weather this summer, while engaged on the Scafells. I had looked forward to this part of the task with much apprehension, because of the relative inaccessibility of places like Wasdale and Eskdale and the fear of a period of bad weather, or even normal summer weather, which could have meant many fruitless journeys and held me up very considerably. Instead of that, however, the weekends have been gloriously fine, with bright sun, visibility simply terrific (quite unusual for summertime) day after day, with the Isle of Man almost permanently on the horizon; no soakings and no wet feet. It's been glorious. A few Saturday nights spent at Wasdale Head and Eskdale, aided by the wonderful conditions, have enabled me to do in weeks what might well have taken months. I still have a few 'mopping-up' operations to carry out in the Eskdale and Screes areas, and will be having a short stay there in August, the book itself will be printed and ready by Easter next year, or a little later.

As always, I am interested to learn of your own recent wanderings. It must have been simply galling to have been laid up with your ankle in Eskdale, of all places. I share your own opinion as to the merit of this delightful valley. The dalehead is magnificent, and the foothills, too, are captivating. It must be the pink granite that makes Eskdale just that little bit more attractive; yet I have been surprised on my recent visits, to find so few walkers based there – in fact, a fortnight ago I was the only one staying at the Burnmoor Inn; a Saturday, too, and mid-July!

27th July

Yesterday (Sunday) I was in Sprinkling Tarn – Styhead Tarn and it rained most of the day – the first wet Sunday for months (I believe first since that wet Easter Sunday when you were at Dungeon Ghyll). Nevertheless, the popular paths from Borrowdale were quick thick with people, but the Eskdale approaches, on such a day, would be almost, if not entirely, deserted. Today, and last night, there have been thunderstorms with very heavy rain; the hills are shrouded in mist and conditions must be very unpleasant for the dozen or mountain tents I saw yesterday around Sty head.

I will most certainly be delighted to send you an autographed copy of Book Four when it is available. In the meantime you should be tending your ankles carefully, because the screes of Lords Rake and Mickledore get worse with every year that passes. Or am I getting old?

Yours sincerely,

AWainwright

LETTER 59: TO BERT MARKLAND, 15 AUGUST 1961

> Henry Marshall
> Low Bridge
> Kentmere
> Westmorland
> Telephone: Kentmere 45
> 15th August 1961

Dear Mr Markland,

It was a great pleasure to receive your interesting letter of 14th July, the first for some time. I had begun to think you must have fallen over a crag somewhere.

Thank you for your very kind comments about Book Four, which of course I enjoyed doing tremendously, magnificent territory, all of it!

I will tell you (in a whisper) that the packwoman's grave is <u>within 20 yards</u> of the track going straight up Rossett Gill, after the old pony route has gone off to the left and before impending rocks force the track into the bed of the gill. It's there all right, on a little grassy knoll. In fact it can be seen from the track higher up, but is probably never noticed because everybody just here is too busily engaged on keeping a footing on the rough ground. Look for it next time, but don't tell anybody.

I don't think I altogether agree with a tax on visitors for the maintenance of paths and bridges, but perhaps I am being a bit selfish here because I personally derive so much interest from tracing them. I work from 6" maps published by the Ordnance Survey about a century ago, before there were any walkers' paths as such but when drove roads and miners' tracks were common. It's fun trying to find them today!

As for the 'cloak of anonymity' I have assumed, it's all part of the game, but, for me, an essential part. I always travel alone (the best way of walking the hills). I never reveal my identity to anyone. I keep out of other people's way. Mind you, there have been some very embarrassing moments, especially on buses and in cafes. It's funny hearing yourself discussed by a stranger on the next seat! Twice only, I have been challenged, and had to own up. Molly Garmeworthy knows me (by sight only) through her association with Kendal C.H.A.

I have had several reports that the cairn on Pike o' Blisco had been rebuilt (which pleases me) but since all my correspondents claim to have contributed to the work, it must be getting quite a height now! I hope some of these good people will give their attention to the Lingmell cairn next. This was a beauty, a slender pile 10' high, but some time ago I heard that it had been thrown down.

I am sorry about my failure to autograph your copy of the Southern Fells. This must have been a shocking oversight on somebody's part. However, repeat the request next time, and if you feel it worth the trouble to send Book Four back for autographing, of course I'll be pleased to do it.

I hope your operation has proved successful, and that your next visit to the Lakes will find you in possession of all your faculties. I hope, too, you will be able to find time for another account of your wanderings. Your letters are a pleasure to read.

Myself, I'm off for a holiday later this week – to Scotland!!!

Yours sincerely

AWainwright

Bert Markland ceased writing to AW in 1961, feeling that AW was now so well known, his books so famous, that he should not bother him any more. He died in 1999, just a few days before his 90th birthday.

In his last letter from AW, in October 1961, AW refers to a 'delicate personal matter' but this was nothing to do with his wife – as AW never referred to her in any of his letters – but to an invitation Bert Markland had issued for AW to to be guest speaker at the annual meeting of the Bolton Photographic Society.

LETTER 60: TO BERT MARKLAND, 27 OCTOBER 1961

Henry Marshall
Low Bridge
Kentmere
Westmorland
Telephone: Kentmere 45
27th October 1961

Dear Mr Markland,

Thank you for your interesting letter. It was a pleasure to hear from you again.

I'm glad you located the old grave all right (and rather relieved to know it is still there). If the grave actually marks the spot where the body was found, it seems that your supposition (that the direct route was in use in those far off days as well as the pony track) is probably correct – I hadn't thought of this before.

I have personal knowledge of the sloppiness of the crossing from Stake top to Rossett top. The 'terrace' route below Black Crag, on the contrary, is very good indeed – although, if coming from Langstrath, a descent and re-ascent would be involved in the use of it.

About the delicate personal matter – no, I'm sorry. It isn't the sort of thing I enjoy – some defect in my make-up, obviously. And I've got to an age when I don't do things I don't like doing. This doesn't mean that I don't think the occasion is going to be anything but a splendid weekend for those present; and it certainly doesn't mean that I am not appreciative of your very kind invitation. I am indeed – you do me a great honour. I just don't happen to be a sucker of honours, nor do I feel I deserve any. Funny old stick!

Sorry to hear your operation was not a success, but disabilities only become really serious when they keep you off the hills.

I've remedied the oversight in the book, which I now return (with apologies for the delay), and hope it will not happen again.

Yours sincerely,

AWainwright

Part 7
Pictorial Guides Letters, 1960-6

The seven Pictorial Guides, which had first appeared in 1955, came out at regular intervals from then on, roughly every two years, until the last one, the Western Fells, was published in 1966. By then his fan mail had grown enormously, with letters coming in every day. He managed to answer every one, though sometimes a month or so late, while still working at his day job as Kendal's Borough Treasurer, and bashing on with his Guides, spending his weekends and daylight evenings in the summer either walking or writing his current book.

Many of his letters are very chatty, friendly and informative, especially about his books and what he was then working on, but he rarely ever gives away any personal information – either about his office job or his family life.

By 1960, his wife Ruth is never mentioned, even when occasionally old friends from the past write to him. It looks as if they have ceased to be on speaking terms, in the same house but living their own separate lives, never going out nor having holidays together.

Peter, his son, born 1933, who until he was a teenager was a regular walking companion with his father, also ceases to be mentioned in any letters. He left school aged sixteen and moved to Windermere, working at the local gas works. In 1959, he moved abroad to work for the Bahrain Petroleum Company where he stayed for the next 15 years. He wrote regularly to his mother, but heard nothing from his father.

AW appeared to prefer communicating with people he didn't know, and was not likely to meet.

One of his earliest long-running correspondents was Len Chadwick of Dobcross near Oldham. He was a member of a local club called the Kindred Spirits Fell Walking Society. (The reference to OT presumably refers to its magazine.)

In a letter to AW in 1960, he happened to mention that he and some others *were planning to spend two weeks climbing the Monros – the 277 Scottish Mountains over 3,000 feet – and enclosed their detailed timetable, routes and plans, all of which AW found fascinating. He himself had become interested in the Scottish mountains, despite his obsession with the Lakeland fells. He wrote back, promising to sponsor him, even though Mr Chadwick had not asked for any money or sponsorship. He even enclosed a cheque for £25 in advance, which was generous, considering the assaults were not going to be attempted till the following summer.*

LETTER 61: TO LEN CHADWICK, 31 OCTOBER 1960
[on Henry Marshall headed paper]

> Low Bridge
> Kentmere
> Westmorland
> Telephone: Kentmere 45
> 31st October 1960

Dear Mr Chadwick,

'Munro's Tables' herewith. I suggest you keep this to work from. It should be the Expedition's Bible!

On looking through this book, I find there aren't quite as many genuine Munroes (separate mountains) as I thought, and I am now rather inclined to your opinion that 20 are as many as could be managed in a fortnight.

I didn't intend my terms to be quite so harsh and am now prepared to extend my offer as follows:

5/- for every separate mountain over 3000ft

Plus

10/ for every top (not being a separate mountain) over 3000ft according to the first two columns of TABLE II. As before, <u>all</u> members of the party must touch the summit-cairn to qualify. Maximum contribution 50 pounds (the same summit cannot qualify both for 1 pound and 10/)

This adjustment should give you rather more scope and augment the funds. You should have some fun with your Scottish maps and timetables this winter!

Yours sincerely,

AWainwright

LETTER 62: TO LEN CHADWICK, 8 FEBRUARY 1961
[on Henry Marshall headed paper]

Low Bridge
Kentmere
Westmorland
Telephone: Kentmere 45
8th Feb 1961

Dear Mr Chadwick

I return the November O.T and am sorry that some delay has arisen in its transit from one reader to another. You wanted it back by January 16th, and it is now February 8th.

I have studied your provisional programme for the Munro Challenge with interest – obviously there has been a great deal of careful planning. It looks very attractive, especially as it introduces territory new to you – but it does mean a fortnight's hard graft. Don't forget that the first consideration should be that you are going up there to enjoy yourselves, and that you are on holiday. We don't want you to come back two stone lighter and with an enlarged heart, not after all you've suffered with your teeth!

Personally, I don't expect you to complete the programme. To do it in full, you will have to strike top form right away and get a fortnight's continuously good weather. Anyway, we'll have to see what happens. Of course I wish you the best of good fortune!

Yours sincerely.

AWainwright

LETTER 63: TO LEN CHADWICK, 10 MARCH 1961
[on Henry Marshall headed paper]

Low Bridge
Kentmere
Westmorland
Telephone: Kentmere 45
10th March 1961

Dear Mr Chadwick,

I am afraid the circulation of O.T never follows your programme of distribution as far as dates are concerned, and here is your December issue coming back to you five weeks behind schedule.

In a couple of months I hope to be in Scotland myself on a much easier mission than yours in the summer. I plan to follow the coast from Lochinver to Kinlochbervie, or perhaps cutting across to Durness, doing about 10.12 miles a day (which is enough for comfort) and hoping for weather suitable for photography.

Yours sincerely.

AWainwright

LETTER 64: TO LEN CHADWICK, 18 APRIL 1961
[on Henry Marshall headed paper]

> Low Bridge
> Kentmere
> Westmorland
> Telephone: Kentmere 4
> 18th April 1961

Dear Mr Chadwick,

Thank you for your letter and newspaper cuttings, which I greatly enjoyed reading. I have a fancy for the Cairngorms, having read much about them but never actually seen them – except from trains at Aviemore. I might possibly visit the area next month.

I was extremely sorry to hear about Andrew's sad bereavement, which must have been a great shock to him and spoilt his memories of a grand holiday. I agree that if he feels he must cancel his Munro arrangements in the circumstances we should not try to persuade him otherwise. If you are disposed to tackle the [illegible] alone, then of course the offer still holds good. Similarly if you decide to take some other companion. Or, if you prefer to do your postponed Ireland trip this year instead, the offer would hold good for 1962. I know what a nuisance a late break-up of holiday plans can be, and I leave it entirely to you.

I should be interested to know, later on, what you have decided to do.

Yours sincerely.

AWainwright

Another early correspondent was Bob Harvey, a research scientist for the BBC, living in Surrey, with whom AW exchanged photographs.

LETTER 65: TO BOB HARVEY, 22 DECEMBER 1961
[on Henry Marshall headed paper]

> Low Bridge
> Kentmere
> Westmorland
> Telephone: Kentmere 4
> 22nd December 1961

Dear Mr Harvey,

I feel I owe you much more than mere thanks for your very kind letter. Your references to my books are extremely generous, and, as I am a man who blushes easily, somewhat embarrassing!

I have always maintained that I compile these books for my own self-gratification, enthusiasm for the job being a flame that needs no fanning by encouragement from others, and this is still perfectly true. But more and more I am coming to realise that others are finding pleasure in my efforts, and increasingly a new stimulus is creeping in – to do my best for the many friends I have won. I number you amongst them, and thank you sincerely for your kindness in writing to me. You have a happy literary style that makes your account of your various wanderings on the hills, of the incidents that happen to you, of the encounters you enjoy (and suffer!) most interesting and pleasant and amusing to read. It kept me chuckling all the way through it – and has done since.

The photograph you enclosed is a masterpiece of simple, effective arrangement – the man, the cairn, the boundless sky – and somehow symbolic, too. It's an absolute gem, and although you don't actually say I may keep it, I am going to assume it is a gift and have it framed to stand on my desk. An inspiration in itself!

I have never been back to Pike o' Blisco since, but several people have written to say that the cairn is now restored, but yours is the first picture I have had and I would say it is now back to its original proportions. Thanks for your help. I didn't know the fine cairn on Sergeant Man had also been wrecked – that was news to me – but a Keswick reader wrote some time ago to report that the slender column on Lingmell had been thrown down, and that he was making a series of visits to try to get it up again. Poor chap – he's over 70!

I am terribly sorry it's taken me such a long time to reply – I feel dreadful about this – but the delay does at least give me the opportunity to combine Christmas greetings with my reply – and the hope that 1962 will be a grand fell walking year for you. Perhaps after your next expedition you could find time to let me know what you have done! It would always been a pleasure to hear from you . . .

Yours sincerely

AWainwright

LETTER 66: TO BOB HARVEY, 19 MAY 1963
[on Henry Marshall headed paper]

Low Bridge
Kentmere
Westmorland
Telephone: Kentmere 4
19th May 1963

Dear Mr Harvey,

I have formed a deplorable habit latterly (due to a chronic shortage of time) of piling up letters received into a cairn on my desk instead of answering them promptly, as decency demands, and only when the edifice topples over do I give some attention to them. I have become adept at making excuses for neglecting correspondence and these are generally accepted (at least the writers write again) but occasionally it happens that I withdraw from the heap, with dismay and shame, a manuscript that, because of its interest or literary merit, deserved immediate acknowledgment – and, alas, I have allowed it to mingle for months with much less worthy material (usually from fond parents asking if its is safe to take their progeny up Jack's Rake, to which I always answer 'yes!'). Such a manuscript was yours, mercifully undated, describing your experience at the Lingmell cairn. You close this letter by wishing me a Happy Christmas. As there hasn't been a Christmas for five months, you can imagine my remorse, for this letter, like the one I had from you earlier, was a classic. I shall treasure it, and the accompanying photograph.

As a matter of fact I have had several letters about the Lingmell cairn, which have left me rather bemused. Some people have claimed my thanks because they have rebuilt it; others have stated that it is still in ruins. However quite recently I had a letter from a scoutmaster (who I therefore assume to be a paragon of virtue) stating that he and his troop had fully restored the height of the cairn and its slender appearance from afar, while admitting to a certain weakness in the structure on the Gable side: this, he assured me, would be corrected on a later visit this year. When you come up in June, therefore, you might (or might not) find an edifice that stands no less proudly that did its predecessor. As an expert in the subject, you will be interested in the reconstructed cairn on Dale Head (photo enclosed) which replaces one recently scattered although not quite in the same place. This is a magnificent, professional job done in cut green stone (which must have been hauled up from Yew Crag Quarry), and is unusual in being wider in the middle that at the base. Take a look at it this summer – before somebody knocks it down!

Yours sincerely,

AWainwright

LETTER 67: TO REG BOND, UNDATED, 1963
[first page of letter missing]

. . . making the correction isn't quite so easy. It isn't a simle matter of the printer taking out one figure and substituting another. The whole of the page (and all other pages in these books) is reproduced from a zinc block which gives an exact impression of the author's original. The correction could only be made, therefore, by my doing the whole page again and having another block made. So far, I haven't found time to do this, but later I may.

Actually, there is a mistake on Scafell Pike 17, too. 'Bus <u>shelter</u>' at Seatoller should be 'Bus <u>terminus</u>' (see Scafell Pike 15). There isn't a shelter – I got wet there yesterday waiting for a bus. I ought to correct this also, but I'm hoping somebody will put a shelter there soon and save me the trouble!

Yours sincerely,

AWainwright

There were also women readers who wrote to AW, such as Joy Ross from Bowness on Windermere. She was a Cambridge graduate, mother of four, and a madly keen Lakeland walker and swimmer who had made her own maps of Lakeland, plotting every swimmable rock pool. She got him going on the subject of maps, especially those produced by Messers Batholomew.

LETTER 68: TO JOY ROSS, 27 OCTOBER 1963

Kendal
27 October 1963

Dear Mrs Ross

Thank you very much for your interesting letter, and its kind (too kind) references to myself. Reading it made me blush, but I am, of course, very pleased to learn that my books are proving helpful.

No, I am not in touch with the Ordnance Survey or Bartholomews about the footpaths on their Lake District maps. Bart's map is just hopeless, dangerously inaccurate and very misleading; no attempt has been made to show paths correctly, and they would have been better omitted altogether. For the Ordnance Survey, however, I have the most profound respect – their maps are my favourite literature, and their surveys and cartography is, in general wonderfully accurate, especially on their large scale maps. Features on the ground (walls, sheepfolds, streams, tarns, buildings etc) are 100% correct. There are three things I am disposed to criticize: first, the hachuring for crags, which is unreliable in many instances; secondly, the contours on the 2 and a half inch maps are often wildly wrong on high ground; and thirdly, the footpaths. In the case of the O.S, however, the trouble is not that they invent paths or smooth out the bends and corners, as Bart's does, but that they do not keep them up to date. They still show paths that have completely vanished, although I don not doubt that they existed a hundred years ago; and conversely, they do not show paths that are not in popular use. These, however, are difficulties arising from too infrequent revision, not from inaccurate cartography.

You will love Lakeland more and more with growing familiarity – the sincerest test of affection – and you will find it equally charming at all seasons. I hope you continue to enjoy your expeditions to the hills, for no experiences are more rewarding. Every day on the tops is different from all others, whether you seek beauty, excitement, lovely views or merely exercise; every day has its individual memories. Even the soakings and weariness and bad moments are pleasant in retrospect!

Thank you for finding the time and taking the trouble to write to me. It was nice of you to do this.

Yours sincerely,

AWainwright

Fancy meeting 31 people on a day's walk over High Street! I didn't see that many in two years . . . by the way, that was a fine walk you did – Shipman Knotts to Loadpot Hill, and a commendable performance indeed. The family must be tough! I should have had to turn back at nan Bield.

In May 1964, AW heard from the son of an old, though more senior colleague from his Blackburn days. Norman Hamm had been senior accountant, later the Borough Treasurer. Alas he survived only a couple of years in that post, dying in 1952, aged fifty-one. His son Roderick Hamm went on to have a distinguished career in local government, becoming Town Clerk of South Ribble Borough. In his letter to AW he reminisced about his father and the Blackburn office.

LETTER 69: TO RODERICK HAMM, 7 MAY 1964

Municipal Offices, Kendal
7th May 1964

Dear Mr Hamm,

It was a great to surprise to receive your letter, and a pleasure too. Thank you for your kind remarks.

Very vaguely I seem to remember hearing of your schooling at Sedbergh, but the last twenty years are a void so far as news of your family is concerned.

Your letter has recalled for me an event that I think must have contributed to the idea of writing a series of pictorial guides. I remember saying farewell to your father as he left the office on the Saturday I finished work at Blackburn, but within a few minutes he returned to give me a book he had just bought for twopence on a second-hand book stall in the market Hall. It was an ancient but handsome volume entitled 'Swiss Pictures in Pen and Pencil'. I still have it. This was a book of drawings of mountain scenes and I think it may have been this that first planted the germ of the idea in my head. Alas, I was never able to tell him so!

Yours sincerely,

AWainwright

AW had taken a camera out on the fells from his earliest walks and used his photographs when working on his Guides – not copying them, but as an aide memoir. He used a cheap camera and the results were not very good. He was always very disappointed when he got them back from the local chemist, so from about 1950 onwards he started taking them to a local photographer in Kendal, Ken Shepherd. He specialised in weddings and portraits, but he had his own dark room. AW got him to make prints for him and also enlargements. Percy is Percy Duff, AW's office colleague, Deputy Borough Treasurer.

LETTER 70: TO KEN SHEPHERD, I FEBRUARY 1965

> Municipal Offices, Kendal
> 1st Feb 1965

Dear Mr Shepherd,

59 negatives from my expeditions to Caledonia in 1964 are enclosed. I should be greatly obliged if you would kindly make 6" × 4" semi-matt enlargements from these, as before, in accordance with the marked prints also enclosed. At your convenience, of course.

MAY: Spean bridge, Mallaig, Kyle, Inverness, Braemar + Edinburgh
            Mainly cold and wet, with heavy rainstorms

AUGUST: Spean Bridge, Mallaig, Kyle, Inverness, Helmsdale, Melrose.
            Mainly bright, but with cold strong winds.

Most of the best of the pictures were taken from moving trains on the west Highland Railway.

Percy tells me you are not quite OK at present. I hope you are soon fit and well again.

Yours sincerely,

AWainwright

With Bob Alker, an old friend and colleague from Blackburn – who had moved to Preston where he became area accountant for NORWEB – he was a lot saucier, reverting to the style of his office magazine. There was still no mention of Ruth, but a lot of suggestive remarks about his sex life, or lack of it.

LETTER 71: TO BOB ALKER, UNDATED, 1965

Dear Bob,

I am a little ashamed to note that your letter, to which this is a reply, was dated as long ago as Sep. 10th, but you cannot expect priority on the strength of past acquaintance (now if you'd been a soft, juicy woman it would have been different). What happens is that I maintain a cairn of unanswered letters on my desk and when it collapses I answer one and build the rest up again. In fact you have been fortunate. I know there are some in the heap dated 1963 and 1964 still awaiting attention, but, of course, none from women, who form the majority of my correspondents. It is my ingrained gallantry (which you remarked in earlier years) that makes me give them immediate attention, nothing else. I offer them no inducements (as a rule), but they keep coming running back for more. All I need to comment is that my knowledge of women's anatomy is derived purely from hearsay, and they cling like leeches. I like them clinging like leeches. I always did.

Well, thank you for all your kind comments. It wouldn't be me if I didn't say they are well deserved. Last time I heard anything about you, you were dying, so that I am doubly pleased to hear from you and to learn that you had started fellwalking. Good lad! After fifty wasted years! You must look out for me – a tall, distinguished-looking figure (to quote one source) recognisable by the long tail of females straggling along behind. How they all hate each other! It's funny, really.

Two pages is as much as any male correspondent gets from me. If you want to write again and expect an earlier and fuller reply, get your missus to write instead and address me as 'Dear Alf'.

You have been warned

AW

A popular topic in letters to AW was the mountain top cairns. AW usually described them in detail in his Pictorial Guides, but of course as the years went on, they were not always as he described – or even still there.

In 1966, Eric Hargreaves, a maths teacher at Cockermouth Grammar School and chairman of the Cockermouth Mountain Rescue team, wrote to him about the Dale Head cairn being damaged.

LETTER 72: TO ERIC HARGREAVES, 19 JULY 1966

c/o Westmorland Gazette, Kendal
19th July 1966

Dear Mr Hargreaves,

I must thank you for your letter, even though it did bring me the sad news of the fate of the Dale Head Cairn. This is a shocking thing to have happened. The cairn was one of the best in the district, and built by a craftsman. It was far too soundly constructed to suffer from the weather and no gale could have brought it down. The only explanation is that it has been deliberately wrecked.

There must have been some maniac about with a dislike of well-built cairns. The same thing happened to the cairn on Pike o' blisco and Lingmell, both outstandingly well built, but these two have been restored by willing hands. Perhaps some working party will do the same for Dale Head.

Sorry news, but thanks for letting me know.

Yours sincerely,

AWainwright

Mr Hargreaves wrote again, this time about the stretcher box on Pillar, as described and illustrated in Book 7, the Western Fells, page Pillar 11 (just published in 1966). AW rarely apologised for anything in his books but he was beginning to realise that objects would not always stay the way were.

LETTER 73: TO MR HARGREAVES, 16 DECEMBER 1966

c/o Westmorland Gazette, Kendal
16th December 1966

Dear Mr Hargreaves,

I am writing (belatedly!) to thank you for your letter of 9th November about the stretcher box on Pillar and to apologise for my long delay in replying – not due, I assure you, to a lack of appreciation of your kindness in putting me in the picture.

Well, of course, the collapse of the box on Shamrock Traverse illustrates the perils of guide book writing – nothing that man does can be relied upon to stay put. Rather oddly, though, when one of your members (Colin Greenhow?) told me of the placing of the box originally, I expressed the opinion that the <u>foot</u> of the Rock would seem to me a better place since people face <u>down</u>, not up.

Yes, of course, the implications of the vanished box (which I described as a landmark to look for) could be serious to newcomers relying on my notes, and I hope nobody falls down Walkers Gully looking for it. If they do the new site of the second box will be singularly appropriate. In the circumstances, since the fault is mine and not yours, it seems an uncommonly generous intention on your part to pinpoint the place by affixing an explanatory tablet. When I can find time I must either re-write my notes or add an erratum to say that things are not as they were when the book was written.

Yours sincerely,

AWainwright

Larry Skillman of Sevenoaks, Kent, also wrote to AW about the Western Fells – and suggested that AW should now turn his attention to Wales. AW wasn't keen, but he did say he was working on the Pennine Way and also, unusually, revealed what his real job was.

LETTER 74: TO LARRY SKILLMAN, 13 DECEMBER 1966

c/o Westmorland Gazette, Kendal
13th December 1966

Dear Mr Skillman,

Thank you for your exceedingly kind letter. I appreciate greatly your very generous comments, and am only too sorry that my long delay in replying may have suggested otherwise. I was interested, too, to read of your preferences for the Western and Southern fells, but hope that when you make your intended long visit next summer you will find time to take a look at some of the other districts, especially, perhaps, Blencathra and High Street, which, even at the height of the tourist season, retain much of the loneliness and solitude that constitutes much of their appeal.

Snowdonia has never had the same attraction for me as the Lakes. I concede that the Welsh mountains are grander; but the trees, the lovely valleys, the colours and the dialect of the natives of Lakeland are all contributory to its particular charm. Several people have, in fact, suggested that I turn my attention to north Wales, but the urge is missing and I doubt now whether my legs could stand the effort. The Pennine Way, on the other hand, is very easy (as far as gradients are concerned) and I am enjoying it greatly.

My day-to-day work for the past 46 years has been in local government, and for the last 18 I have been Borough Treasurer of Kendal.

Thank you again for writing. It was nice of you to find the time and take the trouble to do this.

Yours sincerely,

AWainwright

With all the Pictorial Guides now published, and proving enormously popular, there came an inevitable if minor backlash. Several Lake District experts worried that he was attracting too many visitors to the Lakes, the popular paths would soon become eroded, all these newcomers, the amateur walkers, would probably cause accidents to themselves and each other.

AW got particularly incensed by criticism attributed to John Wyatt, who had become the National Park's first warden in 1960, and was now the Head Warden and also author of several guide books to the Lakes.

Mr Wyatt's criticism was reported in the Westmorland Gazette sometime in 1966, and AW sat down to write a strongly worded Letter to the Editor. He retained a carbon copy of the letter – but it is not clear if in fact he ever sent it.

LETTER 75: TO THE WESTMORLAND GAZETTE, 1966?

Dear Sir,

During a long life I must have read statements more stupid than those attributed to Mr Wyatt in your paper, but I cannot bring them to mind. To say, as he appears to do, that my guidebooks to the Lakeland fells are the cause of countless accidents and are potential killers is really too ridiculous to warrant a reply, but I have been persuaded by indignant readers of his remarks to answer his accusations.

Having regard to the position he holds, My Wyatt must surely know that fellwalking involves rough scrambling, and the joy of it is to get up off the tarmac roads and find excitement and adventure and beauty along the stony tracks and in the lonely places amongst the hills.

Accidents occur, not because of 'out-of-date' guidebooks but because some walkers do not watch where they are putting their feet. Out of date? They will be out of date when the hills are out of date.

I claim that my books have often saved people from benightment and injury, and that there would be more incidents without them.

Does his criticism also extend to the Ordnance Survey maps, which also show the footpaths, and to the guidebooks of other writers? If not, why not?

Really, Mr Wyatt, Give fellwalkers credit for common sense. They are not lemmings!

Part 8
The Pennine Way, 1965-8

In May 1965, AW decided to use four researchers to help with a book he was planning on the Pennine Way. He wanted them to go ahead and walk a particular stretch of the route which he would then cover.

One of the researchers was Len Chadwick of Dobcross near Oldham with whom he had been in correspondence a few year earlier (see Letters 61–4) When it was suggested to him, Len was immediately very keen, and was willing to do it for free, but wanted to involve other members of his walking club KS (Kindred Spirits). AW was against this, saying it should be done alone, sending exact instructions on what to do and what to look out for.

LETTER 76: TO LEN CHADWICK, 12 MAY 1965 (PLUS INSTRUCTIONS)

12 May 1965

Dear Mr Chadwick,

Thank you for your letter and poems, which latter I now return.

All the Pennine Way stuff is here, so if you are rarin' to go you can make a start. Instructions are enclosed.

I note you suggest this is a job the K.S can do as a party, but in my opinion it should be done without distractions by one man travelling slowly and alone.

I will expect to hear from you around Christmas.

Yours sincerely

AWainwright

A PICTORIAL GUIDE TO THE PENINE WAY

Collaborators	Sections
Mr Len Chadwick, of Oldham	Edale to Todmorden–Halifax road
Mr Lawrence W. Smith, of Bradford	Todmorden-Halifax road to Malham Tarn
Mr Harry Appleyard, of Wigton	Tan Hill Inn to Cross Fell summit
Mr Cyril Moore, of Morecambe	Cross Fell summit to Kirk Yetholm

(A. Wainwright will do the middle section, Malham Tarn to Tan Hill Inn)

INSTRUCTIONS

A complete set of 2 and a half inch maps for your section is enclosed. On them, Mr Moore has indicated the course of the Pennine Way by a faint green line, according to the best information available to him. Also enclosed are the related 1 inch maps in the latest editions, which indicate the Pennine Way.

The line of the Way is to be checked carefully. Where there is no evidence on the ground (by signpost or distinct path), the approved route should be verified, if necessary, from other sources – by the various official publications on the subject, by local ramblers' associations or the local authority for the area, or by the farmers over whose ground the route passes. Doubts will arise in only a few places, as a complete right of way has now been established. Where a certain amount of discretion is left to the walker, such as in crossing a pathless moor, the best line should be worked out. Where there are 'official' variations, as with the start at Edale, all variations should be given the full treatment, as below.

The plan is to indicate on the 2 and a half inch maps the nature of the course to be followed. Where the way lies along a motor-road, an unbroken black line should be used ———; where the path is clear underfoot, a broken line ------; where the path is intermittent, a line of dots ·········· These must be indicated neatly on the maps provided, in black waterproof Indian ink.

It is not intended in the book to give detail more than a hundred yards on each side of a well-defined path, but where there is discretion a wider area will need to be detailed. Objects of interest in the vicinity of the Way, say within a mile, such as Roman Camps, tumuli, good viewpoints, waterfalls, etc, will be mentioned and these items numbered to agree with numbers written on the two and a half inch maps at the appropriate places. Apart from the classifications of the footpaths as mentioned in the previous paragraphs, and these reference numbers, no other markings should be made on the maps.

Please return the completed 2 and a half inch maps, the list of notes of interesting places, the 1 inch maps, and any correspondence collected on doubtful matter, by Christmas 1965. A.W will then go over <u>all</u> the ground, a bit at a time, during 1966 and 1967. Publication date: Easter 1968.

Although all collaborators have offered their services out of the goodness of their hearts, it is not intended that they shall suffer any expense, and a cheque is enclosed to cover travelling and subsistence expenses. Payments need not be accounted for; if there is any balance it may be spent in riotous living with A.W's compliments.

A year later, Len started sending his research notes to AW and there began a long correspondence between them, over details of the walks.

They never met and AW knew nothing about Len – whether he married, what his job was – though eventually AW did enquire about his occupation.

LETTER 77: TO LEN CHADWICK, 29 MAY 1966

c/o Westmorland Gazette, Kendal
29th May 1966

Dear Mr Chadwick

I am writing to acknowledge safe receipt of your separate volumes on the southern part of the Pennine way, and do so with sincere thanks for a job very well done. In fact, these books are fabulous, full of interesting detail, and it is a pity, in a way, that they contain far more information than I can find space to use. If I don't make a first-class job of it, after all the trouble you have gone to and all the help you have given me, it will be due to my own short-comings. In due course I will return all your notes.

I with the weather would improve!
Yours sincerely,

AWainwright

LETTER 78: TO LEN CHADWICK, 6 MAY 1966

c/o Westmorland Gazette, Kendal
6th June 1966

Dear Mr Chadwick,

Your remaining PW volumes have arrived safely. Many thanks.

As you can imagine, I had a splendid Whitsuntide in perfect conditions. I was staying with relatives at Penistone, and managed to get done the section from Crowden to the A.640 beyond Standedge including the Wessenden Loop. In bad weather there must be many difficulties of route-finding, but in the clear visibility and sunshine of Whitsun I had no trouble at all and thoroughly enjoyed everything – most of all your notes, which are admirable to follow and which I found absolutely accurate in all details. You certainly did a thorough job and have saved me a great deal of time.

I have now started on the book, and am doing this section first – it will fit into place later.

There is a little additional information needed on a few points I wish to mention, and if you can supply it I shall be grateful. The questions are overleaf.

Thanks again, a lot.

AWainwright

Black Hill's summit also seems to be named Soldier's Lump. Do you know why? (you mention army surveyors) is the story fit for telling?

Am I right in assuming that Hollin Brown Knott was the place of burial of the bodies in the recent trial?

I found the Ammon Wrigley memorial stone on Standedge (but would have missed it completely but for your clear description). Is this rock locally known as the Dinner Stone, as you suggest? The O.S maps indicate the Dinner Stone as being 200 yards from the column at a place where there is a conspicuous and isolated rock with a cairn on it and the letters L.T. Do you know the year of Ammon's birth?

LETTER 79: TO LEN CHADWICK, 14 JULY 1966

c/o Westmorland Gazette, Kendal
14th July 1966

Dear Mr Chadwick,

I am now returning volumes 3 and 4 of your Pennine Way notes, and three of the 6 inch maps you loaned me. The sections, CROWDEN-STANDEDGE, is now completed in book form, and your notes and the maps have been of immense help. The pity is that I have had to condense everything so much and leave out much I would have liked to include. This particular section, for instance, will occupy only 12 pages. Many thanks again for your assistance.

I wrote to Miss Winterbottom and have had her reply. She has given me the date of Ammon's birth, confirmed that the Dinners Stone is the one with L.T on it and not the memorial stone, told me about the Cotton Famine Road, and volunteered an opinion about the name Soliders Lump. As she was not sure about the latter I have addressed an enquiry to the Ordnance Survey and will let you know what they say.

I am still hoping to get down for a few days to do the next section north to Eastwood before the end of the summer but cannot be sure of this yet. Your additional notes on this section will be useful, and if you can find out anything about the line of the TransPennine motorway I should be glad to have it.

I am sorry you didn't get very far on your intended PW walk during the holidays. I agree the weather has been very poor. However, wait until the book is out, and then you can point out all my mistakes!

At present I am doing the Teesdale-Dufton crossing, which is magnificent country. With the help of friends with cars I have finished the walking and am now on the penwork. I must say I am enjoying the Pennine Way far more than I thought I would.

Yours sincerely,

AWainwright

LETTER 80: TO LEN CHADWICK, 9 AUGUST 1966

9th August 1966

Dear Mr Chadwick,

Your letter of 29th July ('proposed changes in the route of the Pennine

Way') was disturbing, but I must thank you for drawing my attention to the mischief that is being planned. I agree that the present route from Crowden to Black Hill is fine and could not be improved upon, so what are they playing at? Please keep me informed if you hear of any changes being approved.

I enclose a letter from the Ordnance Survey about Soldier's Lump, which seems to support your original hunch that the name was given by army surveyors, and that Vera's shot in the dark (that the name derived from the Volunteer Regiment formed to guard Yorkshire from French invasion 150 years ago) was wrong. Please return this letter and map.

Middleton-in Teesdale to Dufton is now in book form.

Yours sincerely,

AWainwright

LETTER 81: TO LEN CHADWICK, 25 OCTOBER 1966

c/o Westmorland Gazette, Kendal
25th October 1966

Dear Mr Chadwick,

I went to Rochdale on Sunday, the 16th, with the object of complet- ing your section of the P.W northwards from Standedge to Eastwood, and spent three days doing just that (average 5 miles a day!) very satis- factorily. I stayed at the Wellington Hotel in Rochdale (super-posh) and made good use of the trans-Pennine bus services both from Oldham and Rochdale. I met no other walkers on any of the three days.

The next section, over White Hill, I found dreary, but the gravel beds of Axletree Edge were much better to walk on and this area, down to the TV station, was rather enjoyable. I didn't like the next bit, over Slippery Moss, and the vast bog of Redmires was a squalid mess: feet and legs soaking. Blackstone Edge was a big improvement, though nothing like as impressive as I had imagined. It was a shock to find the O.S column-boulder defaced for ever by your name! (one way of achieving immortality!). I was uncertain which was the Aiggin Stone. Your notes stated that it was nearly lying on its side, and I assumed it was the one in the enclosed photograph (please confirm and return the photograph). The local library is trying to borrow a copy of 'Roof of Lancashire' for me so that I can give a note of its history. Do you ever remember seeing the stone upright? And in the location it now occupies? (some squared blocks neaerby suggest that they have formed the base of it – see photograph no 2)

The Roman Road was a grand surprise, and in places better preserved than any I have seen. The section across to Stoodley Pike was also a good fast route, and more interesting because of the views. And, although the finish between a pig farm and a sewage works is, as you say, a sad end to your section, the easy downhill road into the Calder Valley was delightful: the sun was warm, the autumn colours of the birch woods glorious. In fact, before industry took over the valley, this must have been a beautiful countryside. I didn't expect it – but perhaps its sweetness is exaggerated in comparison with the many miles of peat moors crossed since Edale. I am always surprised to find that this area is Yorkshire, which seems completely wrong because it is so much identified with Lancashire; geographically it certainly ought to be Lancashire.

As before, I found your notes and diagrams wonderfully accurate and helpful, and I would often have been quite bewildered without them. I will return them when I have completed my pages for this section.

Yours sincerely,

AWainwright

There were of course other things going on AW's life while walking and researching the Pennine Way – and the reference in passing to some friends, not named, giving him a lift is interesting. One of his major concerns from this period was to do with animal charities. Now that he was making quite a bit of income from his Pictorial Guides – as he revealed at the end of Book Seven – he was keen to set up some sort of animal refuge.

LETTER 82: TO MRS BOYLE, 11 NOVEMBER 1965

38 Kendal Green
Kendal
11th November 1965

Dear Mrs Boyle,

I am prepared to enter into a covenant to pay to the Westmorland Branch of the Royal Society for the Prevention of Cruelty to Animals the sum of one thousand pounds per annum for seven years, the first payment to be made on 17th January 1967, for the purpose of providing a headquarters for the Society in Kendal. The annual payments would be made out of income that has already been subject to income tax, and the Society would, therefore, as a registered Charity be able to claim a refund of tax on each annual payment. In round figures the tax refund over the period would amount to about 4,500, and with interest accrued from investment of the annual payments as they are made, I estimate the value of the gift to the Society to be around 12,000 by the end of the seventh year.

This amount should be enough, I think, to erect and equip a small buidling with office accommodation for the Inspector (sufficiently large to be used as a Committee Room), a waiting room, clinic, surgery, store, and inside kennels and cages, opening on to an exercise yard or compound. I have in mind a central site, quiet and remote from private residences, which I hope it may be possible to acquire.

Apart from providing greater convenience for the Inspector, and freeing him from the present need to use his home as an office and animal shelter, the primary object would be to make available a 'hospital' where sick animals and birds could be brought for care and attention without charge, but voluntary contributions would be invited. I feel confident that there would be no lack of voluntary helpers to staff the building, but would expect the professional services of veterinary surgeons to be paid for in accordance with their normal charges.

I have discussed these and other matters with your Hon. Treasurer, Mr Cross, who will be able to explain my proposal in greater detail.

I should be grateful if you would kindly arrange for your Committee to consider this offer and let me know their decision in due course. In the meantime I should be obliged if the matter could be treated in confidence.

Yours faithfully,

AWainwright

Mrs Clara Boyle
Hon. Secretary
Westmorland Branch RSPCA
Eller How
Ambleside

Mrs Clara Boyle, local secretary for the RSPCA, was 'overwhelmed' by AW's generosity, but when the proposal went up to headquarters, it developed into long drawn out discussions and meetings, with the RSPCA becoming worried that AW's plan was too ambitious, would cost at least £20,000 and was possibly not worth it. In the end AW decided he would instead become involved with an existing animal sanctuary in Lancashire, and would have nothing to do with the RSPCA.

Meanwhile, he was still walking the Pennine Way and corresponding with Len Chadwick.

LETTER 83: TO LEN CHADWICK, 21 APRIL 1967

c/o Westmorland Gazette, Kendal
21st April 1967

Dear Mr Chadwick,

Thank you for keeping me informed on the latest 'gen' about the Pennine Way. It certainly does appear from what you say that a change in the route is proposed on the Crowden-Black Hill section. I find this disturbing. I was under the impression that the precise route had been determined and approved long ago, and cannot understand why the Ramblers' Association or any other body should seek to alter it. The present route, as you say, is a good one and could not be improved upon. Please let me know if you hear of any developments. I think it's a bit thick, but as I shall be having a few days in Penistone very soon I had better walk the new line, just in case.

I reached the stake on Alport Low, wet through, but things were impossible: I couldn't take photographs and I couldn't refer to maps in all that rain, so I fled back down Doctor's Gate to Glossop, not without further troubles, for the beck was flooded and I couldn't get across at the ford. So I am no nearer with the southern section. And this explains why your Bleaklow volume will look as though it's had a rough time when you finally get it back. I will try again very shortly.

In complete contrast I had a magnificent day on the Penyghent section last Tuesday – a glorious day, the best of the year so far. I have now completed the whole route between Crowden and Dufton, having made a few trips recently to the Hebden Bridge – Keighley – Skipton area to fill in the gaps. I am enjoying making the book enormously, but if I hadn't the book in mind I doubt whether I should spend my time on places like Ickornshaw Moor.

I am glad you are keeping well, getting new recruits, and still planning bigger and better expeditions. I don't think I ever thanked you for the photograph, which I will treasure. Someday, perhaps to celebrate 'A

Pictorial Guide to the Pennine Way', we must arrange a meeting.
In the meantime, best of luck and good walking.
Yours sincerely,

AWainwright.

In his reply, Len revealed that he worked as a shorthand typist in the office of a Manchester cotton importer. Alas, it later transpired that this job was not all that secure.

LETTER 84: TO LEN CHADWICK, 29 JUNE 1967

c/o Westmorland Gazette, Kendal
29th June 1967

Dear Mr Chadwick,
Thank you for your letter of several weeks ago, written in Kendal on the eve of your expedition to the Howgills, which I hope proved successful. It was useful to have your notes about changes in the Pennine Way, which I will keep by me for the final revision, but I think I must come over again to see what is happening to the Trans-Pennine Motorway and try to find out from the engineer-in-charge how they propose to get the Pennine Way across it. I still haven't done the Edale-Crowden section, but am making good but slow progress northwards where I have now reached Bellingham in Northumberland. A visit to Kirk Yetholm in May was a complete washout – 3 days non-stop rain and mist – but I expect to be up there again in August on a do-or-die attempt, because time is now running out on me. Then I must have another shot at Edale-Crowden, and take a look at he new route to Black Hill although I have seen no references anywhere to the change you have reported here. Who makes these changes, anyway, what authority have they, when the whole route has been approved by the National Parks Commission?
Hope you are having a good year with the Club

AW

LETTER 85: TO LEN CHADWICK, 27 JULY 1967

Kendal, Thursday 27/7/67
JULY 27 – 67

Dear Mr Chadwick,

Thank you for your very kind letter, and offer of further help. It does appear, from what you say, that I shall have to include the new route up Black Hill from Crowden (damn nuisance) and it <u>would</u> be a help if you would kindly reconnoitre it and let me <u>have a few notes before the end of August</u>.

A fortnight ago today I reached the Border at last, just above Byrness, with 20 miles still to do to Kirk Yetholm, and this last lap I hope to finish next month. Everything is going OK.

I was very sorry to hear of the threat of redundancy at work, and do hope that nothing comes of this. It must be very unsettling, at your age, to have a feeling of insecurity about the future, and I sincerely trust your fears prove unfounded.

Yours sincerely,

AWainwright

LETTER 86: TO LEN CHADWICK, 19 NOVEMBER 1967

38 Kendal Green, Kendal
19th November 1967

Dear Mr Chadwick,

Just one final enquiry. Will you please ascertain the correct name of the buildings and masts on the summit of the Denshaw – Ripponden road? In your notes you have referred to this place as the Bleakedgate Moor <u>TV</u> Booster Station and I have done likewise in the book, but a doubt is creeping in. In a newspaper article about the new motorway I find it referred to as the 'BBC Radio Transmitter on Windy Hill'. I wondered if you could look it up in the telephone directory, or ask at the Post Office, or, better still, give them a ring and ask how the place should properly be described.

The book is now nearing completion. I want, of course, to pay acknowledgment to those who have helped me, and should be glad if you would let me know the year of your birth and whether you are an active member of any recognised rambling or mountaineering club, or of any mountain rescue team, or anything else of particular interest. I take it I can correctly describe you as the Hon. Secretary of the Kindred Spirits Fellwalking Society – is this the right title? And your occupation, please.

I will soon be returning all the notes you kindly let me have.

Yours sincerely

AWainwright

Please reply to 38 Kendal Green, Kendal to save time, the Gazette office often hold letters up for weeks.

LETTER 87: TO LEN CHADWICK, 17 JANUARY 1968

38 Kendal Green, Kendal
17 January 1968

Dear Mr Chadwick,

I have now completed the book and got it away to the printers. It will be published around Easter under the title of PENNINE WAY COMPANION. I feel pretty confident that you will like it, and will send you a copy when it is ready.

With regard to The Mystery of Bleakedgate Moor, I have described the contraption as a G.P.O Wireless Telegraphy Station. This seemed safest. There is the authority of the Ordnance map for referring to it as a W.T Station, and I cannot think that the W.T can mean anything but Wireless Telegraphy. And you established that it belonged to the G.P.O. You will note that Holme Moss, which is a T.V station, is described on the map.

I am now returning the remainder of your notes, which were a great help. If they are a bit soiled it is because they were well used. Also a number of letters, which may contain information you might require. These come back to you with my very sincere thanks for a job well done.

I hope you are feeling fitter these days. By a stroke of luck I managed to complete the P.W walking just one week before the fells were closed for the epidemic, otherwise I would have been badly held up.

Yours sincerely,

AWainwright

LETTER 88: TO LEN CHADWICK, I FEBRUARY 1968

38 Kendal Green, Kendal
1st February 1968

Dear Mr Chadwick,

I was extremely sorry to learn from your letter that you are faced with the prospect of finding new employment, which is bad enough in itself but doubly so when it happens at an age when most men want nothing more than to stay quietly in their present jobs and cruise along uneventfully to retirement and a pension. You don't sound hopeful of securing fresh work in the Oldham district, and it may well be that, although we read in the papers of there being more jobs available than men, this does not apply in south Lancashire. In the Midlands or around London you would have a fair chance of getting fixed up quite quickly, but I suppose you are not eager to leave your home territory – or the hills. Neither would I be.

It is unlikely that I could do anything to solve your problem myself. Since retirement I have lost touch and broken my contacts except insofar as they affect my books.

As you are going to have to start afresh anyway, could it not be the sort of employment for which you have a natural flair, something you could really enjoy? I am thinking, of course, of a wardenship of some small youth hostel or similar outdoor institution run single-handed, somewhere in the country, even in the wilds? Or forestry? Or reservoir-keeping? There is never much demand for jobs situated far from the creature comforts of the towns. You would have to sacrifice your clerical training and start something quite new, but does this matter? 'something new' may be something better.

I'm sorry I can see no way of helping, but hope you get fixed up quite soon in congenial work. Please keep me informed.

THE BOOK is starting printing next week. I will send you a copy as soon as available, probably around the end of March.

Yours sincerely,

AWainwright

LETTER 89: TO LEN CHADWICK, 3 MAY 1968

38 Kendal Green, Kendal
3rd May 1968.

Dear Mr Chadwick,

I am owing you three letters, and am sorry I have been so slow in replying. Pressure of correspondence! First let me thank you for your very kind approval of PENNINE WAY COMPANION, which has (so far) had a good reception. You ought to be feeling that you have a proprietary interest in this book, and I hope that you consider the book sufficient reward for the many months of lonely reconnaissance and the miles of mud-slogging and the many doubts and difficulties you suffered on my behalf. Unfortunately I had to be very selective in what I included and what I left out in order to keep the book to reasonable dimensions, and masses of information had to be sacrificed for the public although everything was of inestimable value to myself. Your other letters have suggested improvements to the route, and I am quite sure you are right in saying that alternative passages you have tried out recently give better walking. But it is now too late to think of alterations to the present route: it is here to stay.

I am sorry to learn that you are not yet fixed up with a new job. About two months ago I had an enquiry from the C.H.A about you, to which I was able to reply favourably, and I thought you might have been successful with your application to them, but apparently not. Then I heard, but only in a roundabout way, that the Y.H.A were looking for a warden (single man) for their hostel in Mallerstang, but could not get confirmation of this and so did not write, imagining you anyway as being signed on by the C.H.A. In your letter received this morning there is a hint that your expect to have fresh employment soon, and I hope this materialises if the work is something you could enjoy doing. A Warden in the Lake District was also advertised for recently, I noticed, (850 p.a), but I am afraid age would be against you for this job although there was no age-limit in the advert. However, I hope you will have good news soon.

I am making good progress with WALKS IN LIMESTONE COUNTRY, which I am finding much easier to do than the Pennine Way. Not only is the territory around Ingleton and Settle much pleasanter to walk, and much more interesting, but it also happens to be within close range of Kendal, so that I can pick out the good weather, and not find myself marooned in lodgings in bad weather far out in the wilds.

I am glad to see you are still very active with your walking programme and trust you have a successful year on the hills with no worries as to where your next meal is coming from.

Yours sincerely,

AWainwright

Part 9
Letters to Molly, 1964-6

Molly Lefubure first wrote to AW around 1957 when Book Two came out, correcting him about some point, now long forgotten. She remembered that he wrote back and said he was right and she was wrong.

Later on, she wrote again and this time something sparked off AW's interest in Molly personally – perhaps it was because she was a sparky, middle class, educated, literary lady, of the sort he had rarely met – and so began a correspondence that went on for many years.

Molly went to North London Collegiate School and London University and then worked for three years on a chain of East End newspapers throughout the Blitz, after which, for eight years, she was medical secretary to Keith Simpson, the Home Office pathologist. She married John Gerrish, an old company executive, and had two sons. In 1957 they bought a house in Newlands near Keswick, used by Molly as a bolt-hole to write in and for family holidays. They now live there full time. Molly has written several books on crime and the Lake District, novels for adults and children, as well as biographies of Coleridge and Thomas Hardy.

Their correspondence proper began in September 1964 when Molly wrote to him enclosing an old clay pipe she had found while climbing Robinson. 'I knew he smoked a pipe, as he had drawn himself with one in one of his Guides. In my letter, I said it must be one of his, but he shouldn't leave such litter on the fells . . .'

LETTER 90: TO MOLLY LEFEBURE, 4 SEPTEMBER 1964

c/o Westmorland Gazette, Kendal
4th September 1964

Dear Madam,
Thank you for your kind letter, with its generous comments and

remarkable enclosure. The pipe is no longer serviceable, unfortunately, but your letter was a perfect delight to read, a thing of great charm, quiet fun, vivid imagination, and apt, expressive words.

You put me in a difficulty right away. How should I address you? Simply to say 'Dear Mrs Gerrish' seems an awful damper on your positively friendly, spirited, scintillating and spontaneous overtures to me (if 'overtures' isn't an unhappy word to use here). 'Dear Molly' sounds much better, but would it bring an angry husband rampaging after me? (I have a dread of angry husbands, as of bulls.) You mention a bevy of offspring, unashamedly. I wonder. . . . Oh, what the hell – I always get myself into trouble when I write to women. Better play safe . . .

I am writing now only to acknowledge its receipt. Usually I keep correspondents waiting at least three months for attention – not out of discourtesy, but out of self-defence. I have such a vast heap of unanswered letters on my desk (built up into a lovely cairn – it seems such a pity to disturb it). But you are special. I can't keep you waiting that long.

Please accept this acknowledgement until I can find time to give your letter the full attention it deserves. I'll write as soon as I can.

Yours sincerely,

AWainwright (Mr!)

Some time later, he wrote from Scotland to her, from the Caledonian Hotel in Inverness. No year is given, but it is clearly 1965, judging by the following letter. Molly says he was doing lots of train rides, partly because he was allowed a certain amount of free rail travel as a local government servant. There had been other shorter letters between them before this long letter from Scotland. The reference to Burnbank is about a running argument between them. Molly had said there was an old stone circle on Burnbank he had missed – and he said it didn't exist, she was imagining it. This row, only half jocular, went on for years.

LETTER 91: TO MOLLY LEFEBURE, 16 MAY 1965?

Caledonian Hotel, Inverness
May 16th, I think

Dear Molly,

I must tell somebody, or I shall start screaming. And only from you, with your rich understanding of human frailties, can I expect the warmth of sympathy my present unfortunate circumstances deserve.

I am making my annual railway tour of Scotland solo. The purpose is complete relaxation, mark you. But, but by a cruel chain of coincidences, I am finding myself everywhere given a hotel bedroom next to a door marked 'toilet', with devastating effect on sleep and rest. You must understand that I cannot sleep with a noise going on. I can not only not sleep with clock in the room, I can't if there's one in the next. My watch I have to bury under the carpet and put my rucksack over it. But since I came up here my nights have been punctuated by the crash of waters only the thickness of a brick from my weary head. Things were at their lowest ebb at the Loch Lomand Hotel at Balloch, which had two coach parties staying overnight. All night long they were at it, flushing the poor thing mercilessly. There was never any question of sleep. At 2 o'clock I gave up trying, put the light on and kept a tally on the wallpaper. As the result of this research into the Toilet-Going Habits of the British Tourist in Scotland, I can now produce statistics to show that (by dividing the number of flushes by the number of guests in what might be termed the 'catchment area' or 'toilet zone') the average attendance of the British Tourist between supper and breakfast is 3 and a third. This takes some swallowing, you will admit. O, for the freedom from inhibition of Burnbank Stone Circle! This may be life in the raw, but how much to be preferred! The other hotels have been little better. I feel like a wet rag; my eyes are going bloodshot.

I don't know why I'm here, anyway. The place has been smothered in mist and rain for four days. There is no pleasure in it. The last act of desperation of a man at his wits' end is to go from Inverness to Wick and back in a day – 320 miles – and this I did yesterday. It rained all the time and I had the train to myself. I must be going out of my mind, because nobody in his right senses every goes to Wick. My heart's not in it, either. I cross Rannoch Moor and my thoughts are of Ennerdale, I look at the Cairngorms from Aviemore and see High Stile and Red Pike from Crummock. I climb the bonny braes above Lomond searching for Burnbank's stone circle. The hills are mightier, the lochs vaster, the distances greater, but it is a country without charm. No, lass, this is second best, and a long way short of the best we both know and live.

It is late and I ought to be in bed, but what's the use. Here at the Caledonian I am next door to the plumbing nerve-centre for the whole establishment. Every time somebody turns a tap, or worse, there is a spluttering convulsion in a battery of unseen but nearby pipes, and the gurgle long afterwards like a death rattler. Dawn is hours away. There is no hope for me. I have tried making ear-plugs from tufts pulled from the carpet, and from pellets of newspaper, but nothing works. My eyes are getting bloodshotter and bloodshotter. I feed jaded, weary, shot at. In my extremity, I think of you, and I don't even know why.

NEXT MORNING

I have been to sleep! And slept well!! They say necessity is the mother of invention, but this was pure chance. During restless tossings and turn-ings during the night, after one particular contortion I found my head under the pillow, making a sandwich with the bolster, and all extraneous noises were immediately stilled. Here was the solution! Pressure on the pillow can be effected by some article of bedroom furniture, such as a chair. Tell all your friends who cannot sleep to put their heads under the pillow, not on it. Mind you, it gets a bit warm. And I suppose it could cause suffocation. It's perhaps an idea to work into a murder plot. Now suppose there is this woman novelist on a lonely Lakeland farm. . . . I'll think about it going down to Perth today. I must be lots better. I'm get-ting my imagination back.

Back in Kendal, AW describes the rest of his Scottish tour, and also says he has been to Keswick and climbed Catbells, within sight of Molly's house (referred to as LHS). AW's remark about her husband being 'a fat old boy of 76' was one of his usual teasing references, suggesting she had made a mistake to prefer him to AW. He had never met John at this stage, far less Molly. John in fact was always thin, and at the time was only in his early forties.

LETTER 92: TO MOLLY LEFEBURE, 28 MAY 1965

KENDAL, 28 May 1965

Dear Molly,

My admonition to the Gazette (to deliver to me promptly any corre-spondence with a Keswick postmark) has had a salutary effect, and your letter of the 18th was in my hands by the 20th.

Well, to complete the story, I got home all right, but odiferous with kip-pers (which I had had every morning for breakfast – just for the hell of it, being on holiday and slightly reckless) – one cannot go through an experi-ence like this and emerge unscathed, and after a week of it I was smelling worse than Wick Harbour. I persisted with them, however, finding them effective in ensuring a compartment to one's self, which suited me fine because I like to bob from one side to the other, looking for mountains.

When I got to Perth, the rain it was sluicing down, so I kept on the train to Glasgow, where the rain it was sluicing down, so I changed trains for Stranraer, where the rain it was sluicing down. Stranraer, like Wick, is the end of the railway and the end of hope: the sort of place you would go to commit suicide. At Stranraer I booked in at a hotel that used to be a big house built by Ross the explorer, and I think he too must have been a man easily disturbed by noises in the night: so solid are the walls that not a murmur passes from one room to another. I had a double bed all to myself (a great treat, for I wobble off single ones) and slept like a man in a grave. Beauty is often glimpsed in unexpected places, and it can be found in certain conditions even at Stranraer. Looking out on the harbour from my window at bedtime, I found that the rain had stopped and a yellow band had appeared across the sky to the west, an afterglow of sunset, against which was silhouetted the masts of the Irish steamer that had crept in during the evening and was now ablaze with lights. I looked at this pretty picture a long time. It pleased me.

The following day was all blue sky and white clouds, but perishing cold. I ended it at Dumfries, having earned for myself the cheap distinction of being the last local government officer in the history of the world to travel on the Stranraer-Dumfries railway, which closes on JUNE 14TH. At Dumfries I found myself in a room with twin beds, which seemed a waste; and in any case I can never see any sense in twin beds – they are neither one thing nor another. Between these two was a crevice into which one leg fell and was trapped during the night, but again I slept well.

Next day was spent coming home, and, as so often happens, the weather turned glorious. On the journey from Dumfries to Carlisle the hills of Lakeland can be seen across the Solway, and on this morning they looked delicious under a blue sky with little puffs of white cloud above them. From Carrock Fell to Grasmoor they could all be clearly recognized, old Skiddaw looking especially magnificent from here. Hills of memories! They looked good, so good that from Carlisle I made a bus tour of West Cumberland just to get nearer to them. At Keswick there was time to visit a favourite spot on Derwentwater where nobody else goes and look across to Catbells. Such beauty I had not seen in Scotland. It was good to be back. Real good.

Last Saturday I was back to happy routine with my usual weekly visit to Keswick, although I am only killing time until the summer bus services start. I took a stroll on Catbells. I stood looking across the valley to

LHS, quietly seething with jealously of the fat old boy of 76 you follow around. And me in the full flower of manhood (according to you)! There was no flag flying over the old homestead to warn the burghers (correct spelling) of Newlands that Mr G was in residence, but I turned sadly away, in fact, this correspondence, with its unhealthy tread of sadism, is making it impossible that we should ever meet. You started it, not me. Rubbish dumps, bulls, water closets, murders and kippers – well, at any rate, nobody can ever accuse us of exchanging love letters.

From Catbells I went to look for the Roman Fort at Caermote, between Binsey and Bothel (which a lady on the bus called Brothel, which made my ears prick up intently – so perhaps you are right and I am not yet past the full flower). I couldn't find Caermote, but noticed its pattern later from a neighbouring hillside. Back in Keswick I had a prowl round the new refuse tip, now in its formative stages, but there is nothing to recommend except possibly an old mattress that might do for your guest room, but it is nearly buried and would need a lot of tugging to get it free. The rest was a humdrum miscellany, not really inspiring.

Yes, I know the type of fierce walker you describe, but believe me I was never one such. I have always climbed hills by pulling myself up from one tuft of grass to the next. But I share your dislike, or is it mortification? Heaven preserve us from breezy individuals! The thing to do is to reverse the embarrassment. Memorise a short passage from a book on geology – just a sentence or two chosen at random – and carry a small hammer. Then when you find yourself being overtaken by someone who is obviously going to give you a hearty greeting, even if he doesn't actually slap you on the shoulder, as he strides past, just stop in your tracks and start tapping the nearest stone. The odds are he will pass without comment, but if he should ask what you are doing, look him up and down pityingly, quote your passage, and resume your concentration. He will creep quietly away! I know, I've tried it!

AW

By the end of 1965, AW had finished the manuscript of Fellwanderer, the book about writing his Pictorial Guides, which he is sent to Molly for advice and comments. She had recently published her own first Lakeland book, The English Lake District (Batsford 1964) and was working on another Cumbrian book. She didn't like the proposed shape of Fellander, saying it would stick out of the book shelves and should be shaped like the Guides – advice he ignored. But he did take out a reference to peeing in Thirlmere which he had done because he hated the Water Board for turning it into a reservoir. She said it would encourage other walkers to do the same and the Water Board would then be after him.

AW had teased her about her maiden name, Lefebure, that it was Franco-German. Her grandfather had originally come from France, hence her surname, but Molly had been born and brought up in England. 'There was no German in our family. That was just one of AW's silly jokes, or deliberate misunderstandings.'

LETTER 93: TO MOLLY LEFEBURE, 11 FEBRUARY 1966

Municipal Offices, Kendal
11th February 1966

Molly, I could kiss you. I could you. You must have spent hours and hours on my little manuscript. It was never my intention to encroach so much on your busy existence, and I would never have dared to ask your opinion if I had known you would feel you had to do more than read it through once. But you are obviously nothing if not thorough. You simply had to do your best to make a writer out of me, as in the past you have tried to make a man out of me.

Well, I am tremendously grateful. I think your suggestions are absolutely right. Of course I should have mentioned my introduction to the district – the thing is lopsided without it. Of course I should start at the second paragraph. Of course my discursion on handwriting is too long and out of place and should be cut. Of course, everything else. You are dead right. I will do all these things. And it will be a better book.

As for the Saga of the Stone Circle, you have permitted more than I thought you would, but you will have an opportunity to change your mind if you want to when I let you see the proofs later on. I referred to your father only to make sense of the 'Franco-German sweep' mentioned later – sorry! Yes, I suppose we are being rather abandoned. The association seems even to become a little suspicious when my letters to you are hidden in a cask of rum in a dark cellar and yours to me are craftily concealed in a cabinet of files of strictly local government affairs. Well, let's bring it to the light of day if you are perfectly sure that everything will be all right at your end. I may be in trouble about it, but am inured to trouble. I might find that a private eye is following me around, but, if so, could lose him for ever on Jack's Rake. It will be a jolt to several women who think of me as their soul-mate, but, in any case, I really ought to stop giving them this impression. We might each find people regarding us (individually, of course) out of the corner of their eyes and we might be a source of exercise for the little minds . . . but haven't I read somewhere that writers are permitted some licence? Or does this apply only to poets? Don't worry, love. We'll switch to poetry, if need be.

Funny about that large, yeti-like <u>thing</u> you found prowling around the environs of L.H.S! you know, the description fits me perfectly, and I certainly was in the places you mention, several times, but it wasn't me, I assure you. It couldn't be could it? <u>I</u> wouldn't flee up the fell if an attractive woman spoke sweetly to me, not likely. Instinct would urge me to get down in the bracken with her. Nor was it yours truly you en encountered on Catbells. You were right to belabour him with your tongue. Cheeky devil! No, I don't speak to people I meet on the fells unless they speak first, and then not always. Only once did I lose my temper and berate somebody: a party of townies had strolled up to he head of Mickleden from Dungeon Ghyll with a little yapping dog and they were having great fun watching it chase the sheep around – and this just before lambing time. So I told them off good and proper and left them with red faces. Mine was red, too.

Yes, do please tell me about the funny remark that nearly led to your arrest. The world is getting less funny every day, and people are getting far too serious on nearly every subject under the sun. There's nothing funny about Vietnam, or Rhodesia, or landing on the moon, or teenage morals. People are becoming too earnest, too intolerant, to determind to get things just as they think they should be: they are forgetting how to laugh. I don't think you can plan human life and human destiny by going to meetings and passing resolutions and writing to newspapers and parading through the streets. There are far too many societies springing up with the object of telling people how to live, too much interference with others. You don't live to a prescribed pattern: this would be deadly boring. Life is happy chance, and exciting, and full of humour if you only have the imagination to recognize it. It's the terribly earnest types who commit suicide, those who can see the funny side who most enjoy life. Yes, do please tell me that funny story!

Again, many many thanks for your wonderful help. I won't be dedicating the book to you, nor even mentioning you in acknowledgment, because this might cause a major domestic explosion that would penetrate even my thick skin, but I shall always remember your extreme kindness in the matter, and be grateful.

AW

Molly did not hide AW's letters. That was another of his jokes. Her husband John always read and was amused by AW's – but presumably AW did keep Molly's letters hidden from his wife Ruth, just in case they could be misconstrued.

He was delighted with Molly's suggestion that they should write some sort of book together – especially as he seemed to be getting bogged down in his Pennine Way project.

LETTER 94: TO MOLLY LEFEBURE, 15 APRIL 1966

Municipal Offices, Kendal
15th April 1966

Dear Molly,

I am going to write to you here and now if it kills me. I am disgustingly busy. But never mind the ringing telephone, never mind the queue of dear old ladies who want to see me about rate rebates (they lose their attractiveness to me when they get to 75 to 80, anyway – some queer twist in my make-up, must be), never mind the accumulation of IN papers on my desk, never mind anything. Molly is my darling, and I have three fat juicy letters from her and none of them answered yet. L.H.S must be shaking from her sobs.

Yes, I am 101% (as Sam Goldwyn would have said) behind the idea of doing a book together. I can just see it in Chaplin's bookshop window, with a hand-drawn gnarled, arthritic finger pointing to it with the words 'JUST OUT' – LAKELAND LETTERS OF LEFEBURE AND WAINWRIGHT BEING AN EXCHANGE OF CORRESPONDENCE BETWEEN A SCATTY INEBRIATE AND A SEEDY REPROBATE. The cover, in superb technicolour, would show a couple in silhouette against a westering sun on the shores of Buttermere, SHE obviously once-handsome but now wearied with liquor and child-bearing, HE merely rather distinguished. But it wouldn't have to be a book about ghosts, love. You've only found one, anyway. No, we must battle fiercely on the subjects most in the Lakeland news – wider roads, chair-lifts, public W's in Borrowdale, foxhunting, fell races, water abstraction, and so on – and we must be clever enough to give the impression (between the lines) that although we fight we are really fond of each other. We won't ever say so but we will lead our readers to that conclusion, and then they will think themselves very smart and gossip about it in the Portinscale hotels.

About Moses Rigg. You must be absolutely right. I had previously seen a reference to him with the surname of Rigg, but was influenced to doubt his existence by an informative article, 'Moses Trod', in the Fell and Rock Journal, many years ago, by Graham, who, after exhaustive enquiries, had found no evidence that he ever lived.

I am enclosing a rough proof of the Burnbank incident. This is your last opportunity to avoid the consequences of your high-spirited agreement to its publication, which, at the worse, could mean a future life of shame and degradation to a greater extent even than your past and present. You can alter it if you wish, or you can opt out altogether and say no, better not, Mr G. will play merry hell with me again and I can't take any more. It's up to you, baby. Don't bother to return it unless you make some corrections.

Now for the story of The Most Disastrous Expedition in the History of Exploration. For weeks I had impatiently awaited Easter, because at Easter I was going to make a start on the Pennine Way, working northwards from Edale. The P.W was a new toy, and I was going to play with it for the first time at Easter. Easter came and a lady friend took me down to Buxton in her car. My motives were pure and wholesome – I was going to walk the Pennine Way and write a book about it – but it's funny how pally you can get within the confines of a mini; however, this has nothing to do with the story and is mentioned only to make you jealous. Pure and wholesome I said.

Continued at home, in secret

It was unfortunate that Easter 1966 coincided with the Worst Weather ever recorded at Edale. On Good Friday morning the great moment arrived, although unrecognizable as such. I set a size 10 boot on the first step of the 250 mile trek, and I thought this is it, I've started, I'm on my way. There was no sounding of trumpets, no firing of cannons, no fanfare. In fact, the inaugural step was downright depressing, into three inches of mud and in the unavoidable company of an infestation of strange long haired characters from Manchester and hordes of boy scouts; a drizzle had set in, mist was falling, the path was a quagmire. I thought of Borrowdale, I thought ye gods, what have I done, what am I doing in this god-forsaken spot? 250 miles of this! I must be mad. Well, I got up to the plateau, two miles, and into a wilderness of wet fog and snowdrifts and slimy peat hags, and my heart was in my boots. I turned back, back to the howling crowds and the transistor radios, and fled from Edale in a train packed to the doors with filthy youngsters, everybody cuddling everybody else except me. It's no fun looking rather distinguished! So back to the Palace Hotel at Buxton, which did its best to make me forget the whole sorry business. The fare there is of the very best, the appointments simply luxurious. Going to do your numbers here is a joy out of this world.

Next day was shocking – continuous heavy rain all day. The P.W was never in my mind. I sat for hours in an easy chair in the foyer and gloomily watched the elegant ladies coming in and going out, sizing them up, so to speak, and wondering how each would react in certain circumstances. Later I stirred myself sufficiently to go and have a look at Haddon Hall. This was fine, but it was another wasted day. I dined well and expensively that night. Enthusiasm for the Pennine Way succumbed to the soft easy life of the Palace Hotel.

Next day the same. I could stand no more, and I could afford no more. The P.W was a thousand miles away. I came back, wondering why I had ever said I would walk the Pennine Way and write a book about it. I will do it, of course, but how I shall ache for the old green road on Catbells, the sweet birches of Ashness, the little bays of Sprinkling Tarn. I shall understand how you feel at Surbiton.

Cheer me up, love, and tell me about falling into Dalehead Tarn. You don't have to explain that you had been on the bottle again. I will assume that much.

AW

AW sent Molly a copy of Fellwanderer when it came out in 1966. In it Molly is mentioned by name, and teased once again that she imagined she had discovered a stone circle on Burnbank, which AW mocked.

In this letter, he also teases her about being drunk and destitute, hence he is leaving her money, two other running jokes. But then he also goes rather serious as if becoming depressed. Not that he reveals what the problem might be.

LETTER 95: TO MOLLY LEFEBURE, UNDATED, 1966

Molly love, thank you for your letter, which cheered me up at lot, as you knew it would. You really know me very well. Here is The Book (capitals, like The Bog in Wythburn). The truth is out. You now have my picture, and of course you must have seen me many times, always (curiously) going across to the Gents on Keswick Bus Station. (The nearest factual stone circle being a mile away, on Castlerigg). I prefer the earlier photo, included to arouse the maternal instinct of my lady fans – they will fall for me in a big way now, I expect. (I've stopped hoping). Funny thing, when I am in trouble I always feel as I look in the first photo: very young, very bewildered, very helpless, wanting a soft breast – and soft breasts are hard to come by when you get to my age. However, I will survive. I am never down for long. Resilient, that's me. I hope The Book doesn't get you into trouble, too, at your end.

The dark hours of depression are made darker by my Pennine excursions. I ought now to be seeking rebirth on airy ridges and lofty summits, but, due to mad folly I find myself wallowing every weekend in rural slime on the fringe of industrial Lancashire and Yorkshire. You know the sort of thing: manurial farmyards, tumbledown henpens, grimy rows of cottages, mill chimneys in the distance, cinder paths dotted with puddles and cowclaps, slovenly women, cheeky kids, bus conductresses who call you 'love' and don't mean it and it wouldn't make any difference if they did, more cowclaps. . . .

Sometimes I stop in my tracks and ask myself what the hell am I doing here. This is where I started, this was my first environment, this is what I ran away from, remember? But soon I shall have left the towns behind me and be heading north to the lonely wildernesses of the Border. There will be a message for me there, of inspiration and encouragement. Here there is none. There I shall be able to get away from care and trouble, be captain of my soul, master of my fate and other high-sounding phrases. Free, that's the word. Free to think, free to plan what must be a new life and a last chance.

One day I will go up Catbells and bury 2s 4d for you (4d = cost of living increase since april 1965, and is outside the 'freeze')

Tell me something funny, love. Make me smile. I have been living alone for the past five weeks.

I am famished with hunger

I am too weak to write more

Despite writing all these frisky, teasing, personal letters to Molly, he has not revealed why it is he might be 'free to plan what must be a new life'.

In none of his letters does AW ever mention Ruth, his wife, or that he is married, but once they had started their correspondence, Molly asked around and discovered he was married, but not apparently very happily.

When he had finished all the Pictorial Guides, she had suggested in one or her letters to him that he should buy his wife a new hat to make up for neglecting her all these years.

'He ignored this remark, so I never mentioned his wife again, realizing it was a sore subject.'

Nor has AW so far given any further details to Molly of the 'lady friend' mentioned earlier, the one he said had driven him to Buxton. . . .

Part 10
Letters to Betty, 1965

AW first met Betty McNally some time in 1957 when she was called into his Borough Treasurer's office about an unpaid bill for ten shillings, incurred by a charity she happened to be involved with. He reprimanded her, and told her not to sign things on behalf of other people. She sensed a gentleness despite his sternness, and also noticed the sun shining on the red hairs on the back of his hands. Then she went back to her own life.

Betty was born Betty Hayes in 1922, educated at Casteron School, which the Brontë sisters once attended, did a Speech and Drama course, got married to a Dublin doctor called Paddy McNally and had two daughters, Jane and Anne. The marriage collapsed and Betty returned with her daughters to live in Kendal – where an old school friend was living – and busied herself with good works and cultural activities, bringing up her daughters on her own.

Seven years after that first encounter with AW, some time in 1965, she wrote him a fan letter. By this time she had realised he was the author of the Pictorial Guides, which she had enjoyed reading. He wrote a reply, inviting her to his office to talk about the fells. She was a bit surprised, him being the Borough Treasurer, but a few weeks later, on 20 September, finding herself passing the Town Hall, she decided to pop in and asked to see him. They chatted and he asked her to call again, making a proper appointment this time.

When she arrived, he said he was just going off on a holiday to Scotland with his cousin Eric, but while he was way, he wanted her to read a book which he gave to her.

The book was a typed manuscript which he had written in 1939, an autobiographical story in which he imagines he will one day meet his Dream Lady, that he will sit with her, she will comfort him, resting his aching head on her sweet breast. He had shown no one this manuscript, keeping it totally secret.

AW was aged fifty-eight by now, already thinking of retirement, while Betty was forty-three, still officially a married woman with two young daughters.

But from the moment of meeting Betty, he had decided that she was the Dream Lady, the one he had fantasised about for almost three decades.

LETTER 96: TO BETTY MCNALLY, LATE SEPTEMBER 1965?
[A note to Betty, accompanying his book]

Just read the book first, and make sure it is not a case of mistaken identity with me, and mistaken impression with you. Wait a fortnight, please. Then let me know.

How I am looking forward to my journey tomorrow! Twelve hours alone, without distraction, to sort myself out and think tenderly of you.

. . .

Oh dear!!!!

AW returned from Scotland and got down to finishing off the last stages of Book Seven, the Western Fells, while also thinking of the Pennines, his next project, but unable to get the image of Betty out of his mind.

LETTER 97: TO BETTY, 2 OCTOBER 1965

Dear Betty,

I <u>must</u> write. An eternity has passed since I saw you. Saturday was a complete non-success. It rained all the time, but I hardly noticed it, and as the day dragged endlessly on it began to sit my mood. Silly me, I looked for you on the bus. I walked the streets of Keswick looking for you, although I knew you would not be there. I walked the streets of Cockermouth looking for you, although I knew you would not be there. I went on to Loweswater for no better reason than that you said you had once been there. I walked by the lake; there was not a soul about. I stood under a tree and listened to the rain on the leaves above. I was wretched. For the first time I was not merely alone, but lonely. Desperately lonely. What folly, to have put so much distance between us when every instinct urged me to get closer to you! I wanted you. I <u>needed</u> you. I thought of you all day with such tenderness that I felt I was melting away. As for sorting myself out, I couldn't: I need your help to do that. I sighed the three words 'oh Betty <u>please</u>' a hundred times that day, not quite knowing what I was asking of you. Perhaps simply that you should not forget me. Only hours had passed, by the clock, but it seemed to me that an age had gone by without word or sign from you.

I want so much to be with you again.

Forgive me if I should not have written. But I badly need some reassurance that I have not been dreaming, that I was not wrong in feeling some response from you. You seem worlds away at this moment. How cruel a silence can be when it is not explained or understood! You may have disliked my book and be now disliking me. I know I suggested no contact for a month, but that idea has proved a complete non-success too, except perhaps as an exquisite torture. How can I know what a silence means? I want to hear you whisper that you have not forgotten me.

Alfred (to you)

It is an hour since you rang, and I have spent it gazing out of the window. Thank you for letting me hear your sweet voice again and for being so wonderfully kind to me. Now I know you have not changed. And I am <u>very very</u> happy.

Betty, in her letter back to him, said that she had decided to call him Red from now on, thinking of the red hairs she had noticed on the back of his hand and also as a diminutive of Alfred – which of course he never used or liked.

LETTER 98: TO BETTY, 5 OCTOBER 1965

On Saturday I had coffee at my usual place at Keswick: a nice quiet place of shaded lights and soft music. A lady asked if she could share my table. I said yes, of course. She had a kindly face; she was rather older than I. The background music switched to 'Rose of Tralee', a haunting melody that I first heard John McCormick sing and which always brings me close to tears. I would like this to be <u>our</u> song. I wanted to tell the lady that I had found the most wonderful girl in the world. I wanted to tell everybody, even the man sweeping the street. I can tell only you.

I didn't get to the top of Gable. The weather was glorious and I was infinitely happier than last Saturday, but I had your last letter with me for company, and halfway up I thought I would turn aside from the path and find a quiet hollow in the heather and read it yet again. So I did, and then I felt to dreaming and trying to recall every word you said to me last Wednesday. After which it was much too late to go on and I wandered slowly down to Seatoller in a happy trance

Yesterday I spend on my book, as I always do on Sundays. Sunday is my best opportunity – I can get 10 or 12 hours at it. All day I wondered what you were doing, and ached for your touch again. I have so many ideas for you, for us. In the evening I watched a film on TV, attracted by the title 'Magnificent Obsession', which seemed singularly appropriate. I enjoyed it. The story, a sad one, would hardly bear analysis, but there were nice sentiments in it. It ended happily, as I wanted it to do. Please, B, I want to buy you a TV for Christmas. It would be one way of sharing experiences while apart.

The word I was searching for was not therapy. It was telepathy.

I have ringed two dates in the diary – first anniversaries. But I hope the whole year will record only pleasant events and incidents. You deserve so much to be entirely happy. I like the name you have given me. So simple and so appropriate, yet nobody thought of 'Red' before. Yes, I do like it. Sounds tough! I always fancied myself as a cowboy riding the lonely ranges, and Red is just right for a man who sits tall in the saddle. And this is exactly how I have felt since last Wednesday. Tall in the saddle. On top of the world. A world that has turned upside down in three amazing weeks. And I like it so much better the way you have changed it for me!

Take very good care of yourself in Dublin, love. Remember all the time you are away that there is someone here waiting for you to come back, and wanting you.

Red

Betty was going to Dublin to see her husband, to discuss divorce arrangements, which had been planned, long before AW appeared. While she was away, AW climbed Great Gable with Harry Firth, the printing manager of the Westmorland Gazette, who had been charge of the production of AW's books since the beginning. Cindy was AW's dog.

LETTER 99: TO BETTY, 19 OCTOBER 1965

Monday,

Betty dear, I am missing you awfully. We are separated by distance, with only your sweet letter, received this morning, linking us together. It is a frail bridge across space, your letter, but a comfort in my loneliness. It tells me you are safe, and well, and coming back to me.

The wonderful experiences of last Thursday evening, when for a blissful hour you took me into another world, a world with only the two of us in it, I shall never forget and I shall never try to forget. Everything was just perfect, as I have long dreamed it would be, as I have long known it would be, if ever I found you. It was wonderful, like being on an island away from everything and everybody else. I was conscious of you, and only you. I have lived in a cocoon of happy thoughts ever since. The warmth of your embrace is ever in my mind, somehow protecting me against the unkindnesses and irritations of life, the little niggling things that happen every day. These things don't matter any more. What is important is that when you hold me close, I feel safe. I suppose I am a big baby, really. I want just to snuggle up to you and let you deal with the world outside me. I know you would handle everything competently as you do the car. I want only to hold your sweet body, and cling and cling and cling, while you look after me and kiss me often.

Great Gable was duly climbed last Saturday by an all-British expedition consisting of Mr Firth and myself, our combined ages being 107. I was not an attentive companion, I'm afraid, my thoughts being very much elsewhere, and in fact once, in the car, I found myself gently stroking his knee. However we got to the top all right, and down again. A thick mist hid everything. On the summit I found a place to sit facing Ireland (which Mr F must have thought a bit mad because it was exposed to a drizzling rain and there were better shelters nearby), but visibility was down to 30 yards and never improved. But it was a good day. I was happy, and back in form. Mr F greatly enjoyed it – mist on the mountains was a new experience for him – and asked to go with me again and do the same walk in clear weather. OK, I said. And could he bring his son? OK, I said. Oh how I wished he had said could he bring Betty McNally. OK, I would have said, quite casually, but my heart would have been racing. We have fixed November 6th for a repeat. I have another and much more important engagement on the 30th.

Ten hours on my book on Sunday was enough to finish it, except for revision. I was alone with Cindy all day. I must thank you for understanding so well last Thursday. Telling you my story was the oddest thing! I had been dreading bringing back the old memories, yet you made it so easy for me. You sat quietly listening, so quietly that I felt I was talking to myself. It was a strange feeling, to be talking of things I had always tried to hide, and it could not possibly have happened with anyone else. You gave me your legs to caress, and it was lovely to do this: they were a link between us in the darkness. Today's letter tells me you did understand. Bless you, for this and for everything.

I have found a delightful place in Keswick for coffee on the 30th, and next Saturday I shall make a tour of all the ladies lavatories so that I can be the perfect guide. Nothing must be left to chance on the 30th. I want this to be happiest day of my life. I want to feel you are mine, and only mine. For twelve blessed hours, in surroundings I have come to love. All this, and heaven, too!

Tuesday

I have saved the postscript until I can feel you are really on your way back to me. Such a lovely day for your flight, and such a lovely feeling for me!

Red

LETTER 100: TO BETTY, 25 OCTOBER 1965

Thursday

Better dear,

Before last night I had reason enough to be grateful to you – for being so delightfully friendly, for taking an interest in me, for seeming to understand.

After last night's overwhelming kindnesses I cannot even begin to speak my thanks. The car ride was lovely (I wasn't a bit frightened by your driving); and the coffee (with nothing forgotten) was an inspiration. But these were kindnesses others might have shown me. No, it is of the very special kindnesses that I write, the kindnesses that only you could have shown me. The interlinking of fingers when I tried to start to tell you my story and couldn't go on; the sympathy that seemed well enough expressed by a clasping of hands; and, later, your utter sweetness, your caresses, the touch of your lips, the whispered words of close embrace. There was mystery and magic enough in the night itself, although this would have passed with the morning, but what happened between us cast over me a spell that will be with me forever. Betty dear, I want last night to happen again and again. I wish all nights could be like that.

Monday

Today I came down to work with an eagerness not usually associated with Mondays. There was your letter, shy and forlorn amongst fifty others paying bills, wanting Council houses, and so on. I fondled the envelope and put it to one side to be read quietly when my tea was brought in. Alas for another resolve! By ten past nine I had read it over and over again. All day I have been taking peeps at it. Betty dear, what can I say in reply? Every word if it is charming. I am half-swooning at my desk for love of you. I am afraid the ratepayers are not getting value for money out of me these days at all, at all. How I wish these last few months of service were fled! I am in chains here. This is no place to be, with you in my thoughts all the time . . . I can only answer your letter with my arms around you.

My new Monday-morning habit is to scatter all the mail that is brought to me in an impatient search for your now-familiar writing, and read first of all what you have to say. The rest is unimportant, and can wait. For a few moments I can feel you are with me again, and am suffused in a warm glow. I am all tenderness for you.

Thank you for telling me about your weekend. I had been wondering. I am always wondering. How crowded your life is, really! You have the house to look after, a two-acre garden, the children, the car, your friends, you have lectures, meetings, concerts to attend. Is there really room in it for me, too? Am I intruding in the pattern of life you have chosen for yourself? A fear is creeping into my mind, and I want you to kiss it away!

Tonight I have meetings to attend, but my thoughts are all of tomorrow. Another day of waiting and then we shall be together gain, really together, in the quiet of the evening. I think of the other nights there have been, of the moments of tenderness, of kisses in the dark, of your heart lying against mine. There is still so much to be said, so much to learn about you – but first twelve days of waiting must be rewarded, twelve days of stored-up affection must be expressed, twelve days of hunger must be satisfied. I want to hold you close. It is five weeks since you called to see me – five weeks today, at just about this hour. It is five weeks today since I fell in love with you. Five wonderful, amazing weeks. I try to think what life was like before. I thought it was a full life, and I was content with it. Only now am I beginning to realise how much better it could have been.

Trying to write to you in the office is very difficult. Every few minutes something happens to bring me back to earth with a bump. Visitors, telephone calls, letters to sign, staff enquiries, meetings to prepare for. My time is divided between my desk and White Moss Common; my thoughts flit from one to the other bewilderingly. But now I am going to steal across to the Fleece with your letter, and read it yet again, and then try to read what is written between the lines. It was delightful to see you at midday: you disturb me but re-assure me at the same time.

Until tomorrow, love. I cannot wait, but wait I must. I leave the agenda to you, but first you must be held close. I must go now. When you get this letter tomorrow will have become today. Our meeting will be only a matter of hours, our kiss only a few hundred heartbeats away.

Red

The big meeting took place in Keswick, a favourite spot for their secret meetings as there was less chance of people from Kendal spotting the Borough Treasurer doing any sort of canoodling. Betty arrived in her car. AW came on the bus, as usual.

LETTER 101: TO BETTY, 1 NOVEMBER 1965

Sunday evening
Betty my love,

Yesterday was the most wonderful day ever, and although 24 hours have gone by since we kissed goodnight I am still utterly under the spell. There never was another day like it, from the moment you appeared – or even earlier, when there was the excitement of knowing you would come for me. In terms of geography, our journey covered ground I have covered many times before, but never like this, never like yesterday. How much I prefer your company to my own! How much I admire your competence in every situation, when my own thoughts are floundering in dreams, and your many accomplishments! How I like to hear your sweet voice talking to me – about anything! What delight and comfort there is for me in your lovely little body! Betty dear, thank you a thousand times for making yesterday possible and giving me a memory I shall never forget.

It was all too wonderful to be happening to me, and if I seemed a little quiet and sad on the way home it was only because a perfect day was coming to an end. But you have promised me other days, and much more even than that, you have promised yourself to me, that you will come to me for always if even I can ask you. Oh Betty, if only that could happen! Oh my darling that would be the greatest kindness of all . . . So today I am not less happy although you are not with me. My dream of a future together may be proved idle, but it is so very pleasant to think about!

I can hardly believe the good fortune that brought our widely-different paths side by side. I am still completely bewildered by the happenings of the past few weeks. If I try to think rationally, nothing makes sense. Why should you have taken this interest in me, of all people? Why should the sweetest, liveliest creature I have even seen prefer to eat fish and chips with me out of a newspaper sat in a car in a scruffy side street, than to attend a social banquet as a special guest with the nobility? This is the sort of thing that happens on the pictures, but I am no film star. Why should it happen to me? Why me?

And the incidents in the car, the trembling ecstasies of nearness, the gentleness of your touch, the softness of your lips. Why, of all men, should I be the one so privileged? Not even the gods fared better. But these are questions only you can answer.

Today has been happy, too. I have been studying my maps for a visit to Wuthering Heights, and, from what I remember of the story, our walk across the moor should be done on a wild and stormy winter's day – soon, please? But most of the day I have been doing a drawing for you, because I want you to have something of me in your home that others may see, something that has not be secretly locked away. I like drawing better than writing because the mind can wander, and today it has wandered over every incident of yesterday, and returned to each one time and again – and nothing happened that was not altogether delightful. We talked over coffee, and there was positively not another person in the whole world except yourself – yet when it was time to go I found the room crowded, even our table being shared. I liked shopping with you. I liked the rain. I liked the little walk we had, the plans we made, in our secret valley. I liked you changing your clothes in the back of the car, because this gave me confidence to feel someone rather special. I was glad you were with me to help me out with the conversation at Badger Hill. <u>Everything</u> was just right yesterday. Even the unkind weather didn't matter one little bit, as you said earlier it wouldn't. My plan for giving you a scrumptious meal that would have made your little tummy as tight as a drum went awry, but that didn't matter either, and I wouldn't have missed the interlude outside Ambleside Police Station for worlds. Oh, Betty!! Please let's go on, and on, and on. I love you so very much, and I need you more with every passing day

Red

Monday:
I dared not expect a letter from you today, but there was one for me as usual, and as kind and charming as usual, telling me what I love to hear you whisper, thrilling me, making me want to hold you close for ever. Yes, dear, there will be other days, other meetings, other kisses. There must be. Yes, dear, we will go again to Badger Hill, and write our novel, and snuggle up close in bed. Somehow, we must. And yes, dear, I will come to Fowl Ing. I must. I am riding on the crest of good fortune, and I have a most wonderful feeling that heaven is opening its gates for me, or that you have opened them for me. I stand on the threshold, eagerly – yet a little fearfully because I know I cannot enter, and will never enter, unless you are by my side and holding my hand.

You must never leave me, Betty

Red

AW had taken to wandering past Betty's house, Fowl Ing, even when he knew she would not be at home, or hoping to spot her car in the street. Apart from sweet nothings, they had also been discussing animals, which they both loved, and charity work. He had told her about his RSPCA plan (see Letter 82) which Betty encouraged him to do.

LETTER 102: TO BETTY, NOVEMBER 1965?

Thursday p.m
Dear Betty,
Thank you for your lovely letter. There are times, dear, when my thoughts of you are so intense that there are simply no words to express them. This latest message from you, so kind, so loving, has touched me deeply.
I looked for you today, as I do every day – even when I know you are out of town.
Every day is a month when I do not see you.
I have now committed myself to the R.S.P.C.A idea, and had an encouraging talk with the local Inspector. I didn't lose any time after you had said 'go ahead' because I want this gift always to be associated in my mind with you.
Please try to see me tomorrow. I have been carrying a present for you around the streets all week, hoping to come across KJM 307, and although it is an insignificant present it is a <u>very heavy</u> one. My arms are aching (for you) enough already, without this added burden! Have pity on me!
I love you.

Red

LETTER 103: TO BETTY, 8 NOVEMBER 1965

Sunday evening
Betty dear,
It was charming of you to call to see me on Friday afternoon, to share my tea, to talk to me, to give me yet another glimpse of the heaven it would be to live with you. For me, this was a quite delightful interlude, delightful as all the others have been, but stolen as they must all be. The

time always comes for you to go, and leave me; or for me to go, and leave you. I wish we could be together forever, Betty, never one leaving the other. Farewell kisses and caresses are nice, but, since they prelude a further separation, there is sadness about them. For us there should be not farewells, but only gradual coming closer.

Friday night's meeting was soon over, and I found myself wandering afterwards along Appleby Road, but this was a mistake. I knew you were not a home, but in other company, and quite suddenly I felt miserable and lonely. I wanted you all for myself – I who have no right to you at all! Melancholy set in and I went home, where, at least, I have a right to be.

Yesterday, Saturday, in spite of a cold east wind, was a glorious day although I wasn't feeling quite attuned to it. My chill was worse, for one thing, and, for another, I fear I am growing resentful of anybody being with me if it isn't you. You have sadly spoiled me for anyone else's company! However, I went up Great Gable with Mr Firth and his son Michael and eight hankies, and was in good form (which means I was nearly able to keep up with my companions). On the top, Mr F. produced coffee and mint cake and apples, and this time I sat with my back to Ireland, which is now out of favour with me because I know that Dublin is going to take you away from me. Jim kept coming into my mind all day, and he was out of favour, too, because I don't like Jim intruding in my thoughts when I am thinking of you. Put Jim on the next agenda, please – high on the list. Mr F. was out of favour also, rather unfairly, simply because he wasn't you, and even little Michael was out of favour because he wasn't our red-haired and brown-eyed child, yours and mine. It was a good day, but I wished you had been there instead of the others. You would have enjoyed the walk immensely. The sky was cloudless and the visibility perfect. I was home by seven; the car swept past Dunmail Raise and White Moss as thought they were places of no importance. I like your VW much better: it is a friend, it has sympathy and sentiment, and deserves some frilly little curtains for Christmas.

Today, Sunday, I have finished my book and wondered all day what you were doing. Only a short mile separates us, but when you are not at my side you are a world away. Sunday has become the loneliest day of the week, for it is a day with no contact, when I know there will be no word from you, no sight of you. Sunday has become a day when memories of other days must sustain me. There are many memories now, all of them pleasant to recall, and I like to think back to the 20th September, when you called at the office after I had given up hope that you would, and I fell in love with you; and all that has happened to us since. I try not to think how it will end

Monday
After seeing you this morning, after stroking your sweet little face (you ought to stop me touching you in public) just to make sure you were real, after reading your wonderful letter (surely poetry cannot better your prose?), after thrilling at your hopes for our future, I cannot but feel remorse at the sulky, peevish undertones of the there pages I wrote last night. I feel like tearing them up, but will send them anyway, because I <u>have</u> been despondent this weekend, and jealous, and nasty with the Firths, and I think you should know that your letter has lifted me up and sent me soaring again. Perhaps it was just my cold that got me down a bit, but this is nothing that the soft breasts of my beloved will not cure. Thank you, and bless you, for being the sweetest person I have ever known. You will know tomorrow night how much you mean to me.

RED

LETTER 104: TO BETTY: 22 NOV 1965

. . . nothing was important but you. You were with me, when you could have been with any of your friends. You preferred my company to that of anyone else, and I still don't think you can possibly realise what an honour I count that, and how grateful I am, and how fervently I wish I could, somehow, repay you for all your kindness. I can only hold you close, and trust you to understand what I cannot say.

After such a day there was little question of sleep. I was restless for you, and though a lot about your academic and highly-technical dissertation in the car from Colne to Gisburn. What a lot you know! I learned much I never knew before, and must have taken it all in.

Today I have been drawing, and imagining you endlessly and uncontrollably eating nuts. I have nothing further to report from home. Mrs W. was out when I got home last night (we could have loved each other longer) and today has gone to see Peter's young lady at Staveley.

Take good care of yourself, Betty love, and never never forget that you are the sweetest person in the whole world to

Red

At last, in a café in Keswick, AW was allowed to meet Betty's daughters.

LETTER 105: TO BETTY, 25 NOVEMBER 1965

. . . I loved them on sight, and wanted to put my arms around all three of you and squash you into a struggling limp and hug you all tight. Some day I will do just that. I was home by 7.30, and there was a welcome only from Cindy.

This morning I had to attend the civic Remembrance Service (I remembered it only just in time!) and the rest of the day I have spent sorting out photographs and maps, thinking about you and yesterday and next Tuesday and Saturday, and wanting to love you. I intended to watch Moira Shearer on TV tonight, and pretend she was you but wasn't allowed to. Instead, I am writing this letter.

I am terribly sorry about your own difficult domestic position this weekend. I think I do understand your disappointments and problems.

LETTER 106: TO BETTY, 29 NOVEMBER 1965

Monday afternoon
Betty, my dearest one,
Yesterday, for a Sunday, was more tolerable than usual. Last Friday night was not so far distant that I had lost comfort from it: I could still feel your touch and your kisses still warmed my heart. It was so nice to come to you again, and find you waiting, so delightful to walk together into the darkness, away from the bright lights and away from people. Just to be with you would be enough, just to hear your voice and see you smile would be more than reward for the devotion I have for you. But you give me much more, and willingly, and then I know, in the blissful moments of embrace, that I must hold you forever, that there is not, never has been, and never can be anyone else. You are so wonderfully kind to me, I who deserve nothing of the happiness you bring me.

And yesterday was more tolerable, too, because I was designing my own Christmas card to you – a little thing, and a poor thing, but I was pleased to feel I was doing it for you. It brought you nearer.

On Saturday I went to Keswick, chasing a 1000 to 1 chance that you would appear to have tea with me. I ought to know by this time that 1000 to 1 chances don't happen, but it was a hope I clung to till 4.30. Such a state am I reduced to that, for a meeting with you, even for no more than a glimpse of you, I would do anything, go anywhere. I might not have gone, otherwise, so bad was the weather early on, but it improved magically and transformed the scene. At Low Wood, across a deep-blue Windermere, the mountains looked as though carved in white marble: a picture beautiful beyond belief, and I wanted you there with me to see it. The road was clear, but two miles out of Keswick the bus broke down (the driver said he'd 'lost his air', whatever that may mean), so I got out and walked the rest of the way. I had lunch at The George, where our sacred corner was being profaned by a bunch of noisy youths, visited Friars Crag, which was quite deserted, and then walked around the suburbs of Keswick three times, killing time until 4.30 (no climbing, she said – as if I would take any risk that might keep us apart!) at 4.30 I entered the Keswick Restaurant to find it completely empty of customers, as it remained for the hour I was there. I listened for the door to open, but it never did. I listened for the patter of tiny feet, but they never came. The place was warm and cosy, the soft music nostalgic love songs. I pretended you were there with me, and I told you how I thought it should happen to us, that act of love you have made me want so much. Oh Betty, shall we ever know each other completely? You agreed with me, so sweetly; and then I went out in the dark and the cold and felt suddenly desperately alone. What have you done to me, dear girl, that I can now find restfulness and comfort only in you?

I have read you letter this morning over and over again. You have no idea how lonely and out of it your account of a happy weekend at Fowl Ing makes me feel, how much I would like to be there, sitting quietly in a corner of the kitchen, watching you all the time and perhaps being allowed to touch you now and then. For this, for the right to sit by your fire in my slippers, for the right to go upstairs with you, I would give everything I have. Ambition has narrowed to this – to be with you, to have you for myself, to be yours, to show you how much I love you. I am so very sure, now, that with you there would be perfect happiness for me: I get a glimpse of it every time I see you in the street, a real awareness every time I hold you close.

The weather is dreadful today. When you emerge from your snug nest tomorrow night mind you don't get blown away over Benson Knott!

Oh, my love, I can't wait . . .

Red

When AW started on the Pennine Way, he began to use Betty – and other friends – to give him a lift in their car. He also got Betty to take him to Blackburn, in her little VW Beetle.

LETTER 107: TO BETTY, 6 DECEMBER 1965

In the car, I am so well content to listen to your sweet voice telling me things I never knew before, and later, after dark, to experience again the very special pleasures that only you can give me. I enjoyed every single moment, even the wild ride across the Lupton ice-cap, where driver and car came through a severe test with flying colours. Being an innocent in things mechanical, I probably didn't fully realise how capably you handled the situation, but then, I knew you would. I had no fears, no doubts. I never had a guardian angel before, but I have now. You never fail me.

Thank you, dear, for taking me to Blackburn. It is a town of little attraction, and it was kind of you to suggest it. It was interesting to me to see once-familiar places again, but the old feeling has almost gone. I am a stranger there now, and I see with the eyes of a stranger. I could never go back to stay. The past is dead and done with. Home for me now is the five-foot-nothing of Betty Hayes. Life for me now lies in her warm bosom and sheltering arms. This is my new home, and the best. I hope I shall never be turned out, and I shall never stray. When I am there, warm and cosy, I want nothing else. What else is there to want? Comfort, happiness, love, are, for me, all to be found in your sweet body. This the foot of my personal rainbow. My search has ended in your arms.

I liked Whalley. I liked the quiet of the abbey ruins, and I liked kissing you there. Someday, in summer, we will go back and climb Pendle hand-in-hand.

LETTER 108: TO BETTY, 13 DECEMBER 1965

Sunday evening
Better dear,

The hours pass quickly when I am with you, but how slowly when I am without you! Today has dragged, I have been alone most of the time. I have drawn. I have looked for you on television, in vain. I have checked the proofs for Book Seven. It has rained all day. No bright little face appeared over the garden wall to cheer me up. But I have had our meeting last evening to think of, and I cannot be other than happy when I think of you. So many meetings now, so many places with special memories! I have always been happy with you, from the first moment. I found comfort in your company not after long acquaintance, but from the very instant of our first coming together. I did not then, and have not since, felt any shyness, any awkwardness, and strangeness, with you.

I have hidden nothing, nor wanted to. I have no secrets from you, nor wanted to have. It could not be like this with anyone else. You are the one, the only one. Falling in love with you has been the most natural thing in the world: it was bound to happen to me if ever we met. I waited a long time for you to come along, too long. I lived almost a lifetime, missing you and wanting you. I knew you must be around somewhere because you were more real to me than the people I met every day. But the years went by. You never came, and I never found you, until a few weeks ago. And at once everything changed. I had been lonely and now I was lonely no more. I had kept other people at arm's length, you I wanted against my breast. Nobody else understood, but you did. You knew exactly, and you knew at once. You passed into me, and became part of my being, and from that moment the world became a happier place and living a happier experience. You will never leave me. You cannot. If I were never to see you again you would still be with me. You are everywhere. All the time I can feel the touch of your lips, so softly caressing, and hear your whispered endearments. You have brought a magic to existence and made living worth-while and thrilling and exciting, you have transformed everything. You have made me love you, utterly. You have made me very very happy, and I shall always bless you and be grateful. I hope the day will come, and come soon, when I can show you how much you mean to me. That day will be the happiest of all.

Red

By Christmas time, it had been three months since their relationship started – and the romance was growing stronger than ever, even though Betty was caught up in her family Christmas while AW was still mooching around on the bus, walking his old haunts, or going past Betty's house, gazing at the lights.

LETTER 109: TO BETTY, DECEMBER 1965

Sunday evening
Dear Betty,
   On the face of it, yesterday was a day like so many others have been. I caught the 8.30 bus to Keswick, as I invariably do. The weather was poor, not fit for the tops: a grey day with some rain: so many have been like that. At Keswick I had coffee, following long custom. Then I went to Cockermouth on the bus, a journey I have often travelled, and at Cockermouth I had a look in Smith's, as usual, and killed time with

a short walk, finishing at Ouse Bridge to catch the return bus. And at Keswick I had the meal I have had, without variation, for five years past. It was a day spent as I have spent so many others, and, in the things I did, a very ordinary day. Yet there was something about it that made it not an ordinary day at all, but one quite different and special.

There was no letter for me yesterday, and I worried about it. Perhaps you had been called away to Manchester. Perhaps another door had fallen on you and broken your right arm – no, both, because you are a clever girl and can write with your left. Perhaps you had told me you wouldn't write and I couldn't remember. Or, perhaps more likely, the Christmas post had delayed it. I felt anxious.

This morning your bedroom light shone brightly through the slight mist and cheered me up wonderfully, and when I arrived at the office your letter awaited me. I kissed it. Now I could send mine. I feel grand again and very much in love.

R

Part 11
Letters to Betty, 1966

The new year, 1966, started off well for AW. It began with his final Pictorial Guide at the printer, and he was finishing off writing Fellwanderer, researching Pennine Way, and there was Betty McNally, the light of his life, stealing time with her, arranging secret trysts, experiencing the sort of joy he had never known in his life. He was growing a bit more daring, 'accidentally' meeting her in the street, even contemplating inviting her to local functions which he had to attend. Life was so exciting that he had even forgotten that his fifty-ninth birthday was coming up on 17 January.

LETTER 110: TO BETTY, 10 JANUARY 1966

Monday

Thank you for your letter, Betty love. It wasn't really expected, because we hadn't said we would write, and its warm reassurances were not really necessary, because I am now utterly convinced that our love for each other is deeper by far than any word could tell, but it was very welcome, as any sign or sight of you must always be.

Oh Betty, Saturday night! Yes, I was happified too. I wanted desperately for you to appear so that I could say I was sorry for Friday, and you did and we had tea and we loved each other in the darkness. Another wonderful day.

Yesterday I spent re-writing FELLWANDERER ready for typing. I'm still not sure about this and think it safer to get a few opinions before it goes to the printer. Yours first, please.

Mr Firth has just been in with the last rough proofs for Book Seven, and I am enclosing the 'personal notes in conclusion' for you to read.

Betty dear, it's bitterly cold again.

Do <u>please</u> go <u>now</u> and buy an electric blanket (the best; <u>not a cheap</u>

one) as a gift from you to you. Promise the girls one each if they do well in their exams.

The chastity belt can wait a while.

Look! It's working. . . .

BETTY DEAR
I LOVE YOU
RED

LETTER III: TO BETTY, 17 JANUARY 1966

Dear Betty,

Until I saw you in the street this morning, I hadn't realised it was my birthday. It was sweet of you to appear so unexpectedly, and to wish me many more, and to offer me flowers for my desk. I could have kicked myself afterwards for not taking your flowers after you had taken the trouble to bring them, but they would have been too great an embarrassment. It was a lovely thought, and I spoiled it for you. I'm sorry, Betty, really I am. In fact, I didn't behave at all well this morning. I was unkind. I had much on my mind. A cloud has settled on me and I can't get rid of it.

Your card, and J and A's [Betty's daughters], are the only ones I have received, but Miss Thompson (typist) brought me 20 cigarettes and a box of matches, and Mr Duff bought me a blackcurrant tart which was a beastly thing to eat and squirted all over the desk and my clothes and dripped on the carpet. I went to Blackburn on Saturday morning (never did your bedroom light shine more brightly!), spent the afternoon with Doris [Snape], and came back very disturbed. Things are not all right with the business, and I may have to go over again. I told her about you, up to a point, and this was a bad mistake.

Yesterday I sorted out many old photographs, and have put some at one side to show you next Saturday. I tried to sort myself out a bit, too. It was a poor day. I was still disturbed about my visit to Blackburn.

Miss Thompson typed FELLWANDERER for me over the weekend, and I will let you have a copy next Saturday and would value your opinion as to its impact on lady readers. There is a letter today from Molly Lefebure, agreeing to read and criticise it from the point of view of a professional writer. Donald James, Librarian, has agreed to look through it for obscenities. And the fourth opinion, I think will have to be Mr Firth's, representing the man in the street. I ought really to ask Mr Griffin, but he talks far too much.

Thank you for your charming letter is morning. It did me good to read of your simple faith in me, after a weekend of doubts in myself. I am so glad about the blanket: it must take my place for the time being. Already I am jealous of it!

I have had two 'backwords' for the Old Folks Treat and cannot make up my mind about inviting Margaret and yourself. I seem to have got myself into a mood when I cannot make up my mind about anything. I think I had better not. It isn't really convenient for you, anyway, and may not be at all for Margaret. I have others I can ask.

Thank you, too, for the supplementary birthday presents. I will bring these on Saturday so that you can tell me how they work. You've no idea how my heart sinks when I see the word DIRECTIONS.

I am missing you terribly, Betty. It isn't so much that I want my arms around you; I <u>need</u> <u>your</u> arms around <u>me</u>. Today I feel just a bit that circumstances are getting me down, but I'll be alright by Saturday. If I'm not, Upper Long Churn Cave will cure me, for you can't take worries into caves, and if Upper Long Churn Cave doesn't, you must. Perhaps all I need is happifying, and only you can do that for me. It's been a long long time to have to wait, Betty. Maybe I love you a little too much. I can no longer manage without you.

Your equipment for Saturday should include a hatpin!

With all my love,

X: today
X: tomorrow
X: Wednesday
X: Thursday
X: Friday

Red

Oh golly, I can't wait!

LETTER 112: TO BETTY, FEBRUARY 1966

Monday afternoon

Betty, my own and only-ever sweetheart,

I know how you feel, love, because I feel just the same way. I too am obsessed. I too am hungry for an experience. I too want the companionship of my beloved <u>all</u> the time. I too find Sunday a day of no hope.

I know when it dawns that it will be a blank. Every other day has its prospect of a meeting, by chance or planned, but never Sunday. I gaze up the valley and think of the last time and the next time: the last time with tenderness and the next time with eagerness. I am empty, and aching, and wanting you; but happy. As long as I know there will be a next time I shall always be happy.

Cindy is in worse case. She is staying in for a week or two and being courted zealously by a white poodle from Underley called Pepi, who appears every morning soon after daylight with his tail wagging and waits patiently through out the day on the doorstep, going home at dusk with his tail drooping. His is, however, a great optimist and most faithful in his daily attendance, and Cindy is tremendously excited.

I love you as you love me, Betty dear, and cannot tell you how much, but I long for the time to come when I can show you, and then you will know.

Saturday was wonderful, every moment of it. I loved the delightful intimacy (non-technical) of the bus journey, with all the other passengers intent on going about their business and paying no attention at all to their two fellow-travellers intent only on each other. I think Mr James [Donald James, Kendal Borough librarian] would permit the word 'cocoon' (of happiness) in this instance, although of course he wouldn't understand and would completely disapproved of our secret caresses – on a public transport vehicle, too! The very idea! But you are so sweet: I must keep touching you and cannot help myself. The iron discipline is melting away.

LETTER 113: TO BETTY, 14 MARCH 1966

Betty dear, I am terribly and wretchedly sorry for behaving so badly. The very last thing I ever wanted to do was to cause you any distress at all. You must believe that.

But things have gone tragically wrong. I ought to be right on top of the world, but find myself suddenly in the bitterest depths. I am in bad trouble, and must find a way out of it myself. Nobody can help me in a positive way (although I wish someone would show me how to fry an egg!) and, in the circumstances, you least of all. Thank you for your kind letter, but please do not try. You can help only by being there when it is all over.

I am grateful for six months of the most wonderful happiness. I was not entitled to this, and now, for a time, I must pay for it.

I am too confused in my mind to explain anything yet and sorely troubled by a conscience I had forgotten I had. I feel like a man who has been betrayed, but in fact know I have been caught in my own betrayal.

There have been dark passages in my life before, but I have always emerged in the sunshine. This will happen again. In the meantime you will not hear from me; but, Betty please, you must trust me to do what I think is right.

Red

What had suddenly gone wrong? From his reference to trying to fry eggs, it looks as if he is on his own – so presumably Ruth, his wife, has left him. It would seem as if she has found one of his love letters from Betty, or some kind neighbour has reported spotting them together somewhere.

He decides to bash on with his Pennine Way research and agrees to the offer of a lift to Buxton from another female friend, Mary Burkett, who became Director of the Abbot Hall Gallery in Kendal in 1966, and thus had quite a bit of official business with the Borough Treasurer. He is not in any way romantically attracted to her, but it shows that he had can and does have female friends, all perfectly respectably. So much for any gossips.

LETTER 114: TO BETTY, 18 APRIL 1966

The Palace Hotel, Buxton, Derbyshire

Thursday night
Dear Betty,

I am in room 72 in this very palatial establishment – and guess who's next door in Room 73? Yes, you're right. Destiny has played another of her tricks. It's Miss B. I can, and will, explain everything when I see you.

The drive down was OK – no touching, positively! – but we ran into bad weather, mist and rain, before arriving here at 9 o'clock. Prospects aren't too hopeful for tomorrow.

Wish you were here

After several weeks of not meeting, communications start again with Betty, and arrangements to meet her. AW is still on his own but his son Peter has returned on leave from Bahrein.

LETTER 115: TO BETTY, 21 JUNE 1966

Wednesday evening

Betty dear,

Thank you for your nice long letter, love. It was sweet. Even the written lines were decidedly friendly; what lay between them, unsaid, I hope I interpreted correctly.

I have read it over and over again. With the family united once more, these will be happy days for you, shortened though they are, unfortunately at present, by your hospital duties. Three brilliant women under one roof, each scintillating in her own sphere! A home of erudition and scholastic attainment, of academic study and learned conversation. (or do you throw things at each other?). to think I so nearly became a paying guest! What field of knowledge I have denied myself! What intellectual discourses I have missed! What a barren desert is my life now, and how it might have flourished under the tuition and example of three lovely goddesses of wisdom! (or do you bicker?). Betty love, you have much to be thankful for and much to be pleased about. You have more than repaired the damaged past. You have built something finer out of the ruins. I wish I could have helped and been more, much more, than a late witness.

Of course I will be in a seventh heaven of delight to see you on Friday. I have often vowed to myself that I would go to the ends of the earth to see you and it seems odd that I should now suggest that Orton is too far. In the short time available to you, I mean. Tell you what, love: I will be at Fox's Pulpit, if I can find it, from 2.45 to 3.45, reaching it by road from the Sedbergh bus at Black Horse; the easiest way for you would be by Appleby Road, Docker Garths, Lambrigg road-end and Firbank (narrow but surfaced road). There is a bus back at 4.15, so you could be home in good time, by 4.30. But if you find it is inconvenient after all, or if Jane wants you with her, please don't try to come. It would be O.K with me. I want to visit Fox's Pulpit, anyway.

Peter was over to see me on Saturday, and has been here again yesterday, all day, and today, morning. He intends to come tomorrow and Friday, so I have had to tell him I shall be away both days. He has brought a tape-recorder and is building up a library from my records, which will make his visits frequent. His appearances are not likely to follow any pattern, and there is no prospect of a love-in yet. He has hired a car (110 pounds for 10 weeks). On the 25th of this month a friend is coming up to join him, a youngish man I have met and like, and I have suggested that he can stay here with me: I have found some more blankets. The ulterior motive, not yet disclosed, is that he can pay for his keep by Hoovering the house.

AW then thinks of a really clever cover. An American fan called Ade Meyer, a wealthy widower, who has been reading the Pictorial Guides from the beginning, is coming on a visit staying in Grasmere, and wants to have a walk with AW. How perfect it will be if Betty comes along as well, a harmless threesome of middle-aged persons, walking the fells . . .

LETTER 116: TO BETTY, 23 JUNE 1966

Dear Betty,

Your letter today did me a world of good, and I must write and thank you for it. I feel much better in my mind after reading it, and re-assured. I need to see you and I need your advice, and there is little time to lose. I am troubled, but not so troubled that I cannot see a way opening ahead to a fuller and better experience of life.

Saturday is definite; it must be. Mr F. is back at work and has promised to help with his car. Ade is still keen, and will pick me up at 9.15. Please be ready at 9.25. You will need your boots.

See you then, love

Red

The walk with Ade and Betty goes well, and they do it again, as Ade seems to get on so well with Betty. AW hopes they will all be friends. In fact he encourages Betty to have a walk just with Ade. Meanwhile he is taking the first stages in getting a divorce from Ruth.

LETTER 117: TO BETTY, 27 JUNE 1966

Monday

Betty dear,

The days I spend with you are the happiest I have ever known. They are, to me, like days on parole from prison; days in the sunshine after long confinement in the darkness. Saturday was such a day, a wonderfully happy and (in spite of everything) carefree twelve hours. The unpleasant things didn't seem to matter while you were with me, and I could forget them. You are a constant delight to me. Perhaps it was as well that Ade was with us. If we had started loving each other at Cauldron Snout, or in the Moss Shop Shelter, or in the black sinister gorge (all likely places) – ! we were late enough as it was.

I shall always associate you with Upper Teesdale, and for me there is sadness in the thought that our work there is ended: but I hope we shall go again, the two of us, and walk again amongst the flowers. Promise!

I want you to go out with Ade, as much and as often as you like. He is hard work at times, I know (he reminds me of an old St Bernard dog), but really a delightful man and I greatly admire his determination and independence. Quite obviously and understandably he is fond of you. He is a stranger in a strange land and has need of friends. Yes, please go with him, and make him happy – up to a point (there must be no sprigs of heather sticking in your jumper when you come back to me!). Show him your home, your daughters, Krishna [Betty's cat]. . . . Besides, I have the idea of suggesting a pact – that the three of us do the John Muir Trail together in 1968, and I'm serious about it. For you and me this could be a heavenly holiday. But it depends on how well you and Ade get along during the next few weeks. It depends on nothing else. The barriers are falling.

Mr F. has been in. He was greatly impressed by High Force. Mr F. wants to come with us again, definitely. Super, being with three men, you said.

I cannot solve the mystery of the letter of last November, which is now deepened because I was quoted as mentioning Jim by his full name (i.e. surname). The man who came to see me said that the solicitor had the original, and this appears now to have been a trick. The whole business mystifies me. Your suspicions must be right. Somewhere I have been careless. Perhaps it was because this particular piece of evidence was so tenuous that, having mentioned it, it was not brought up in discussion again. However, thank goodness you are not involved. You are much too precious. I would never do anything to cause you distress.

Thank you for your letter. I have today spoken to the Lancaster solicitor on the telephone. He sounds very nice. He will start the ball rolling by asking JrB to submit a draft agreement, incorporating their client's wishes, and then I will have to go to see him.

I had better not see you again until 9.30 July 9th, love, desperately though I want to. If I do not write again before then assume that everything is going smoothly, and please, please, do not worry. My own initial anxiety is turning into profound relief.

Go out with Ade, and be in high spirits. Remember (if you like the idea) that you are working for an adventure in the High Sierras for us.

How proud Ade would be to play host to us in his own territory! I enclose the map of California. Take this with you and let him show you where he lives.

Oh Betty love, just think ahead a year. . . .

Red

LETTER 118: TO BETTY, 14 JULY 1966

Kendal, Thursday

Dear Mrs McNally,

I said I wouldn't write, but you must have known I would have to. I think I did, too. The days are so long and empty, the nights so lonely and troubled. I am only half a man when you are away from me, and half a miserable wretch prey to all sort of fears and apprehensions. You cannot know what a comfort to me you have become, but it is no longer a comfort that satisfies me across a distance: you must be near. Your letters help, and I must thank you for finding the time to write. I didn't fully realise that Ade had become a problem to the extent that you are now really disturbed about him. I am sure he will want to talk about you next Saturday, and I will make it an opportunity to give him advice such as befits my seniority in age and my longer friendship with you, but of course I must do this without letting him suspect that you have already confided in me. I'm sorry things are going awry. Leave it to me to straighten them out. You won't need to do or say anything. Was the parting caress in the car last Saturday staged for his benefit, or mine? On Thursday, feeling rather miserable, I thought I may as well go down to Lancaster and make myself completely so, which I did. I will tell you about this visit, on the 23rd. I found your name (twice) in the Gazette report, and felt very proud!

I now have the photographs of you and Ade on the High Cup journey last Saturday and a fortnight earlier. These are good, but there is unmistakable devotion in his eyes as he looks at you in two of these pictures and an obvious urgency in the need for me to talk to him. He must be stopped before he too begins to wonder what it would be like; it would be cruel to let his thoughts carry that far. Two other pictures are very good indeed – how bonny you are! – and from these I am having enlargements made for both of you. I will let Ade see them all next Saturday and then send them to you on Monday with news of the day's events. On the office photograph now enclosed, Miss T is on the right of the front row, and prim and proper as always.

Next Sunday I shall devote all day to the drawing of Fowl Ing House, and have it ready for your return. The evenings this week are being spent gradually working up-river from Middleton, on paper, in a state of mind excited by memories and a lot of maudlin sentiment. You are walking ahead of me as I trace the path through the meadows and along the riverside. Sometimes you stop and wait for me. I remember, with misty eyes, every awkward stile, the place where we rested (if rest is the word). The places where you vanished into the bushes. It is a tortured pleasure to do this, with you so far away . . . Betty love, when I am gone you must go back there often and walk amongst the flowers again. If there is any sort of after-life at all, it is there, by the Tees, I will come back to you.

Put me out of my misery. Have a good time. Don't worry about anything here. Now just look out of the window and along the busy street – and think of the lonely moor around Maize Beck, and poor Ade stuck in the bog, and the little cave we found when, for a minute, we were alone and hidden from the world. And make your choice.

Come back, chick, come back!

Red

. . . 14th, 15th, 16th, 17th, 18th, 19th, 20th, 21st, 22nd, ⟨23rd⟩

AW, alas, had never told Ade that he, AW, was romantically involved with Betty, so the inevitable happened . . .

LETTER 119: TO BETTY, 18 JULY 1966

Sunday evening

Betty dear, this letter will be the most difficult I have ever written. I won't like writing it, and you won't like reading it. But, after yesterday, there are some things that must be said, and quickly. I am sorry to have to say them in a letter, when you have no chance of immediate reply, but you happen to be in Dublin and I am sat here in a lonely house, with a heart turned to tears, and cannot wait until I see you again.

It concerns Ade and yourself, of course. Nothing I say must lead you to think that I have changed my opinion about Ade in any way. He is the most generous, most considerate man I have ever known. A gentleman, as I always wanted to be – and never made it. Nor have I changed my opinion about you. You are the sweetest woman in the whole world, and always will be. Yet yesterday Ade and I came near to having a blazing row. As I expected, our Saturday walk was all 'Betty this' and 'Betty that' (except that I do wish he would say Betty and not Beddy!) and at first I was wagging my tail, mightily pleased, because there are so few people I can talk to about you and because compliments about you always make me feel so proud. But then he went on to tell me about his more personal relationships with you – the late evenings you had had together, the telephone calls, the places you had visited in his company, your calendar of future engagements – and I could feel my innards shrivelling up. He was brutally frank and open about everything, brutally so only because he did not know my feelings for you and may also have assumed that you may have mentioned these events to me anyway already. Betty, this affair has gone much further than I imagined from the very little you have told me. With pleasure he reported that after Dufton ('I don't want him to come home with me' you said) he was with you until 11.35. In the car coming back you will remember that he mentioned the 'beautiful ladies' who were joining him on the following day. Guess who they turned out to be? How stupid I was about that! Why didn't you at least tell me? It was no kindness, if that was your intention. I wouldn't have been hurt. I would have been happy for you, and pleased about it – but not when you are being deliberately secretive. We have never had secrets from each other before. That is what hurts.

Our main discussion was on the seat provided by Mrs Lewis on the summit of High Pike. (I was going to take you there one day, remember?) Ade told me all his plans for you, more that he has yet told you, and certainly more than you have told me; and he told me of other arrangements made with your knowledge and consent. There is Place Fell and Sharrow Bay, a family party, the day after Cross Fell, Blencathra at your request. You are to have dinner with him at the George, Keswick. He intends to see you, or at least speak to you, every day during the remaining seven weeks of his stay. He is going to insist that you visit San Francisco this autumn. He has suggested you have a few days with him in London. Oh Betty love, why didn't you tell me? Why did I have to find out like this? What is going wrong between us?

I don't object to what you are doing (because I asked you to see him as often as you wanted, and make him happy), and can't (because in Ade lies your best chance of happiness). But I wish you had told me. I was shocked into silence. He didn't know, but his words were slowly killing me. I had no idea you and he had become so close.

He has wonderful plans for you, and is absolutely convinced and absolutely sincere. He told me his financial position, as though I were your guardian instead of merely a cast-off lover. I gave him my consent. A really wonderful new life is being offered to you, by a generous man who loves you. You should accept it.

I ought not to be in the picture at all, not even in the background. The solicitors are meeting on Tuesday next to consider figures that will leave me 5 pounds a week to live on (after meeting commitments such as tax, mortgage, etc) plus what I can get from my books (they may want some of that, too). And smoking costs me 2 pounds! There is clearly no future for me and certainly none for you with me.

Saturday was a bonny day, but Ade took all the sunshine out of it for me. After hearing him, how could I tell him that I loved you more than he ever could, that I had known you in dreams long before we ever met? Nor could I tell him of my own troubles. I had very little to say all the way back. There seemed nothing I could do but tell him I would pull out of the trinity, leaving the two of you to sort yourselves out. This I did when we got to Grasmere, and he was dreadfully upset (still not realising why) and in fact we spent the evening in the car park at White Moss (of blessed memory), arguing about it.

I'm sorry, love, but it seems the only thing to do. I am desperately unhappy – the past week has been wretched, with you out of reach, and the next will be worse. I am so terribly alone. Last night I had no sleep at all. I feel like a sinking ship after everybody has left it.

Ade will tell you the story. He is visiting you on Friday for a 'late night' if he is not allowed to collect you in Liverpool. I have said, only after much persuasion and only after he had threatened never to see either of us again, that I will turn up on Saturday for Cross Fell to explain to you what I feel. But really there is nothing more to be added, except thanks for all you have done for me and for giving me the happiest days of my life. Please <u>don't</u> ring me on Friday. There is nothing I can say over the telephone, and in any case Ade will be with you all day if he brings you from Liverpool.

I enclose the photographs. Ade has ordered more enlargements. He wants me next Saturday to take a picture of him kissing you, so you see how impossible things have become. He may get his kiss, that's up to you; but it will certainly not be recorded on <u>my</u> camera.

Please don't worry. I will see you on Saturday at 9.30, as so often before, but for the first time I shall not be looking forward to it. I will bring the drawing of Fowl Ing: I have been working at it since 8.30 this morning and will finish it before then. As for the Pennine Way, I don't know. The spark has gone.

This is a hateful thing to do to you, I know. But I am hopelessly in love with you, and 'hopelessly' has now become he operative word. I <u>ache</u> for you, but it would get worse, not better, if we carried on as before. I have one satisfaction, the way things have turned out – that I never kept my promise. On my dying day I will still be wondering what it would be like!

Sorry, love, sorry

Red

LETTER 120: TO BETTY, UNDATED, JULY 1966

I didn't bow out very gracefully, did i? I'm terribly sorry now. I had a rough bringing-up, and the grittiness still comes out at times.

Betty, you don't have to reply to a letter that should never have been written. If I do not hear from you at all, I will get the message, perhaps better than if you tried to tell me.

Let's end it romantically, as it started, please, love. Let my farewell present, very appropriately, be this record of the theme music from Dr Zhivago. Please play it when the house is quiet, and mark well the words, for these are the words I wanted you to hear from me. I was clumsy and cruel. So try to forgive me.

With all my heart, dear, I hope you find the happiness you never found with me.

Red

However, Betty wrote back at once, telling him not to be so silly. There was nothing between her and Ade. AW was just imagining it was more serious than it was.

LETTER 121: TO BETTY, 22 JULY 1966

Friday morning

Betty love, your reply filled me with remorse, but did me a world of good. I didn't mean to slap your face so hard. I have been so terribly lonely without you. An age has passed since Bowes Moor. All week I have been distressed, heart-broken, that our friendship should end so unhappily. It has needed Ade's intervention to teach me that I could not face a future in which you had no part. I love you, and only you, and always shall. If you had to take a whip to me you could not alter that.

I am sorry for some of the things I implied in my letter. I was always a bad loser. But last Saturday I was given the impression that you had encouraged Ade in his hopes, although you had led me to think differently. Betty, it was a nightmare experience. I was having to listen to the last things I wanted to hear, and there was no escape. He was so confident, so possessive. He had asked you to get a divorce, and then all you had to do was sign on the dotted line. It was as easy as that.

I don't blame Ade. In his position, I would have been in a seventh heaven of delight, too, and wanting to enthuse about you to others. Ade is a go-getter: it is his training, and a national characteristic. But I have since had misgivings. He is offering you wealth, security, servants, good social contacts, city amenities. Think hard, love. Isn't this where you came in, twenty years ago? Please be very sure of yourself, and please, please don't make the same mistake again. Don't be hustled into a trap. Don't be taken for granted. If you want to consider him seriously, play for time. Ade could not give you the sort of love you <u>need</u>, as I could, but the trouble with me is that I have so much love for you and so little else.

Sweetheart, I didn't want to believe that you could forget so easily the pledges we made to each other last winter. I didn't want to believe that your thoughts were now all of San Francisco and no longer of Kirkcarrion, or that our plans of a cottage by a stream were not really important. And I just couldn't believe that the unexpected final caress in the car a fortnight ago, about which I wondered, was a Judas kiss. You could never do that to me!

Perhaps I could have a few minutes alone with you tomorrow? I will not stay in your company long, having no wish to witness Ade's courtship. You could drop me off at Orton Scar, and I will have a walk along the limeston edge to Asby and Appleby, and return by bus. You and Ade will want to talk, and make arrangements for Sunday.

I shall be with you an hour or so after you receive this letter, and it will make me a lot happier to see your sweet face again. But let it be smiling, Betty, not sad, so that I can think, at least for a little longer, that I have not lost you after all, and that our love for each other is still running pretty high (mine for you is in full spate!). Tell me with your eyes what your lips may not have a chance to say.

Red.

*Over the summer, all three continued to meet and go for walks – as AW had
still never got round to telling Ade that Betty was his chosen one. Then on 3
August, Betty rang AW at work to say that Ade had proposed . . .*

LETTER 122: TO BETTY, 3 AUGUST 1966

Wednesday

Arising out of your telephone call today –

Betty love, listen. <u>You are worrying your pretty little head over a problem that does not exist. A man has offered marriage.</u> You do not love
him. You know, and I know, that you never could. <u>Why can't you see the
answer as clearly as I do</u>, or as Laura would? <u>It must be no</u>. It cannot be
anything else.

You confuse a simple issue in your mind by thinking that <u>I</u> am
involved. Love, I am not. Your answer to Ade has nothing to do with
me. I am separate from it. My own misgivings arise from your muddled
thinking. You are giving me the impression that if I say yes, your answer
to Ade will be no. and conversely, if I say no, your answer to Ade will
be yes. From what you tell me I am sure you are giving Ade the same
impression. You are driving some sort of a bargain, and showing little
sense about it. The shrewd, mature, intellectual woman is behaving like a
silly schoolgirl. Remind me to smack your bottom on Saturday.

Ade is ready to settle for marriage without love. He has suffered a
rebuff (which he is not accustomed to) and his instincts are in revolt.
He had a business arrangement, all planned, and it has collapsed. No, of
course he won't like it. He wants a wife (preferably, but not particularly,
you), and just see if he doesn't get one within the next year or so. And
then you lecture me about his strong moral fibre! Snap out of it, love.
Send him home to his Jewish mistress. Moral fibre, indeed!

You <u>must</u> tell him that the more he persists, the less you like him. You
<u>must</u> tell him, the next time he parades his worldly possessions before
you, that you are not on sale to the highest bidder. Just close your eyes for
a minute, and picture the slobbering old fool smirking at you at bedtime,
not one night, but every night. And me in a lonely bed at the other side
of the world. You would end up screaming. You must be crazy, even to
think of him. <u>Remind the man of his noble resolve not to come between
us. You see now what it was worth.</u> Moral fibre, indeed!

I am not offering you love. I am giving it to you, as I have for the
past thirty years, and I always shall: I can't help it. It is <u>you</u> I want, not
any woman. Just you. More than love I cannot promise. <u>You must trust</u>

<u>me.</u> When you persist in asking for assurances, you make me doubt, not myself, but you.

When you are in Keswick tomorrow night, and Ade is showering his gold and frankincense and myrrh on your lap, spare a thought for me slaving away (I wish I could say in a garret) on the Pennine Way – I shall be in the vicinity of the sinister limestone gorge where my heart was crying out 'Betty, <u>please</u>', not knowing then that the man who was spying on us was your new lover – and remember that I am working not for <u>my</u> future, but <u>ours</u>. It may only be a small cottage, and there may not be much to eat, and the ricketty bed will squeak like mad, but, oh Betty, it will be a place with so much love in it that it will flow out of the windows and up the chimney and lose itself in heaven. Spare a thought, too, tomorrow night, for Kirkcarrion. My memory is better than yours: for me, Kirkcarrion means 'for ever'.

Oh golly! Sometimes I even wish I didn't love you so much. But not really. I love to love you. I want you to love me the same way. Just for the love of it. Now off you go to Keswick. Let Ade see the lovelight in your eyes, and let the doddering old clown know it is not there for him.

You <u>are</u> a funny little thing. All winter you profess your affection, and show it, and then when a man walks past with his pockets bulging and gives you a wink you wriggle out of my embrace and go after him and I have to get to my feet, exhausted by your attention and pull you back. Hold me close for ever, you said. Yes, I will, but do stop trying to break away!

Your bedroom light, on at 8.30 this (Thursday) morning, would tell me you remember Kirkcarrion, and send me to work happy and assured.

Red

It would seem that Ruth at this stage had not completely gone, but was returning home from time to him. But then she did leave – and he was left to look after himelf, all alone.

LETTER 123: TO BETTY, 8 SEPTEMBER 1966

Thursday afternoon

Betty dear, please do not see me or ring me tomorrow (Friday). There has been another hysterical outburst at home and a stated intention of leaving me on Saturday of this week. I am very worried about these latest developments, and am finding myself in a situation I cannot control. I know very well that in these circumstances I should ask you to cancel our Saturday arrangement, but I want to see you so much and tell you what has happened. There is nobody else I can talk to. If you think it better that we should not meet on that day, don't come and I will understand. There is a danger of becoming implicated. Circumstances on Saturday morning may prevent me from turning out myself, although I desperately want to get away from events for a few hours. If anything should happen tomorrow that makes it clear that I shall not be able to keep our rendezvous, I will write again tomorrow.

LETTER 124: TO BETTY, 12 SEPTEMBER 1966

ON LIVING ALONE

Well, of course, my spirits took a nose-dive as I watched you drive away through the rain. I felt bleakly that you were leaving me forever, leaving me in a sea of troubles of my own making. I was depressed, and frightened. Yours was the hand I wanted to hold, and I no longer could. You had gone. There was a bus waiting for Settle, and so I went to Settle and had a meal big enough to last me until Monday in the dining-room of the Golden Lion, where you and I dined last November after a visit to Haworth. Out in the street I ran into Harry Robinson and wife (alibi!) and another woman (which I suppose is all right if your wife is present). Rather oddly, they had been doing the Settle-Carlisle railway journey, and return. I was in a bad state of mind on the journey home, naturally, and extremely apprehensive as I approached the house. Surprisingly, the lights were on and the lady of the house in residence. Supper was served and nothing was said.

I had a wonderful night's sleep, for which you must take full credit. You are a clever girl. You've got the know-how, somehow! Nothing had gone from the house. A busy day's work had been done. In addition to the week's washing, the summer curtains had been taken down and the winter ones put up. The television set had been moved to its winter position, nearer the fireplace. Everything was neat and tidy.

This morning I carried on with my book (Wyther Hill to Middleton) while a busy morning's cleaning and cooking was going on. I had an excellent dinner, and returned to my book. The dinner plates were washed up and put away, and Cindy prepared for going out. THEN, at 1.30, she announced her departure to her new home in Kentmere and there ensued a fairly rational conversation, at last. She has rented School Cottage, just by the church, for a few months, furnished, at the reasonable rent of 3 pounds a week. The cottage is the converted school-house and very attractive. Peter will stay there when he comes. I offered to pay her 10 pounds a week while she is there (which she accepted, and protested it was much too much) and gave her 40 pounds for the next four weeks. Her intention is still to go to Blackburn to live, and I then asked whether she would say how much a week she would want from me then, after I had retired. Would she not agree a figure with me now, and save all the unpleasantness and expense of solicitors? Yes, all right, 7 pounds. All right, I said, 7 pounds. We are to inform our solicitors accordingly, but ask them to leave the matter in abeyance until she has discussed her position with Peter.

Had she kept a key? Yes. Would she come in once a week to do the washing? Yes, if the solicitor said it was all right for her to do so, she would come every Saturday (the only day when there was a bus) and wash and bake for me.

I felt dreadfully sorry for her. She is obviously in a state of extreme nervous depression, probably ill, and confused and unhappy. Off she went, in the rain, after doing everything she possibly could for me in the house and writing out full instructions about the milk and newspaper and coal arrangements, on how to de-frost the fridge, and so on. She has gone to a place where she will be desperately lonely, where he winter months will be severe, where there are no shops and no link other than the Saturday bus. She has no TV, but hopes Peter will provide one.

She has gone, a tragic figure, a faithful wife who can no longer live with her husband because of his conduct. I have driven her to this. I am relieved that we have reached an agreement, and grateful for the further delay. It seems there will be no scandal now for people to gossip about, that I need not now have to explain what has happened, or, if I have to, can tell a plausible story that she is away for a time for reasons of health.

Selfishly, my first concern is for myself, and I am pleased I have come out of this trouble fairly satisfactorily, or look like doing. If I had anything of my conscience I should now be in a desperate state of mind, but I honestly haven't, and I am not. I am deeply sad that she had found it necessary to go, particularly so because Kentmere is not a place where she will find happiness, but only an awful loneliness that, I am sure, will not bring the improvement in health and mind she badly needs. These things she can only find amongst her many friends in Blackburn.

So that's it, love. Next Saturday I shall go out with Mr Firth, or, if he is not available, to Gargrave alone. I cannot see you just yet – it would be quite wrong. I will write again next Sunday.

A funny thing – this conversation I have reported interrupted my notes on Kirkcarrion! I am not feeling too good, but, as you said, I am resilient. I will get over it.

Red

Monday
Thank you for your letter. Please do not trouble to write again until you hear from me next week.

Part 12
Letters to Betty, 1967

In January 1967, aged sixty, AW retired as Borough Treasurer of Kendal. To give himself an office to go to, and a place where he could meet people instead of inviting them home, he did two days a week at the little Kendal Museum where he was Honorary Curator. He was still struggling with the Pennine Way which was proving harder than he had expected. He was seeing Betty only occasionally, aware that he should not be linked with her in case she might be named in his divorce case, though that appeared to be progressing smoothly if slowly. Ade had returned to America, which was a relief for AW, but he was now beginning to worry that the heat had gone out of their romance.

LETTER 125: TO BETTY, 3 JULY 1967

Monday afternoon
Betty dear,

Thank you for your letter. I think I ought to reply at once.

Yesterday was completely wasted – except perhaps that in the morning I cleaned the house, even doing some Hoovering, and changed the flowers – in anticipation. From 2 o'clock until 10 I did nothing but pace the house, waiting for you. I had such a lovely tea ready, every item personally selected for your delectation in Carlisle on Saturday.

The endless hours of waiting did, at any rate, give me plenty of opportunity to think about you and about us. It is now perfectly clear (to both of us, surely) that there can be very little, if any, room for me in your crowded life. You must devote yourself to the essentials – work, home and family – and ration such leisure hours as you can afford between your older friends and older interests. You must set your priorities and work to them. Time has become very precious and you cannot afford to waste any on non-essentials, such as me. There is now a real danger that

187

you may make an appointment with me that, when the time comes, you wish you had never made because of something else you would rather be doing instead. I would never want you to spend time with me that you prefer to be spending elsewhere. I should hate to feel this was happening. I don't want to be a friend on sufferance.

I am writing to let you off the hook. You have no duty to me, and you mustn't feel you have. I have sensed a change in your feelings recently – one or two things you have said. They were happier days for me when we saw or wrote or spoke to each other almost every day. When you kept a light in your bedroom window ... sometimes I wish I hadn't such a good memory. I remember I was Priority No 1 then! Now, if I am only going to be allowed odd minutes with you, always with an eye on the clock (and I can see no other way) I really think you would be kinder to me if no further promises were made, at least for the present.

I will manage fine, and always be grateful for all you have done for me. Nothing will ever alter my esteem: you are the most wonderful woman, the only one for me, the one I have always wanted. I will keep myself busy, and get on with the book. I will get a divorce, and then see how you feel. If any emergency arises, of course I will let you know, and if you want me for anything at all, you know I will always be at home in the evenings, alone, and glad to see you.

Red

Betty wrote back to reassure him all was well, that he was worrying unduly – but then he learned some worse news.

LETTER 126: TO BETTY, 6 JULY 1967

Thursday morning
Dear Betty,

Thank you for your card. I hadn't meant to shock you, and if my words were clumsy, I am sorry.

I had a dreadful shock myself on Tuesday, when I was unexpectedly served with fearful-looking papers to attend High Court in connection with a petition for Judicial Separation. So either I have been double-crossed or my solicitor has bungled matters. The charge is cruelty, and the allegations are so grossly untrue, exaggerated and misleading that I must defend the case. It is unfortunate that those that are untrue deal with aspects I cannot disprove, but they must certainly be denied.

It is <u>very</u> important that you should be kept out of this, for your own sake more than mine, and therefore better we should not meet. To your friends 'in the know' you can quite truthfully explain that our business arrangement is now ended and I am doing those sections of the Pennine Way, beyond the reach of a car, on my own; and that, in any case, your new circumstances give you no time to help further.

I am naturally very upset, but trying to concentrate as much as I can on the book. I am making good progress and have got as far as Thirlwal Castle with the drawings and notes. Soon I shall need the Border Forest Guide, and should be glad if you would kindly send it when you write.

I want desperately to get away for a few days and may go up to Bellingham next Tuesday to distract my mind, if I am allowed to. Tomorrow I am going to Lancaster to see my solicitor.

This is the worst crisis yet, but it is one I must face alone. I have a host of wonderfully happy memories to sustain me, but these are not enough. Without you, I shall be utterly desolate.

Take very good care of yourself until we meet again. Remember Kirkcarrion. It is forever.

Red

AW had hoped Ruth would disappear quietly, agree to a modest amount of money, and nothing would ever come out. In this next letter to Betty, he addresses her as 'Kirk' – short for Kirkcarrion, where something significant happened between them.

LETTER 127: TO BETTY, 10 JULY 1967

Monday afternoon
Kirk dear,

I do not want to weary you with letters, but must thank you for returning the guides and writing so sweetly.

You ask to be kept informed of events. These are likely to be harrowing and I would not wish to sadden you with details nor cause you anxiety. I saw the solicitor only for a few minutes, my call not being convenient, but felt rather better for the visit. At least he was a friend, when all others seem to have fled. His attitude was 'Not to worry. It is for the opposition to prove their case, and we have a good man in Peter Leaver' (the barrister, presumably). He asked me to let him have my replies to the charges, a marital history and any other observations.

These I prepared on Saturday, a most distasteful and disagreeable task that made me very unhappy. The day was a nightmare of self-reproach and indignation confused together. I felt completely wretched. I wanted you to come and tell me what to do. The enclosed envelope contains the specific complaints, my replies, a marital history and one or two other observations: bad copies through a worn carbon, but all I had. Love, you need not look at these if you don't want to. You can say to yourself that it is none of your business. You will not like me any better for what they contain. Please return these papers. If the envelope is unopened I will understand.

I think I will go to Bellingham on Wednesday, staying in Tuesday to take in the groceries. I hope this outing clears my mind. I am very depressed and miserable. This wretched affair has knocked the heart out of me. I have collected the gooseberries and forgotten what you told me to do. The electric fire has broken down. The house needs cleaning, but what the hell? Who is to see it? I am alone, a recluse on parole only on Monday and Thursday mornings. I have even felt like putting 'P.W. Companion' in the dustbin, but then I have remembered from past experience that I recover quickly from a stunning blow and that the present bleakness of my existence will be followed by happier days, happier perhaps than any I have known in the past.

I saw Eric this morning. He recalled our visit to Teesdale, your kindness. This is his only memory, poor man, but I am blessed with many that, at the time, turned despair into a wonderful happiness. The must go on doing just that.

I don't want to burden you, love, but please write to me sometimes. Tell me about your work. Tell me what Jane and Anne are doing. Tell me where Ade took you for that last supper. Tell me about Diddy and Pocca [Betty's parents]. Tell me anything! I have lost touch. Already you are a world away. I want you near, and a word from you now and then would help a lot. Don't worry about me, please.

Red

LETTER 128: TO BETTY, 17 JULY 1967

This was not only a successful day on the P.W, but a most satisfactory one in every respect; the other business was nearly out of my thoughts. But perhaps the highlight was the bus ride over Carter Bar (rather like Shap) in the early evening. The sky had now cleared of clouds and there was a view from the summit of the road that covered half Scotland, the Highland standing up all along the horizon – one of the best views I have ever seen. I was in Hawick soon after eight, with four hours to wait. I wrote cards to you and Molly and Cyril, flitted in and out of snackbars and then went to the Chinese Restaurant for a very good supper. The waitress was a Chinese girl, and I studied her out of the corner of my eye and decided there was no truth in what I had been told about Chinese women when I was a boy at school.

The bus was late in, and unexpectedly, was crowded with Scottish people going on holiday, but I got the only vacant seat amongst a lot of crying infants. I had expected to fall asleep as son as I got in the bus, but instead, although dog-tired, I remained bright and alert all through the journey, and, in fact, did a mental compound interest sum to test myself. At Penrith, unfortunately, there was an hour's rest for the driver, but it was delightfully mild and I stood on the pavement smoking and thinking what a fine holiday I had had.

Coming over Shap, there was a wonderful display of sheet lightening ahead, over Kendal, and by the time the bus got in, about 4.30, a deluge had set in and the streets were swimming in water. There was nothing for it but to face the downpour and the lightning and the thunder, and I was soaked when I got home. I went to bed and slept for an hour.

On Friday I went over my maps and notes, and yesterday and today I have worked hard on the book. I would like you to look through the Cross Fell and Roman Wall pages before the book goes to the printer: you will find I have borrowed an idea of yours about the old lead mines.

I have heard nothing more from the solicitor. I think the case is likely to be heard at Carlisle, and I suppose there could be a delay of two or three months. This interval, if it means not seeing you, will seem a life-time; but at least it will give you a breathing space to come to a decision about me. Absence, they say, makes the heart grow fonder, but absence long continued can make the heart forget. Betty love, be fair to yourself. As I said, I know you have lost the first rapture, which was only to be expected, and if you find in your heart that it has not been replaced by something more enduring, then it's curtains for me. In due course I shall ask you, and you must tell me, honestly and don't worry. I'll get by!

Thank you for telling me all the news. I was especially pleased about Jane's wonderful success, and can imagine how delighted and proud you must be.

Red

AW received another shock when Betty told him she had started a nursing course in Kendal which would last three years. Now that her two daughters, Jane and Anne, were growing up, with Jane away at university, she wanted to become as independent as possible.

LETTER 129: TO BETTY, 28 JULY 1967

Tuesday evening.
Dear Betty,

It was good to hear from you again. A voice from the past, an age-old past! I was glad to have your news, and followed your Sleagill walk on the map: an ingenious route, this, appealing in its conception and no doubt brilliantly executed: who thought of it? As for Jane, I can understand your anxiety: things must be pretty bad over there and seem to be getting worse. God's Own Country, they call it. This will be Jane's longest absence from home, and she can be sure of a great big welcome when she gets back. I know how much you miss her. You seem to be enjoying your work, although it sounds completely unattractive to me, handling entrails and mopping up blood all day. I have a better idea: come and be my part-time secretary-housekeeper. Good pay. Short hours. Holidays with pay. Typewriter and aprons provided. Pension scheme. Genial company. Free meals.

I hope you will not mind my writing to you. Please. I have nobody else and the days do drag. I would like to send you a weekly bulletin, if I may.

Great strides along the Pennine Way (in the living-room) have brought me to Bellingham; all is now complete up to this point, and I hope to have the penwork a breast of the fieldwork by the time my cousin arrives on the 9th. (we are now fixed up for four nights at Coylumbridge and two at Kirk Yetholm, the latter booking in the hope that I can do the last twenty miles with him). I am rushing the book a little now, and would again ask if you will be kind enough to check the pages on Cross Fell and the Wall and see whether I have missed anything? The end of the book is now within measurable distance, and latterly I have been searching in my mind for something to succeed it, something to do with maps, something to do with hills. The proposed book of drawings will not occupy me enough. I have thought of the Howgills, but a book about them would be too slight an effort. I have thought of the limestone hills of Craven (Ingleborough, Penyghent, etc), which would give me great pleasure to explore thoroughly, but here, too, in lesser degree, the area is not quite big enough to make a decent book, and besides, Craven has no boundary and is difficult to define. But now the inspiration has come: 'A Pictorial Guide to the Yorkshire Fells' on the same pattern as the Lakeland series: routes of ascent, maps, panoramas, and so on. Definition is given by the boundary of the Yorkshire Dales National Park, which contains all the high ground, there being 200 fells over 2000 feet. The advantages are that all the fells are in the north-west of the county, between Lune and Wharfe, and therefore convenient to Kendal and bus services; that the Howgills and the Craven Hills, my favourites, would be included as part of a greater whole; that the work would take me back, with a mission, to the places I was happy with you; that popular appeal is assured. I have mentioned this to Mr Firth and, as a Yorkshireman, he is very keen on the idea.

I set the seal on this new enthusiasm last Saturday with an ascent of the Calf, the highest of the Howgills, above Sedbergh. It was simply glorious, one of the best-ever mountain days. Everything was just right except that I was badly wanting my favourite companion. The path up, around Winder, was delightful, like walking on velvet. The views were superb: a vast landscape, covering the Pennine Way from Penyghent to Cross Fell inland, and, facing the sea, the long crinkly skyline of Lakeland, from Black Combe to Blencathra. The larks were quiet, but the still air of the summit was full of darting swifts. A couple, man and wife(?) – the only persons I met – were resting by the cairn, and I waited for an hour for them to depart, which they finally did, leaving me alone to take a series of photographs and draw the Lakeland panorama – for my <u>new</u> book. The thought of another lease of two years studying maps and climbing hills excites me. There will be sentimental journeys among those I shall have to do – Great Shunner, Penyghent, Ingleborough, etc. – and I shall halt in reverence at the places where you found it necessary to halt, and there will be many bitter-sweet moments of remembrance. But I shall pretend you are there, walking ahead just out of sight. That way, you will help to keep me going.

Mr Firth had an hour with me at the Museum last Thursday, and brought me a great many letters. Two of interest I enclose.

Cyril Moore called on Monday, bringing the last of his P.W papers, including some cuttings about the lead mines, which I also enclose. He also brought the latest issue of the Fell and Rock Journal, which belatedly reviews Books Six and Seven favourably but gives me a fearful slating for Fellwanderer.

Wednesday evening.

There were letters this morning from Peter, Doris and cousin Eric. Eric is a faithful old soul. I had told him were going to Kirk Yetholm so that I could do the last part of the Pennine Way, and that if the weather was not good I would be staying on to get it finished. Today he tells me that he has arranged to extend his holiday, and will stay on with me as long as is necessary.

Doris has been making some discreet enquiries from a local tailor about the correct wear for my visit to London. She reports 'black hat, morning coat, striped trousers;. The tailor will fix me up if I want, for three pounds fifty (hire, not purchase). She says she would consider it a proud privilege to go with me. So there, you see.

Peter confirms his arrival on leave on September 7th. He is hiring a car again, and will therefore be able to hep me with that final and ill-starred walk up Knock Fell from Dufton. Later that month I must go down south and get Bleaklow and the Peak done. (Something has gone wrong with the typewriter: the ribbon has stuck – it should jump up and down when you hit the keys).

I always read your letters over and over again, squeezing every ray of hope out of them but without gaining much comfort these days. Now you promise soon to explain your 'rather complex feelings'. There you go again, hurting me! Have I become a problem? See, love, the issue is dead simple, not complex at all. Either you do or you don't. That's all you have to decide, and you don't have to do it right now. It's nothing to get all mixed up in your mind about. It isn't, anyway, a matter for the mind to work out; it isn't a matter of cold calculation, it's an affair of the heart. It there are complexities, there are doubts. If there are doubts, commit yourself to nothing. That makes sense, doesn't it? Anyway, forget I asked. We drifted together and we can drift apart if you want it that way. It's just up to you. You have a very full life now, lots to do, lots of friends. If your new life, besides being full, is also happy with things as they are, well then, why take on a bad risk? Spare me an explanation of your rather complex feelings, please: it could only make me unhappy.

I'm sorry if I seem peevish. I have just been reading that last bit again. It sounds like sour grapes. Maybe it is. I am not rebuking you, or being unkind, not intentionally. Oh Betty, please understand! I am deprived. I am sick of an old passion. I have grown used to you and miss you terribly. I, for one, still do. I, for one, always will. Kirkcarrion has no double meaning, for me. The turn of events distresses me. Change the subject! In the garden, the philadelphus (mock orange) has blossomed and faded since you were last here. The hydrangeas are putting on a fine show; they must have heard you say you didn't like them. The lavender is in bloom, and the first nasturtium is in full flower. But the garden is a wilderness, and the Virginia creeper is climbing up the windows and even coming through the slates on the roof. Reminds me of the old neglected house in 'Rebecca'. Next year I really must get down to tidying up. Too late now for this year.

Thursday evening.

Miss B___t called to see me at the museum this morning, full of her Scandinavian tour and very bright and cheerful. Quite obviously she has no idea that her name is being taken in vain, the bastards! I hope she never finds out.

As there had been no word from the solicitor, not even an acknowledgment of my Homeric effort, I rang him up from the museum. He says (a) everything is in hand, (b) he has filed a 'blanket' denial, i.e a complete denial of all complaints, (c) he has consulted the barrister, who has expressed the view that the complaints are too thin to be supported; we are all to meet in September, (d) that the Courts are now in summer recess, and he does not expect the case to be heard until around Christmas, and (e) that I have no cause to be despondent about the outcome. Christmas! Five months!

I was never adamant about not seeing each other; or if I was, I am weakening every day. No, my concern was, and is, that you should not become involved in my troubles. If I cared for you less, I should concern myself less. If you were involved, you would never forgive me and I would never forgive myself. I would not have you hurt for anything. I would rather sacrifice your friendship altogether than have you (and Jane and Anne) made unhappy because of me.

I have worked hard this week and am now some miles north of Bellingham. Tomorrow I'll take a day off, and go to Morecambe to do some shopping (soap, of all things, not records) and see 'The Sound of Music'. I'll work Saturday and Sunday, unless Saturday happens to be a beautiful day in which case I'll explore new routes up the Calf.

The privations of these past months are taking their toll on my tummy. I'll be lean and slender and more distinguished-looking that ever when you see me again. And hungrier!

Funny thing about the typewriter. I shall miss it. Buggar, buggar, buggar.

R

Miss B___t was Mary Burkett, Director of Abbot Hall, and an old friend of AW's
— who was not aware that there were rumours circulating round Kendal, heard
apparently by Ruth, that she was the woman AW had been having an affair with.
    The reason for visiting a tailor was that he had heard that Harold Wilson's
Labour Government had awarded him an MBE and he was planning to go
London to receive it later in the year.

LETTER 130: TO BETTY, 3 AUGUST 1967

Friday evening.
Dear B,
    Today I have been to Morecambe, a place that depresses me, especially
when crowded with visitors. To escape the glare of the promenade, which
hurt my eyes, and get away from the Lancashire dialect, which offended
my ears, I took a ride on the Sand Trail Express, a daring thing for me to
do – this is an open wagon with seats, driven by a tractor dressed up as
a train engine with a long funnel like Stevenson's Rocket. Do you know,
I enjoyed it, just as I enjoyed the pillion ride. I was taken on a two-mile
ride across the sands, for 1s 6d; and from way out in the bay, Morecambe
doesn't look too bad, while the view across to Lakeland, on this day at
least, was very good indeed.
    Then I went to see 'The Sound of Music' and was no longer depressed
but quite wonderfully uplifted. There were only two other people in the
balcony, and nothing to distract attention from a very beautiful, very
happy and yet very moving film. It was <u>fab</u>. If I could make a film like
that I would consider it my life's work. At times the screen went misty
and tears rolled down my face, and it didn't matter because there was
nobody to see; but mostly I was enthralled by the wonderful happiness
of the story and the glorious scenery. Julie was magnificent: she was <u>you</u>,
when I have seen <u>you</u> happy. I enjoyed it tremendously. I sat transfixed.
It did me a power of good. I felt a heel for having written to you as I
did. I knew now that I had said things that were hurtful, and if I had not
already posted my letter, I would now not.

    Red

LETTER 131: TO BETTY, AUGUST 1967?

It is a habit of mine to watch for your car whenever I am out, even
in the most unlikely and impossible places. I remember sitting on the

parapet of the bridge at Bellingham, for instance, watching the traffic as intently as if I had a rendezvous with you. And the times my heart has missed a beat at the approach of a car that looks, at a distance, like yours!

Today I have worked hard on the book since 9am, and slowly my hand is catching up with my boots. When it does I am resolved to clean the house thoroughly, so that when my cousin arrives next week he will not feel sorry for me. I have no appetite for this coming holiday at all. I have said not a word to anybody about my domestic affairs, apart from yourself and recently, briefly, to the solicitor in the thesis you saw, but it seems inevitable that my cousin will have a few questions to ask, and I am not disposed to say anything.

It has been a cheerless day, with the rain lashing the windows and the hills obscured in a pall of wet mist. I have badly wanted you to call; I listen for the gate opening, but it never does. On a miserable day like this, when I am housebound and rather lonely, the Pennine Way is a blessing: without it to pass the time I should feel completely lost. Where is my life drifting? What aims have I left? What is to be the end of it all? These are the questions I ask myself. I do not know the answers. Bedtime now. The electric blanket is operational again.

Betty then informed AW that it looked as if she would not complete her three-year nursing course in Kendal, as she had expected, but would have to continue it in London, at Whipps Cross Hospital – another reason to make AW alarmed.

LETTER 132: TO BETTY, UNDATED

Monday evening.

Not much has happened today. At the museum two boys called to have books autographed and then Mr Firth appeared with my cheque for royalties for the first six months of the year (562 pounds) and discussed details for printing 'Pennine Way Companion': in particular the colour of the Rexine cover. This I had intended to ask you to select, but I think you will approve my choice of turquoise. It is your colour. It will match. You will be able to sit in your turquoise car, wearing your turquoise dress and turquoise earrings (inter alia) with a turquoise book on your lap, and you will look right bonny.

This afternoon I did a full page of drawings in 3 and a half hours, which is good fast progress, and am now only six miles short of Byrness.

Tuesday evening

Your letter arrived this morning, and was more welcome than a cheque for a fortune. It was Magna Carta: it freed me from my worse fears. Not only that, it transported me, made me feel good again. Oh B, it was sweet, and charming. I had deserved reproach, but reproach there was none – only kindness.

Yes, I understand now, perfectly. I will not ask again for too much, to have you wholly; but you will not mind if I go on dreaming my favourite dream, without ever mentioning it again? Yes, love, we will have it the way you want it, for as long as you want it. You put your case with sweet reasonableness and I have no counter-argument. You win. Your intention to work for your own security is admirable, and, because there is really no compulsion to do so, noble – but please don't ever again suggest that your life up to now has been wasted or unfulfilled. It is a fine thing to be independent, but it is also a fine thing to have others dependent on you, knowing they can rely on you, and this has been your position these past 19 years. This is really the fundamental role of a woman and a mother, and surely there is more fulfilment of life in this than in being concerned only with a career? Don't be <u>too</u> humble and penitent. You have made a lovely and intelligent woman out of the little frightened girl who went to Casterton School; you have made a charming and devoted mother; you have failed in nothing. Feel <u>proud</u> of your accomplishments, as you ought.

Yes, love, we will do anything you say and everything you want. See each other, be loving companions, walk together. We must. Your letter inspired me, and I have worked today like a man possessed. I am trying to get up-to-date so that I can send you all the pages you haven't seen – Cross Fell to Byrness – before I go away. I will post them to you next Wednesday, then you needn't rush and could return them when you call. When you call! How nice to be writing that! I will enjoy my holiday but look forward eagerly to coming back, not to an empty house and an empty life, but to you, my sweetheart.

Wednesday evening.

More good progress today; am now within 2 miles of Byrness. This is going to be a splendid book, the sort I would have wanted for my own as a boy.

I have been studying the map of the Yorkshire Dales National Park and find the area too big – it is a big as Lakeland – to be dealt with in a single volume, so have reverted to my original idea, the Craven district only. The difficulty of having no boundary to work within can be overcome by a change of title: 'The <u>Limestone</u> Hills of Craven', so that I can confine myself to my favourites (north of the Kirkby L–Settle road: Casterton Fell, Gragareth, Whernside, Ingleborough, Penyghent and a few more), which are, better still, easily accessible – and omit the soggy peat moors I like much less. This will be a fascinating task.

Apart from the usual explorations and ascents, there are some 300 caves and potholes to be discovered and plotted exactly; and, as you know, the whole area is delightful walking country. Envy me the next two years. This book will give me tremendous pleasure. And it will be good because I shall enjoy doing it. Yes, love, come when you can, and help me. I will save the best walks for the days you can come along. The area is so handy that half-days would be OK, and so convenient that even the short days of winter can be put to good use. It will be great to have you with me. Mrs Newsome, here we come! Oh, no, we daren't – they'll ask about the children. Many, then, at Goat Gap? No, not until we have our divorces. Never mind, chick, I'll go this very Saturday* and look for a new place. Oh Betty love, aren't you excited? It will be wunderbar (pron. Vunderbar).

Of course Doris is not going to London with me, silly.

Now will you please let me know if you two working girls, plus Diddy, can manage a night out to see 'The Sound of Music'? I know it won't be too easy for you. The evening performance starts at 7.15 prompt, and so does the picture (nothing else is shown) and the opening shots must NOT be missed, so you would have to be there at 7.10. Do try, please. I could go down for the tickets next Tuesday, otherwise after I return from Scotland.

* more probably Friday, Ingleton gets so crowded on Saturdays

No misunderstanding – <u>I</u> shall not be in the next seat. I shall weary you if I write more, but gosh! How nice it is to write to you and have you in my thoughts now that we are good pals again!

So do I!! as if you didn't know!

R

LETTER 133: TO BETTY, AUGUST 1967?

NEW READERS START HERE

Red, a rather distinguished-looking local government officer, and Eric, who beggars description, are engaged on a tour of the Scottish Highlands. Although beset by difficulties of travel, they are pushing on with their programme and contriving to live elegantly en route. In our last instalment they had reached Oban and were about to start the hazardous voyage to Mull.

NOW READ ON

OBAN
Saturday night (in bed)
I have enjoyed today.

The weather could not have been better for a first visit to Tobermory, and the place lived up to expectations. This quaint village (capital of Mull) lies around the curve of a land-locked harbour in a single line of clean and colourful shops and cottages facing the bay, with a background of steep wooded slopes. I think we'll have a fortnight here. My honeymoon plans now cover nine weeks.

I have a lovely room at the front, with the quaint white church on the left and the river curving round on the right. Before I pulled the curtains there was a sickle of moon over the hills. Your letter was handed to me as I came in. Thank you for being so faithful to my wishes. I loved it – except for the pencilled postscript, which disturbed me with its reference to domestic crisis. I hope this is over whatever it was. Don't worry, love. What you need is a man in the house. Me. This must end my news from Scotland, Betty. I will be on my way back to you when you get it. <u>Please</u> come to Tebay, and <u>please be just as I remember you</u>.

It seems so long

Red

LETTER 134: TO BETTY, UNDATED

KIRK YETHOLM, six o'clock in the morning. Tuesday.
Have super holiday, you said.

I am simply fed up to the teeth. The weather is <u>awful</u>. It rained all the way down from Aviemore (where we had a look round the Sports Centre (brochure enclosed), opened since your visit last year). It was raining when we arrived at Kirk Yetholm, and now 12 hours later, it still is. The mist is down to the fields around the village and the hills are invisible.

I do not like the Border Hotel, where we are staying. The building itself is charming, raftered externally in Tudor style, part of the roof being thatched, and it is well furnished in oak and brass inside, but mine host is inane and inefficient, an ex-Squadron Leader complete, after the fashion of his kind, with widespread moustachios. I was half-expecting trouble, his letter in reply to mine about accommodation (for which he kept me waiting three weeks) caused misgivings by its untidy and illiterate style; and I was not really surprised on arrival when he disclaimed all knowledge of the booking, saying he had never received my confirmation (which I had sent by return post). The woman who waits on the table told me afterwards that she had no doubt he had blundered again, as he was always doing. You will understand the mentality of the man from the card (enclosed) that greets visitors in their bedrooms. However, the room was available and we could have it.

I ham unhappy here. After the spaciousness of the Coylumbridge this place gives me claustrophobia. The rooms are small and overcrowded with furniture, and there is no privacy at all. There are nine people staying here and the tiny lounge is congested. The others talk endlessly of their homes, their cars, their families, their holidays, each trying to better the others, while Eric sleeps and I creep further and further into my shell. Worse, there is only one lavatory.

LETTER 135: TO BETTY, 2 OCTOBER 1967

NOT TO BE READ IN A HURRY.
SAVE IT UNTIL BEDTIME.   Sunday morning.

Dear Betty,

You must have known I would have to write again, after last night. My purpose is not to try to revive anything that we agreed should be buried, and I am not going to be petulant. I want this to be the nicest letter I have ever written.

Something went wrong around midnight. I did not want our friendly association to end in tears. It had always been such a happy affair. Together we built up a little heaven for ourselves that nobody ever knew about. It was ours, yours and mine, and nobody else could have shared it or even understood. I cannot think that any woman was ever loved more. You were an angel to me. I had never know such wonderful happiness as you brought me, and I had never thought that a woman could mean so much to a man. You made bright for me a period when, without you, I would have been sunk in black despair. Your smile and your kiss chased away the shadows. You were always a rainbow of hope for the future. In our own little world, together, we could forget the tragic past and the present held no secrets. We understood each other well. As we said so often, we were just right for each other. I am sure you felt as I did, until changed circumstances changed you too. You began to be restless in my arms and started peeping over my shoulder at the world we had left. You began to feel you must play a part in it. You had a longer future to look forward to then I had and your life might be uncertain and troubled unless you equipped yourself to meet it. I was selfish and didn't want you to go, but I had nothing to offer and could see the sense in your new intentions. Yet I am convinced that, for a blessed interval in time, you were happy with me, and that, if only other considerations had not pressed so cruelly, we could have built together a life of mutual tenderness and affection.

What I was trying to say myself, and bungled it as usual, was that, knowing you so well, I have realised instinctively, without being told, that your old feelings for me have withered. I honestly believe, and you have confirmed it, that this has not happened because of anything I have done, or omitted to do. It's just one of those things that can never be properly explained and for which an explanation is better not attempted. I don't honestly think either that I was becoming a hindrance in your very busy life. But I was someone who kept cropping up in your mind, and you may have been feeling some obligation or duty to me because of what we had been to each other. This is what I was trying to get across: that you owe me nothing and that you can put me right out of your mind and, if you want to, forget that I exist. One thing less for you to worry about! I also wanted to say that I shall not, and could never, change my regard for you. I shall always love you; I can't help it. If ever you want me I shall be here, always ready, always willing, always wanting you. Promise you will come to me if ever you are in trouble or serious doubt. To me, please, not to your other friends. All I can now ask is that you should continue to think of me, not as one of many friends, but as someone rather special. I don't want you to class me with Dick and Margaret and Jim and Sheila, but as someone who loves you even more than these, and, even more than these, would want to help. There is one particular way in which I could help (no strings) if only you would let me. Don't ever let pride stand in your way. Give me the chance, please, to express my devotion in a way that would give me as much joy as our day on Ingleboro. We must not break our ties completely. That would be too much of a penance for both of us, I think. We will abandon Kirkcarrion but keep in touch. I will let you know of any exciting events, and hope you will do the same. But we will not see each other, except when you really want to, and we will not correspond regularly. You don't ever have to sit down to me when there are dishes waiting to be washed, you know that. This letter calls for no reply, but I wanted you to have it so that you might better understand my faltering words last night. Today I feel shrivelled by your tears, and the outlook is as bleak as the weather. But I have my books to do, fortunately, and a host of wonderful memories of you. There will be reminders of you everywhere when I go out. I shall never see a birds-eye primrose or a purple saxifrage again without thinking of our search for them together. I will take pleasure in going again to the places we visited together; you will be everywhere. There will be many anniversaries, too, to recall. Next Wednesday night's meeting at the Museum will be the second of our very first expedition together, to Paddy Lane, and coming back along Oxenholme Road I remember suggesting that we should write love letters to each other purely on the basis of a professional literary exercise. Well, this present letter is not within that category. It is written from the heart. . . . I will no longer listen for the doorbell as I have these many months past. But someday I will write a novel set in the places where we were happy, and if you don't recognise yourself in it my pen will certainly be failing. I may even include myself – in a very small part. It will have a happy ending, just as I want your life to have. Never feel, if you do not hear from me for some time, that I have forgotten you. Betty dear, you know I never could. There's Christmas and your birthday. I will send remembrances, and you will know that as long as these arrive I shall be thinking of you and with no less tenderness. I have so much to be grateful to you for, so very much.

My eyes are filling. I said I wept not at sadness but at happiness. Perhaps because there has been so much sadness, so little happiness. So it must be the memory of a blissful partnership that brings today's tears. It is ended, but nothing could ever make me forget our days in the heaven we made for a little while. Few men can have loved as I have, and no man is the worse for loving as I have. Thank you, Betty, for everything.

Whenever I hear of Doctor Zhivago I shall think, not of the Russian revolution, but of a country lane near Sedgwick on a September midnight in 1967.

Please remember all I have said, and most of all that I will always love you dearly.

Now turn out the light, and curl up and go to sleep, chick, and try not to worry. Be patient, and lasting happiness will come to you. Don't make the mistake of going out to look for it. It will come to you, in its own good time. Sweet dreams. Goodnight, love, and goodbye. God bless!

Red

LETTER 136: TO BETTY, 8 OCTOBER 1967

Thursday afternoon

Dear Betty,

Last Saturday was a wonderfully happy day. It was delightful to be with you again, to walk and explore together as we used to, to wander awhile in a world upeopled by others, to talk to you and to listen to you and even to have my spine chilled by the details of your men's-surgical-ward experiences, to have you all to myself, to turn away and not look while you made little waterfalls – oh yes, love, everything was as I had remembered it. I was reassured. I was left feeling that nothing had really changed. Saturday brought me back to normal, and I have been happy since. I can keep going now until the next time.

On Monday, Cyril called at the Museum (for two hours), with stories of his preliminary excursions to the Limestone Hills of Craven, with new maps for me, and with a copy of 'A Guide to the Pennine Way', just out. I am sending this for you to look at as and when you can find time over the next few weeks. I have only glanced through it myself, sufficiently to form some conclusions. It is attractively designed, well printed and nice to handle; it is well written and the author has delved deep into avenues of research for his interesting side-notes (history, botany, architecture, etc), and in fact for a boy of 23 it is a remarkable achievement of which he ought to be very proud. It is a good book, love, but ours will be better.

Cyril also produced a letter from Her Majesty's Stationary Office saying, in reply to his enquiry, that the OFFICIAL guide to the Pennine Way is to be published early in 1968. Ours will be better, love.

On Monday there was a letter from Doris, distressed by recent events, so on Tuesday I went over to see her, staying overnight and combining with this visit an expedition to the new motorway being constructed across the Pennine Way on the moors east of Rochdale, which was something I had to do anyway. But first Doris. I don't know why, but I seem to have a tranquillising effect on her. She was tearful and unwell and full of woe when I got there, and with reason (I'll tell you later), but a few simple enquiries at an opportune moment on the best way to make coffee, to polish furniture, to grill bacon, etc. led to a two hour demonstration on housewifery in great detail that took her mind off other matters and before bedtime the smiles and her old sense of fun were back again. She has the knack of recounting a story, even a trivial incident, most entertainingly, with word for word conversations, and is a wonderful mimic.

I don't have to contribute anything but an attentive ear. Just occasionally I have to lead her from one story to the next, but 'Has Eddie been to see you lately?' or 'What did the Vicar say when he called?' is enough to produce another entertaining half-hour. We also looked through some of her old photographs, another sure-fire way of getting her to reminisce on the past and forget present misfortunes. She gave me the enclosed picture of herself and Derrick as I first knew them, when she was being urged to become an opera singer. She asked about you. I had some success, too, with her little dog Cindy, who, by devoted nursing, she has kept alive when the vet said there was not hope. Cindy has recovered from pneumonia but is left with a very weak heart, poor little thing, and cannot yet walk without stumbling; for two months she has lain at deaths door, her toys untouched, but for just a few minutes that night I got her tail wagging as we wrestled for possession of her squeaking cat on the carpet. She is all the world to Doris, and I do hope she recovers.

I have had a letter from the solicitor (enclosed) and have fixed up the appointment he requests.

I am satisfied now that the cavity where we had our coffee was in fact the place we were looking for, i.e. the exit of Long Kin Cave with the entrance to Long Kin Pot directly opposite, although these apertures could not clearly be seen from the surface. But I am still puzzled by the absence of the stream linking the two. I will go again with Peter (home tomorrow) and we will get down the hole and investigate.

This morning's post brought me details of a new medical encyclopaedia, which, it seems, is a <u>must</u> for every pupil nurse in her mid forties, especially if she has a lovely face and has come out top in her first written examination. I know it isn't Christmas, and I know it isn't your birthday, but may I get it for you, please? Please, chick. Besides, I want to look at the bits on female anatomy. You have me at a disadvantage these days. You are getting all the breaks and I am learning nothing. I feel stripped naked by your incredible stories of the men's ward. Are you quite sure you get all your facts right? Sometimes I think you are pulling my innocent leg. I never heard of the things you tell me.

R

P.S about the encyclopaedia. It doesn't have to be a present. I would order it in my name and it could belong to me, coming to you only on permanent loan if this arrangement would suit you better. Please say yes and return the order form.

Enclosure:

_____ 'A Guide to the Pennine Way' by Christopher John Wright
_____ Letter from the solicitor dated 4th September
_____ Cutting from the Lancashire Evening Telegraph, 5th September
_____ Photograph of Doris and Derrick, taken about 1939
_____ Packet of Doublemint Chewing Gum.
_____ Details of the New Illustrated Medical and Health Encyclopaedia

On October 23 AW sent Betty two letters – the second in his assumed persona as her wise uncle Hans.

LETTER 137: TO BETTY, 23 OCTOBER 1967

Thursday evening
To the sweetest woman in the world:

Dear Betty,
Sentimental, you said I was. It was not sentiment, Betty, that made me kiss your letter this morning. It was gratitude, for writing so kindly, for understanding me so well, for letting me know and love you. It was more than a letter. It was a reprieve from a death sentence. It came after the four most wretched days of my life, four days empty of all purpose, four days when I had no will or wish to do anything but think and think and think of the events of last Saturday night. Betty, love, I was heartbroken. I could not bear the thought of losing you. I had hurt you, else why the tears? I was four days in the house, with no callers, with nothing to deflect my thoughts. The newspapers held no interest: it was last Saturday evening, the night of the long knives, that was important, not Vietnam or the Labour Conference. I watched TV, but the picture I saw was your tearful face. I badly wanted Peter to come and provide a distraction, but he did not. The house was a condemned cell, and I a guilty man.

Reaction to Saturday night did not set in until after I had written to you on Sunday morning, after a night of little sleep. I was utterly dazed, unable to comprehend that I might never see you again. I simply could not believe that I would never again feel your sweet body nor the caress of you lips. It was unthinkable. I loved you so much. How could it be that we had parted? What had happened between us? The reaction came slowly. You know how a bad knock or fall brings no pain immediately. Rockclimbers have told how they have fallen from great heights and been badly injured, yet have felt no pain until some time afterwards. Medically

I believe this is a first consequence of shock, but you will know. That's the way it was with me. Sunday dragged on as I tried to recall all you had said, searching desperately in your words for some gleam of hope to check my rising doubts. But I could find none. The more I reflected the more I despaired.

I had been so utterly sure that in you I had found the girl I had dreamed about for forty years, so who so often comforted my loneliest hours. She was a fiction, until you came and made her real. You were this girl, exactly. In the way you looked, in everything you did and said, in the way you loved me. I was never more sure of anything. The girl was you. You were the girl. Betty, I could never find the words to ell you, but I worshipped you. You were so right for me. I had waited so long for you to come, and when you came you were sweeter and lovelier than imagination had pictured you. But – after Saturday night, could it really be that I had been wrong? No, no that was unthinkable. You, the woman I revered and respected, could it be that you had feet of clay? No, I refused to believe it. How could you destroy so perfect an image? . . . No, not disappointed, Betty. Disenchanted is the word. And it hurt. Well, I concluded (trying to console myself) there's no fool like an old fool; everybody knows that. Well, I said (still trying to console myself) at least I've got a bit of iron in my soul now, and I shall be a better writer through bitter experience; forget about that love story and I'll do one about the duplicity and deceit of women. Yes, that's what I'll do. To hell with dream girls anyway. They don't exist, how could they? They are the stuff of imagination. More damn fool me, to think one would come to life, just for me.

So my thoughts ran on. Betty love, I am truly repentant. You see what powerful influence you have on me. The four days were hell. But today has been altogether different. Your letter came, and if I had dictated it to you it could not have said better just what I wanted to hear. My black mood fell away completely between your first sentence and the last. Quite suddenly, in the short time it took me to read it, I was a happy man again, the happiest in the world. I sang 'Oh what a beautiful morning; as I washed up. Peter came and I could have fallen on his neck with joy. The sun is shining, I said, and you said you would take me to Knock Fell to finish the Pennine Way, and I am feeling great; come on, let's go. So we collected his friend Arthur and off we went. The day remained fine, and I filled in the last gap in my Pennine Way journey. We took the car up to the brick hut on Great Dun Fell, the one we have abused so often. Peter and Arthur climbed Cross Fell while I went the other way, over Knock

Fell and down to Dufton, reversing the route to save climbing. All went well. When I came down to Swindale Beck I had completely walked the Pennine Way. The rest of the walk into Dufton I had done with you, and here started the memories, which yesterday would have had irony in them but today were joyous indeed. Look, there's the patch of heather near the high stile where we lay together, heart against heart (we must have been mad: it was trying to <u>snow</u>); and the railway wagon near the path where she disappeared for a minute (clever girl, she always knows when she wants to do it); and the little clapper bridge where she sat and munched an apple and watched the stream, in her funny rain-hat and cape, not knowing I was regarding her with devotion and thinking how adorable she was; and that muddy lane where we sheltered against a wall during a minor blizzard and I kissed away the snowflakes as they fell on her sweet face. Betty McNally, <u>surely</u> you must realise that no other man could love you as I do? My whole world lies in your sweet body. Please, please never leave me . Peter and Arthur were late for our arranged rendezvous in Dufton. I had had wings on my heels, they hadn't. What was described as a celebration tea was agreed; the others though it was to celebrate the completion of the Pennine Way, but you and I know different. I didn't take them to Mrs Barker's – she would have asked how my wife (or daughter) was, and my American cousin. We had tea in the new café in Appleby and then came home. A wonderful day. I have been in a state of ecstatic chuffiness ever since the postman called. Oh yes, a wonderful, wonderful day. And a wonderful evening, writing to you when I thought I might never again do so. And it will be wonderful going to bed; I shall be able to think of you before going to sleep, as I used to before last Saturday. I shall put in a bolster to hug.

I am thrilled and excited, but I haven't sought to give you the impression that I am assuming we will resume our pre-hospital friendship. I know that cannot be, dear, and I am reconciled to it. I am happy today because your letter has told me you want us to remain good friends. I am not expecting more. And what I wrote on Sunday is still true. I would never try to hold you if you wanted someone else, never. You can <u>buggar</u> off (where did I get that dreadful word from?) whenever you feel like spreading your wigs and flying away.

But I am glad, really glad and relieved, to have your assurance that you will step warily. I don't want you ever even to contemplate doing anything shabby because I know my dream girl never would and it would hurt me. Don't look back into the past, love. Looking back is for old people, like Ade. Not for you. Please don't keep a candle burning in the window for what is dead and done with; there are only ghosts in the past. You are young (which is why I like to call you chick) and for the young happiness lies ahead, not behind. You will not find it by raking the ashes of dead fires. You may miss seeing it when it comes if you are looking back over your shoulder. For you, love, the promise of a fuller life and complete happiness lies wholly in the future. It will come, of that I am sure. Bet you five bob! All right, ten. But do cheer up. I want you to be smiling when I see you again. The only tears a sweet woman like you should shed are tears of happiness. Those are the only tears I ever want to see in your lovely eyes.

You do need your bottom smacking a little bit, though. I couldn't bring myself to do it, and anyway my smack would soon turn into a caress, but I have persuaded your Uncle Hans in Utrecht to do it for me. His letter is enclosed. It will jolt you: his hand is heavier than mine. His is not a letter to read in bed. His is a letter to read when you feel like throwing things: it will add power to your arm. I know that nothing infuriates more than to be given advice and told it is for your own good, and I am not claiming this for anything Uncle Hans has written. He has said what he has because he loves you, as I do.

Golly, love, it's nearly two o'clock in the morning. And I was supposed to be going to bed with a sympathetic bolster. But it really has been nice, spending a long evening with you after such a wonderful day.

I got a letter from you this morning that ended 'My love as always'. That's why it's been such a gloriously happy day for me.

Red

LETTER 138: TO BETTY (FROM 'UNCLE HANS'), 23 OCTOBER 1967

Utrecht, Holland. Thursday evening.

My very dear child,

You will be greatly surprised to hear from me. I have played no part in your life, living as I do in another country. You will have heard of me, a long time ago, from your father, but your recollection will be vague, if indeed you remember me at all. I am old now, and long retired from work, but, thanks be to the good God, I keep very well. I have my garden, which keeps me busy, and now and again I still win a prize at our annual show with my flowers. Joanna, too, is blessed with good health although her sight is failing somewhat (a great trial, since she was always so fond of embroidery). The children, of course, are now grown up and scattered, and we see little of them. Gretel has two lovely children.

I have always taken a great interest in you. I have on my writing desk (you will hardly believe this) a small framed photograph of you when you were at school – must be over thirty years ago. It has always stood there, between the two inkwells. Your father sent it when you first went to boarding school. I love that picture. You were so small in your new uniform, so neat, so tidy. The expression on your face always brings a smile. You look so serious, my dear! And just a little fearful, as might any child at a new school. There is an elfin wistfulness about you that is very appealing. And, if you don't mind my saying so, you ears did stick out a bit, didn't they? I am sure you did everything you were told in those days, and observed strictly what must have been a strict school discipline. Life has its disciplines, too. You were no rebel against conventions in those days, of that I am sure, but you have become one since. This is why I am writing.

You grew into a beautiful woman. You were talented, intelligent, charming, but never lost the bubbling mischief and curiosity of the young girl. I heard of your marriage with profound pleasure and my heart warmed towards your husband for his good taste in choosing my favourite niece for his bride . . . I was shocked when, a few years later, I learned that you had left him and returned to your parents with your two babies. I felt you should not have done that. I heard the story, but it seemed to me, judging the case from a distance, that the man was ill of a sickness that needed not the attention of a hospital but the care and devotion of his wife. You gave him that for a time but were not prepared to go on doing it. You broke a vow made before God, and that can never be right. You made two mistakes, the first in marrying a man you did not wholly love, the second and greater in deserting him in his trouble. With patience you could have made him well, but instead you left him to rot. I myself was once very ill with a sort of nervous and mental exhaustion, for a long time – it was during the Occupation, when I lost my business and we all suffered not only privation but a great loss of pride – and I must have been quite insufferable. But Joanna never left my side, and you see I am today winning prizes at flower shows and a happy man. Joanna does not know I am writing to you: she is sitting by the fire, knitting something for me for the winter. It has been a good life, with her. I am very grateful.

Back home, you spent the early years bringing up the children. They were your whole life, and you spared yourself nothing and sacrificed much to prepare them for the world they must enter. You were a devoted mother, and not only a mentor but a companion. The two girls, now grown up and attractive and confident and assured, are themselves testimony to what they owe to you. They are a mirror of yourself. All of us who knew the unhappy background, the loneliness you must often have felt but had to hide from the children, feel wonderfully proud of you. You showed rare courage and determination. Your children do you credit.

It was the natural instinct of a mother that prompted your care and attention for Jane and Anne. But you had another natural instinct: the instinct of a woman to show tenderness and affection to people to whom you were attracted, sometimes because of their own inherent charm, sometimes because of some attribute that appealed to you.

I now hear, with dismay, that you are sick of an old passion. I beg of you to say no. You are not entitled to any man but your husband. You are not entitled to say that life has given you a raw deal and you must find happiness where you can get it. Can you look at Jane and Anne and truthfully say that life has given you a raw deal? Can you think of the hundreds of women in your own town who must envy you the opportunities and achievements and experiences you have had, and still say that life has given you a raw deal? Of course it hasn't. You have a better life than most. It is not complete, but it would be folly to wreck what you have and opt for anything less permanently satisfying. You are approaching the age when you will want only to be peacefully settled in your own home, to enjoy the security you have earned and have the love and respect of your children and friends. You won't want men throwing pebbles at the windows. The present unrest you feel will die, and when it does you must not find yourself stranded in strange surroundings. To embark now on a voyage of endless drifting with no harbour in sight, to jettison dignity and pride and self-respect as you go, is asking for shipwreck. Please don't do it. If you hurt yourself you hurt Jane and Anne and all of us. You are a limb of the family tree; when you are distressed so are we all. We love you.

Stay with old Red. He's dotty about you, we know. But at least he's harmless.

Joanna has been looking at me over her spectacles these past few minutes, but saying nothing. She must be wondering what I am doing. I have lost track of time while I have been writing, but dusk has fallen and the street lamps are lit. It must be past the hour for supper, so I must end my letter before Joanna gets too curious. I has been just between the two of us, this letter, you and me. You will have decided that I am an old busybody, meddling in your private affairs when I have no right to. But I have, dear. I have that right because I love you. And I want to go on thinking of you as the embodiment of all a good woman should be. That's why I've written. I know you will not disappoint me.

Your devoted Uncle Hans

Betty replied in the same style, as if she were his niece, trying to explain her worries and confusions about her feelings for AW – and for other people.

After months of being convinced it was all off, that Betty was moving out of his life, the year was ending on a better note, apart of course from the divorce procedings, which were growing nastier all the time.

LETTER 139: TO BETTY, 23 NOVEMBER 1967

Wednesday

Betty NcNally, I am going to hug you next time we meet. Yes, strong and purposeful, that's me. A man who does not waver in his intentions, a man of iron resolution . . .

My mind was quite firm. I had asked her not to write, and I was determined that, if she did, I would return the letter unopened. Without hesitation, back it would go to her. This was an inflexible decision . . . what was the point, anyway, in listening to anything she had to tell me? I had no way of knowing whether to believe or disbelieve, and I had been on the rack of doubt and despair long enough. For deceit there can be no forgiveness, and for untruths no pardon. Yes, I would send it back unopened. That would teach her a lesson she would never forget. But, Betty, I was also a man in love, and a man in love cannot be disciplined. Sight of your familiar handwriting on the envelope was too much to be borne with indifference. Your letter was torn open eagerly, as all others have been. It was not addressed to me, even, but I claimed a power of attorney for your uncle, and besides I wanted desperately to know what you had to tell him. You are a very clever little girl. You respect my wish not to correspond, but write to me by proxy. That lets me out of my iron resolve, too, and without loss of face, because how could I return a letter that was never sent to me?

So I read your letter with no sense of eavesdropping. I cannot now forward it to your Uncle Hans. He died while I was reading it. Betty love, it was a beautiful letter. You chose your words with great care and you meant exactly what you said. It was written at some cost in anguish of mind, and not without some heart-burning. I know, love, I know. You had to refer to past episodes that must have been painful to recall and relate. It was courageous of you to write so openly and frankly. I could not but regard it as an expression of your trust and confidence. I am humbled and contrite. Betty love, I understand now. I didn't before. It had been a bad time for both of us, because when I hurt you, I bleed too. Each of us has something to forgive. I cared for you more than you wanted me to. I was roughly forging ahead too far while you were gently applying a brake. We have been pulling apart . . . of course you are right. It is a matter of balance and adjustment. Somewhere midway we had found a common ground of respect and friendship and affection. We have both strayed from it recently and lost track of each other in a lonely and frightening wilderness. It has made me realise that a life in which you have no part is a life without meaning. You too found, in lesser degree, that you were losing a friend you valued. Now you have called me back, and I come gladly.

Yes, we have our differences of character and outlook and, above all, background. I think you are shallower and more superficial than I, more cautious, but only because you are afraid to venture, to risk a mistake. You don't permit yourself dreams. You are capable of great depth of feeling, but lack the sense of security that would let you express it freely and fully. I too like to keep my feet firmly planted – you have seen me climbing a wall – but that does not stop me from indulging the most heavenly flights of fancy. My dreams become very real, and for two years they have been centred on you. Your influence on me is too profound, I know. I ought not to be so obsessed, I know. But I have liked to have you in my thoughts all the time. When we are friendly, this helps a lot to make a lonely life tolerable; it keeps me happy and inspired even when I am not seeing you. When we are not friendly it makes life hell for me, for I have lost the knack of shutting you out. You are everything to me. I would give my life to save yours. There are social differences of which I am acutely aware: you belong to a class where the common term of affection is 'darling', overworked until it becomes meaningless; in my world we say 'luv' and mean it. Yes, of course there are differences between us, but one complements the other. What I lack, you have. What you lack, I have. Together we are complete.

I will always remember October 1967, not because it was the wettest on record, but because it was the gloomiest. I could not work at the book. I tried once or twice but my gaze would wander through the window to the hills or at the sodden garden. I watched TV without seeing it. If I went out I took my thoughts with me, and they were bleak. Every night I tortured myself by playing Lara's song before going upstairs. There must not be another October 1967.

Let's forget this misunderstanding, please love. Let's not mention it again, and roll a heavy boulder on the buried past. Let's meet again as though it had never happened. I never stopped loving and wanting you in the darkest hours. I declined to see you last Saturday because it seemed to me that another meeting would have meant another parting, and that I could not face. I have a thin skin, and bruise too easily, as you now know. Yet I spent the afternoon hovering around Goat Gap with two apples and a box of liquorice allsorts, just in case. I wanted you to come to me.

Please let me see you soon. Please use the enclosed letter card to tell me when – it is designed to save you time in correspondence. Any time, any day, but soon. I have no other news, except that I have bought a new pair of braces and go to the Palace on November 23rd. I am not given an alternative. Ordinary suit will do. Wish you were going with me to make sure my flies were buttoned up.

In my darkest hours of depression I kept recalling a saying I heard when I was boy, and have never forgotten:

'keep a green bough in thy heart,
And God will send thee a singing bird'

He has, with your letter and gift of books. Bless you.

Red

The card AW enclosed was for them to meet at Ingleton – and he also invited her to the pictures at Morecambe to see South Pacific. But she said she had already seen it.

For his trip to London to receive his MBE he went with his son Peter, who happened to be in England at the time.

LETTER 140: TO BETTY, UNDATED
[On a postcard]

Thursday 12.30pm

WRITING THIS ON EUSTON STATION, HOMEWARD BOUND. UNEXPECTEDLY, EVERYTHING REALLY HAS BEEN SUPER,

AFTER ALL * FAST, QUIET TRAIN * COMFY HOTEL * FIRST
JOURNEY ON THE UNDERGROUND * GOOD MEAL IN LEICESTER
SQUARE * WALKING TOUR OF CENTRAL LONDON * SAW
CAMELOT * GOOD NIGHT'S SLEEP * SAW PETER OFF (RATHER
SADLY) * BUCKINGHAM PALACE INTERIOR MAGNIFICENT *
HAT (3 POUNDS) UNNECESSARY * BUTTONS DOUBLE-CHECKED
* ONE-THIRD IN LOUNGE SUITS * CEREMONDY GLORIOUS, LIKE
HOLLYWOOD SPECTACULAR IN CINEMASCOPE * NOW, BEST OF
ALL, BACK HOME TO MY LOVE, TO COLLECT A PROMISE. SOON,
LOVE X

Part 13
The Divorce, 1966-8

The separation and divorce turned out longer and more complicated than AW had ever expected. He wrote copious letters and notes to his lawyers in Lancaster – picking a firm well away from Kendal, in case there might be any leaks – and kept exact copies of every letter, and their replies, filing them away carefully, as a good municipal accountant should. He was used to writing such letters in his office work, and well understood the bureaucratic mind, but it did not spare him from anger and fury and personal comments when things turned against him.

Things got complicated when Ruth decided to fight the case – and accuse him of various misdeeds. Financially, there were also complications in connection with his charitable contributions – and by now he was giving away a great deal of his royalties to animals. Ruth suspected this might be a ruse to keep money away from her, or was the work of the 'Other Woman', not that Ruth appears to have known who Betty was until it was all over. References to Mary Burkett and her status in the town were mentioned several times in the legal letters flying back and forwards as that rumour continued.

LETTER 141: TO HIS LAWYERS, OCTOBER 1966

38 Kendal Green
Kendal
Your ref: GCH/EM   October 1966

Dear Sirs,

Thank you for your letter of the 12th.

Referring to your first paragraph, it seems that perhaps you read too much into my previous letter, when I said that it appeared likely that my wife and I could agree on my terms. I did not suggest that a reconciliation was likely.

I have given some thought to the two exceptions to my original offer, mentioned in your second paragraph. Dealing with (b) first, this is the matter that led me to say previously that I thought agreement could be reached. Yes, I will give way on this point and offer 7 pounds a week from the date of separation (instead of 5 pounds increasing to 7 pounds at age 65). I must say, however, that I regard the amount as excessive, since it provides much more for my wife than it leaves me for living expenses out of my Corporation pension and especially as she has stated her intention of obtaining employment, but I will concede (subject to what I say later) in expectation that I shall continue to derive royalties during the next five years. If this latter source of incomes ceases I shall be in an impossible position, but the risk is one I am prepared to take to bring these distressing negotiations to a close. Perhaps it would be permissible to draft an 'escape' clause?

With regard to (a), my offer was to provide up to 1000 pounds to buy a house in Blackburn, the title deeds of which could be in joint names so that in the event of the death of one the title would revert to the survivor, and, further, that no rent would be payable for long as my wife remained sole occupier. This offer is so obviously fair and indeed generous that I am completely at a loss to understand why exception is taken to the conditions, which seem to give my wife absolute security. I think I am entitled to an explanation of the reason for the exception taken on this point, and should be pleased if you would try to obtain one.

My wife is not, in fact, now living with me, having left me six weeks ago to rent a cottage temporarily outside Kendal. She is determined not to return, and in view of her insistence on what seems to me an excessive demand, I intend to start divorce proceedings with your kind help and advice. It must be clear that the agreement finally arrived at does not preclude me from taking such proceedings (you have promised to safeguard my position in this respect), and I am wondering further whether the whole agreement should not be stated as being operative pending the hearing of a divorce action – but perhaps you would consider this superfluous.

I am sorry to write at such length, but wish to avoid a further visit to your office at the present time.

Yours faithfully,

AWainwright

LETTER 142: TO HIS LAWYERS, 8 DECEMBER 1966

Dear Sirs,

In reply to your letter of yesterday's date, I confirm my agreement to the removal from 38 Kendal Green of the items listed in the schedule enclosed therewith.

I am pleased to learn that the preparation of the Separation Agreement is proceeding. There is one matter (which need not delay it), namely, that I want it clearly understood by my wife and her solicitors that I consider myself the aggrieved party in the separation, that I refute absolutely as groundless all allegations of immoral or inconsiderate behaviour admitting only to an incompatability of temperaments, and that the separation has taken place against my wishes and requests. If possible, I would like to see this embodied in the document above my signature; if not possible, I will attach a signed statement to this effect to the document to be read as part of it.

List of goods to be removed from 38, Kendal Green, Kendal
1 display Cabinet including china, glass and wooden utensils in it.
1 Oak Gate leg Table
1 small mahogany Bedside Table
Small table at present in cellar
1 Sinke Oak Wardrobe (property of Mr. Peter Wainwright)
1 tin bedding chest
Ornaments and collection of China and glass and wood animals
Brass Candlesticks
Washing Machine
Personal effects still at 38 Kendal Green.

[Signed R. Wainwright (Mrs)]

LETTER 143: TO HIS LAWYERS, 22 FEBRUARY 1967

38 Kendal Green, Kendal
22nd February 1967.

Dear Sirs

Thank you for your letter of the 20th instant. I note, with some disappointment, that it contains no report of progress towards completion of the maintenance agreement.

Yes, please inform Messrs. Temple and Bargh of my intention to go ahead now with my proposed covenant with the R.S.P.C.A. in view of the long delay that has taken place. I intend to sign a covenant before the end of the current tax year, but costs of erecting the proposed building have first to be worked out. It appears that the cost will be considerably less than I had originally thought, because of a restriction in layout imposed by the Society's Headquarters, and the amount of the covenant will, therefore, probably be less than the amount I first offered. If Messrs Temple and Bargh still wish to restrain me from legitimately spending money I have legitimately earned they must be prepared to argue the point with the Society's legal advisers in London. I think you should inform them also that when I originally offered a covenant (to be paid exclusively out of royalties on my books) my wife stated that she did not want any of this money for her own use. I doubt whether her solicitors are aware of this.

I think you should inform them also of my intention to start divorce proceedings, my wife having now informed me that she has no intention of returning to me, and that I am persuaded to this course of action in order to disprove publicly the untrue and unfounded allegations she has made to support her unjustified desertion.

You will already, no doubt, have made known to my wife's solicitors the contents of my Will, made ten years ago, leaving everything to my wife. I can understand that this disclosure must have been disconcerting to them having regard to their insistence that I bequeath her only a part of my estate. Please return this Will in due course.

I think we have been on the defensive long enough and should take over the offensive. If you have no explanation of the delay that is occurring please seek an early acceptance of the terms offered.

Yours faithfully,

AW

Messrs Holden and Wilsons,
Lancaster

LETTER 144: TO HIS LAWYERS, 18 MARCH 1967

38 Kendal Green, Kendal
18 March 1967

Dear Sirs,

Thank you for our letter of the 17th instant., enclosing a copy of Messrs Temple and Bargh's letter of the 15th.

As you had previously suggested, it would now appear that the hold-up in the negotiations is due to my expressed intention of taking divorce proceedings. If this is in fact the case, I am surprised. You will recall that the draft agreement prepared by Messrs Temple and Bargh with the approval of my wife made provision for her in the event of my remarriage and therefore divorce was obviously presumed. If, now, there is objection to divorce, am I to assume the possibility that she might at some future time wish to return to live with me? The impression she has given me is that she will not. Please ask for a definite statement of her intentions.

In my view, there is clearly no possibility of reconciliation and the marriage should be ended. The question of re-marriage is not at present in my mind, but, as I have said before, I want to be in a position to re-marry if my future circumstances should make this desirable, the obvious example being some failing in health that makes it difficult for me to continue to live alone.

Please communicate my comments to Messrs Temple and Bargh, or send them a copy of this letter if you prefer. Please ask them to say definitely, yes or no, whether my offers for a private settlement are rejected, and, if they are, urge them to refer the matter to Court with as little further delay as possible. My objection hitherto to a reference to Court has been due to a reluctance to submit testimony against my wife, but I am now more inclined to the view that the matter should be brought into the open and both sides of the story heard. I question, but do not really know, whether the Court would have jurisdiction to restrain me from taking divorce action, which seems to be the object in mind.

I have no knowledge of my wife's present state of health, which has not been good recently, and if it would cause her further distress if I were to commence proceedings in the near future I would be prepared to wait until after the end of the three-year period of desertion and then rely on the grounds of desertion only unless the petition was contested. This is the only concession I am prepared to make in the matter of divorce.

Please request an early decision, one way or the other.

Yours faithfully,

Messrs Holden and Wilsons
Lancaster

LETTER 145: TO HIS LAWYERS, 15 NOVEMBER 1967

38 Kendal Green, Kendal
15t November 1967
Your Ref: GCH/EM

Dear Sirs,

I am disappointed to learn from your letter of the 9th instant that my offer for a financial settlement arising out of the proposed divorce proceedings has been rejected. This offer, taken as a whole, was in my view generous, and it is now becoming clear from my wife's uncompromising demands that her intention is not so much to secure an adequate allowance for herself as to deprive me, to the fullest extent she can, of the rewards earned from a working life of 47 years. I now propose to accede to her demand for an annual maintenance of 500 pounds.

I repeat the offer to pay to my wife for her own use the sum of 4000 pounds upon the divorce becoming absolute, and accept the fact that this money will be entirely at her discretion. The suggestion that she would derive no income from it is patently absurd, unless indeed she is so improvident and irresponsible as to dispose of it at once upon receipt. The object of the capital sum is obviously to ensure additional income from its investment during her lifetime, particularly in the event of my prior death. I have no doubt she will be so advised by her solicitors.

Additionally I will pay an annual maintenance allowance of 500 pounds gross, half-yearly in advance from the date the divorce becomes absolute. It will be appreciated that, as this would be in the nature of an annual payment of fixed amount, I may be required by the Inland Revenue to deduct tax at the standard rate and pay over such deductions to them, in which event my wife would need to make an annual claim for repayment.

Additionally I will provide for a weekly allowance of 2 pounds to be paid from my estate upon death and to continue thence during my wife's remaining lifetime.

The position we have now arrived at is that my wife will have an allowance equivalent to 10 pounds weekly, plus 5 pounds interest on her capital, a total of 15 pounds, disregarding entirely her potential earning capacity, which, at this stage, I do not wish to press. (incidentally, the weekly amount agreed between the parties at the time of desertion was 7 pounds). I myself would be left with the balance of my pension, 10 pounds, which, after deduction to tax, is sufficient only to meet the cost of maintaining the house. For living expenses I would be entirely dependent upon an uncertain and variable income from royalties, and in the matter of continued publication of my books I am at the mercy of my publishers; quite clearly I must go on working as long as my health permits in order to secure a standard of living that must, at best, be inferior to that of my wife.

With regard to the deletion of certain clauses in the present petition, I am sure an acceptable compromise can be reached, but it is interesting to note the view expressed that, without their inclusion, the petition would probably not succeed. What is being said, in effect, is that if the untruths were omitted no cause for desertion could be established. Clause 7 (e) is known by my wife's solicitors to be untrue, and clauses (c) and (d) will also be disproved if the petition is heard. Clause (b) is so wickedly untrue that, if the truth were disclosed in Court, as it certainly would be, it is likely that the petition would be dismissed on this point alone. I appreciate that deletion of these clause would create a difficulty for my wife's solicitors in sifting the hallucinations from the facts, but the only assurance I can give is that I would not defend any other complaints that my wife honestly believes to be true and is prepared to testify on oath, although no doubt I would probably privately disagree.

The revised proposals contained in this letter meet my wife's demands and I expect them to be accepted, but if they are not, there will be no point in continuing negotiations out of Court. In this event I would like an assurance that she fully understands the consequences of non-acceptance.

Yours faithfully

Messrs Holden and Wilsons,
2 Castle Hill, Lancaster

*In December, AW was asked to give his own account of his marital history –
and also to reply to some allegations about him which Ruth had made. He let
Betty read his account before he sent it off to the lawyer.*

LETTER 146: TO HIS LAWYERS, DECEMBER 1967

FURTHER OBSERVATIONS OF THE RESPONDENT
The marital history generally:

The marriage, contracted in Blackburn in 1931, has never been entirely happy, but was reasonably so for a few years, especially after the birth of the child. The husband was deeply involved with studies for professional examinations, which, at a cost of my years' sacrifice of leisure time, he finally passed successfully and with distinction. Having completed his studies he found himself unable to relax and turned his attention to other pursuits, particularly writing and drawing. He advanced in his profession and was disappointed that his wife did not improve herself educationally and go forward with him. Both preferred a quiet life: the wife had her own friends but the husband made few social contacts, being of a more solitary nature. The War, however, brought changes that took him out of the house much more: overtime due to staff shortages and Home Guard duties, for example, but more particularly he became involved in the formation of the Blackburn Rovers Supporters' Club, as Secretary and Treasurer, which not only took much of his spare time but introduced him to many friendly people with a very different way of life, these new contacts leading to many late nights out. Because of this, his wife left him for a short time in 1941 but returned.

On his transfer to Kendal in 1941, and now amongst strangers, life was very quiet and the family went out more together, then the husband was given extraneous duties in connection with the war effort, which took up much of his spare time, but as the wife was now friendly with many of the neighbours, life went on fairly smoothly. After the War the husband returned more seriously to landscape drawing, going out on the fells for his subjects with his son as constant companion. Upon appointment as Borough Treasurer in 1948 it became necessary to vacate his Council house and he had a house built in another district of the town, a change the wife was to regret. With his duties now more onerous, and the need for an 'escape' from them in his leisure time to occupy his mind, the husband developed an idea he had long had in view, and started to write a series of guide-books to the Lakeland Fells, devoting to the task almost every hour of his leisure. These books were successful, bringing him in due course a national repute that was finally recognized by the award of the M.B.E in 1967. They also brought a spate of correspondence and he was kept fully occupied. In 1968 the son, having also done well in examinations, obtained a post overseas, and this undoubtedly brought an emptiness into his wife's hitherto-active life. She had no interest at all in her husband's leisure activity but did not appear to resent it and developed her own interests and friendships. The husband, now nearing retirement, completed his series of book in 1965 and started others. Towards the end of that year, and quite unexpectedly, he was utterly shocked to be told by his wife that she wanted a separation. She had not been well for some months, being in a mood of depression, and moved into her own bedroom, the husband raising no objection. The matter of separation was not again referred to until, several months later, the husband was distressed by a visit from a local solicitors' agent with the news that the wife, unknown to him, had instructed them to start proceedings. Finally, against his wishes, she left the house on September 11th 1966.

The marriage has broken down for various reasons. The husband has always led a very full and active life, which the wife could not, or did not want to, share; she was, however, quite contented until the withdrawal of the son from the home, which left her lonely. She was always a devoted mother and an excellent house-keeper, but a disappointing wife. There was no true communion with the husband and: they had grown away from each other. The only welcome the husband got on coming home from work was from the dog. Never did she ever say she was proud of, or even pleased with, the husband's achievements; there was never a word of encouragement or congratulation on his efforts. There was, probably, a growing sense of frustration that he should be kept so busy while she had so few outlets and interests, and the husband's view of her subsequent desertion is that she ran away not from his shortcomings but from her own while in a state of mental or nervous depression.

– – –

On the specific complaints:

(a) see previous comments on the marital history

(b) no further comments, but I admit to a liking for a shapely leg!

(c) The proof will be available around 1970 (probable publication year).

(d) The woman concerned is highly respected and occupies a responsible post which could be jeopardized by scandal. As a completely innocent party her name (which is known to the 'opposition', as she herself is) must be kept out of the proceedings. This was no secret mission! Her staff turned out to see us off.

(e) This was to have been a reward to my wife for her forbearance! Because of it she circulated stories that I did not intend to make provision for her. This is disproved by my Will of 1956, which leaves every penny to her, and by my forfeiture of part of my personal pension to provide a widow's pension in the event of my prior death.

(f) My wife, who is terrified of cancer, had a bad scare about two years ago when she suspected a cancer in the neck which happily proved to be not a cancer at all. I date her subsequent depression from this time. It is not stated in the Petition that she ceased to live as a wife much earlier than the date of desertion.

And (g) no further comment

ALLEGATIONS

That the Respondent has, since the celebration of said marriage, treated the petitioner with cruelty

(a) that the Respondent is a man of selfish, withdrawn and sullen personality and disposition who, for long periods of time, has refused to converse with the Petitioner; who has shown scant and increasingly less interest in her, her happiness and general well-being and who has regarded the Petitioner as being but a housekeeper, domestic worker and convenience.

RESPONSE: This complaint is exaggerated and misleading. Respondent agrees that he has always been pre-occupied with his own interests, which have, for the past 15 years, been confined exclusively to his work and the writing of books, but the Petitioner did not complain of this at any time although she did not, and could not, share these interests. He had never refused to converse, but agrees there has been no exchange of confidences between them for many years, partly because of the nature of his appointment as a public official. He admits to having a quiet, reserved and withdrawn manner, but is neither selfish nor sullen, being of a generous nature and of a happy disposition, as his books testify.

LETTER 147: TO HIS LAWYERS, 6 DECEMBER 1967

38 Kendal Green, Kendal
6th December 1967

Dear Sirs,

I have received your letter of the 5th instant, and am pleased to note that the financial arrangements for an undefended divorce petition are agreed. This I regard as the major difficulty out of the way. (Please confirm that you stated the 500 pound annual allowance as a <u>gross</u> payment; if, however, you forwarded a copy of my letter containing the offer, this point will be clear).

The <u>grounds</u> of complaint I regard only as a minor difficulty. I have already said that I will not defend any allegations my wife honestly believes to be true and is prepared to testify on oath (whether true or not), and I abide by my word. In order to secure an early divorce, and assuming it is understood that acquiescence is not necessarily an admission of guilt, I am prepared to accept the decision of Messrs Temple and Bargh in this matter.

I now trust that a final agreement can be quickly reached and that the present petition will be withdrawn and substituted by one for divorce.

Yours faithfully

LETTER 148: TO HIS LAWYERS, 12 DECEMBER 1967

Your Ref: GCH/EM   38 Kendal Green, Kendal
12th December 1967

Dear Sirs,

Now that the terms of divorce are settled, I would like an assurance from Messrs Temple and Bargh that I may enter into covenants or make donations to charities without interference on their part.

Yours faithfully

AW's divorce became official on June 24 1968. He was found guilty of mental cruelty and had to pay Ruth a lump sum of £4000 and £500 a year during her life time.

Betty was by now also divorced, so they were able to go openly on holiday to Scotland. Betty had now decided not to go to London to complete an extra year for her SRN training.

In October 1968, AW rewrote his will, which he presented in an envelope to Betty, but with strict instructions that she should not open the envelope until his death.

LETTER 149: TO BETTY, 14 OCTOBER 1968

To be opened only upon the death of Mr A. Wainwright

Mrs Betty McNally
Fowl Ing House,
Kendal

Not to be opened by any other person

<u>To Mrs Betty McNally</u>   14th October 1968

Dear Betty,

I have today made a Will in which I have provided that the residue of my estate and all income from royalties after my death shall, subject only to the deduction of the expenses of my Trustees, accrue to you and, after payment of income tax, be applied at your absolute discretion,

Firstly, towards maintaining the standard of life to which you have been accustomed;

Secondly, in continuing the annual payment of 15 pounds to Mr P.J.L Hindle of 3 All Souls Terrace, Haley Hill, Halifax, to enable him to take a holiday each year in the Lake District;

Thirdly, in replenishing from time to time the fund administered by the management of the Border Hotel, Kirk Yetholm, for Pennine Way walkers

Fourthly, in making anonymous donations to animal charities which have as their primary object the care of animals, especially working animals, that would otherwise be put to sleep.

These are my wishes, but you are free to use the money entirely as you think fit.

In the event of your not wishing at any time to undertake this distribution please inform Mr C.G. Howson, of Messrs Holden and Wilsons, Solicitors, 2 Castle Hill, Lancaster, and let him have the enclosed envelope to pass to Mr Firth (who will continue to act according to the instructions it contains) without disclosing to Mr Firth that you have hitherto been the recipient of this money.

Goodbye, love, and thanks for a thousand kindnesses.

If there <u>is</u> another life, I will be waiting for you.

Red

Part 14
Letters to Molly, 1968–70

While all these personal dramas were going on, AW was still working away on his books. The Pennine Way Companion was published in 1968 and he then started working on a series of Lakeland Sketchbooks.

In 1968, he also agreed to do the illustrations for a children's book which Molly Lebebure had written. He was still in contact with Molly, still without having met her, writing her amusing and sometimes flirtatious letters, despite the arrival of Betty, but he never mentions Betty by name or refers to his divorce.

Molly had written a story about an expedition of cats to a great mountain – on the lines of the Everest Expedition, only set on Scafell. She sent him the manuscript and he did her some sketches. Her agent had never heard of AW, but her publisher had, Livia Gollancz, who was a Lake District lover.

There then started a lengthy correspondence about the illustrations with AW being rather stroppy, trying to impose his views and knowledge. The book was originally going to be called 'Red Rowan's Paw of Friendship', which AW hated. Miss Gollanz did not it like either, and the title was changed to Scratch and Co. It was published in the UK in 1968 with some success, and in France and the USA. (In those countries, the publishers had not heard of Wainwright and commissioned their own illustrations.)

LETTER 150: TO MOLLY LEFEBURE, UNDATED, 1968

THE DIAGRAM OF THE ROUTE OF THE EXPEDITION
You persist in calling this a map, which it isn't. It is a diagram.

I have made the snowline occur at about 2000', just about the level of Sprinkling Tarn. You were right about snow being easier to draw than fields of boulders; in fact, snow doesn't have to be drawn at all. The result is that the higher mountains are left white except where smooth ground

is interrupted by crags or heavy scree, and this permits a clearer definition of the route.

I had many doubts about the Cat Kingdom flag. Reading your letter
of instructions it seemed that you had intended to let me have a rough
design but omitted to do so; then, on a second reading, it seemed that you
wanted me to have a shot at it, which I have done; but now I am wondering whether the narrative itself contains details of the design and I failed to
notice the passage. If this is so, you must amend the story, or make it clear
that a special expedition flag was used in addition to the national flag.

You may notice a small patch on the diagram near Stockley Bridge.
This hides a burn mark caused by my pipe spilling onto the paper in a
moment of tense excitement, but will not show on the printed picture.

The diagram has been drawn to bleed, but if Livia wants a margin
half-an-inch can be sliced off the left-hand edge without loss of anything
material except the name 'Esk Hause', which is not really important,
being mentioned once only in the story.

THE BOOK JACKET

It's the title that gives me the pip. It is clumsy, and too long. Worse, it
must be spread over two lines, the first ending in a blessed apostrophe-
ess, which is shockingly bad. 'Red Rowan's Paw' on the first line and 'Of
Friendship' on the second is worse still. The book obviously should be
titled RED ROWAN, quite simply; then it could appear in bold stark lettering. I, too, have conducted a consumer research in the matter, my sample
for interrogation being a most attractive woman, and she agrees with me
absolutely. I think your title is untidy, too long to endure into immortality, and ill conceived. RED ROWAN is good, pithy, remilerable.

You know I have doubts about the drawing appearing in colour. You
have already told me that the bookshops insist on coloured jackets for
children's books. My own view is that you are more likely to sell well
by being original and not conforming to pattern, certainly not a pattern dictated by booksellers. In this particular case, you are describing
a bold adventure, an expedition into (for cats) uncharted territory, and
the cover should suggest something of the old scrolls and maps used
in Drake's days, which were roughly hand-drawn with flourishes, and
certainly not in three or four colours. As I have told you before, if you
leave the colouring to a printer who has never seen anything higher than
Box Hill he will paint Scafell Crag a violent green, which no part of it is:
it is grey and brown and ochre, never green. He will colour Red Rowan
in puce, not recognising him as a fox (can't really blame him for that),

and he will colour our lovely snow-covered ledges and terraces daffodil yellow . . . well, it's your pigeon. You've decided on colour. So be it. I disagree.

LETTER 151: TO MOLLY LEFEBURE, 2 DECEMBER 1968

38 Kendal Green, Kendal
2nd December 1968

Dear Molly,

Can you ever forgive me?

I take back all I said. I was ruthlessly unkind to you.

I have just seen your photograph in an Ambleside bookshop.

Such an open and frank and honest countenance.

Such grace, such charm. No trace of the ravages of alchohol.

Such a well-proportioned figure (upper half only visible).

Indeed, such beauty. An Anglo-Franco rose, no less.

I have been a blind fool. What do scraggy thighs matter, after all?

I think you are super.

Incidentally, there is a Scottish terrier in the picture with you. Hamish, no doubt. But the caption to the picture says 'Molly Lefebure and Scratch'.

Enclosed is a review of 'Scratch & Co' from the Westmorland Gazette of a few weeks ago, which you may not have seen. I hope the book is selling well.

I had a wonderful holiday in Scotland, the best ever. Partly and primarily due to the attractiveness of my companion, who has all your good looks and thighs as well. We went in a car, she driving, me tickling her ears and enjoying the scenery. Which, even as late as the end of October, was superb. After the mild summer, the leaves were still on the trees, making a most gorgeous riot of yellows and reds and bronzes. I withdraw what I have said before, that Lakeland is lovelier than the Highlands of Scotland. It isn't. In fact, after seeing the Scottish glens in autumn, it beats me why people rave about the Lake District.

Tell me I am forgiven, even after saying that.

Tell me we are good friends again.

Tell me anything, except that you have gone off me.

I think you are super.

AW

The photo AW had seen of Molly shows her with her dog Hamish.

AW and Molly then made plans to do further children's books set in the Lake District, though only one more was ever published: The Hunting of Wilberforce Pike, which came out in 1970.

LETTER 152: TO MOLLY LEFEBURE, 2 APRIL 1969

38 Kendal Green, Kendal
2nd April 1969

Dear Molly,

No, I'm not dead.

I've been frenetically busy, that's why.

But really I should have replied to your last letter much earlier than this, and thanked you for the gorgeous photograph. It's super. Such an appealing pose, such grooming, such charm, such wistfulness and yearning in those soft eyes! Yes, I could fall for Hamish. You're not half bad yourself, either. Thank you for this picture.

I've been frenetically busy because a deadline has been set for the two books I am doing, and, as usual, I am pressed for time. I have undertaken to finish A LAKELAND SKETCHBOOK (which, incidentally, is now planned to be the first of a series of five companion volumes – if enough people buy it) by June 30th for publication on September 30th, and WALKS IN LIMESTONE COUNTRY by the end of the year for publication next Easter. In addition I have resumed my assault on the garden, and, in an attempt to make the desert blossom as the rose, I have turned over much virgin ground and planted 600 bulbs and plants, not a single one of which is as yet showing any signs of life. Waiting to be done is the laying of a parquet floor, and the writing up of an acquisition book for Abbot Hall Art Gallery.

So I received your commission for the illustrating of two new Scratch books with some consternation. You know jolly well I can't refuse you anything, and I'll have a shot at hem, utterly regardless of my own convenience, but I do hope you'll proceed tardily with the writing of them. Yes, Dove Crag would be a fine place for the wilful murder of the cat-thieves by Scratch and Co., and there are some mammoth boulders crowned with lush vegetation just below the rocks that would serve as hiding places and vantage points for the ambush. I should need to go there again for pictures, not having any photographs of the crag (it's almost always in deep shadow). Or there is Deer Bield Crag in Easedale

– another good spot for a dark deed, with Easedale Tarn handy to throw the bodies in. Or what about a chase up Jack's Rake on Pavey Ark, which everybody knows and would recognise from your description, with a watery bier in Stickle Tarn? Let's make it a really gruesome murder – eyes scratched out, ears torn off, guts hanging out, etc., I think that cat-thieves should suffer horrific deaths. And folk who send dogs for vivisection. So I am all for a bit or moralising.

For the third book I am not so sure about the Coniston mines. Remember that these are mainly straight shafts and therefore could not be used by cats. (You might get into trouble, too, for giving publicity to these death traps, as happened to me; there's talk of filling up the holes, anyway). Better for feline adventures would be the Tilberthwaite or Little Langdale slate quarries, where access is gained by horizontal tunnels – there are some beauties on the fellside above Slaters Bridge, and here too is Lanty Slee's Cave, in which you could have an hilarious interlude as Scratch and Co. try their hand (paw) at whisky distilling.

Sorry you won't let me do a drawing of L.HS but I will, someday, just the same. I'll come heavily disguised, with an unshaven chin, limping and wearing a tattered raincoat (perhaps not such a heavy disguise, now I come to think of it). I may knock at the door and ask the way up Robinson. Merely to get a peep at dear old Hamish, of course. Such a sweet little fellow. Such grooming, such charm . . .

AW

LETTER 153: TO MOLLY LEFEBURE, 30 MAY 1969

> 38 Kendal Green
> KENDAL
> 30th May 1969

Dear Molly,

Correspondence between us would be more facile if I knew where the hell you were living at any given time. You send me a letter from Surbiton and I naturally reply to Surbiton and then you write from L.H.S to ask why haven't I written and then I write to L.H.S to say I have and then comes a letter from Surbiton to see if I'm ill. THIS letter I shall address to Surbiton. I expect your next to come from L.H.S . . . No, I am not ill. Judging by recent performances of one sort of another I am in the prime of life.

The letter I am now replying to came from Surbiton and was written in your very best vein, full of choice turns of phrase ('swirling cloud which occasionally lifted sufficiently to show the magnificent Mrs Shepperd perched like a sentinel on the ridge') with scant regard for grammar ('which' should be 'that' in the quote); of graphic description ('off into the sluicing downpour we sloshed'); of juicy anecdotes in the dialect ('it were t'muck smoking, like') of word inventiveness ('edentulous'; 'yoiked'). A richly humorous letter describing hilarious situations: the sort you do better than anyone else. I don't reckon much of your children's books even though they go mad about them in Chicago (it's the illustrations that sell them, I always think), and in your serious delvings into history and tradition you are merely following others, less worthy no doubt, but your true forte is humorous story-telling and I am surprised you do not launch forth as a female Jerome K. Jerome and beat him hollow at his own game. 'Three Women In A Tent', set in flooded Borrowdale, is simply crying out for your attention. I have kept all your correspondence. I wish you'd be quick and die and then I could pick up a fortune by publishing posthumously 'The Letters Of Molly Lefebure', They'd go mad about this in Sarawak.

Incidentally, I don't want to charge you with double-crossing me, but didn't we agree that the Cumbrian Literary Society was a collection of undersexed morons, or something of the sort? You only have to write a four-line 'Ode to a Pansy' to get into that mob, and it needn't even rhyme. Yet I find that, according to their syllabus, they are to be addressed this summer by Mollie (yes Moll_ie_) Lefebure, the author (sic.). Shame on you, turncoat! If you see in your audience a man not wearing a white carnation in his buttonhole it won't be me. I stick to my principles. Anyway, since you have committed yourself, don't forget to remind them that Wainwright's Guides are obtainable in all good bookshops in the district. I don't know what's come over you. Even Griffin has addressed the Cumbrian Literary Society, and you can't get any lower than that.

Yes, as I promised before (I don't change my mind) I will do you the honour of illustrating your second cat book, but not until the end of July. I will do a jacket showing the cat-thief hanging on to an imaginary precipice on Striding Edge with a bunch of cats hissing and spitting at him and clawing his clutching fingertips (they'll howl in Lyons when they see this). I will draw a map of their wandering for a frontispiece. I will do up to a dozen tailpieces. Livia's generous fee should be sent to the Bleakholt Animal Sanctuary, Ramsbottom, Lancs, the patron of which, by the way, is the Duchess of Argyll, Margaret, the third existing of that ilk, of whose exploits you will doubtless have heard. I have met her by invitation at a remote rendezvous on a desolate Lancashire hillside (what better place for it?) and returned unsullied from the encounter. Livia's fee will buy food for her poor unwanted animals, for which she has a quite genuine compassion . . . So, you see, I can now number the nobility amongst my acquaintances as well as lesser fry like authors of cat books.

Love and so forth, as you so naively put it. Old Gerrish won't last for ever. Hand in hand we may still climb Dale Head together, just you and me and the magnificent Mrs Shepperd.

AW

AW could be rather cruel about Molly's childrens books, but she said she was not upset. It was just his way. AW really did meet the Duchess of Argyll, through the animal charity Bleakholt Animal Sanctuary, of which she was the Patron. He and Betty helped them a lot, after he had finally fallen out with the RSPCA and the collapse of his suggested animal refuge.

The reference to Mrs Shepperd concerns a rumour about a well known member of the local hunt. According to local gossip she and her husband slept with a badger in their bed, which led to various confusions in the night.

LETTER 154: TO MOLLY LEFEBURE, 2 AUGUST 1969

38 Kendal Green, KENDAL
2nd August 1969

Dear Molly,

Please confirm that you are not dead.

If you are, there is not much point in reading further, and I would just like to say how deeply sorry I am. Right in the prime of life, too, and at the peak of performance. I am sadly distressed.

If you are not, then I am writing to say that I am ready to draw cats, having just completed my book of drawings and before I resume my shelved epic on the limestone country.

I feel very alone. I haven't heard from you for ages. I know you can't write to me if you're dead, but damn, after all we've been to each other, you might at least try to appear before me as a spirit.

Farewell, if necessary,

AW

LETTER 155: TO MOLLY LEFEBURE, 8 APRIL 1970

38 Kendal Green, Kendal
8th April 1970

Dear Moll,

They say exchange is no robbery, and here is my swap for the copy of your classic CUMBRIAN HERITAGE, which is very good indeed, obviously the result of much painstaking research and unrecognizable as the product of the same brain that gave birth to the much less distinguished legends of Scratch and Co. I enjoyed it immensely, and my apprehension that you may have courted notoriety by denouncing me as a fake who describes as coachroads rough tracks where coaches have never passed was, happily, without foundation. You are very kind to me. You could have exposed me as counterfeit, but you generously refrained. I am still sceptical about the gutter on Sty Head Pass, which I prefer to regard as a pristine part of the original roadway. However, a very fine book, the result of much hard work and an entertaining and instructive account of Cumberland as it used to be. Now say something nice about WALKS IN LIMESTONE COUNTRY, out this week.

Also enclosed, in a separate envelope; couldn't squash everything in one, to make you furious with rage, is the newly-issued Directory of Northern Writers, which includes your friend Dudley Hoys but excludes yourself. But you are in good company. Griffin, too, is omitted.

Your extremely kind and cordial invitation to LHS at Easter touched me deeply and my callous disregard of it may well mean that it will never be repeated. But in fact the opportunity never arose; the bitter weather kept me indoors, drawing and rugging, and although I am now almost back to normal (i.e., back to smoking) I have only once ventured out into the country, this to walk the Whinfell ridge between Shap and the Tebay roads for a couple of miles or so to give me a start on WALKS ON THE HOWGILL FELLS. I felt none the worse, but my powers are disgustingly diminished, what with bronchial pneumonia and wedlock.

Incidentally, while honeymooning at York, I paid a first visit to the North Yorks Moors area. Not bad, not bad. I might yet do a COAST TO COAST WALK, St. Bees Head to Robin Hood's Bay, crossing Lakeland, using the newly-created Dales Way into Yorkshire and ending with parts of both the Lyke Wake Walk and the Cleveland Way.

You will be dying to learn of my progress with the rug, and I am pleased to report that, as a result of diligent application, over 20,000 knots have now been completed and the whole should be finished within a fortnight. Then I hope to have it displayed on exhibition at many of the provincial galleries. It is by far the greatest of my accomplishments. If I am remembered, it will be because of the rug.

I assume you have now fled the bitter Northern weather are now back in suburbia.

AW

AW and Betty got married at Kendal Town Hall on 10 March 1970 – so at last AW started writing about Betty by name. Molly invited him and Betty to her home – but so far AW had not managed to get there.

The references to the Cumbrian writers Dudley Hoyes and Harry Griffin are all scurrilous – AW amusing himself by suggesting Molly was having affairs with them. She hadn't even met them.

The correct title of Molly's latest book was Cumberland Heritage published by Gollancz in 1970. 'Mr A Wainwright' is listed in the Acknowledgements.

LETTER 156: TO MOLLY LEFEBURE, 24 MAY 1970

38 Kendal Green, KENDAL
24th May 1970

Dear Molly,

Thank you for two entertaining letters and a well-deserved congratulatory telegram. I would have written earlier but found that a further period of convalescence was necessary after my rug affliction. Following such a sustained effort with a latchet hook I was quite unable to manipulate either pen or typewriter. I was making knots in my sleep and seriously disrupting normal marital relations. My fingers still sometimes go through the motions.

The really bitter pill was that the damned thing, when finally completed, couldn't be used as intended because it slipped all over the parquet floor and was in fact positively dangerous. It is doomed to spend its days ignominiously under a table firmly pinned down by the table legs and four chairs. Never again. I keep seeing better rugs in the shops at half the price. Ready made, too. 220 hours of my life have been wasted.

Otherwise I am just about back to normal (i.e. smoking like a chimney) and getting around again. Latterbarrow (803') and Hallin Fell (1291') have both been conquered in recent weeks without undue distress. I have remained modest about these achievements and kept the news out of the press. And last week I paid a first visit to Black Force near Sedbergh in furtherance of my super new book (not yet started): WALKS ON THE HOWGILL FELLS. The going was arduous without the encouragement and help of a faithful, devoted and admiring new wife this expedition might well have failed. I must say I am enjoying having a faithful, devoted and admiring new wife (with a car). Not without good reason, she thinks I'm wonderful.

Betty is more than ever determined to get me up to L.H.S after learning of your extremely kind invitation to me to meet Livia there. But I'm afraid Livia must be denied the pleasure of meeting the man who has come to mean so much to her. Because on Tuesday the 26th we are off to Scotland for ten days, touring the west and north in general and Wester Ross and Sutherland in particular. In the car, of course, with my f, d, and admiring new wife driving and me rubbernecking. Not for me any longer the bourgoise discomforts of bus and train travel. So I'm sorry, but Livia must suffer a wretched frustration. I feel a bit sorry for her, not seeing me. Of course there's always Dudley Hoys, who would do anything for you, or even, as a last resort, Griffin.

I await with impatience he appearance and world preview of THE HUNTING OF WILBERFORCE PIKE, but meanwhile am applying myself diligently to A SECOND LAKELAND SKETCHBOOK, which is well up to schedule and will be out in the autumn. In one drawing in this book L.H.S appears unobtrusively in the background ('Robinson and Hindscarth from Catbells') No, let's get it right: 'Hindscarth and Robinson from Catbells'. Sometime this summer I shall be taking a long look at Newlands Church with the same purpose in mind.

With much of the tourist traffic drained off into limestone country the Lake District is strangely quiet this year, and this has undoubtedly contributed to the nesting of a pair of eagles with two eggs that are due to hatch this weekend. The area is being patrolled by wardens, but the actual site is being kept a dark secret. I know where it is, but all I can tell you is that it is amongst the eastern fells.

Talking about cats, part of the nuptial package deal was that I should take over a feline named Krishna, who has quickly established himself in the household and become the terror of all living creatures in the garden. He is no ordinary cat, but a four-legged monster with an extraordinary penchant for climbing. You don't look for Krishna curled up on the floor somewhere; you look for him on the tops of wardrobes and cupboards and on high windowsills and on any projections from the vertical conveniently near the ceilings. It is somewhat disconcerting to suddenly notice him surveying your steadfastly from some lofty vantage point far above your head. You can't help cowering a little with Krishna. The point is that I now have a model to pose for the illustrations in your next cat book. I have nothing to learn about baleful feline glares and snarls and expressions of utter indifference to entreaties. In repose he sleeps with a big fat smile on his face. No wonder. He's the boss in this establishment and right well he knows it.

I hope you have better weather than you had on the occasion of your last visit. Don't get too involved with Dudley.

AW

AW had taken up rug making after a serious bout of pneumonia and had been told to stay indoors and not do any strenuous exercise for a while. AW hated doing it. When he had eventually finished his rug, he laid it out on the living room floor which was made of highly polished wood. He slipped when walking on it the first time – and injured his leg. So much for recuperative therapy.

LETTER 157: TO MOLLY LEFEBURE, 9 AUGUST 1970

38 Kendal Green, KENDAL
Sunday afternoon, 9th August

Dear Molly, or Molly dear, whichever you prefer

So I finally completed my convalescence the other day with an intrepid ascent of Great Gable from a car parked on Honister Pass and accompanied only by my faithful and adoring new wife, realizing full well that I might drop dead or be smitten by a stroke or develop a palsy or yellow fever or something as a result of the unaccustomed exercise following my long lay-off. I kept glancing at Haystacks where my charred embers will some day be decently scattered, and thinking not yet, buggar; and in fact I not only didn't pass away from lack of breath but completed the ascent in fine style and had enough puff to visit Green Gable, Brandreth and Grey Knotts before returning to the car. I was mightily pleased with my performance. I am a fellwalker again.

Mind you, the summit of Great Gable was no place to be that day. All the decent walkers are doing the limestone country this year, of course, unfortunately leaving in possession of Lakeland an untidy and noisy rabble of school parties and dropouts. You would have thought there was a Pop Festival going on top of Gable. There were hundreds of near-humans draped all over the summit, an noisy, uncouth, illiterate mob with transistors going full blast, and after a brief visit to Westmorland Cairn we fled the place. Green Gable was little better, but Brandreth and Grey Knotts were havens of peace. It was heavenly to recline again in a bed of heather and be damned to the passage of time.

Yesterday I sent off to the printer the last few pages of a super new book entitled A SECOND LAKELAND SKETCHBOOK, and when I have finished this overdue letter to you I shall get cracking on WALKS ON THE HOWGILL FELLS, which, although you have never heard of the Howgill Fells, is likely to become the standard book of reference to that area.

After looking through A CUMBERLAND HERITAGE only cursorily when I first received a copy (due to other pressures at the time) I have recently spent my evenings, apart from watching Coronation Street of course, in a detailed study of the book. The amount of time you must have spend in digging out all that forgotten information is truly amazing, and you have produced a classic here greater even than Scratch & Co. I could have wished you hadn't been so confoundedly dogmatic about the old so-called coach road over to Dockray, or that original unspoilt bit of the Sty Head track, or about the so-called memorial stone to John Bankes, but I suppose you must be right and I should be grateful that you preferred not to name the cheapjacks who spread their spurious fictions around and call them truth. Congratulations on a splendid book. I hope it sells well, but the price of books in general is becoming frightening to those of us who live by the pen, don't you think? And will get worse. From July 1st printing costs jump by 30%, mainly due to big wage increases and paper prices. Books like this last one of yours are gong to cost the public around three guineas in future and even your best friends will sneak off to the Public Library to borrow a copy. Anyway, Jennie Lee said that authors are soon to get royalties on books borrowed from public libraries, so perhaps you will be able to continue to live in the manner to which you are accustomed, booze and all.

You can't tell me anything about the eagles in the Lake District. I know all about them. They have built three eyries for use in alternate season and I know exactly where they are, but I am not going to tell you because you would want to go rubbernecking. This year the hatching was half successful, one baby being reared successfully and it has already taken to the air. I don't think the secret will keep much longer. A Cumberland newspaper has already published a photograph of the nest, or a least of the crag where the nest is.

Your account of the guided mission to Scafell with a distinguished professor from California was a delectable piece of writing. Molly the Sherpa certainly did her stuff all right all right, and Professor Omygosh must have had an adventure he will never forget. No, I can't honestly say that any foreign researchers have ever asked me to guide them. Nor has anybody else, come to think of it. But you are hardly fair to dear old Dudley in saying he doesn't know one end of Cam Spout from t'other. He does, you know, he knows Eskdale better than anyone. Anyway, why so spiteful with old Dudley all at once. Not long ago you were as thick as thieves. He could do no wrong in your eyes. You turned to him when I jilted you in favour of Betty and for months you rammed his virtues down my throat, not that I cared. Now clearly it is all over between you, and posterity will be left not knowing what your true association ever was. There will be speculation, of course. Sometime in the 21st century an avid woman researcher, probably living in a remote farmhouse in a Lakeland valley, will start digging into the dusty logbooks and visitors journals at L.H.S and the Woolpack and interviewing the oldest inhabitants to discover what their grandfathers ever told them about the shriveled little man and the big bosomed florid woman who for a fleeting period of history were thrown together in a mad romance that ended abruptly in mutual abuse and recrimination (I did hear tell as how the woman was half-French).

Each morning I await my free copy of THE HUNTING OF WILBERFORCE PIKE from Livia. It never comes.

LETTER 158: TO MOLLY LEFEBURE, 16 DECEMBER 1970

38 Kendal Green, Kendal
16th December 1970

Dear Molly,

I received your letter, smelling vilely of gin, which no doubt accounted for its general incoherence. The message it purported to convey, if message there was, suffered from a welter of crossings out and misspellings and although I was generous enough to accept your apology for the haste in which it was written, I am left unhappy that your mind could have been in such turmoil and am still confused as to the role I am supposed to play with regard to the third Scratch classic, (sic) which I received safely a few days later. Hitherto your instructions have been reasonably explicit; they must have been penned in lucid intervals when you were off the bottle, but on this occasion you have thrown the thing at me and left me to work out for myself what I'm supposed to do with it.

Nor can I understand your mention of Mr G's desire for the Siamese cat drawing from Wilberforce Pike. I said yes to this request almost a year ago, and in any case never got those drawings back from Livia, not that I wanted such reminders of a shameful episode in my artistic career.

It is good to know, however, that the book has been so well reviewed (can't think why) and my sympathies are with the Halifax reviewer who thought Wilberforce Pike was 2634'. The trouble is that these flattering eulogies only spur you on to do more. I wish you would stick to your Cumberland Heritages and so do something worthwhile for posterity. Scratch and Co are amongst the banalities of life.

Meanwhile I am ranging far and wide over the magnificent Howgills, treading where no man has trod before but where multitudes will tread from Easter 1972 onwards. Now I see that a 168-mile footpath, Offa's Dike, is to be opened next year. This will surely call for a super guidebook, but piling up for early attention are Walking the Border, The Pennine Watershed and a Coast-to-Coast Walk (St. Bees Head to Robin Hoods Bay). I am also committed to one Sketchbook per annum. These, coming on top of the marital duties I am now expected to perform, would exhaust a lesser man. Even so, time presses hard and you can imagine my rage and fury when you blithely command me to illustrate yet another cat book. You have me under your thumb, and well you know it.

All right, then, tell me what you want me to do, and say whether a deferment until 1985 is possible. If Scratch is as immortal as you seem to think, time is of little consequence. But Offa's Dike is urgent and soon there will be a clamour for a Companion to it such as has not been heard since guidance was provided for the Pennine Way.

Okay, okay, what do you want me to do with Loona Balloona apart from the obvious?

Thank you for a lovely Christmas card. You said you weren't going to send any more, you rotten thing. A shilling, this one's cost me.

AW

Molly eventually did meet AW – she thinks probably around 1971. They then planned to do a book about the old packhorse roads of Lakeland and did some research together on various routes – along with Betty, driving them.

While investigating an old road over Shap, Molly said it was one way, AW said another. They shouted and argued, each insisting they were correct.

Finally in exasperation, Molly yelled at him 'That's the fucking road down there!'

AW was silent before replying 'I thought you were a lady.'

Molly says AW didn't speak to her for two years, but they did become friends again, though the joint book never happened. (In 1985 AW did a slim book on his own called Old Roads of Eastern Lakeland.)

AW and Betty visited Molly's house in the Newlands valley house and Molly and her husband visited AW and Betty at home in Kendal.

'When we arrived at Kendal Green for the first time, AW opened the door and said "Did you have to bring him?" John didn't mind. He took our Great Romance in his stride.'

Part 15
Fan Letters, 1969–80

During the 1970s, AW published twenty-two books – a sudden spurt, partly due to the fact that he was now happily married and domestically settled and had his own chauffeur – but also because a lot of the books were quite short, with usually more drawings than words.

It meant his fan mail grew even larger, but he still insisted on answering every letter, if not always immediately. And of course he still did not give away his home address to ordinary readers but continued to use the Westmorland Gazette as his address.

Most of the letters are from readers who love his books, and just want to tell him; others are informing him about their own walks and experiences; some pick holes in his spelling or routes, and they mostly get short shrift.

Once he retires in 1967, and begins to feel he is getting on a bit, he often uses this as an excuse not to take up suggestions and invitations made by readers or old friends. He also begins to harken back to the old days in Lakeland, before all the cars and tourists. He wrote a letter in 1969 – undated – to the Westmorland Gazette, complaining about what was happening to Kendal. In 1969 there was also a letter to an old friend from the past, George Haworth, who had been with him at Blakey Moor secondary school in Blackburn. He had gone into the Post Office, not the Town Hall. He was hoping AW would join them at an old boys reunion dinner.

LETTER 159: TO GEORGE HAWORTH, 16 SEPTEMBER 1969

> 38 Kendal Green, Kendal
> 16th September 1969

Dear George,

Thank you for your letter and its very interesting enclosure. I return the latter in case you want it before the dinner on the 19th.

I shall not be there, nice though it was of you to suggest that I attend. It would be just too overfacing to have to meet some forty white-haired and bald-headed old gents who professed a former acquaintance when I couldn't recognise a blessed one of them. In fact, not more than half-a-dozen names on the list ring a bell, and those only faintly, but three (Barker, Tatlow and Wolstenholme) were subsequently colleagues in the Borough Treasurer's Office. You can give my regards to Lawrence Wolstenholme, if you will; he was the only one I knew well.

No, I can't bring J.C. Pye to mind at all, but H. Rydings I remember well if in fact he was a teacher at the time I was there. I'm surprised, if he it is, that he is still kicking around (but don't tell him so!). Of the other teachers I recall Abbott, Mellor, Moulding and a Miss Almond, and of course Mr Boddy, but I could not mention any other names. H. Parker was in my class, I think – he came from Mill Hill – but I fancy that most of the others would belong to a different period.

My congratulations on your ascent of Cust's Gully. To tell you the truth I never managed to get up that awkward pitch after trying on both sides of the gully, and in spite of being on a rope. There was nothing frightening about it but I simply could not bend my legs enough to get up the places where movement is constricted. It is, I would think, generally not true that long legs are a help in climbing and certainly not when climbing rocks. I had an awful job in Jack's Rake for that very reason. It's not that your feet are a long way removed from your brain, it's simply that you can't bend a three-foot leg in a two-foot crack. However, you clearly had no such troubles. Anyway, I suppose you just daren't fail a task that your own offspring had accomplished. How interesting that she is taking a Mountain Leadership Course! I'd better enrol as a pupil if she can guarantee to get me up Cust's Gully without bloodletting.

I hope you have a very successful evening on the 19th.

Yours sincerely,

AWainwright

LETTER 160: TO THE WESTMORLAND GAZETTE, 1969?

38 Kendal Green, KENDAL
To the Editor
The Westmorland Gazette,
Kendal.

Dear Sir,

THE FUTURE OF KENDAL
Amongst all the clamour for big changes in Kendal now that the by-passes are almost with us, may a small voice be heard?

The clamour is for a radical change of purpose, for modern development and new facilities, for more industry, for greater attractions for visitors, for more car parks – lest the town stagnate. Kendal is a delightful place, paradoxically say those who would change it.

Yes, it is. It is a delightful place because it was not planned, because it grew up anyhow over the centuries without interference from a surfeit of authorities and developers and consultants and outside advisers.

And why the hurry? Kendal has been here for the best part of a thousand years. Why is the year 1969 so important for decisions about its future? Kendal, even yet, is unique. Destroy the features that make it unique and they are lost for ever. There can be no going back to things as they were if a mistake is made.

Prosperity, the plank of the argument, is not altogether a matter of big turnovers and thronged shops. Prosperity has to do with contentment and tranquillity, too. If stagnation means quieter and safer streets and less noise I am all for it.

Visitors come to Kendal because they like it as it is, not because it has super camping sites and multi-storey car parks and all the fun of the fair. Introduce these things and you introduce a new type of visitor, less discerning and less appreciative.

I, as a resident, like Kendal as it is. I liked it even better twenty years ago before the planners were let loose on it.

I cannot believe that I am the only one out of step.

Yours faithfully

LETTER 161: TO MR HANCOCK, 12 JANUARY 1969

c/o The Westmorland Gazette
Kendal
12th January 1969

Dear Mr Hancock,

Thank you for the interesting letter enclosed with your Christmas card, and for your good wishes. I didn't know that the Lake District had an admirer who was prepared to travel by train all the way from Edinburgh and back again just for the joy of spending a few hours in Borrowdale and its other delectable places. Many people do in fact travel similar distances with the same in view, but they have cars and motorways to help them along (Birmingham is now only a three-hour journey by road) but I have not heard of anyone else coming regularly across the Border and committing himself to public transport. In your case I suspect that much of the attraction of these outings derives from the pleasure of travelling on the Waverley line, which, incidentally, I also know well and always enjoy.

In beseeching me to come up to Scotland and sample its glories, you do me less than justice. As a discriminating seeker after grand scenery I have long been addicted to the Highlands, especially those along the western seaboard, and for the past fifteen years have spent all my holidays up there, usually with a Freedom of Scotland railway ticket, but more often latterly in the company of a friend with a car. I claim, in fact, to have completely surveyed the Highlands with a camera and have a collection of around 500 enlarged photographs to prove it. Scotland is magnificent (north of Glasgow) but I have never conceded that it is more beautiful than Lakeland – until last October, when I got a late chance to make yet another tour by car, and, not having been up there so late in the year before, was absolutely spellbound by the glorious autumn colours. Lock Lomond, in sunshine, was a dream of delight, the birches in Glen Garry showed a beauty out of this world, Loch Maree was a fairyland. The whole place was lit up by colours I had not suspected from summer visits. I was enthralled.

Earlier, in August, with a Freedom ticket (not to be issued in future years) I went over all the railway lines likely to be closed, even going up to Thurso in case the opportunity never came again. As regards the Waverley line, I always make a point of using it for the return home, invariably spending a last night at Melrose. As you suggest, it is a journey to make with your nose to the window.

I must thank you for your kind references to my books. I'm glad you find them helpful. If I were forty years younger I'd just love to do the same for Scotland. I have a vague idea of doing a book on walking the Border line from the Solway to Berwick, but, this apart, must content myself with places nearer home. Such as the Pennine Way. Ugh!

Thank you again for writing.

Yours sincerely,

AWainwright

LETTER 162: TO MR RIMMER, 2 JULY 1969

c/o Westmorland Gazette, KENDAL
2nd July 1969

Dear Mr Rimmer,

Thank you for your interesting letter about Cust's Gully, damn it. The letter has been held up somewhere, otherwise I would have replied earlier.

Honestly, I don't know what you're bellyaching about. I told you that the first pitch had defeated me, and that I had retired to lick my wounds, never to return. Warning enough, surely, to expect some trouble? Therefore, not having done it, I couldn't describe what terrors lay beyond the first pitch. But, from my reading of other descriptions, I feel sure your account of a horrific second pitch must be exaggerated. When I was there I had with me a companion who managed to get up the lower pitch and completed the ascent of the gully, returning to me down the branch gully. He looked ashen-faced upon his return, I admit, but said nothing of having met any further difficulty higher up the gully. Looking up it from my dishonourable place of waiting, I could see nothing above but a choke of stones. The rock-climbers guide mentions the one pitch only (as dead easy!). I think it likely, therefore, that a recent fall of rocks may have built up into a second pitch, especially as you say it was all loose.

Nay, damn it, don't blame me. I told you not to go.

Yours sincerely,

AWainwright

LETTER 163: TO MR VIPOND, 21 NOVEMBER 1969

c/o The Westmorland Gazette
Kendal, Westmorland   21st November 1969

Dear Mr Vipond,
    Your kind letter of 5th November has been passed on to me by the
Gazette office.
    Yes, you are right to criticise the title 'Boardale' for the drawing num-
bered 50. I was in the greatest doubt myself before deciding to use it and
did so only because I could not think of one more suitable. I know the place
well, and have always come across it myself after descending Boardale, as
many people will have (unless arriving by the infernal internal combus-
tion engine, to quote your description). Martindale, to me and to most
people, runs higher into the hills from the old church. The foreground to
the drawing is a sort of no-man's-land, neither in one valley nor the other.
Perhaps your suggestion of 'Howe Grain' might have been better, after all.
    I share your great regard for this corner of Lakeland, even though, at
weekends, the motorists seem to have discovered it as a place for a nice
picnic. Which it is, but I wish they could have left it alone and undisturbed
for those who get there on foot. I remember it as a place of absolute peace
and tranquillity, a very lovely backwater known to but few.
    In fact, present trends being what they are, we may have been fortunate,
people of our generation, in knowing the Lake District at its very best, and
it may never be the same again for those who follow us. More's the pity.
    Yours sincerely

    AWainwright

*Some of these readers were regular writers and often it turned into a
correspondence which lasted many years.*

LETTER 164: TO MR DOUGHERTY, 8 AUGUST 1970

c/o The Westmorland Gazette
KENDAL
8th August 1970

Dear Mr Dougherty,
    Thank you so much for your extremely kind letter of 5th July. This

really deserved a much prompter reply, and I am sorry that circumstances have prevented me from giving it earlier attention. Your comments on my books are very generous and of course I greatly appreciate all you say.

With regard to Litt's Memorial, yes, the inscription has been deciphered and communicated to me by several correspondents, and in every case agrees word for word with your translation. The word MEREOILL has in all other cases been given to me as MEREGILL, which is what it should be. I should express particular thanks to your wife, who, in the interests of knowledge, kept her face pressed into a bed of sheep droppings for twenty minutes. This I was not prepared to do myself. And the say men are the tougher sex!

As for you kind suggestion about North Wales, no I am too old now. If I were thirty years younger (how often I have said that!) it would give me pleasure to go over those wonderful hills with a small-tooth comb, but I'm afraid the task is quite beyond me now. In any case, the Highlands of Scotland (a lifetime's work) would be my prior choice. Wales never appealed to me quite so much. The mountains are fine, of course, but the surroundings haven't the appeal for me that Lakeland has. Wales, I always feel, lacks the soft beauty of Lakeland and always seems to me untidy: the sprawling quarry heaps, the pylons, and so on. It hasn't been cared for and jealously guarded as has Lakeland. I'm not too fond of the Welsh accent either, if I must be honest: it would be a source of irritation if I had to spend much time there. But these are excuses. I am past it, that's the sombre truth.

I read with interest your list of some of the lesser well-known fellwalks you have done, and I was pleased to learn that you have enjoyed these equally with the classic climbs. So did I, at the time. And nowadays, with many more people on the hills, even more so. The crowds aim for the better-known heights, Helvellyn, Gable and so on, but many of the smaller ones continue to be unfrequented and remain quiet and here one can sit and meditate undisturbed by others. The last time I was on Gable, a few weeks ago, the summit was overrun by noisy parties, transistors blared and it was a relief to get off it.

Thank you again for finding the time and taking the trouble to write to me. It was nice of you to do this. Your letter was very kind and I shall treasure it.

Yours sincerely

AWainwright

LETTER 165: TO MR DOUGHERTY, 20 MARCH 1971

. . . I appreciate very much all you say, and never more in evidence than in your references to caravan sites. Of course I agree absolutely. These ghastly eyesores are authorised by people who would recoil with horror if somebody slashed a Constable landscape. I think myself that they should be prohibited in any area of natural beauty. Individual protests are unavailing, and the only hope lies in organised objections by the associations who care for rural England. I have sent the appendix to your letter to the Secretary of the Friends of the Lake District, who shares our views most strongly and has often appeared as an objector on behalf of his association when applications for the development of caravan sites are under consideration.

It was nice to hear from you again.

Yours sincerely,

AWainwright

LETTER 166: TO MR DOUGHERTY, 23 OCTOBER 1974

Dear Mr Dougherty,

I have just been looking and lingering, for the umpteenth time, over the delectable view-cards of the Dolomites you were kind enough to send me after enjoying your fabulous holiday amongst real mountains. The pictures are superb. They stir the imagination almost to screaming point. Why, oh why, have I never ventured to leave these shores and go in search of my own Shangri-la? Perhaps because I was never certain where to look. Now I know. The foot of my personal rainbow would be found in the Dolomites, of course. Where else?

But I doubt whether I would ever, even in the distant days of youth, have been able to emulate your own fearless wanderings around those magnificent peaks. You did amazingly well for a mere fellwalker apprenticed to English molehills.

Perhaps it has been the fear of frustration that has kept me from venturing too far afield. It must be galling – at least I would find it so – to gaze at some soaring peak, and want to climb it, and know you can't. Red Screes I can, and Bowfell, an even Scafell Pike, with the comforting assurance that I cannot fall off into space or be halted by an impassable rockface or be swamped by an avalanche, and that I will not get lost or benighted, and that I can reward myself at the end of the day with a rousing meal and a comfy bed. I am timid, I admit. I like to tackle something I know I can finish.

The Doughertys, obviously, are of tougher fibre. Not for them the simple paths on easy foothills. The challenge is too strong. For them, the dizzy heights, the call of the unknown, the privations, the ultimate triumph.

... Perhaps, after all, if I keep looking at them, as I most certainly will as a daily routine, I shall find a pleasure not greatly less than an actual visit would give me. Aided by a vivid imagination, which I do not lack, I can now do the skyline of the Gruppo Di Brenta, be home for tea, and sleep in my own bed.

Thank you again for the conducted tour. I appreciated and enjoyed it.

Yours sincerely,

AWainwright

LETTER 167: TO MR DOUGHERTY, 6 MARCH 1976

... At present, however, I cannot rid my thoughts of Scotland, and am due to spend a few days at Easter in Skye with two particular expeditions in mind on the Black Cuillin. I last climbed there in 1954, enjoying a heavenly week of perpetual blue skies, and the memory of those wonderful mountains has haunted me ever since. Here, without any doubt, are the finest peaks in these islands, not up to Dolemite standards but of compelling appearance and with the added advantage that you can at least get up on to most of the summits and needn't just stand and admire from a distance.

The second Scottish book is being published next week. I cannot remember whether you ever asked for a companion to Coire na Feola, but just in case you would like another I have asked the Gazette to enclose details with the leaflet they will be sending to you in a few days.

With very best wishes for rapid return to full health. You will feel a lot better when the daffodils come up in the garden and the sun has some warmth.

Yours sincerely,

AWainwright

LETTER 168: TO MR DOUGHERTY, 29 DECEMBER 1980

... Your descriptions of Ireland's scenery are mouth-watering. My wife, who lived there for five years, is always begging me to go and see the delights of the island for myself, but so far the unrest there has put me off. However it is on my itinerary for the next few years and has been brought forward by your account of the pleasures to be found along the western seaboard. 1982 perhaps ...

In Book Six – the North Western Fells – first published in 1964, AW described how he had spotted a young rowan which had secured a precarious foothold on Hassnesshow Beck, on the way up to Robinson. He asked any kind readers if they would let him know in 1970 if it was still alive and well.

In 1970, lots of people did write to him, including Tommy Orr from Whitehaven, who had gone up with a party and taken photographs.

LETTER 169: TO TOMMY ORR, 7 MARCH 1970

38 Kendal Green, Kendal.

Dear Mr Orr

I was absolutely delighted to receive your confirmation that the young rowan on the way up Robinson from Hassness is still alive and well. Indeed it is flourishing exceedingly, judging by the photographs you were kind enough to send along with your amusing illustrated report. The last time I saw it, in 1963, 'twas but a tiny two-branched sprig. From time to time, since then, I have been kept aware of its progress by other walkers who have passed that way, but yours is the first notification in 1970 and the first photographic evidence that has been supplied. The presentation of your report shows commendable initiative and talent, and I shall treasure it. Clearly the weather conditions were such that only the most intrepid of alpinists would venture forth on those cruel slopes of snow, and the whole party is to be congratulated on a performance that can surely seldom have been bettered. I have a new respect for the inhabitants of Whitehaven and especially its females.

Write again in 1980 and tell me the rowan is still there. Please!

Yours sincerely, with many thanks,

A Wainwright

In 1980, Tommy Orr sent another drawing and information to AW. By then, he was being inundated by sitings and reports. According to AW, 'no single feature I have mentioned in my books has brought me more letters'.

LETTER 170: TO TOMMY ORR, 26 JANUARY 1980

38 Kendal Green, Kendal

Dear Mr Orr,

Thank you, thank you, thank you for the graphic account of your New Year's Day pilgrimage and the accompanying photographs and nail biting illustrations. What fortitude, what courage your party displayed in their determination to confirm the survival of my rowan! Congratulations to all, and especially the ageing cripples.

I am so touched by your devotion to the cause that I have sent off to the Editor of 'Cumbria' the 20-year saga of the rowan with two of your photos, '1970' and '1980', and demanded that he publishes it.

If any of your party are capable of submitting a report in 1990, please do so. I may have gone to the happy hunting grounds by then. But the rowan will still be there, bless it.

Yours gratefully,

A Wainwright.

In writing back to Trevor Davys, AW gave away his home address from the beginning – which was unusual.

LETTER 171: TO TREVOR DAVYS, 29 AUGUST 1970

38 Kendal Green, KENDAL
29th August 1970

Dear Mr Davys,

I must beg forgiveness for what must seem a rather shocking neglect to reply to, or even acknowledge, your kind and very interesting letter of a month ago.

I appreciate your kind references to myself; the rest of your letter takes on the form of a brief autobiography to which my own experiences of life in relation to Lakeland are an answering chord, although the moment of 'impact' for me, happened forty years ago. I think you will find, as I did, that although the revelation comes suddenly it is no transient thing that passes away with familiarity, but an experience that recurs, fresh and vital as ever, each time acquaintance is renewed. I sacrificed something to live my life here, and it was the best move I ever made. It could be for you, too.

Thank you for finding the time and taking the trouble to write to me. It was nice of you to do this. I enjoyed reading your letter.

Yours sincerely,

AWainwright

LETTER 172: TO TREVOR DAVYS, 5 MAY 1971

38 Kendal Green, Kendal
5th May 1971

Dear Mr Davys,

Thank you for your interesting letter and accompanying sketch.

First let me deal with your enquiry about Rake's Progress on Scafell and tell you that it is no place for your 2 and a half year old daughter, although I have no doubt she would be game enough to try it. The Progress is a rock ledge, not quite continuous, running across the face of Scafell Crag at a higher level than the pedestrian route, which skirts the base of the crag. You have shown its course perfectly on your sketch. It starts exactly at the point where the Mickledore ridge abuts on Scafell. The pedestrian route here goes steeply down scree along the base of the cliffs; the Progress starts to climb broken ledges upwards to the right before trending down to run parallel to the pedestrian path and some fifty feet above it: the ground between the two is very steep but not vertical as is the crag above. At the far (west) end the Progress descends easier ground to join the pedestrian route. There are a few bad steps along it that rule it out for ordinary walkers, but climbers use this terrace to reach the start of some of the rock-climbs on the Crag. If I were you I would leave it alone.

I have amended our sketch to show the route normally taken up Lord's Rake. The turn left you show is the West Wall Traverse, a refinement of the original way. Both routes are quite feasible, although extremely steep and rough. It would be as much as you could manage to look after yourself without having a young daughter in tow, so with reluctance I must advise you to let Lord's Rake wait for a few more years – unless, of course, you have an opportunity of going there alone first to spy out the land. This area is tremendously exciting, and I can understand your eagerness to go there. I felt the same myself, long before the chance came. One other warning – don't try to come down either West Wall traverse or the full length of Lord's Rake before you have been up them. This was the mistake I made on my first visit: I reached the top of Scafell up the easy slope from Eskdale, couldn't identify the head of Lord's Rake and got into trouble looking for it.

I hope your Whitsuntide is a great success. I am sure it will be if you leave Scafell alone, but it could be a tragic non-success if you ventured there with a young child. She deserves commendation for getting as far as Kern Knotts but Scafell Crag is a much tougher proposition.

Yours sincerely,

AWainwright

Trevor Davys, who lives in Nottingham, says he was grateful at the time to AW for his advice and warnings. 'My 2½-year-old daughter was Rebecca. She loved the Lake District and made her holidays there in later life. She got an MA in Library studies and read all AW's books. Sadly she died aged thirty-seven.'

LETTER 173: TO JOHN BOOTH, 12 JUNE 1971

38 Kendal Green, KENDAL
12 June 1971

Dear Mr Booth,

I am glad you have found my books helpful on your visits to the Lakes and the Penyghent area and I warmly appreciate all you say. I especially like your idea of the miniature ornamental cairns, and often wish I had brought home with me a single stone from every mountain summit I have visited, and neatly labelled and dated it. But if I had down this, the house would now be cluttered up with stones, so perhaps it is as well!

I assume, from the mention of your recent marriage, that you have almost a full lifetime of happy hill-wandering to look forward to and I hope you have a great many wonderful days on the mountains in the years that lie ahead. But you must go easy on the cairns. They take a lot of dusting!

Thank you again for finding the time and taking the trouble to write to me and doing it so nicely.

Yours sincerely,

AWainwright

LETTER 174: TO JOHN BOOTH, 5 JULY 1971

38 Kendal Green, KENDAL
Westmorland
5th July 1971

Dear Mr Booth,

There was a delightful surprise awaiting me upon my return the other day from a holiday in Wester Ross (which explains my delay in acknowledging it) – a replica of the Lingmell cairn, no less, and all in one piece. This gift was completely unexpected, and I assure you is greatly appreciated and will be treasured. It now stands on the edge of a high shelf in my room, so that I have to look up at it as I have looked up at so many cairns in my time. Up on the shelf, peeping over as though on the edge of a cliff, it gives the impression of being about a hundred yards distant, which is just right – I always really enjoyed the last hundred yards to any cairn: the hard work finished, the reward almost within reach. It is a splendid addition to my collection of mountain trophies, and I prize it highly. I look up at it often. It is an inspiration. Thank you so much for the kind thought.

Yours sincerely,

AWainwright

By his third letter back, AW was addressing the Booths as John and Odette, which was very personal. Mr Booth had tickled AW's interest by sending him a replica cairn. He made them by taking small stones from the real cairns then gluing them together. He was very pleased to see in Memoirs of a Fellwanderer, published 1993, that on page 151 there is a photo of AW at home with his replica Lingmell cairn on the window sill behind him. It proved that AW was not simply being polite in his letters. Mr Booth worked all his life on the railways, starting as a signalman and finishing as a safety manager. During his years writing to AW, he moved from York, to Chester and to Reading, before retiring in Swindon.

LETTER 175: TO JOHN BOOTH, 11 JUNE 1972

38 Kendal Green, KENDAL
Westmorland
11 June 1972

Dear John and Odette,

Thank you for your letter. It was nice to hear from you again and to learn that you are still building cairns. The one you kindly sent me is still in prefect condition. Not a stone out of place or even loose! I see Lingmell every time I raise my eyes from my desk, however wet and misty it may be through the window. Incidentally, now that you have finished the Three Men of Gragareth I have another to suggest that will keep you occupied for months – Nine Standards, where there is a fine collection of cairns, the best I have ever seen. They are most impressive, and look like Stonehenge as you approach them. Trouble is, you would need a large mantelpiece to display them, and dusting would be a delicate operation. So perhaps you shouldn't bother. But do go and look at them sometime. You know where they are – between Kirkby Stephen and Keld, and easily reached from the top of the Birkdale road.

I have just finished my book on the St. Bees–Robin Hood's Bay walk, and thoroughly enjoyed it. This gave me my first introduction to the Cleveland Hills and the North Yorks Moors, which I found a delectable area, largely because most of my walking there coincided with the heather in bloom. I was there again a few weeks ago, to see the daffodils in Farndale and re-visit a few places that had specially appealed to me.

Thank you for your very kind invitation to visit you in your new bungalow. I do not see any early possibility of this, but perhaps if you were ever to report that the Nine Standards had now been repeated on top of your TV set I think I would simply have to call next time I was in your area!

Thank you again for keeping in touch.
Yours sincerely,

AWainwright

LETTER 176: TO JOHN BOOTH, 10 APRIL 1973

c/o The Westmorland Gazette
KENDAL
10th April 1973

Dear Odette and John,

Thank you for your letter. It was a pleasure to hear from you again. Before I mention more mundane matters, let me say how pleased I was to hear your big news, although the arrival of the newcomer will certainly mean a stop to cairn-building and fellwalking for some time afterwards, but not, I hope, the end of these activities. You enjoy your expeditions too much, and they should be even more exciting with three in the party. Some proud new parents have reported from time to time that their off-spring have bagged a peak before they could walk (carried on father's back). So let's set a target for you. Roseberry Topping (the Cleveland Matterhorn) before John Junior is a year old.

I had wondered whether you had ever taken me up on the Nine Standards idea, and am glad to learn that you did and that the work is proceeding well. Thank you for your invitation to call and see the masterpiece. I may just do that sometime when Junior is house-trained. My own Lingmell cairn, on the window-sill beside my desk, looks fine, with not a stone out of place.

LETTER 177: TO JOHN BOOTH, 26 MAY 1974

38 Kendal Green, KENDAL
Westmorland
26th May 1974

Dear John,

Thank you for an interesting letter, and congratulations on being not the first but nearly the first to do the St Bees–Robin Hood's Bay walk. I'm glad you enjoyed it. You probably had super weather conditions – it's been a wonderful springtime – and it is rather a relief to learn that you did not encounter opposition at any stage except from the Moor House barbed wire. So did I when I was there, as a result of which I wrote to the County Clerk at Northallerton about this particular section and received the most solemn assurances that a through route would be established here and the farmers told of the right of way – obviously nothing has been done. It was clear to me at the time of my visit that nobody had used this right of way for donkeys years, an opinion confirmed by the farmer at Brompton Moor, to whom I spoke about it. Others who have done the walk have not reported any difficulty here and I had hoped that the County Clerk had been as good as his word. Apparently not. I haven't been to York or its vicinity since last you wrote, but I bear in mind the wonderful array of cairns waiting to be inspected. One of these days! My own Lingmell cairn remains in pristine condition – not a stone loose or out of place.

Yours sincerely.

AWainwright

LETTER 178: TO JOHN BOOTH, 31 DECEMBER 1974

38 Kendal Green, KENDAL
Westmorland

Dear John,

Thank you for your letter and kind references to the Scottish mountain book, I have taken all my holidays in the Highlands for donkeys years, latterly making three visits every year, in spring, summer and autumn, and, without doing too much walking, made myself very familiar with the terrain. These visits are proving the highlights of my retirement and I greatly look forward to them, especially now that I am working to a set plan of campaign. I envy you the experience that awaits you, of a first expedition, a first tour of those wonderful mountains north of the Border. The two cardinal rules to observe are, first, to get into Wester Ross and Sutherland, because the further north you go the greater is the reward, and, secondly, to keep to the west side rather than the east.

I must congratulate you on your promotion, although personally I would prefer York to Chester, but at least the more will bring within range a whole new series of mountains tops and a fresh decade of cairn-building, although I think it unlikely you will want to reproduce Snowdon's highest inches, which looked quite a mess when I was last there a couple of years ago. However, I hope all goes well in the new job and hat the added responsibility leaves you free to get out into the hills as much as ever.

The Lingmell cairn still adorns my desk and remains in pristine condition. Not a stone has fallen from it, not a stone is loose.

Thank you for repeating your kind invitation to me to drop in to see you someday. I rarely turn my face south, but perhaps I will someday. Chester is high on the list of places I must see when the call of the hills becomes less insistent, but, touching wood, that has not happened yet.

With kind regards,

Yours sincerely

AWainwright

LETTER 179: TO JOHN BOOTH, 26 JANUARY 1976

38 Kendal Green, KENDAL
26 January 1976

Dear John and Odette and Jamie,

I'm sorry that I cannot let you have a copy of WESTMORLAND HERITAGE. This was a strictly limited issue, one thousand copies only, and I was not even given a simple complimentary copy. In fact, all I have is a printer's proof. You will be less disappointed when I tell you that the book was priced at 11.50!

Sorry to hear that cairn-building has come to a full stop, at least pending a change of environment. Nine Standards still awaits attention and is, I assure you, a much better subject than Ill Bell. My own Lingmell cairn still stands proudly on the window-sill above my desk, the perfect monument. Not a stone out of place. Not a stone even loose. Better than the original!

Yours sincerely,

AWainwright

LETTER 180: TO MR BISHOP, 7 MARCH 1974

c/o The Westmorland Gazette
KENDAL
7th March 1974

Dear Mr Bishop,

Thank you for your very kind letter, which deserved a more prompt reply but unfortunately was held up in the Gazette office and has only just reached me. Sorry about the delay!

I read of your travels from Coast to Coast with considerable interest, and especially so because yours is actually only the second letter I have had that reported completion of the walk, the first coming some months ago. This apparent lack of interest has surprised me, because I receive literally hundreds of letters a year from walkers who have done the Pennine Way. Maybe more will be following in your footsteps this coming summer. The book has in fact sold extremely well.

However, as I say, I was most interested to learn that you had accomplished the walk and am pleased to note that you enjoyed the experience (even the Vale of Mowbray?). Of the two diversions you made, I approve the Ullswater-Howtown alternative, which is pleasanter than my own route over the ops, but am sorry you preferred to follow the Swale downriver from Keld. My own preference here is certainly to cross the hills by way of the old lead mines, a splendid walk of fascinating interest; indeed, apart from the crossing of the Lake District, I considered the Swaledale lead mines and the North York escarpment to be the highlights of the journey.

Congratulations on doing the walk; I hope it is the forerunner of many more expeditions and that you enjoy happy seasons on the fells long into the future. And thank you again for taking the trouble and finding the time to write to me.

Yours sincerely,

AWainwright

LETTER 181: TO MR MORRIS, 8 APRIL 1974

c/o The Westmorland Gazette
KENDAL, Westmorland
8th April 1974

Dear Mr Morris,

Thank you for your extremely kind letter and generous comments.

I have noted your ambition to climb all the 214 Lakeland fells, and I have checked your arithmetic and found it to be faultless, but I am mightily perplexed by your intention to repeat the performance 15 times. There must be a reason for this but it eludes me. You would certainly qualify for inclusion in the Guinness Book of Records if you accomplished the feat, but I don't honestly think you ever will, certainly not from a base as far away as Essex. What I would advise is that you tackle every one of the 214 over the next few years, plus 56 lesser fells I have listed in a book called the The Outlying Fells of Lakeland due to be published in a few weeks, thus making 270 in all. This task is enough to keep you actively engaged until the '80s, after which there are 560 mountains in Scotland over 3000' awaiting your attentions.

So while I would not like to discourage your present plan, I believe it to be far too ambitious and virtually impossible of attainment and would strongly suggest the modified target I have mentioned. Whatever you decide, you may be assured of my good wishes. I can think of no better way of spending leisure hours than by walking over the tops according to a set plan and choosing your weather. Days spent thus are all happy ones. I hope you have a great many such, with fair winds and good walking conditions, over the nest few years.

Yours sincerely,

AWainwright

LETTER 182: TO MR GREEN, 4 AUGUST 1974

c/o The Westmorland Gazette
KENDAL, Westmorland
4th August 1974

Dear Mr Green,

It was a pleasure to hear from you again, and I really must hasten to congratulate you on your successful assault on the Aonach Eagach ridge – an objective I have had my sights on for donkeys years but never ventured to attempt. I have grown old looking at it from a safe distance, and now the effort is beyond me. You are one up on me there, all right!

As it happens I have already done a drawing of the mountain in advance for the third volume of Scottish drawings, which means, as the first is only now being printed, a wait of another two years, but you can have it, with pleasure, when it becomes available. Since my memory, like my legs, is no longer capable of sustained effort, I beg of you to remind me nearer the time.

There are still stirrings of life in me. In June I climbed two Munros in the Glen Affric area. Easy ones. Nothing like Aonach Eagach.

You must be a proud man. I would be, if I were in your boots.

Yours sincerely,

AWainwright

LETTER 183: TO MR GREEN, 27 SEPTEMBER 1975

c/o The Westmorland Gazette
KENDAL, Westmorland
27th September 1975

Dear Mr Green,

Thank you for your reminder. I expect to be able to let you have Aonach Eagach quite early next summer. I have just got Volume Two off to the printer, having been delayed for more than a year by a desire to do a sort of requiem for dear-departed Westmorland, which too is now finished, so that I am ready for Volume Three and rarin' to start, although, as I think I told you, the drawing of A.E and a few others are already done. In two weeks time, I go up to Glencoe to finish off the fieldwork for that area. I go there in some apprehension, actually, having booked a caravan in Glencoe and being unaccustomed to this type of accommodation. But hotel charges are really getting out of hand. I shall know later whether the suffering is worth the saving.

You are obviously a good deal tougher than I am. How often have I looked up lingeringly at A.E. and An Teallach and Liathach and the rest and how much I have read of their terrors for the timid pedestrian, and how often I have turned sadly away. I am getting old. I like a clear and easy path. I will be in touch in a few months if I survive the caravan.

Yours sincerely,

AWainwright

LETTER 184: TO MRS DEKETELAERE, 14 JUNE 1974

c/o The Westmorland Gazette
KENDAL, Cumbria
14th June 1974

Dear Mrs Deketelaere

Thank you for your very kind and friendly letter of May 30th. It was a pleasure to hear from you, and to learn of some of your expeditions and experiences on the hills. These left me a little envious. It must be great to be only 58. I've forgotten; so long ago!

I still have very long legs, but nowadays I would approach Easy Gully on Pavey Ark with considerable apprehension and would certainly need a shove on the awkward step.

North Wales, no, not for me. I admire the mountain scenery but am annoyed and frustrated by the pronunciation of their names. No Blencathras and Glaramaras and Helvellyns in Snowdonia. And too many people go. Two years ago I climbed Y Wydffa from Pen-y-Pass in a procession of at least three hundred others. No, I am turning more and more to Scotland, and especially Sutherland and the Far North. You must go and look at Suilven before you are 70 because you will most certainly want to climb it.

By your reference to Mollie's husband, I assume you must mean Molly Lefebure's. He permits his wife to correspond with me.

AWainwright.

AW was also still in correspondence with Len Chadwick, who had been one of his researchers on the Pennine Way. Len got very depressed when he lost his job as a shorthand typist – then later his home. AW tried to cheer him and also find him a job as a youth hostel warden. Len died alone in a home in Oldham in 1987.

LETTER 185: TO LEN CHADWICK, 11 JANUARY 1974

c/o Westmorland Gazette
KENDAL
11th January 1974

Dear Mr Chadwick,

Well, thank you for writing, but I must say your letter made rather depressing reading! Hardly the inspiring and optimistic message one expects at the beginning of a New Year. Nothing seems to be going right for you – bad weather, flu, three-day week, notice to quit and nowhere to go, lack of funds, loss of prestige, inability to interest people in brilliant ideas, a spoiled Christmas, and so on. A catalogue of doom.

There must be a glimmer of hope somewhere. The present may be black but the future must surely hold some promise of better times. Are you so depressed and downcast that you haven't noticed the daffodils coming up in the garden? This has been a bad winter for everyone, and things can only improve. I have never known you so gloomy. Cheer up. Who knows, come springtime you might be right on top of the world again, perhaps married to a wealthy widow, living in a comfortable home with four good meals a day provided, no worries at work, leading fifty-mile marathons at weekends, perhaps seeing the 'latics at Wembley. 1974 could be the best ever.

Me, I have finished the outlying fells and am just putting the finishing touches to a first volume of Scottish mountain drawings.

Next time you write, I hope you have better news for me and are in a much brighter mood. Never give up used to be your motto, and I think that when the sun gets a little warmer and your flu is cured and the curlews come back to the hills, it will be again.

Yours sincerely,

AWainwright

LETTER 186: TO LEN CHADWICK, 8 APRIL 1974

c/o Westmorland Gazette
KENDAL
8th April 1974

Dear Mr Chadwick,

I was glad to have your further note telling me that you had been discharged from hospital and been able, through the kindness of a friend, to get temporary accommodation for a few weeks. This will have relieved your immediate worries and given you a short breathing space for further enquiries which, I hope, will produce a permanent and satisfactory address.

Your infirmity is obviously going to take quite a time to cure, but if you are patient and do as the doctors say there is probably no reason why you should not get back to near-normal after a few months and be able to resume your work or some lighter duties. The 50-miles marathons, however, are out, but I have found myself as much pleasure in pottering around the country, resting often and taking things easy, and I am sure you will, too.

As for sorting your papers, I will do that if they are sent in a parcel, not too big, I hope, because my own quarters are chock a block with maps and books.

The Outlying Fells will be out soon after Easter and I will send you a copy to help pass your time.

Yours sincerely,

AWainwright

AW continued to be upset with the RSPCA, after his generous offer of funding back in 1967 came to nothing, and he was looking round for other animal charities and causes to support instead, but it was not until 1974 that he officially resigned in a furious letter. It was after this letter that he became involved with a local Kendal charity, Animal Rescue, and decided to help their campaign to build their own animal shelter.

LETTER 187: MRS NORTON, 20 JULY 1974

38 Kendal Green
Kendal
20th July 1974

Dear Mrs Norton

When I was elected President of the Westmorland Branch of the R.S.P.C.A. at a recent meeting, I accepted the office, but with some reluctance, mainly on three grounds: first, because I have long been of the opinion that the work of the Branch has been impeded by the old age and resulting loss of enthusiasm of some of those in charge, and I am myself afflicted by advancing years and would have preferred the appointment of a younger person; secondly, because I am aware that the serious defects in administration of the Branch have been, and are increasingly, a matter of local concern; and thirdly, because I know, by painful personal experience, that the charges of arrogance and indifference that have gained so much press publicity recently are well founded and by no means confined to Headquarters. However, I accepted office, intending it to be for a short period only, during which time I hoped to be able to restore public confidence and in particular see that much more was done for the welfare of distressed animals – an aspect of the Society's work in which the record of the Westmorland Branch is deplorable.

You were present at the Branch meeting last Tuesday and witnessed the events. Orderly proceedings were disrupted from the start by the insistence of a paid officer of the Society to make a statement in complete disregard of the Chair, a breach of etiquette I have never known in forty years of continuous committee work. The statement alleged a trivial contravention of the Society's rules, a technicality, nothing more serious than the dates on which certain named members of the Committee had paid their subscriptions. Rather unfortunately for him, and due to local mismanagement, the officer's information was inaccurate, as was pointed out to him. Nevertheless, when I asked if he was inferring that those members had no right to serve on the Committee, he affirmed that such was the case. When I asked why their ineligibility had not been mentioned at the meeting at which they were appointed (at which he was present) he could not give a satisfactory answer. When I asked if he was trying to say that those members should not be in the room at all, he said they should not. The members named then left the meeting, as indeed they had no alternative – and these were the same people, all willing helpers, who had organised and run last Saturday's flag day when other members and office-holders had not even put in an appearance.

I considered the matter had been grossly mishandled and was a calculated affront, planned in advance with the connivance (as I later discovered) of others present. If there had been substance in the objection, surely it would have been kinder and more proper to have explained the position by letter in advance of the meeting and spared the members concerned the humiliation and embarrassment of being taken completely by surprise at their denouement in front of other people. When adult humans behave like this, even the animals have cause to be ashamed of them! So I left the room also, only to be insulted by later entreaties, from the same officer, to return to the meeting with certain named members who had, only a few minutes earlier, been told they had no right to be there. So much for his insistence that the rules be adhered to! Apparently they can be ignored to serve a purpose, as indeed they have been on other occasions. I found the whole business quite sickening.

I have no wish to preside over an assembly where matters are so obviously deliberately going wrong, where mismanagement is actually supported by paid officers of the Society, where some members can sit in silence without protest and see fellow-members shamefully treated, where personal animosities and witch-hunting are practiced, and the welfare of suffering animals neglected as a result. Nor do I think the presence of so many paid officers is at all necessary: I regarded their attendance at this meeting an extravagant waste of money subscribed in good faith for the prevention of cruelty to animals, not to the building up of a bureaucracy bound by red tape and Parkinson's Law.

As President of the Westmorland Branch, I request you to send a copy of this letter to all persons present at the meeting last Tuesday, including the Society's officers, and to the Director of the R.S.P.C.A. with a request, which I expect him to ignore, that an investigation be held into the affairs of the Branch and the conduct of his officers at that meeting. When you have done this, then I ask you to report my resignation to your Committee.

Yours faithfully,

AWainwright

In 1971, AW started a correspondence with a dog called Meg who lived in Southport and was apparently a very keen fell walker.

LETTER 188: TO MEG, 5 JULY 1971

38 Kendal Green
Kendal
5th July 1971

My dear Meg,

I know you never bothered to learn to write, and I am sure you never bothered to learn to read, either. How could you when you have been so busy climbing hills? First things first! But perhaps your old Daddy will tell you what I say.

I think you are a super little girl. You are the tops, really and truly. Yes, a few others have climbed all the 214 hills, but they were big strong men. The youngest I know of was a boy from Carlisle, but he was 16 (sixteen, not six). So you hold the record and ought to get Daddy to write to the papers about it and get you on television. People have got medals for less!!! You have done very well indeed, especially as you have been slowed down so much by your Daddy. It's time he gave up, at his age. Why, he's nearly as old as I am!

What next? Well, there are 533 mountains in Scotland higher than Scafell and Helvellyn. I've only been up two of them, but if I was a little boy (or girl) of 6 I'd be wanting to get started on them. Learning to read and write can wait until you are really old, say about 30.

It must be awful for you, having your old Daddy with you all the time, crawling along like a snail under all his heavy clothes and boots and not letting you run after the sheep. Can you not get a rope and pull him along faster? Really, these grown-ups! They make you sick . . .

But never mind, love. You have many years ahead of you. They'll be happy years if you spend them amongst the hills. I wish I were seven, and you would go with me. What fun we would have, chasing the sheep, and blow your old daddy. He could wait in the car with your Mummy. Wouldn't it be super?

Love from AW

LETTER 189: TO MEG, 31 DECEMBER 1974

c/o Westmorland Gazette
KENDAL
31st December 1974

Dear Meg,

I know you are a truthful little girl and I believe everything you tell me, but I must confess that your letter the other day, informing me that you had now climbed all the Lakeland fells for a second time, was a great surprise to me. It is a truly remarkable performance. You ought to go down into history with Scott and Amundsen and Drake and Marco Polo. Never before in the records of fellwalking has there been such an achievement as yours. I myself was nearly sixty before I could claim to have climbed all the fells – you were six. And now you have done them all again, and are still only nine and a bit. You make me feel I have wasted my life, but I haven't really, because as you grow older you will find that there are other things to live for, other interests, other targets to aim for, other ideals, perhaps not so exciting but no less worth while. You must work hard at your lessons and be as good at them as you are at fell-walking. And I hope you will write again sometime and tell me of your progress in other directions.

In the meantime, congratulations on a wonderful performance. Daddy should pin a row of medals across your chest.
Yours sincerely

AWainwright

Thank you for the lovely photo. Best wishes for 1975

What AW didn't know was that the man behind the dog letters was her owner Max Hargreave, a chartered accountant in Southport. He didn't take up fell walking until he was fifty but he became so keen on AW's guides that he took it upon himself to stand on the top of various Lakeland fells and collect signatures for AW to be awarded an honour. He then sent the petition to the Mayor of Kendal and, lo and behold, in 1967 AW was awarded at MBE.

AW never knew this until he received a letter from a Mrs Sutcliffe of Otley who told him about the petition raised by Mr Hargreave. AW still did not realise he had in fact been in touch with Mr Hargreave for some years – or at least with his dog.

LETTER 190: TO MRS SUTCLIFFE, 17 OCTOBER 1977

c/o Westmorland Gazette
KENDAL
17th October 1977

Dear Mrs Sutcliffe,

Thank you so much for your kind letter of the 12th.

This clears up a ten-years-old mystery, because I had really no idea of the circumstances leading up to my award of the M.B.E. I remember that, some time before the official notification was received, the Town Clerk of Kendal told me that my name had gone forward as the result of a petition, but when he went on to add that the signatures had been collected by a man on the summit of Great Gable I thought he was pulling my leg good and proper, and not until I received your letter had there been confirmation of this story. Now I learn from you that there was such a man and that he was a Mr Hargreave of Southport, with whom, incidentally, I have never exchanged correspondence. As, at the time, he did not make his identity known to me, obviously preferring to do his good deed anonymously, I think perhaps I should not communicate my thanks at this late stage, but I will keep a note of his address for future reference.

Your letter was intended to give me pleasure. It did just that. Thank you for taking the trouble to write to let me have the information.

Yours sincerely,

AWainwright

AW then heard confirmation from Mr Hargreave himself.

LETTER 191: TO MAX HARGREAVE, 5 NOVEMBER 1977

38 Kendal Green
KENDAL, Cumbria
5th November 1977

Dear Mr Hargreave,

Well, thank you for clearing up a ten-year mystery! I had long ago given up all thought of ever finding a solution to it. Then, out of the blue, came the letter from Otley, from a complete stranger, giving me the clues I had thought would elude me forever.

I am glad to have the story straight from the horse's mouth (if you will forgive the expression) and get the facts right. Apparently the garbled version I got at the time was substantially correct but inaccurate in detail. Now I know exactly how things came to pass, and am at last given the opportunity to express my thanks for all the time and trouble you took on my behalf.

What happens in the case of an award such as this, is that you receive a very official letter from the Prime Minister (dear Harold, in my case) informing you of his intention to include your name in the next Honours List and asking you whether you are prepared to accept. You say yes, and subsequently you are invited to attend at Buckingham Palace for the occasion. But never, either by letter or verbally, are you told why you have been selected. And certainly you are never told on whose recommendation, or how your name came to the P.M.'s notice. So I went, and I got it, and I never knew why for sure until a lady in Otley told me.

Of course I remember Meg, and actually have been expecting to hear from her with a report that she has completed the trinity. Since she first wrote I have had scores of letters from correspondents proudly announcing that they have climbed all the 214 fells, and asking if they have broken a record. I never fail to tell them about little Meg (which seems to deflate their ego because they never write again). I hope she keeps well and still has a fond liking for the high places of Lakeland.

Thanks again, a lot.

Yours sincerely,

AWainwright

At the end ot the Pennine Way Companion, published in 1968, AW promised a free pint to all walkers who had done the whole route and arranged with the landlord of the Border Hotel in Kirk Yetholm to send him the bill every year.

When I interviewed AW at his home in Kendal in 1978, by which time 100,000 copies of the book had been sold, he was signing a cheque for £400 for the previous year's bar bills. In those ten years a pint had gone up from 1/6 to four shillings, but he said he didn't regret it. If people had done the 270 miles, they deserved it. But when he completed A Coast to Coast Walk, published in 1973, he said there would be no treats this time.

He personally was not all that thrilled by the Pennine Way as a walk. But he always kept up the payments on the Pennine Way, almost to the end of his life, which meant he was continually getting letters about it – usually thanking him for his generosity.

LETTER 192: TO DR TOM PATTERSON, 26 MARCH 1974

. . . You are very welcome to the pint, and well earned it. In fact, being a bit cynical about the Pennine Way (believing there is much better walking to be found elsewhere in this fair country of ours), I consider that anyone who walks the Pennine Way from end to end and lives to tell the tale, deserves shares in a brewery.

Yours sincerely,

AWainwright

Miles Rhodes of Moulton, Northampton, wrote in 1975 to confess that he had rather cheated when claiming his free pint. He had done the walk in two stages – first half in 1971 and second in 1972, not realising the free pint was only for those who had walked it all in one go.

LETTER 193: TO MR RHODES, 22 OCTOBER 1975

c/o Westmorland Gazette
KENDAL
22nd October 1975

Dear Mr Rhodes,

Thank you for a delightful letter, which I appreciate greatly. It has more than earned you absolution from your innocent mistake in claiming a free drink at Kirk Yetholm. Indeed, so generous are your comments that a block of shares in a brewery might have been a more adequate reward. Certainly you need have no further qualms of conscience. Your comments on my books are so generous that I feel I am the gainer from this brief acquaintance.

Although there is a note of pessimism in your letter about your future walking prospects, I am sure that if you are capable of walking the Pennine Way, as you have proved, you will have before you many more happy seasons in the open countryside. I hope you have, and that you enjoy fair weather, pleasant company and rewarding experiences on all your expeditions.

Thank you again for finding the time and taking the trouble to write to me. And for doing it so nicely.

Yours sincerely,

AWainwright

Meanwhile, AW was still receiving occasional letters from his old friends from the past, such as Bob Alker, whom he knew from his days in the Blackburn Treasurers' office.

LETTER 194: TO BOB ALKER, UNDATED, 1975

... I am pleased to learn of your success as a superb photographer and lecturer. You ought to get up to Glencoe or Torridon or Sutherland with your camera. These are now my favourite stamping grounds since inundating the Lake District with fellwalkers: the mountains here have become crawling ant-hills. Caledonia stern and wild – this is the place to be.

It is distressing to find you still belly-aching about Great End 8. I intend to make the necessary alteration the last thing I do before I lay down my pen for good, in about twenty years time. Tell your missus to let me know when you die. I might be able to attend the funeral, but I doubt it. I fear I will be much too busy, but at least I will be reminded of Great End 8.

If there's any of the old gang left, apart from Maudsley and you and me and possibly Arnold Haworth, do please give them my regards if you see them.

AW

[At bottom of this letter he has sketched a 'before' and 'after' self portrait.]

LETTER 195: TO PHILIP COOPER, 24 MAY 1976

c/o Westmorland Gazette
KENDAL, Cumbria
24th May 1976

Dear Philip,

The Westmorland Gazette have passed on to me your very kind letter of a month ago. I am sorry about the long delay in replying, which has been caused by absences from home (working on location).

I found all your comments interesting, and it is good to know that you have taken up fellwalking in earnest and already have a commendable record of expeditions to your credit. In a way, I envy you your early start; mine came much later in life. Like you, I have enjoyed all my days on the hills, my one sad regret being that circumstances prevented me from tackling all the Scottish Munros: now, alas, such a feat is quite beyond my powers, and time is running out for me. But what a target for a young man looking for fresh fields to conquer (or hills to climb)!

The main purpose of your letter was to arrange a meeting, but this, I am sorry to say, is just not on. I find myself overwhelmed by similar requests to such an extent that I have reluctantly had to call a halt to interviews in order to concentrate on my books without interruption. As I said, there is not much time left for me to do all I want to. So, at least until I have laid down my pen for ever, I must ask to be excused.

Thank you for writing to me. I hope you enjoy many many more seasons of happy fellwandering and mountain climbing.

Yours sincerely,

AWainwright

In a letter to Roger Elsom of Southampton, an Ordnance Survey employee, who had just done his first long distance Lakeland walk – from Thirlspot to Ambleside, via Helvellyn, Nethermost Pike, Dollywaggon, Fairfield and Great Rigg – AW revealed something he would liked to have done in life.

LETTER 196: TO ROGER ELSOM, 8 SEPTEMBER 1976

c/o Westmorland Gazette
KENDAL, Cumbria
8th September 1976

Dear Mr Elsom,
Thank you so much for your very kind letter.

I am always interested to learn of the reactions of anyone sampling the Lakeland Fells for the first time, and, with never an exception, I find that all newcomers to the district seem to fall immediately under the spell and thereafter become confirmed addicts to fellwalking. The route you chose for your initiation was a good one, lengthier in fact than anything I have ever accomplished in the course of a day's walk along the tops, and the stage seems set for similar and equally enjoyable excursions in the future. But don't expect fine weather every time! It has been known to rain up here.

I was especially interested to hear of your association with the Ordnance Survey, in praise of which I was never more sincere. I admire their work immensely, being lost in admiration of all their work. Their maps are, as ever, my favourite reading. Only once or twice have I had occasion to question their accuracy, these instances being quite trivial except for one bad boob on the Howgill Fells. I think, if I had my time to do over again, I would try my best to get on the staff. But I might have let the team down, for I could not have contributed more to the general excellence of the maps. They are a fine example of dedicated effort and meticulous accuracy. My private sanctum at home is crammed to the ceiling with Ordnance maps, most of the them dog-eared with over-much use but all loved and respected and handled with reverence.

I wish you many many more happy seasons of fellwalking, and thank you again for finding the time and taking the trouble to write to me.

Yours sincerely,

AWainwright

Part 16
Letters to Richard Adams and Others, 1976-9

Once AW was becoming well known outside Lakeland, and rumours of his massive sales started leaking out, several London publishers tried to tempt him away from the Westmorland Gazette, or to contribute illustrations to their books. In the main he refused all offers, apart of course from doing the drawings for Molly Lefubure's two childrens books.

In 1976 he received a letter from Richard Adams, who had achieved international success with his first novel, Watership Down, in 1972. He was a Lakeland lover and had bought AW's guides from the beginning. He had written a novel set in Lakeland about two dogs who have escaped from a laboratory where animal experiments are being held – exactly a subject which would appeal to AW, though Mr Adams had no idea when he first wrote that AW was even an animal lover.

He sent AW his manuscript and they exchanged several letters – though they never met. AW became very enthusiastic, so much so that he offered to do the job for no money – though Mr Adams thinks that Peter Carson of Penguin the publisher did insist he had to receive some money for his work.

AW also took it upon himself to help Adams with the plot, not just the artwork.

The Plague Dogs came out in 1977 and contained 20 of AW's drawings and 8 diagrams, including the endpapers.

LETTER 197: TO RICHARD ADAMS, 2 OCTOBER 1976

> 38 Kendal Green
> KENDAL, Cumbria
> 2nd October 1976

Dear Mr Adams,

I was rather under the impression that your absence in the U.S.A would mean a hiatus in the arrangements for publication of 'The Plague Dogs' and that nothing much would be happening until your return after Christmas. But events are clearly moving apace. I have had three communiqués from you since I got back from Scotland with a streaming cold after a week of rotten weather and have also now heard from Mr Carson – proposing an early meeting to discuss the illustrations. Enthusiasm is clearly running high, and impatiently.

Referring to your letters. That of September 15th dealt in detail with the comments I made after reading the manuscript and there are now few points on which we differ. But (pages 39 and 42) there is no doubt that the beck flowing into Coniston Water from the east is Yewdale Beck, not School Beck. The use of place-names in the dialect is all right in conversation, but in ordinary narrative is too likely to make the reader think he has spotted a mistake, especially as the accompanying maps will use only official Ordnance spellings – however, your proposed introductory note should explain this. Perhaps I have the impact on the general reader too much in mind: for instance 99% or more will think 'thorough the fog' (page 66) is a printer's mistake, and 'Low Door' (page 243) an author's mistake; very few will recognise the sources you use and I would have thought it better to write down to the general standard of your reading public. I still maintain that a shooting party coming up from Hall Dunnerdale would be seen from the summit or west side of Caw but not from the east (page 137). Otherwise I think we are pretty well in agreement.

Not with any thought of influencing your preference for introducing actual persons and actual places into the story, I still personally doubt whether these touches of authenticity are worth the risk of upsetting those who are spotlighted, especially as they mean nothing to any but a handful of your readers. I still quake when I think of all the potential trouble that could arise from your mention of Lawson Park.

I thought the comments of John Guest, enclosed with your letter of September 24th, were really splendid. First mention of A.R.S.E. is funny, but it ceases to be when kept up through 400 pages. And I think the quote on page 33 he objects to is just a bit too contrived, to artificially clever, and unnecessary in the context. We don't mind giving offence to the bureaucrats and politicians, but not the dear old ladies who leave their money to the anti-vivisection societies. We want to enlist sympathy, not alienate it by the use of expressions never heard in Leamington Spa. Yes, I agree with John. Less so on the potted biographies of the secondary characters, which to me coloured the story and did not hold it up at all.

I think the reference to Duncan Sandys should be omitted – dangerous ground, this. And, most of all, I do so agree that the book should end with the re-union of Snitter and his master. This is the perfect end to the story. To carry on thereafter for a few more pages gives the impression that, having recounted the tale and brought it to a natural and logical conclusion, you were reluctant to say finis. The interest of your readers is fully satisfied by the re-union of Snitter and his master. After that, nothing else matters. Let them put the book down with the happy thought of the re-union, and ponder that eminently satisfactory end with closed eyes for a few minutes. Any other written words are an interruption of a train of happy thoughts.

Anyway, I am really writing to let you know that Peter Carson is seeking a meeting with me to discuss the illustrations when he gets back from a holiday in Spain. This seems to me rather premature because the author himself has not yet seen, and approved or not approved, the proposed drawings and diagrams, and I have therefore suggested to him that I should send them on to you to look at while he is away from home, and give you a chance to express opinions or choices. On the diagrams the route followed is indicated by a dotted line; if Peter agrees to a thin red line I shall have to take the dots out and draw the route separately for overprinting in red. If there are other changes resulting from revision (e.g. the omission of A.R.S.E.) these amendments will also be necessary on the diagrams. In fact, I think you should regard the diagrams merely as drafts at this stage, and I will do them again when all doubts are settled. Having looked at them and decided what you would like to include, and what not, perhaps it would be a good idea to send them on to Peter to await his return on October 22nd so that he too can be studying the matter before we meet.

I hope to be in touch with Gerald Gray within the next few days.

It's Vermont I would most like to see at this time of year!

Yours sincerely,

AWainwright

AW could spend just as much time and energy writing to ordinary readers, not just famous authors, and give his forthright views and opinions

In March 1976 a Mr Brian L. Kershaw of King's Heath, Birmingham, clearly an early computer buff, took issue with a sentence in AW's Fellwanderer where he wrote 'Machines are monsters and they produce little horrors.'

Mr Kershaw said they could do worthwhile things, and to prove it he had fed into his computer details of all the fells in the seven Pictorial Guides, along with the grid references, summits and starting points. He then produced a computer print-out that must have been a massive document – horrifying AW.

LETTER 198: TO BRIAN KERSHAW, 6 MARCH 1976

38 Kendal Green
KENDAL, Cumbria
6th March 1976

Dear Brian,

To say that I was struck dumb by the remarkable document accompanying your letter of 26th February would be to put it mildly. Here was the enemy, suddenly attacking me when I was unprepared for shocks, at first bemusing and confusing me as do the unintelligible hieroglyphics on electricity bills, but gradually my dazed eyes started to recognise names I knew well. . . . Esk Pike, Crinkle Crags, Three Tarns, Cam Spout – these were Lakeland names, surely, and the long columns of figures, daunting at first sight, took on a meaning when I studied them more closely. Perhaps I should have read your letter first, and been warned!

Well, you seem to have proved something; I'm not sure what. I didn't realise these modern mammoth contrivances had a human streak, after all, and it is rather a revelation to find the monsters wrestling with the relative statistics of ascents of the Lakeland Fells. 1984 is with us. A computer installed on Esk Hause will tell you all you want to know. Should we go on to do Scafell Pike, or feed into the machine weather prospects, physical condition of each member of the party, time of day, and see whether it think it would be safer to turn back and go home? Fellwalking made easy, at last!

I think you have done a wonderfully imaginative job, but a rather frightening one if it is a foretaste of the sort of planning we might expect in the future. No, not for me. Give me my old dog-eared maps, which I can understand and which never go wrong.

I concede that you have certainly proved something, but nothing that has any appeal for me. If anything you have confirmed my impressions of new-fangled machines and in no way induced in me a liking for them. This document you have produced is the stuff of which nightmares are made. Heaven help us if these soul-less instruments take over the planning of our leisure as well as all else.

Your achievement is inspired and indicates a fertile imagination that, if applied instead to matters beyond the compass of computers, could well contribute to the sum of human knowledge. This horoscope is free.

The document is quite amazing and opens up all manner of possibilities. But not for me. I am too old-fashioned, thank goodness.

As you say, it must be the way you are built.

Yours sincerely,

AWainwright

However Mr Kershaw wrote back saying that he was still an ordinary human being, who loved steaks and smoking a foul pipe which makes ladies cough, and that the point of computers was that they were the future but they should remain our slaves.

LETTER 199: TO BRIAN KERSHAW, 24 MARCH 1976

c/o Westmorland Gazette
KENDAL, Cumbria
24th March 1976

Dear Brian,

Your second letter pleased me much more than your first. In fact, it delighted me immensely, not so much for its sentiments, which coincide with mine, but for the artistry with which you can use words. There is a compelling literary talent in your choice of expression, in your linking of phrase and passage, in your observation of the seemingly trivial (sheep suddenly spotting a walker) and inspired interpretations (question-mark floating above its head), the whole being a joy to read and deserving a wider public. You have the rare knack of translating simple incidents into a jolly good prose that reads better than poetry and since your subject is the Lakeland everybody loves your words could strike a chord in the hearts of the multitudes of inarticulate admirers of the district who think the place lovely but do not notice the little details that build up into the complete picture. Curtains of rain, lambs calling for their mums, a raven circling a crag: these things are the essence of Lakeland. These are the things many visitors never notice, a few never forget.

You are mis-employed, wrestling day after day with four computers, even though you do contrive to get some fun out of them. I noted your originality previously, and it shines through your second letter, embroidered this time with a beauty of expression and command of language that lifts you far above the common herd. Maybe it's dealing with robots that has sub-consciously determined you never to become one. Even your typing is meticulous, perfect.

What I am saying is that, on the little evidence I have, you have a talent you should be using not on programming computers but on writing for the greater joy of kindred souls, Lakeland lovers, who would hunger for your every word. First write a best-seller, an original epic of Lakeland. Then quit your job. (I hope your missus isn't looking over your shoulder). Then go all romantic: take over Millican Dalton's cave under Castle Crag; live like a hermit; give to an adoring world the best that is in you.

I could be wrong. Your letter reads as though written without hesitation, the words coming easily, not laboured. If so, I think I am right.

Sorry about this, Mrs Kershaw. But I do feel that you should be prodding Brian to get away from his wretched machines and settle in lovely Borrowdale.

AW

I hope this letter makes up for my first reaction!

The ones pointing out mistakes, or what they believed were mistakes, still got proper replies. A Mr K.K. Gibbs wrote to say that from the top of Barrow he had not been able to see Fleetwith Pike, which was what AW had indicated, and in fact he had checked with others and they had not been able to see Fleewith Pike either. In his reply, AW for once is a bit weaselly, suggesting he realised he might not have been totally accurate.

LETTER 200: TO MR GIBBS, 13 AUGUST 1977

c/o Westmorland Gazette
KENDAL, Cumbria
13th August 1977

Dear Mr Gibbs,

Thank you for the kind comments in your letter of 30th July, addressed to the Westmorland Gazette, and the interesting enquiry it contains.

I am unlikely to have an early opportunity of re-visiting Barrow to check the accuracy of the published view, but have been consulting the map again and looking at the contours. I think most certainly that Fleetwith Pike is visible from the summit, and that, on a clear day, it will be seen backed and overtopped slightly by Kirk Fell. A lot depends on weather conditions, but I think it most likely, after reading your letter, that the distant peak was Kirk Fell and that you did not notice Fleetwith Pike in front of it and slightly lower in elevation. Although my views cannot be comprehensive simply because of lack of space I usually selected the most prominent in cases where one summit was overtopped by another. Or it may be that on the occasion of my visit Fleetwith Pike stood out clearly while the higher Kirk Fell was obscured by mist or haze.

I notice that in my views from Fleetwith Pike and Kirk Fell there is no mention of Barrow. This is understandable because from these viewpoints it appears quite insignificant against the background of Skiddaw.

Yours sincerely.

AWainwright

At other times, he was adamant he had not made a mistake.

LETTER 201: TO MR SWALLOW, 14 JUNE 1977

c/o Westmorland Gazette, KENDAL
14th June 1977

Dear Mr Swallow,

I read your letter with profound dismay.

It is inconceivable that I made an error in quoting the O.S. number on Wild Boar Fell's column. My eyes are not all that good, and the numbers are placed in an awkward place and not always easy to decipher, but I cannot believe that I got my figures wrong.

There are two possibilities to account for the discrepancy you mention. One is that I got on some other summit thinking it was Wild Boar Fell. The second is that you did the same. Neither is even remotely likely. The answer can only be that the number has been changed since my visit.

This opens up the dreadful possibility that the numbers of other trig columns in the district may also have been changed, with dire consequences for me. Therefore I should be extremely glad if you would check the numbers I have quoted when engaged on other expeditions in the area, and report if you find any changes.

I agree about the walk up from Aisgill. But just at present Wild Boar Fell is out of favour with me. But thanks a lot for writing with the sad news.

Yours sincerely,

AWainwright

LETTER 202: TO MR SWALLOW, 19 NOVEMBER 1979

c/o Westmorland Gazette
KENDAL, Cumbria,
19th November 1979

Dear Mr Swallow,

There has been a sequel to our correspondence about the number of the Ordnance column on Wild Boar Fell.

A few weeks ago I had a letter from a walker who told me that I had made a mistake in the chapter on Black Combe (in 'The Outlying Fells') where I quoted the Ordnance column number as 2953. The number, he reported, was 11602. I was confident that I had not been in error, and told him so.

Unknown to me he then wrote to the Ordnance Survey to settle the matter, and has just sent me their reply, from which I learn that all their columns are inspected every ten years and repaired if necessary. Latterly they have been finding many vandalised and the number plates stolen, no doubt as mementos. Their records show that an inspection of the one on Black Combe in July 1976 showed that a complete rebuilding was needed and this was done. As the former number plate 2953 could not be found, a new one with the number 11602 was affixed.

The same thing must have happened on Wild Boar Fell – we were both right!

Yours sincerely,

AWainwright

By the end of the 1970s, AW was beginning to complain even more about getting old, about his eyesight fading, and his lack of enthusiasm for ever going abroad.

LETTER 203: TO MR HOUGHTON, 1 SEPTEMBER 1978

38 Kendal Green,
KENDAL, Cumbria
1st September 1978

Dear Mr Houghton,

It was nice to hear from you again.

Yes, the Cuillin from Elgol is reserved for you. I have now finished the 5th and 6th Scottish books and sent them to the printers. The 6th includes Skye, and I expect publication next spring, after which I will be able to let you have the drawing. During the making of the book I visited some of the Western Isles that were quite new to me, and I can recommend to you Harris in particular, Jura and Mull rather less so and Islay not at all.

I must be an old stick-in-the-mud, having never greatly wanted to leave for foreign parts, and, being now well into my seventies, cannot work up enthusiasm for going abroad although my wife is always urging a visit to Switzerland. Someday, perhaps. Thanks for the invitation to see your film. Someday, perhaps.

Watendlath drawing? Well, someday, perhaps.

Yours sincerely,

AWainwright

In a letter to a Mr Simmons, who was planning a directory of something called viewpoint indicators, AW generously says that he can publish anything from his books. This must have had his publisher screaming, if they ever found out.

LETTER 204: TO MR SIMMONS, 12 DECEMBER 1977

c/o Westmorland Gazette
KENDAL, Cumbria,
12th November 1977

Dear Mr Simmons,

I have received your interesting letter of 21st November, and am sorry it has taken me so long to reply.

I am a little puzzled, however, by the nature and purpose of the directory you are planning. I am not sure that I understand what you mean by 'viewpoint indicators'. There are, in fact, not more than half a dozen view-point indicators on the hills of the United Kingdom, certainly not enough to need a directory, and I am left wondering whether you mean the triangulation columns of the Ordnance Survey, of which, of course, there are several hundreds but which cannot be described as viewpoint indicators. A viewpoint indicator shows and names the most prominent objects in view, the details usually being engraved on a circular brass plate or recorded on paper protected by glass, but, as I say, there are very few in number.

The Ordnance columns, on the other hand, are customary features of mountain tops, and there are many of them. If these are what you intend to list, you should have the information vetted by the Ordnance Survey before your directory is published.

If you wish to publish anything from my books you are welcome to do so, but should bear in mind that many of the books were published some years ago and will not now necessarily be up-to-date.

I do not wish to discourage your efforts, but must say that, if I have interpreted your letter correctly, I cannot really see much need for what you propose to do.

Yours sincerely,

AWainwright

One of the simmering problems caused by the success of AW's books was not just the increased numbers of fell walkers on popular paths, and the possibility of erosion, but the danger of trespassing. AW could be a bit cavalier in his suggested routes, often not being aware or ignoring the possibility that he was leading people over private property. He began, privately, to get several legal letters of complaint on behalf of owners, but no one in fact took legal action as by now AW was such a respected, popular and increasingly national figure.

LETTER 205: TO LAWYERS RE BRYERSWOOD ESTATES, 12 SEPTEMBER 1979

> 38 Kendal Green,
> KENDAL, Cumbria
> 12th September 1979

Dear Sirs,
    Re Bryerswood Estate:
<u>Three Dubs Tarn</u>

The Editor of Westmorland Gazette has passed on to me your letter of the 7th for my observations. I think it might resolve the matter in question more quickly if I reply directly.

I am profoundly sorry if my mention of Three Dubs Tarn has caused inconvenience to your clients, and of course I will correct my reference to it to meet your wishes.

You will probably be aware, and no doubt your clients also, that people have walked over Claife Heights and occasionally visited Three Dubs Tarn since Victorian times. The Tarn has long been a subject for artists and photographers, and my own memory of it goes back fifty years. It was with this knowledge that I assumed that the owners had no objection to walkers visiting the tarn and that therefore there was tacit permission for them to do so, as is the case with so much privately-owned land in the district. I have, however, never seen or heard of any specific permission to do so.

Fortunately the book you refer to is continually re-printing and there should be little delay in having a correction made in future editions. I am not quite clear whether your client's grievance is simply the statement that permission has been granted when in fact it has not (in which case it appears that all I need to do is delete the words 'but walkers are permitted on them'), OR, more seriously, whether they now seek to exclude all walkers from the area, in which case I would propose to delete entirely the paragraph headed 'A shorter version of the walk' at the foot of page 82, substituting a note to the effect that the Tarn and approaches to it are on private land to which walkers are not permitted, and adding to the map on page 83 the word 'private' to the two paths leading to it.

Kindly convey my apologies to your clients, and, if you will please let me know what you want done it will be done.

Yours faithfully,

AW

Proof of AW's growing national fame had been his MBE in 1967, and after that, several universities wanted to give him honorary degrees. He accepted an Honorary MA from Newcastle University in 1974 but from then on made a point of investigating whether they experimented on live animals in their laboratories, in which case, he preferred to decline, which was what he did in 1977 when Lancaster University offered him a D. Litt which at first he had accepted.

LETTER 206: TO MR CARTER, VICE-CHANCELLOR, LANCASTER UNIVERSITY, 24 MARCH 1977

> 38 Kendal Green,
> KENDAL, Cumbria
> 24th March 1977

Dear Mr Carter,

I have heard recently, with dismay, that animal experiments are conducted at Lancaster University as part of the curriculum of the Biology Department, and a recent press report, of which you will be aware, confirms that vivisection is practised. I was unaware of this when accepting the Senate's invitation to receive an honorary degree in July next.

I deplore, and abhor, experiments on animals, and, as Chairman of Animal Rescue, Cumbria, cannot possibly agree to any association with an institution that encourages such practices.

Therefore I wish to give you notice that I hereby withdraw my acceptance of the Senate's invitation. I regret the circumstances that have decided this action, but please understand that I cannot be persuaded otherwise.

Yours sincerely,

AW

Part 17
Letters to Margaret Ainley, 1971–80

One of AW's longest correspondences, again with someone he never met, was with Margaret Ainley. Almost from the beginning he was very affectionate, if not quite as saucy as in his letters to Molly, except on rare occasions. Perhaps it was because she was a young married woman, a primary school teacher aged twenty-seven. She was living in Brighouse, Yorkshire, with her husband Richard, an industrial chemist, who worked for Nu Swift, fire extinguishers. In her second letter, she reveals she is pregnant.

The letters began in 1971, when she wrote to say that it was now possible to reach Spout Force without the need for a machete, and continued for twenty years, right up to 1990, by which time the second generation Ainleys had taken over, as their daughter Catherine was now writing to AW. Altogether, they received thirty-three AW letters.

Margaret told AW about their walks, her family, sent him photos, and AW always responded enthusiastically, telling of his holidays with Betty and the books he was working on.

LETTER 207: TO MARGARET AINLEY, 20 MARCH 1971

c/o The Westmorland Gazette, KENDAL
20th March 1971

Dear Mrs Ainley,

Thank you so much for your very kind letter.

Correspondents are, as a rule, quick to tell me where my books have gone wrong, but nobody, until now, has written to give me up to date information about Spout Force, and I was still under the impression that you couldn't approach it without a machete and heavy armour. So I am grateful for your news and propose to adopt your welcome suggestion that the subject should be included in a future Sketchbook (which would give me the opportunity of an explanatory note) – but it will have to be in the Fourth, not the Third which is already finished and at the printer's.

Your other suggestion, about the Yorkshire Dales, is, I fear, beyond my powers, which are declining fast although I am currently working on a guidebook to the Howgill Fells (near Sedbergh, in case you have never heard of them) and planning a Dales Sketchbook. I'm getting old, that's the trouble. How I wish tempus wouldn't fugit so much!

Thank you again for writing, and for finding the time and taking the trouble to do so. And for doing it so nicely.

Yours sincerely,

AWainwright

LETTER 208: TO MARGARET AINLEY, 6 OCTOBER 1971

c/o The Westmorland Gazette, KENDAL
6th October 1971

Dear Mrs Ainley,

It was a pleasure to hear from you again and learn, amongst other interesting facts, the thrilling news written at the very end of your letter – almost as a postscript (although I am sure it takes first place in your mind!)

I haven't yet re-battled my way to Spout Force but have every intention of doing so to get an illustration for a book I am currently preparing. Just lately I have been exploring (of all places) the North York Moors from a base in Whitby and next week I am gong to Helmsley for a few days to continue the operation. This does not imply a desertion of the places we love most of all but is merely a temporary distraction to enable me to complete a guide to a long walk right across the north of England, from St. Bees Head to Robin Hood's Bay. I must admit, however, that I found the heather moors of Cleveland extremely attractive and colourful when I was there last month.

The Howgill book is finished and at the printers. I enjoyed doing this immensely. Whether it will sell or not is open to doubt. In the twelve months I spend in the area I did not see more than a score of other walkers, and then only in the vicinity of Sedbergh and Cautley. Everywhere else is wilderness populated only by ponies and sheep, but if you like solitude the Howgills are hand-tailored for you. Walking on these lonely hills is quite delightful. The book will be out next Easter.

I am so glad you found the limestone area to your liking, apart from the bulls and the thistles. I hope your expedition to Smearsett Scar included a visit to the Celtic Wall which I personally found very impressive. I return the transparency herewith after noting with satisfaction that the subjects included not only Margaret Ainley, the cairn, the Ordnance column, but also her favourite guidebook to the area.

Now you must wait in patience to see what news next April brings. I applaud your resolve to get Ainley junior on the hills as soon as he or she can walk, or even earlier – you see so many babies being happily carried over the tops in rucksacks these days. I hope you have many many happy seasons on the hills in future, and I am sure you will find that three can be very good company.

With very best wishes,

Yours sincerely,

AWainwright

LETTER 209: TO MARGARET AINLEY, 27 MARCH 1972

c/o The Westmorland Gazette, KENDAL
27th May 1972

Dear Margaret,

I regret having delayed my congratulations so long. Yes, I fully realise that the birth of Catherine is the most wonderful thing that ever happened and I agree absolutely that it is, no doubt about it; yet I have other pre-occupations that have pressed me for attention since you sent me the glad tidings and only now can I find time to say how pleased I was with your news. I am sorry it has taken me so long to get round to it. However, Catherine, although a bright little thing, is yet too young to be hurt by my apparent indifference; and her mother will, I hope, understand.

Thank you for letting me know. Now all energies must be concentrated on a plan of campaign for getting her to the top of Smearsett Scar before the end of 1972. It can be done by concerted effort. It must be done.

By a coincidence, I had another letter in the same post as yours from a man whose firstborn has just entered this world, in which he says that his prime object is to get his new son to bag a peak before he can walk, and he is adapting his rucksack as a mobile cot for this purpose. Something of the sort is surely not beyond Dick!

Your account of a winter weekend in the Lakes in January made excellent reading, and you are to be complimented on a sterling performance with the odds weighted heavily (if you don't mind me saying so) against you. I suppose it is true to say that Catherine has already been over Sty Head Pass although she won't remember much about it. Someday soon you must take her there again and let her see the scene of her first fellwalk, carried all the way. Wasdale Head in winter is impressive, and I am glad you saw it in the right conditions.

I look forward to receiving an account of Catherine's first visit to a summit. And when she is old enough to have a rucksack of her very own, I hope you will let me provide it.

You have many days on the hills to look forward to, the three of you. I trust they are all happy ones.

Yours sincerely,

AWainwright

Margaret wrote back to ask if when Catherine was old enough, she could come to his house and collect the rucksack. Almost by return post, a parcel arrved from AW containing a little rucksack. Despite all the personal chat and affection, AW dreaded the idea of strangers arriving at his house.

LETTER 210: TO MARGARET AINLEY, 14 SEPTEMBER 1972

c/o The Westmorland Gazette, KENDAL
14th September 1972

Dear Margaret,

Thank you for your letter giving advance information about the proposed Great Five-Man All-British Expedition to Smearsett Scar. I look forward to a detailed and illustrated account in due course. I hope you are all good runners: a correspondent has reported a bull on that part of the approach route known as The Happy Valley. But I am sure that, after all the preliminary preparations and planning already done, nothing, repeat nothing, will be allowed to prevent a successful accomplishment of your objective. Catherine's first peak!

I can imagine the wonderful day you had on the Howgills. I have had many such; days of wonderful visibility under clear skies, days of fine walking across the tops. The view from The Calf is, in my opinion, the most extensive in the country.

I am glad to know that Catherine is thriving, and I have no doubt at all that she is a lovely child. Yes, the rucksack came from me: it wasn't quite the type I wanted, but the only small one they had. Catherine herself, I thought, would fit snugly inside it until she is big enough to wear it.

I was having a week at Fort William, and tomorrow we are off to a rented cottage near Loch Carron for yet another visit to my beloved Wester Ross, where some of the mountains are even higher than Smearsett Scar.

I cannot wait to hear that this redoubtable summit has again been conquered. I think, in the circumstances, you may be forgiven if you scratch the initials 'C.A. 1972' on the Ordnance column. It would have an historical significance to a few of us.

Yours sincerely,

AWainwright

LETTER 211: TO MARGARET AINLEY, 8 NOVEMBER 1972

c/o The Westmorland Gazette, KENDAL
8th November 1972

Dear Margaret, Dick and Catherine

A conquest indeed! An epic in the annals of mountaineering!

Considering the immaturity and inexperience of a vital member of the expedition, and the hazards met and overcome on the journey, I cannot but rank your successful ascent of Smearsett Scar with Whymper's climb on the Matterhorn; in fact, since it was accomplished without loss of life, I think your performance was even more epic. Now for the North Face of the Eiger. Are you listening, Cath?

The photographs without exception are quite delightful, and they illustrate graphically the dangers of the terrain, the supreme moment of achievement, the exhaustion of certain members on the return to base camp. I return them in haste: Half Brighouse must be panting to see them.

History has been made. No doubt about that!

Yours sincerely,

AWainwright

LETTER 212: TO MARGARET AINLEY, 21 JANUARY 1975

c/o The Westmorland Gazette, KENDAL
21st January 1975

Dear Margaret,

Thank you for your letter and New Year greetings. It was nice to hear from you again and have an up to date report on Catherine's latest peak-bagging successes. The youthful conqueror of Smearset Scar is obviously destined for much greater heights. Catbells and Knott Rigg are merely stepping-stones to bigger and better fells, and I confidently expect to hear from you within the next two years that Great Gable and Scafell Pike have succumbed to her tireless feet. It won't be long before her parents are puffing along in the rear. Even so, she is going to have to pull up her socks to beat the record of one of my correspondents, this being a little girl of six years, from Southport, who wrote to say she had climbed all the 214 fells in the seven books, and last week sent me further word that, now at nine years of age, she had done them all a second time.

I am the very last person you should ask for advice on the pronunciation of Gaelic place-names. I simply have no idea. In fact, I have been badly cut down to size by a Scottish reviewer of the book, who considers me down right rude in suggesting a simplification of the names of the Scottish mountains. No, love, it's no use asking me. Is there no Scotsman amongst your acquaintances who could help? I sometimes think the reason for the great popularity of Ben Nevis is its simple name; walkers do like to be able to say where they've been! One advantage of Gaelic names, the only one that I can see, is that you can adopt your own pronunciation without much fear of contradiction from others who have no idea either and may even come to look upon you with respectful awe.

The second book is being delayed because I am frenetically engaged on a 500-page saga of Westmorland at the present time, but I hope to resume Scotland during the coming summer. When Catherine has polished off everything in Lakeland, you too should cast your sights further north. I should be the last to decry Lakeland, but how flat it seems when you are returning from Wester Ross! This sounds like sacrilege, and of course Lakeland is lovelier by far; but I think a measure of solitude is essential for a full appreciation of mountain scenery and Lakeland is terribly overrun by tourists while the western and northern Highlands are still, for the most part, quite virgin and immeasurably grander then anything between Keswick and Windermere. When Catherine is able to spread her wings a little more and becomes determined to ascend Ben Nevis, I will let you have some useful addresses.

Keep me posted on her progress. I enjoy hearing from you.

Yours sincerely,

AWainwright

LETTER 213: TO MARGARET AINLEY, 5 MARCH 1975

38 Kendal Green, KENDAL
5th March 1975

Dear Margaret,

Since you have discovered that I live in a house and not in a room at the Gazette office there seems little point in further pretence. Yes, write to me here if you prefer but don't get too affectionate; my wife grabs the post first.

So they are Sgoor nan Eech and Sgoor nan Clash yeala slurred together. Clever of you to ferret this out, and from no less authority than Hamish Brown, the man whose review of my book in 'Mountain Life' left me squirming with rage and humiliation. What right have I, from south of the Border, to criticise Gaelic spellings and pronunciation: what rot the fellow writes; what a cheek to suggest a Royal Commission to agree on uniformity of Scottish mountain names; what if there are five ways of spelling a name for 'white mountain' – the Scots understand and like it that way; I am quite wrong in thinking Blencathra and Glaramara are sweeter-sounding names. And so on, and so on. . . . Mind you, I was expecting criticism of this sort. I suppose I was being cheeky. But I still think that life should be made more tolerable for earnest English moun-tain-lovers in the Highlands. On the mountains, more than anywhere, there should be no closed shops. If you have now got really pally with Hamish, you can tell him so.

But for Hamish the mountaineer I have the greatest respect. The enclosed cutting will tell you why. All the Munros in one long walk! Now there is an objective for the Ainleys when Catherine gets in the tiger class. I'm glad, though, that you have set your sights on the Highlands. When Catherine sets foot on the summit of Liathach (Leegak) Smearsett Scar will seem almost a shameful incident in her life. You have some wonder-ful years ahead of you.

Incredibly I managed two Munros myself last summer in a glorious week based on Glen Affric, a feat of which I am inordinately proud and which has encouraged the hope that I might reach the tops of one or two more during my three planned expeditions this coming summer. I have gone off hotels now, just as I went off boarding houses years ago. Heaven in the Highlands consists of being under your own exclusive roof, and hired cottages and well-sited chalets where you can get your maps spread out all over the floor without fear of disturbance, provide this opportunity. Fellow-lodgers, I have decided, are a menace to enjoyment. And especially so if they speak the Gaelic.

Please don't trouble to return the cutting. Pin it up on the kitchen wall and plan a great future for the Ainley clan.

Yours sincerely,

AWainwright

LETTER 214: TO MARGARET AINLEY, 23 OCTOBER 1975

38 Kendal Green, KENDAL
CUMBRIA
23rd October 1975

Dear Margaret,

I am sorry for the delay in replying to your interesting (and entertaining) letter, but it arrived just as I was about to depart for the third time this year to the far north. We had hired a caravan in Glencoe, this being a new experience for me (I mean the caravan, not Glencoe) and it proved enjoyable, even so late in the year, largely because the weather was so mild and there was no rain at all. It was a six-berth, roomy enough for me to spread myself with my maps, the only 'inconvenience' being the extremely restricted W.C., which was so small that I could not even enter it let alone enter it and sit down. Catherine might just have managed it.

You really must get up into Caledonia before she is much older and before the tourist hordes swarm north. You would all enjoy it immensely. The scenery all along the west coast and inland of it is quite superb. Lakeland looks almost flat on the return journey south. When Catherine is old enough to go to school, not long now, she should take Gaelic as a second language: it will be a great advantage, and avoid you much embarrassment when you fall into the company of people like Hamish.

The second Scottish book will be out early in the New Year and the third will follow in the early summer, 1975 having been a rewarding year for the necessary fieldwork.

I'm sorry the weather was none too good for your Keswick holiday, but you seem to have got around quite well, the highlight being the Haystacks – High Stile day; yes, despite Gamlin End, still one of my favourite expeditions. The paths, as you say, are becoming a problem in many places, some of them, once narrow trods, having acquired the dimensions of a motorway. I don't know what can be done about this, short of abandoning the paths altogether and finding your own virgin routes to the tops (which actually is much more fun).

I went through Brighouse on the bus a few weeks ago, but saw no sign of little girl who looked as though she might have been on the top of Smearsett Scar, nor did I notice any street-sign for Castlefields Crescent although I imagined to be on the new estate going up the hill towards the M.62.

Thank you for writing and keeping me in touch.

Yours sincerely,

AWainwright

LETTER 215: TO MARGARET AINLEY, 21 NOVEMBER 1975

38 Kendal Green, KENDAL
21st November 1975

Dear Margaret,

Well, fancy you wishing I had called on you during my travels through Brighouse! You must have masochistic tendencies. No, the thought never once occurred to me. I wouldn't dream of making an unannounced appearance. I was never one for unexpected confrontations. Besides, what would your husband say, you entertaining royalty while he was slaving his guts out at Nu-Swift away in Elland? No, no, I was well content to sit in the bus and search the faces of the passers-by for someone, child or woman, who looked as though they might once have climbed to the uppermost inches of Smearsett Scar. But I saw no-one who looked, even remotely, as though they might have been inspired to undertake such an adventure. None of them even looked happy. You live in alien surroundings, love. Don't let your roots go too deep. There are better places than Brighouse. Couldn't Daddy persuade Nu-Swift to open a branch at Sty Head or Honister Pass?

I have drooled over your lovely transparencies and now return them for the family album, and I have taken to heart your regretful assertion that Lakeland means less to me that it did and Scotland more. Perhaps you are right.

Lakeland is utterly lovely and charming, a heavenly paradise on earth – but oh the crowds! There is no fun in walking in procession, not even in delectable scenery. I remember Keswick when, even in summer, you saw only a few of like kin, fellwalkers out for a day's adventure on the hills; when the only place of refreshment after a hard day was a chip-shop. No, the old romantic atmosphere has quite gone. Only in the depth of winter do you get a reminder of things as they used to be, and only in winter can I be persuaded, these days, to re-visit the places that once I loved almost to distraction. You will see what I mean when at last you find yourselves in Torridon, or on Stac Polly, or by Loch Hourn. Then I think you might agree. Be quick and grow up, Cathy!

You must, I implore you, restrain your impulse to call at 38 K.G. Not only would you be disappointed because, having lived like a recluse for so long I have developed the eccentricities of one, but, more important, I have a wife who is also consumed with insatiable curiosity, not only about female callers but even about female correspondents. You see, I have a secret past, or so she suspects, and what is worse, I continue to enjoy a virility far beyond my years. You'd best leave me alone to get on with my writing.

With very best wishes for a happy Christmas and new peaks in 1976,
Yours sincerely (well, partly what),

AWainwright

LETTER 216: TO MARGARET AINLEY, 26 JULY 1976

38 Kendal Green,
KENDAL, Cumbria
26th July 1976

Dear Margaret,

Thank you for your latest letter and the opportunity of seeing a few of your slides, all of which I enjoyed despite a sneaking feeling that the one of Husband on Lion Couchant was designed to take the mickey out of me although I was consoled by your admission that your own attempt on this perilous climb failed, otherwise I could indeed have taken umbrage at what I must have regarded as a cheeky exercise to emphasise my own failure. <u>You</u> must never climb the Lion Couchant, promise me that. I could never live with myself if you did. Then there's young Catherine, coming along by leaps and bounds as a seasoned fellwalker. She must never do it either. A man has his pride, you know.

How Catherine has grown! Seems only months since she was 'expected', only weeks since she startled the world with the first infant ascent of Smearsett. Already she is conquering giants like Ard Crags, and names like Ben Alligin and Liathach are entering her vocabulary. I don't mind that. It's the Lion Couchant you must keep her away from.

This projected trip to Wester Ross is good news. This is where you really start to live. The world will have a new dimension for the Ainleys next year.

My switching of favours from Lakeland to places north merely demonstrates that there is nothing partisan in my make-up, that I can appreciate the beauty of mountain landscapes wherever they may be. And not only of mountain landscapes. I will now make you swallow your criticisms, your charges of infidelity, your unfounded claim to have detected a change of loyalties, your accusation of fickle devotion, by announcing that for several months I have turned my steps time and again to, guess what, the Yorkshire Dales, and in a few weeks will have completed A DALES SKETCHBOOK, for publication later in the year. This news should make you writhe with shame. Why, only last week, hours after receipt of your letter, I was making a study of Shibden Hall, and going on from there, past innumerable road signs that beseeched me to turn aside to Brighouse, to Kirkstall Abbey. Shame on you. After all, remember that I am going ultimately to the shore of Innominate Tarn, not of Loch Carron. I haven't changed my affections, not really.

Yours sincerely

AWainwright

LETTER 217: TO MARGARET AINLEY, 13 AUGUST 1977

38 Kendal Green, KENDAL
13th August 1977

Dear Margaret,

Thank you for the latest news from Brighouse, of which perhaps the most important item is not the failure of the washing machine but Catherine's ascent of Glyder Fawr, a superlative performance. Who would have thought it likely five years ago? Then, Smearsett Scar was the primary objective! As for the ascent of Snowdon by railway, let not your conscience be troubled. In Glen Shee a month ago I was carried up a mountain by chairlift for the first time ever. So much easier. Wown bookshy don't all mountains have them?

I share your opinion about Wales. Grand mountains, but harsh and unfriendly, quite lacking the beauty and charm of the Lakeland hills. But what I cannot stomach about Wales is the speech of its inhabitants. Imagine being in a community where everyone talks like Clive Jenkins! This is what really puts me off about Wales, and why I never go.

We were back in Plockton again in April, finding it as devastatingly beautiful as ever despite an ugly oil rig across the bay. And a few weeks ago we paid a very successful visit to Braemar, a most delightful area and one you should seriously consider if ever you acquire a tent because there seems to be very little restriction of campers, who we saw scattered along the banks of the Dee in glorious surrounding and all apparently without charge. But keep out of the hotels, which are everywhere in Scotland now very expensive. My week in Braemar, for two, cost around 200 pounds all told.

Yours sincerely,

AW

LETTER 218: TO MARGARET AINLEY, 18 SEPTEMBER 1979

38 Kendal Green,
KENDAL, Cumbria
18 September 1979

Dear Margaret,

Thank you for your letter. I am sending 5 packets of notelets, but unfortunately cannot let you have more of one subject without upsetting the system.

I'm sorry 1979 has not been a good year for the summits but hope 1980 makes up for it. The cottage on Loch Awe sounds delightful.

We went up to Plockton (9th year in succession) at the end of April with the firm idea of climbing Ben Alligin at last, but all the mountains were completely plastered with snow and in fact there was new snow and bitter winds every day. We had often wondered what the Highlands were like at Christmas – now we know. We went north as far as Kinlochbervie.

The white landscape was beautiful but it was never fit to leave the car.

We were more fortunate at the end of June, enjoying the only fine week of the summer on a first serious visit to Wales. We had a cottage at Dolgellau, remarkable for its lack of necessary equipment and furnishings, but had a splendid week nevertheless, the highlight being an ascent of Cader Idris – a splendid mountain, but avoid the Foxes Path if ever you do it. We have a cottage booked at Beddegelert for next May.

I hope you are all well despite the traumas of 1979. Your move to a new house sounds exciting. Has it a view of a noble mountain?

Yours sincerely,

AWainwright

LETTER 219: TO MARGARET AINLEY, 25 JUNE 1980

38 Kendal Green,
KENDAL, Cumbria
25th June 1980

Dear Margaret and family,

Thank you for the eight-page account of your second Loch Awe holiday, all of which made good reading apart from your vindictive attack on innocent caterpillars – sweet little things, I always considered them. You really must learn to love your fellow creatures.

We had better fortune with the weather than yourselves for our week at Beddgelert, a charming place (May 10–17); in fact it was absolutely super. Cloudless skies and unbroken sunshine every minute of every day, and not a drop nor even a hint of rain. You went to bed every night certain that the morrow would be exactly the same, perfect. It is not often one can set off for a day on the mountains unimpeded by protective devices against wet weather, but so it was during that memorable week. The idea of setting forth armed with waterproofs and rain-gear and over-trousers was just too ridiculous to think about. No waiting for the mist to lift or the showers to pass. It was just perfect. And reassuring for me because I found I could still get up on the tops, although slowly, and enjoy the summits as much as ever. Five savage peaks were trodden underfoot and 80 super photographs obtained. The cottage we hired was clean and well-equipped – we enjoyed this too, and have booked it again for the end of September. All told, this was probably the best and most rewarding holidays I have ever had.

Yes, do try Lochinver next year. A charming place with a strange and exciting landscape. A good new restaurant has opened recently and will provide you with splendid evening meals at reasonable cost. And there are NO CATERPILLARS at Lochinver. Only midges.

Photos returned with thanks. It seems incredible that eight years have gone by since you first broke the news of an interesting event in the family and that soon afterwards you reported the successful ascent of Smearsett Scar by a very young Catherine. Now she looks almost a veteran hiker!

Yours sincerely,

AW

[He has drawn caterpillars all over this letter.]

Part 18
Letters to Chris Jesty, 1973-80

AW also conducted several long correspondences of a more technical and work-related nature, connected with his books, or other people's books. They show the amount of work and thought he put into his own books – and also his strong opinions on the work of others. Most of all, they show how generous he was, keen to help others in a similar field.

Chris Jesty first wrote to him from Wales in 1973. He had worked with the Ordance Survey as a cartographer and was now drawing and publishing his own maps, though not with enormous success. To make a living, he was working as a taxi diver.

AW was most impressed when Jesty sent him his panorama of the views as seen from Snowdon – and addressed him as Chris in his first letter, a sure sign of acceptance, though it wasn't till his third letter that AW revealed his home address.

He offered help and advice to Jesty and in 1978, co-operated with him on a Guide to the View from Scafell Pike in which he agreed his name could be used. He put in about 100 hours of work, but refused to take any money.

From time to time, AW tried to be matey, making jocular and teasing references to a woman called Margot whom Chris had happened to mention – but alas, Chris had only admired her from afar and there was never a relationship.

LETTER 220: TO CHRIS JESTY, 26 APRIL 1973

c/o The Westmorland Gazette
KENDAL
26th April 1973

Dear Chris,

It is a pleasure to report safe receipt of a copy of your Snowdon panorama. Many thanks for sending this along to me.

You have my most sincere congratulations on the success of a mission I would have thought no man would ever have the resolution to tackle even if equipped with the necessary powers of intelligences, topographical knowledge, draughtsmanship, ability to record facts with meticulous care, and, perhaps most of all, incredible patience. All these qualities you must possess with an over-riding love of Snowdon.

I have never before seen any project conceived with such care and dedication. It must have been like planning a military campaign.

I confess I have never seen Lakeland from Snowdon, or, more surprisingly, North Wales from Lakeland. Therefore I cannot vouch for the details of your view, but, from careful study of the map, contours and altitudes, I see no reason for doubting your findings. I have only two comments: first, Lad Stones is an insignificant shoulder of Wetherlam, which, seen from the south, overtops it, and, since Lad Stones is a name hardly used locally, I would have preferred this sighting to be named as Wetherlam; and secondly, Little Hart Crag is a minor height dominated by neighbouring Dove Crag and Red Screes, which, I feel, should have been named instead.

Having tried to do panoramas myself on a much less ambitious scale, I can well understand the amount of painstaking work you have put into the task and all the frustrations and doubts that must have arisen, quite apart from all the homework converting miles to metric and measuring distances. I don't know whether you have seen Shearer's panorama from Ben Nevis, done in 1895 (if not, I'll send it on for you to see): this too was a considerable effort, though lacking the precision of yours. It is interesting to note that, after first being published, it was subsequently revised, which can only mean, since the panorama could not change, that the original contained errors. I think you must expect some doubts to be expressed about your own conclusions, in some respects, although my own feeling is that the wealth of detail, so obviously compiled with great care, inspires confidence in its accuracy.

Your printer, too, has done an excellent job. Not even Waterlow and Sons could have done a better.

I hope Margot has recovered from her ordeal. The things some women will do for men! This caps all.

If I may, I would like to keep the copy you sent me. I have a number of friends who will be interested, mightily so, and it will be a joy to me to let them see what you have done.

Yours sincerely,

AWainwright

LETTER 221: TO CHRIS JESTY, 10 MAY 1973

c/o The Westmorland Gazette
KENDAL
10th May 1973

Dear Chris,

Thakyou for your further letter of the 1st.

When I suggested that Wetherlam should be substituted for Lad Stones on your Snowdon panorama I did so without reference to maps, feeling in my bones that Wetherlam was sufficiently east of Coniston Old Man to be visible from Snowdon, south south west. Now, roughly aligning my maps, I find you are right: Wetherlam is hidden. But if the 1500' contour on the Old Man is in direct line with the 2000' contour on Lad Stones I would expect the latter to be overtopped by Fairfield or very nearly so, and not separated as much as your diagram suggests. But I haven't got the right maps or instruments to be sure about this. I take your word for it.

No, I am sure I have never seen Snowdonia from Lakeland, but this summer will be making several trips to Black Combe for another purpose and will keep a sharp lookout with binoculars.

Shearer's panorama is by no means as detailed as yours (no mileages, etc) and probably far less accurate. If you ever wish to borrow my copy, please let me know. Bear in mind, before you get too involved with Ben Nevis, that the top is in cloud for 300 days a year.

Margot would go raving mad if she were to see the last paragraph of your letter. There would be no question of her living in the observatory ruins on Ben Nevis with you for three weeks or more. I am beginning to feel a little sorry for Margot, poor kid. I think she must have a rough time of it.

Yours sincerely,

AWainwright

Off tomorrow for a week in a rented cottage in Wester Ross. The weather reports from there are appalling.

LETTER 222: TO CHRIS JESTY, 14 JUNE 1973

c/o The Westmorland Gazette
KENDAL
14th June 1973

Dear Chris,

Thank you for your further letter, which relieves my apprehension about Margot considerably.

I enclose Shearer's panorama from Ben Nevis. This you may keep for as long as you wish.

While I am sorry you are not finding much demand for your Snowdon masterpiece (which it is), I am not greatly surprised. It lacks visual appeal. A drawing of the panorama, after the fashion of Shearer's crude effort, or, better still, a composite photograph, would be more attractive to the general public, and would sell in thousands to the hordes who frequent Snowdon. The effect of your style of presentation must be to scare most people off. They need to study it carefully, and careful study is not a popular pastime. They want things that can be seen and easily understood. You have, in my view, tried to cram too many statistics in. The result is that your panorama looks as though it has come out of a computer. A simple but accurate drawing on a long folded strip would have proved more popular. Friends I have shown your panorama agree with this opinion while lost in admiration of your prodigious effort. As I said before, you made a wonderful job of it, but I think fell into error, so far as the ordinary observer is concerned, by including too much detail. People don't like complications. No, I think a drawing, a la Shearer, would have sold better, but better still a composite photograph with a really good camera. I have books of mountain panoramas published by a W.M. Docharty, which contain some real beauties, mostly from Scottish summits, and built up from upwards of twenty prints all joined together so precisely that the joinings can hardly be distinguished. Mr Docharty's books were each limited to 250 copies and given to his friends, so that they cannot be purchased. His panoramas are quite magnificent, presenting the scene exactly as it appears, clouds and all. Unfortunately these books are large and heavy volumes or I would have sent you one to see.

Four times in the past two weeks I have been on Black Combe. On no occasion was there the slightest chance of seeing Snowdon. I am now reconciled to the fact that I shall never see North Wales from Lakeland.

You will never do the panorama from Ben Nevis, but it might be an excuse for getting Margot up there with you.

Yours sincerely,

AWainwright

LETTER 223: TO CHRIS JESTY, 13 JULY 1973

38 Kendal Green
Kendal, Westmorland
13th July 1973

Dear Chris,

Thank you for your interesting letter of 28th June, which arrived while I was on holiday with a camera in the Torridon and An Teallach areas, hence the delay in replying.

Your ideas and comments give much food for thought. Panoramas based on colour photographs would be superb provided the viewpoint gave good depth to the foreground so that the view is downward (into the valleys) as well as distant. The trouble with photographs is that they tend to flatten out the verticals, and, short of using a telescopic lens (which distorts distances) there seems no answer to this problem. It is important that the viewpoint should be sharply elevated above its surroundings on all sides; a flattish summit is useless.

I would like to see your panorama from Aran Fawddy very much but, because it is way off the beaten track of tourists, it would never be a commercial proposition, and in fact could be expensive to produce, colour work being very costly. If you care to send it, you may do so to my home address (as above), and I will have a talk with a local printer about the possibilities including costs.

I don't think you should entrust the Schulthess photograph to the post, just as I would not like the Docharty panoramas of mine be subjected to the risk of loss. There may be an opportunity later on to exchange opinions on these.

Incidentally, before going to Scotland, I climbed Black Combe four times in the space of a fortnight only to find each time that the distance was shrouded in haze: on only one occasion was there a sight of the Isle of Man, and that but faintly. I have now abandoned all hope of ever seeing Snowdon from Lakeland.

One thing that always strikes me forcibly every time I go to Scotland is the stark clarity of the distant views. The mists and hazes that shroud the Lake District for so much of the time are quite unknown in the Highlands, where fifty-mile vistas are a common experience even under a cloudy sky. I did not have particularly good weather on this latest trip, most days having a high cloud ceiling, yet the distant views were always starkly clear. Even in rain the mountain tops often remain free from clinging mists.

I will look forward to seeing the Aran Fawddwy [*sic*] photographs.

Yours sincerely,

AWainwright

LETTER 224: TO CHRIS JESTY, 13 DECEMBER 1973

> 38 Kendal Green
> Kendal, Westmorland
> 13th December 1973

Dear Chris,

Thank you for treturning the Shearer panorama from Ben Nevis. I think your slight criticisma of this effort are probably justified and that a detailed check on the spot would be likely to reveal many more defects, the fact that it has once been revised (although the subject matter remains static) suggest original discrepancies which, I feel sure, have not been wholly corrected.

I wouldn't mind having a shot at drawing the foreground for some future distant panorama of yours, provided I can do it from photographs and am not expected to sit on some freezing mountain-top waiting for the clouds to lift, but I must express the opinion again that a single panorama without a narrative or walkers' routes to the summit would never be a commercial proposition except possibly for Snowdon or Ben Nevis. A booklet devoted to a single mountain, giving routes, illustrations, notes on botany and geology with a panorama that opened out might just pay its way, and I think you should plan on these lines. The subject would, of course, have to be a popular one such as Snowdon.

Yours sincerely,

AWainwright

LETTER 225: TO CHRIS JESTY, 18 NOVEMBER 1977

38 Kendal Green
Kendal, Westmorland
18th November 1977

Dear Chris,

I have just been looking at your Scafell Pike panorama, and am quite overwhelmed at the magnitude of the task you have set yourself, the amount of distant detail you have included being amazing. Perhaps the wealth of information rather tends to crowd out the Lakeland part of the panorama in the headings, and much of it will never be seen on most days of the year; however, I have no doubt that all the items you give are visible in exceptional conditions and should therefore be included.

I had expected the titles to synchronise with the drawings, but of course they are on different scales and I couldn't determine that there will be perfect alignment in the finished job, so I must leave that to you. Nor have I attempted to check the distant horizons nor the names outside the Lake District.

I return everything unaltered. My signature is affixed to this letter; perhaps you would place it as you wish.

I enjoyed looking at your sides. Some of them, especially those from Ben Nevis, are out of this world, really excellent. Why not a book of your best mountain photographs?

Yours sincerely,

AWainwright

LETTER 226: TO CHRIS JESTY, 3 FEBRUARY 1978

38 Kendal Green
Kendal, Cumbria
3rd February 1978

Dear Chris,

I have examined the proofs of the Scafell Pike panorama and now return them. This is really a tremendous effort (on your part, not mine) that has obviously required amazing concentration and research and painstaking penwork. I wouldn't have thought it possible to include all the detail you have managed to squeeze in. You must be the only person in the country with the dedication and patience to attempt such a panorama, let alone complete it. The printers too deserve credit for their contribution.

The distant views merge into the Lakeland scene very neatly. I have not checked anything outside the Lake District, but your accuracy on the places I know inspires confidence in the whole.

If the blank spot on Sheet Four is touched up, the printing should come out all right, and probably the faint lines missing on the proofs will register in the finished job.

I have not made any notes on the proofs but attach a list of items at which you might look again. These, however, are trivial and possibly not worth correction.

People are going to wonder how you tackled this remarkable task, and I think a summary of your experiences (number of visits, time spent on the summit, nights out, number of photos taken, etc) would be of great interest: however, there seems no room for this – a pity!

I hope the sale does well enough to repay your expense and provide a deserved reward. I continue to be sceptical about its success, but I think it might help if you were to include my name in your publicity and especially when visiting the Lakeland shops. You should let the magazine Cumbria (Dalesman Publishing Co. Ltd) have a copy for review, and I am sure Border Television would be glad to give you an interview and feature the panorama.

Perhaps you would kindly let me have half-a-dozen copies of the finished panorama when the time comes for publication.

Yours sincerely,

AWainwright

SHEET 1: My signature looks much too prominent compared with yours. Either it should be reduced in size by one-third, or your own should be given much more emphasis in larger type.

SHEET 2: Grisedale For is rather an unfortunate abbreviation. There seems no room for the word Forest and perhaps it should be omitted. A message from the publisher to the reader: writing <u>in</u> would be better than writing <u>up</u>

SHEET 4: On the map on Sheet 4 SFP is an unfortunate abbreviation (remember that 90% of your readers are dull-witted). Is it necessary to include it, bearing in mind that all the lines converge at this point?

LETTER 227: TO CHRIS JESTY, 14 MAY 1978

38 Kendal Green, KENDAL
14th May 1978

Dear Chris,

Many thanks for the copies of the Scafell Pike panorama. These were awaiting my return from a visit to the Outer Hebrides, hence the delay in acknowledging receipt.

The finished product is excellent and I hope you do well with it. There is one spelling error I forgot to mention: note 34 on Sheet 4 – unlikelyhood should be unlikelihood. And I think you have given my name too much prominence and your own too little.

But I really is a magnificent achievement, one of which you can feel very proud, and great tribute is due to the printers, who have done a difficult job very sympathetically.

You will be sending out review copies, no doubt, to publications such as 'Climber and Rambler'. I think the editor of 'Cumbria' (Dalesman Publishing Co., Clapham, via Lancaster) might be glad to give it a mention, especially if accompanied by an article on your trials and tribulations and methods and general experiences during compilation of the data. I will send a copy to the Editor of the Westmorland Gazette for comment in his newspaper. It would be worth your while to make a tour of the Lakeland bookshops and get them to display the sheets in their windows.

I hope it is successful. You deserve success.

Yours sincerely,

AWainwright

I seem to remember Mark Richards telling me that your cottage at Dolgellau is available for holiday lettings. If it is, I might be interested in a week next year (for a book of Welsh Mountain Drawings).

LETTER 228: TO CHRIS JESTY, 14 JANUARY 1979

38 Kendal Green, KENDAL
14th January 1979

Dear Chris,

Please book me for the week commencing 23rd June this coming summer. My cheque is enclosed. If this week is not available the following week will do equally well.

I hope the Scafell Pike panorama is doing all right. You seem to have a good distribution system! I notice it on sale in many unexpected shops!

Yours sincerely,

AWainwright

LETTER 229: TO CHRIS JESTY, 26 OCTOBER 1980

38 Kendal Green, KENDAL
26th October 1980

Dear Chris,

Thank you for your letter and interesting suggestions for revising the Lakeland guides. I think, not yet, and probably not until after my death (now surely imminent), when Westmorland Gazette might well be interested. I agree, however, that some revision is desirable and will bear your ideas in mind. The specimen pages enclosed are certainly very nicely done and I would have no doubts on that score after seeing your painstaking and accurate work on the panoramas, which I hope continue to do well. In the meantime I will let the Gazette see your efforts.

This year, blessed by good weather, I have had two splendid mountaineering holidays based on Beddgelert. My book of drawings is now well in hand and will be published in the spring next year.

Yours sincerely,

AWainwright

Part 19
Letters to Ron Scholes, 1979-84

Ron Scholes, a primary school headmaster living in Staffordshire, came into AW's life by giving to AW's favourite charity, Animal Rescue, rather than the normal way as a fan: writing a fan letter. Ron, aged fifty in 1979, married with two sons, gave an illustrated talk in Kendal in 1979 about a long-distance walk he had done and donated the fee to Animal Rescue. AW was fascinated by Ron's long walks, his attempts to write a book about them, and also of course his interest in Animal Rescue.

LETTER 230: TO RON SCHOLES, 8 APRIL 1979

> 38 Kendal Green
> Kendal, Cumbria
> 8th April 1979

Dear Mr Scholes,
    Very many thanks for your kind donation of fees for lectures.
It was good of you to do this, and your generosity is greatly appreciated.
Yours sincerely,

AWainwright

LETTER 231: TO RON SCHOLES, 5 NOVEMBER 1979

> 38 Kendal Green
> Kendal, Cumbria
> 5th November 1979

Dear Mr Scholes,

Thank you for your further remittance to Animal Rescue, a receipt for which is enclosed.

And for your generous offer to give an illustrated talk on the Cambrian Way. I was immensely interested to learn that you had done his walk because some five or six years ago a Mr Tony Drake of Cheltenham asked me if I would do a detailed guidebook to a Cambrian Way he had devised and for which he was then trying to get the blessing of the Countryside Commission and the necessary permissions from landowners. I was mildly interested, sufficiently to get 2 and a half inch maps of the whole route as he described it to me, but told him that I thought the distance much too great for the average walker and suggested that the less attractive southern section should be excluded entirely, starting the walk at Aberystwyth, and further that an alternative to the Rhinogs should be adopted, feeling that the inevitable novices and school parties may run into trouble on this rough ground. I never heard from him again. Two or three years ago I met a friend of Mr Drake who told me that he was making little progress with the idea, since when there has been silence about the whole project.

It was therefore a surprise to find that you had in fact done the walk, and indeed the whole of the original route as he planned it. I had not heard of anyone else doing the full walk, and it does appear from your letter that it has now been recognised as 'official'.

For this reason I should be very interested to hear your talk and see your slides, another reason being that I am planning a book on Snowdonia: really a portfolio of mountain drawings, and with this in mind spent a week in Dolgellau this past summer and have booked a cottage at Beddgelert for next May.

Now about your very generous offer. I hesitate to ask you to give your talk publicly until I have sounded out the possibilities. My Committee on Animal Rescue is wholly female and probably have little interest in the Cambrian Way, but there is in Kendal a group of CHA and RA members and also a long-distance fellwalking club, as well as a Mountain Rescue team, from all of whom I would expect support. I would hate to ask you to come to a sparse attendance. May I therefore suggest that we leave the matter in abeyance until I have made some enquiries?

Thank you again for your continuing help for the Charity.

Yours sincerely,

AWainwright

LETTER 232: TO RON SCHOLES, 24 FEBRUARY 1980

38 Kendal Green
Kendal, Cumbria
24th February 1980

Dear Mr Scholes,

My 'agent' has now reported a sufficient enthusiasm amongst local walkers to warrant my going ahead with arrangements for your proposed talk on the Cambrian Way. I think we may expect an attendance of around 100, and I intend to have this number of tickets printed for selling in advance at 50p.

Assuming you are still willing to do this for us despite the long delay, perhaps you would kindly give me a few dates (in order of priority) so that we can look for a suitable room. Booking may not be easy at short notice and I would suggest April as the best month if this is also convenient for you. Presumably you will want a room that can be blacked out?

I believe you said you could provide all necessary equipment but if there is anything at all I should be doing, do please let me know.

Again many many thanks for your kindness in this matter.

Yours sincerely,

AWainwright

LETTER 233: TO RON SCHOLES, 12 MARCH 1980

38 Kendal Green
Kendal, Cumbria
12 March 1980

Dear Mr Scholes,

I am terribly sorry, but after taking a Gallup poll amongst the supporters likely to attend your lecture I find that the three dates you give are unsuitable to them. They point out that April 3 and 4 are Eastertime, when many will be away, and that the Saturday April 19 is not a good date either, Saturdays being their usual day for expeditions. I am glad to report, however, that there is considerable enthusiasm for your lecture and none seem to want to miss it.

I really think now that we had better leave it until later in the year, perhaps when you can conveniently combine it with a visit to the Lakes.

There seems to be a good choice of suitable rooms in the town, and a Thursday evening is the popular choice.

Have a good time in Wales. I shall be there May 10–17 and greatly look forward to it. I shall be looking at sections of the Cambrian Way.

Yours sincerely,

AWainwright

LETTER 234: TO RON SCHOLES, 3 SEPTEMBER 1980

38 Kendal Green
Kendal, Cumbria
3rd September 1980

Dear Mr Scholes

I am writing to inform you that I have booked the Kirkland Hall in Kendal for your talk on the Cambrian Way on Thursday evening, 23rd October.

I am not familiar with this Hall, which was formerly a Primary School, but I understand that it is quite nice, having recently been decorated, and seats about 80–100 people. The Natural History Society in Kendal often use it for lectures.

I propose to have tickets printed for sale in advance and to charge 50 pence for admission.

I will write you again nearer the date to see if you want any arrangements making. I assume you will not want hotel accommodation or overnight hospitality, being only an hour's run from your base in Wensleydale, but hope we will be able to have a meal together before the talk.

Yours sincerely,

AWainwright

After almost two years of correspondence, AW invited Ron to pop in, should he be passing, an honour indeed. A year later, he was even addressing him as Ron. Ron did go on to visit AW and Betty several times – and once stayed overnight at Kendal Green.

LETTER 235: TO RON SCHOLES, 11 JANUARY 1981

38 Kendal Green
Kendal, Cumbria
11th January 1981

Dear Mr Scholes,

Thank you for your cheque and letter.

As regards the three books on loan, I am in no hurry to have them back and it will be quite all right for you to keep them until you are next in the vicinity of Kendal.

As regards the project you had in mind, and which we discussed during your visit here in October, I am now of the opinion that you have missed the boat as far as a comprehensive summary of <u>all</u> the long-distance walks is concerned. My attention was recently drawn to an article in Climber and Rambler in which it was stated that Pan Books had commissioned a young fellow of the name of Westmacott to do the sort of thing you had in mind, and although I do not like his style of writing, the vast resources of the publishers and their wide distribution agencies could kill off competitors. There has also just been published 'The Big Walks', an absolutely superb volume in colour of 56 of the toughest walks in the U.K., priced at 16 pounds and worth every penny for the pictures alone. You could not possibly compete with this. Further, I think I told you that Geoffrey Berry's book of long-distance walks had had a disappointing sale. From my own experience, it is <u>guidebooks</u> that sell, books giving intimate detail that walkers can take in their pocket, not the books that give only a scanty indication of routes and are intended for fireside reading. Therefore, if I were you I would abandon the idea of a brief description of all the long distance walks and concentrate on a detailed step by step guidebook to one only – and that one should obviously be the Cambrian Way, for which there will soon be a big demand and for which you already have much of the detail. You must, however, be first in the field, for there is no doubt that other writers will have the same idea when the route is declared official.

I hope you have now settled in your new address, and like it.

Do please call when next your travels bring you to this part of the world.

Yours sincerely,

AWainwright

LETTER 236: TO RON SCHOLES, 25 JANUARY 1981

38 Kendal Green
Kendal, Cumbria
25 January 1981

Dear Mr Scholes,

Very good! Your detailed and interesting descriptions make me want to follow in your footsteps.

I certainly think you should go ahead with the idea and be first in the field as soon as the Way is approved officially. Then you should get Tony Drake to vet it.

Westmorland Gazette would be interested in publishing but have so few distribution agencies that it might be better to try Pan or Penguin.

However, we can discuss these points when you call. In the meantime I will retain your papers and photos.

Yours sincerely,

AWainwright

LETTER 237: TO RON SCHOLES, 10 FEBRUARY 1981

38 Kendal Green
Kendal, Cumbria
10 February 1981

Dear Ron,

Bad news, I'm afraid. Mark Richards, who is in regular touch with Tony Drake, called to see me last weekend, and reports that a RICHARD SALE already has prepared a complete manuscript of the Cambrian Way, which is to be published as soon as the route is made official.

I think you should speak to Drake before doing any more work on the book and I should be interested to learn his views.

Yours sincerely,

AWainwright

LETTER 238: TO RON SCHOLES, 1 MARCH 1981

38 Kendal Green
Kendal, Cumbria
1 March 1981

Dear Ron,

Your interview with Tony Drake seems to have been much more encouraging than I feared. Apparently he is not committed in any way with Richard Sale, and from what you say seems to agree that you should go ahead with your own manuscript. He appears to be pessimistic about early prospects on an official blessing, but of course there could be no objection to the publication of a guidebook without the sanction of the Countryside Commission so long as you keep to rights of way and areas of open access, and describe the book by some title other than 'the Cambrian Way', e.g. 'A Long Walk in Wales'. From your report of the interview it certainly appears that you have the green light to go ahead.

I still think that the walk should be from Aberystwith to Conwy to get the best of the scenery and only the best. Further not many walkers can manage the three weeks the full route would entail and would be deterred by this. Starting from Aberystwith it could be done comfortably in a fortnight.

However, you probably feel that your proposed manuscript should fit exactly with the official pronouncement of 'The Cambrian Way' when finally made, and in view of the publicity which will herald the official 'opening' this must be better from the point of view of sales.

You have certainly got a big job in prospect. You will become engrossed in it. No more telly for the next year or so! You have the best withes of Betty and myself and our eleven cats (or is it twelve?).

I have now booked the same room as before for your talk on 'The Pennine Way' on Thursday evening, 29th October. Thanks again for offering to do this for us.

Yours sincerely

AWainwright

For Aberystwith read Aberystwyth

LETTER 239: TO RON SCHOLES, 22 MARCH 1981

38 Kendal Green
Kendal, Cumbria
22 March 1981

Dear Ron,

Thank you for your letter and kind donation.

Of your two suggested titles I like 'From Cardiff to Conwy – A Long Walk', which describes the contents exactly. I don't like 'Cambrian Ways', which gives no indication of the nature of the book. 'Ways' has other meanings (habits, for instance), and another objection is that this title suggests a poaching of the name of the official route, and if the latter ever gets off the ground, may result in confusion.

It is a good idea to tackle first a much more modest book, to see what the problems are, and the proposed publication of local walks just fits the bill. Presumably Radio Stoke would publish it?

Yes, I shall be pleased to do any drawings you want, from photos to be supplied later.

Many thanks for your further donation
Yours sincerely

AWainwright

LETTER 240: TO RON SCHOLES, 6 JUNE 1982

38 Kendal Green
Kendal, Cumbria
6 June 1982

Dear Ron,

Thank you for your letter.

Yes, it will be quite all right for you to use the drawings you have listed. Two comments – first, I note that those you have selected are all large drawings, about 8" × 6", and you should bear in mind that they can be reproduced to a much smaller size if so required to fit the dimensions of the book. I think myself that they are improved by reduction. As an example of what I mean – the drawings used for the Animal Rescue notelets are all full-size drawings severely reduced to about 5" × 3". specimen of Buttermere enclosed – this is reduced from 8" x 6". Secondly, I still think the book will seem unbalanced because all the drawings are of northern parts of the country and the southern parts are illustrated by photographs only. To correct this I will, if you wish, do about half-a-dozen drawings of subjects in the southern counties if you will send photographs. For instance I was much impressed by the burial chamber at Pentre Ifan near Cardigan on our recent visit to South Wales, and there are places such as Stonehenge and Avebury that would lend themselves to pen-and-ink illustration.

It is still just possible that I may be able to get down to the Peak District later in the year for some pictures for your proposed guide and my own proposed Peak Sketchbook. If so, my visit will be outside school holidays and therefore I shall not avail myself of your kind offer of hospitality and transport. If this visit materialises I shall probably base myself at Casterton and get around by bus (Betty will not be with me).

Sometime within the next two or three months will you please let me have a list of the places you want illustrated for the purpose of your book? I would then visit those I could get to from Casterton and have to rely on your photographs for the remainder. If I cannot get to Casterton this year I would then have to use your photos throughout, assuming of course that you want to make a start on the book this year and cannot wait until 1983 when I may be able to have a longer stay with my chauffeur.

I have just received my copy of CLASSIC WALKS – a super book, free to me as a contributor.

All goes well here. I enclose a copy of the latest A.R. Report, as you request, and look forward to seeing you in October if not before.

Yours sincerely

AW

Our South Wales holiday was very successful, the weather being mainly dry and sunny. I still think the best scenery is around the Wye and Usk valleys. Gower, except for Worm's Head, was rather disappointing.

LETTER 241: TO RON SCHOLES, 25 JULY 1982

38 Kendal Green
Kendal, Cumbria
25th July 1982

Dear Ron,
Many thanks for your very informative letter. I have written to the

Palace Hotel for their current tariff.

I have beaten the printer's deadline and will be able to prepare your drawings rather earlier that I expected, say by mid-August.

I may make a quick trip to South Wales in a fortnight's time, taking advantage of my Senior Citizen's Railcard to have another look at Cardiff and Swansea, which we rather skipped earlier this year, but do call if you are in the area; otherwise perhaps we could have a drink together at Buxton when I am there.

Sincerely,

AW

LETTER 242: TO RON SCHOLES, 12 DECEMBER 1982

38 Kendal Green
Kendal, Cumbria
12th December 1982

Dear Ron,

Many thanks for your cheque for 15 pounds in payment for 'High Crag' (for which, incidentally and much to my surprise, there were twenty applications). In fact I am having to do several repeats of the drawing for disappointed people. Thank you too for the cheque for 6 pounds earned by the talk.

Yes, please book yourself for a talk at Kendal on October 27th. We are rather spoilt for choice of subject, but will let you know later.

Good news about Book Two on long-distance walks, but in this case you have 'Long Walks', splendidly produced and illustrated, to compete with. I doubt very much whether Moorland can match it for quality of production, and I think you will need to devise some different style of presentation and compile a book that sells much more cheaply and has photographs not inferior to those in 'Long Walks'. Nor can it be a book for the pocket. A walker doing one of the long-distance walks will not want to carry around with him a book that also describes twenty others. My own view is that instead of doing something that has already been done by others, and done well with no expense spared, you should persuade Moorland to let you go ahead with your proposed 'Walking in the Peak District', which, although more local, would be assured of a good sale in the district.

Good news about Rex. Is he your new walking companion? How he would enjoy the Roaches!

Best wishes for a happy Christmas and a prosperous 1983.
Yours sincerely,

AW

LETTER 243: TO RON SCHOLES, 6 MARCH 1983

38 Kendal Green
Kendal, Cumbria
6 March 1983

Dear Ron,

Many thanks for your letter and two cheques.

You are now enrolled as a fully-paid member of Animal Rescue for the present year. Which entitles you to no privileges other than a copy of the Annual Report and an invitation to the next A.G.M. You don't even get a badge!

Yes, do please send a sample of your Cambrian Way material, please. If it remains your intention to travel with your readers from Cardiff to Conwy, I still think you should do it in two parts, and try one part on the public first before committing yourself to the other. This would cut your time initially by a half and the price by nearly half. Of course I will see Mr Firth about publication, but the trouble with the Gazette is that they have no agents or distribution in Wales. My own books on Wales have, so far, been a dead loss. No booksellers there (except for Joe Brown) will touch them. However, if you are able to slip over for a drink while we are at Buxton, we can discuss matters at length – Mr Firth and his wife are accompanying us. We are now definitely booked in at the Palace Hotel for the week May 14–21. The tariff, by the way, has gone up to 139 pounds per person per week.

Yours sincerely,

AW

BBC2 say the TV programme will definitely be shown soon but cannot yet give a firm date.

'A South Wales Sketchbook' will be out in a week or so.

Part 20
1980s Fame

AW had been approached about appearing on TV several times, once his books had become best sellers, and always refused, but in 1983 he got talked into appearing in a half-hour documentary about himself and his books for BBC North East. He appeared in the first programme for just a minute or so at the end. It went down well and two years later he agreed to appear in a more ambitious programme, as the presenter, which then developed into several series of programmes, with him walking with Eric Robson in the Lake District, the Pennines and Scotland. These programmes went out nationwide and were hugely popular. By the age of eighty in 1987, AW found that he had become a TV star.

Around the same time as his first tentative TV appearance, there was another exciting development in his life. A mainstream London publisher, Michael Joseph, managed to tempt him away from little old folksy Westmorland Gazette with an interesting project.

In March 1983, Jenny Dereham, a Director of the firm, wrote to him with the suggestion of an illustrated book about the Pennine Way, with photographs by Derry Brabbs. She saw it as a follow up to a highly succesfull book Derry had been involved with called James Herriot's Yorkshire, which had sold 650,000 copies.

LETTER 244: TO JENNY DEREHAM, 20 MARCH 1983

> 38 Kendal Green
> KENDAL, Cumbria LA9 5PP
> 20th March 1983

Dear Miss Dereham,

Many thanks for your kind and most interesting letter of the 11th. It opened up a prospect I find quite thrilling.

I am a proud admirer of the work of Derry Brabbs. On countless occasions during the past couple of years I have picked up JAMES HERRIOT'S YORKSHIRE with the intention of reading through the text but always I find my attention transfixed by Derry's beautiful photographs and spent many rewarding hours just looking at them and remembering my own experiences of the scenes he depicts so well. Indeed, although I am ashamed to admit it, I have never yet read the text! But drooling over the pictures has become an evening pastime. Others with whom I have discussed the book feel the same. It is the photographs, more than the text, that make the book.

A Pennine Way book of Derry's photographs would be a tremendous success, no doubt about it. It would appeal most to those who have already walked the Pennine Way and be a best-selling souvenir of their journey. They number hundreds of thousands and (apart from a minority whose sufferings and privations were such that they have no wish to be reminded of an ordeal they want only to forget) it would be a most welcome refresher of the journey and a memory-stirring reminder they would treasure for the rest of their lives. But let me emphasis again – it is the photographs that would appeal more than the text. Having already done the walk and become familiar with terrain the text would have little of interest unless it could be presented in a attractive form also. In any case, a written description would be looked at only once, but the superb photographs would be referred to often. It is the pictures, not words, that evoke memories.

So my opinion is that the book would have its greatest appeal as a souvenir of a memorable experience – because of Derry's photographs. A written description to accompany them would be of interest mainly to those readers who had not yet done the walk but were planning to.

While I would be thrilled to bits to collaborate in the proposed book, I would, to be honest, be inclined to give Derry all the credit by writing the text himself, making it his own effort exclusively. But if you really prefer me to be in on it, then doubts arise as to the best way of making the text a suitable accompaniment to the pictures. Although I would be highly gratified if you were to make use of excerpts from PENNINE WAY COMPANION and it would be a pleasure to give you permission to reproduce any of its material, I cannot quite see how this could be done. The microscopic detail of the guidebook would be inappropriate and there are few passages that could be lifted out of context. The danger would be that the text would be too bitty and incomplete to serve as the sort of commentary you need.

My own view, after much thought, is that new text should be written, not one that Derry would follow with his camera, but the reverse: a text that would describe the scenes he chooses while maintaining a continuity of the route. We must accept that any text would be secondary to the pictures. If Derry for some reason is unwilling to tackle the writing of a commentary I could do this if you wished me to. The text would conveniently break up into chapters, each describing a section of the walk, these being in sequence from the start at Edale, and each chapter-heading could have as a small decoration a thumb-nail line drawing from the Companion. Added interest would be given by a complete set of strip-maps of the journey indication only the salient features illustrated by Derry and the nearby towns and villages and omitting irrelevant detail. By using scale maps, however, you may run foul of the Ordnance Survey, whose demand for royalties on a big printing could be considerable, but to avoid this contingency the route could be indicated

In his next letter to Ron Scholes, congratulating him on at long last getting a publishing deal with Moorland Publishers, AW told him about his own bit of publishing news.

LETTER 245: TO RON SCHOLES, 6 MAY 1983

38 Kendal Green, KENDAL
May 6th 1983

Dear Ron,

Thank you for your letter and enclosure.

Moorland Publishing are in a bigger way of business than I thought, with many distribution outlets for their publications, and seem well able to give your book all the publicity it deserves. I am sorry to learn that you are still struggling to get it finished but the day will come when you take it to Moorland and say 'That's it'. And what a relief it will be to get it off your hands! Life will seem suddenly empty. But when the first copy is in your hands the effort will all seem to have been very worth while.

Out of the blue recently I was approached by Michael Joseph's, the publishers, to collaborate with Derry Brabbs on a book on the Pennine Way. Derry is the photographer whose pictures in HERRIOTT'S YORKSHIRE were such a joy. The idea is that Derry will do the pictures and I will write an accompanying narrative with many quotes from PENNINE WAY COMPANION. The firm clearly anticipate a prolific seller and have made a generous offer too good to miss. And today, having seen the TV programme, they want to talk about a similar proposal for a Lakeland book. A director of the firm and Derry are coming up to the Palace at Buxton to discuss details with me on the weekend of May 14–15.

You will be sorry to learn that Harry Firth has been attacked quite suddenly by angina. His first instinct was to cancel his visit to Buxton but a diet of pills has eased his pains considerably and he has now resumed his part-time work on Gazette publications and intends to accompany us as first arranged. We all look forward to seeing you at the Palace some evening during the week.

Until then I must leave you. The TV programme has brought a spate of correspondence that I must reply to before Buxton.

Yours sincerely,

AW

AW met Jenny Dereham and Derry Brabbs at the Palace Hotel in Buxton, where he was staying while working on his Peak District Sketchbook. The deal was then done, in fact AW offered them another book first, about Lakeland (which became Fellwalking with Wainwright, published in 1984). Ideas and plans for the books, plus layouts by Michael Joseph's designer Susan McIntyre, then started whizzing back and forward – but very soon AW was complaining that he was not happy with the way things were going. He was also not pleased when Sheila Murphy, Michael Joseph's publicity Director, outlined the interviews and promotional work she had lined up for him

LETTER 246: TO JENNY DEREHAM, JUNE 1983?

Dear Jenny,

I must thank you for your letter of the 3rd, but must also say that my reactions to its contents are of surprise, shock and even horror. Here am I, getting along like a house on fire, and then you suddenly explode a bombshell that stops me in my tracks.

Surprise

I am amazed to learn that you have pre-determined the number of pages in the Pennine book and presumably of the Lakeland book. Surely the number of pages should be that required to contain the full narrative and the photographs needed to illustrate the text? If you were publishing a novel or a biography you would let it run its full course even if it was over-running the number of pages you earlier had in mind; you wouldn't cut out a chapter or two because it proved to be longer than you intended. Similarly I think that the narratives and photos of our two books should be given all the space necessary for the production of complete and unabridged books.

Shock

I have been working under the impression that you wanted books to match the Herriot book in size, format and printing area on each page, and my layouts have been prepared with this in mind. You now say that your designer plans to make the Pennine book slightly smaller than the Herriot. Slightly smaller? The proposed reduction in printing area is dramatic. Herriot has a printing area of over 50 square inches per page. Susan plans 35 square inches only. That's why my layouts don't fit her drafts. As a matter of fact I have been intending all along that each book should be of 224 pages, as you suggest, but they were to be pages having a similar printing area to the Herriot, and my layouts would have slotted into place very nicely had they been adopted.

Susan wants her bottom smacking for implying that some passages should be cut out and some photographs omitted. This is unfair both to me and Derry. As for counting the characters and spaces of my type-written lines, how can you assume that my typewriter characters and spaces between lines are going to coincide exactly with the printer's type and spaces? As for single or double columns for the text, I rather favour single: your letter to me, and this one to you, have lines about the same length as a single column, and of course are quite easy to read as well as easier for a printer to set up, and fewer hyphens would be needed.

Horror

I am horrified at the emphasis being given to the cost of publication, by the counting of pennies. Your intention should be a perfect book, full stop, not a book as perfect as finances permit. By cutting costs you could lose the sale of 10,000 copies. Where's the saving?

Please turn over;

I haven't finished yet.

In general, I think I know from long experience what fellwalkers and Pennine wayfarers like to read and the sort of photographs they like to look at, and it is with their preferences in mind that I have been working. They are outdoor people: they like spaciousness around them and they prefer books that have the contents spaciously arranged, not cramped. They prefer large photos that make them feel they are out in the open, not pictures reduced to snaps and crowded in restricted space.

You have knocked the stuffing out of me. I like to feel free to do as I think best, not work in harness imposed by designers who may never have been out on hills and have no feeling for them.

I am sorry to be so forthright but am sure you are on the wrong tack. I have no interest in doing a book I cannot feel proud of. If you persist in taking advice from your staff, and not from me, I am afraid I must consider pulling out of our arrangement, much though I need the money for a good cause.

I think now that we are not going to produce bestsellers. Just books.

Despite all this acrimonious argument, please be assured that you still have my very best wishes.

AW

LETTER 247: TO JENNY DEREHAM, JULY 1983?

Dear Jenny,

My ideas on layouts are that they should be informal and not all be to a set pattern, which tends to become monotonous and even boring. The reader should not know in advance what the next page will be like when he turns over; let it come as a surprise and so maintain his interest. I have never in all my books had two pages together that look exactly alike. Every turn of the page is fresh and exciting. Further, the narrative on every one of my pages ends in a full stop, so that each one is complete in itself and gives the reader a chance to pause and study the illustration on that page, these being closely related to the narrative. I dislike intensely sentences that run from one page to the next, or overleaf, as in a novel, which tend to keep the reader's attention on following the text rather than on the equally important illustrations. This is the way I plan our two books, and you will be simply thrilled to bits when you see what Derry and I have done to uphold the proud traditions of Michael Joseph Limited.

Each book will be of 224 pages, including the eight blanks at the beginning for the titles, a publishers foreword and a list of contents. A final index will not be necessary for the Lakeland book but may be advisable for the Pennine one.

Only innate modesty has prevented me from suggesting the inclusion of a few small black-and-white drawings instead of photographs to fill awkward spaces, and I am therefore glad to learn that you have the same idea. I am all for large photographs only. Colour photos reduced to cigarette card size never give the effect desired, are unfair to the photographer, and are a needless waste of money, but small drawings are not only more likely to attract the eye of the reader but can be quite decorative and much less costly to reproduce, and moreover they can show detail that the camera cannot capture; for example the view from High Street with all the distant features named. I have in fact sprinkled a few of my own illustrations in the chapters I have done so far in cases where the subject is beyond the scope of the camera but needed to illustrate the text. So I agree absolutely.

It's you who doesn't need to worry, not me. Derry and I are providing you with books that will be highlights in your publishing career. You'll see! So don't worry. Everything will be alright.

With best wishes,

Yours sincerely,

Derry, who agrees with me in all things except in the matter of pipe versus cigars, tells me he is visiting you shortly and has craved my permission to smack Susan's bottom on my behalf. So that no further misunderstandings will arise in Bedford Square I think I should confirm to you that I have given him such permission if, after seeing Susan, he still wishes to exercise this rare privilege.

LETTER 248: TO SHEILA MURPHY, 5 MARCH 1984

38 Kendal Green, KENDAL, Cumbria
5th March 1984

Dear Sheila,

Thank you for your letter of February 28th.

I know you mean well, but, being an honest man, I must say that I found no pleasure in reading it, well written though it was, but only a mounting horror as I read through your several ideas for publicity.

Jenny will have told you what an awkward devil I am, and I hope you will not be too surprised to learn that I reject all your suggestions entirely. Your overtures have only driven me further into my shell.

I'm sorry to disappoint you but I would derive no enjoyment at all from taking part in any of your proposed interviews. Ballyhoo makes me squirm. As you say, I have many fans, and I love them but only at a distance. Nobody gets within a very long arm's length. You might adopt a different tack: that I am a very private person (rare in these days) who prefers to keep out of the public gaze. Mind you, it's not because I'm bad-looking; indeed, Jenny will confirm that compared for instance with

Derry Brabbs I am quite presentable.

Being oldfashioned, I think a book should sell on its merits, not on the personal idiosyncrasies of the author.

Don't worry about it. I seem to be always upsetting somebody at Michael Joseph's.

Yours sincerely,

AWainwright

Despite all his moans and quibbles, AW worked happily with Jenny Dereham for the next eight years. Meanwhile he had not forgotten Ron Scholes, suggesting ideas for him and keeping him up to date with his own books, his state of health and the plans for Kapellan, the property Animal Rescue bought to convert into an animal refuge in 1984.

LETTER 249: TO RON SCHOLES, 28 FEBRUARY 1984

38 Kendal Green, KENDAL
28th February 1984

Dear Ron,

I expect to finish my book by the end of March to coincide with your final touches to the Countryside book??? Then I would like to try the first three maps of your Cambrian Way as a test to see whether I can do them satisfactorily for reduction to a scale of one inch = one mile. I will get Andrew to print them on a reduced size and let you see the result.

I have been thinking more about Frank Rodger's books, which makes fascinating reading. This is the sort of book you would do extremely well and thoroughly enjoy doing. So what about a new series by Ron Scholes:

STAFFORDSHIRE ODDITIES
SHROPSHIRE ODDITIES
CHESHIRE ODDITIES

All these you could do without having nights away from home.

The Planning authorities have told me that they have received several objections to our proposed use of the property we are aiming to purchase, so it is by no means certain we shall get it. Their decision will be taken on March 13th. We might be back to Square One.

Sincerely,

AW

LETTER 250: TO RON SCHOLES, 22 APRIL 1984

38 Kendal Green, KENDAL, Cumbria
22nd April 1984

Dear Ron,

Good news and bad news.

The good news is that we have been granted planning permission to kennel dogs and cats at the premises we have provisionally agreed to purchase, despite objections by the neighbouring farmers, and so we are now free to go ahead. Betty is over the moon. We can now hope to be settled there within a couple of months. Next time you come over we will take you around the property, in which, of course, you have very right to feel you have a stake.

Other good news is that I have finished the Peak District book and got it off to the Gazette.

The bad news is that I have clearly come to the end of the road as far as close pen work is concerned. After a frustrating three weeks struggling to hand-write the captions, being unable to see properly what I was doing, with my writing constantly straying from the pencil guide lines, I had to give up and ask for the captions to be set in type. This disability does not augur well for the set of Cambrian maps you require, although I would still like to have a shot at it. Mentioning this to the Gazette, they say 'Why doesn't Ron do his own maps?'. Apparently, unknown to me, they have seen some maps you have done in connection with the book, and they say they are very good.

Another bit of bad news is that I have had an attack of bronchitis over the past few weeks, which left me totally disinclined for effort of any kind and did not help in completing the Peak District book. I am getting over this now and beginning to feel more normal again.

Now what about your Countryside book? Tell me it is finished!

Yours sincerely,

AW

LETTER 251: TO RON SCHOLES, 16 MAY 1984

16th May 1984

Dear Ron,

Having received your version of these few first maps I will see what I can do to copy them, but I still think that (quite apart from the fact that I can no longer see to do close work) your own efforts would be preferable to mine, if only because of your intimate knowledge of the terrain.

I am now quite well again, thanks, as I hope you are. You will be greatly relieved when the Countryside book is finally out of your hands. We are off to Galloway this weekend. I will keep all the maps you have sent in safe custody but do nothing with them until I hear from you again.

Sincerely,

AW

Cannot even see my typewriter lettering now!!

LETTER 252: TO RON SCHOLES, 15 AUGUST 1984

38 Kendal Green, KENDAL
15th August 1984

Dear Ron,

Thank you for your letter received today. I am sending you a well deserved complimentary copy of the Peak District book – not one with which I am particularly pleased (age is telling) and not helped by the Gazette printing the 'list of books' opposite the title page instead of at the front. Things at the Gazette are in a muddle. There has been a 3 months delays in getting the book out, due to staff shortages and now Andrew has been off sick (vertigo) for some weeks and nobody else there seems able to take over.

I saw two eye specialists, and neither gave me any hope of a cure. The trouble is not cataracts, as I thought, but damaged retinas at the back of the eyeballs. A symptom of old age, they said . . . so I have come to the end of the road as far as close penwork is concerned. Latterly, as an experiment, I have been trying to draw maps, and find it quite impossible. Not only cannot I see what I am doing but am getting blind spots as I work. I am afraid I will not be able to do the Welsh maps for your, and am sorry about this because I would have liked to help.

Michael Joseph's seem pleased with the initial response to the Fellwalking book, and have commissioned two others. As these will require only a written narrative and no close work I will probably be able to manage these.

The work of adapting Kapellan is proceeding apace. Betty is up there every day, painting and acting as clerk of works.

Thank you for all the enquiries you have made about a venue for an exhibition, but please cancel the tentative arrangement at Hanley and do nothing further at present. I will await the response to the leaflet, sell as many drawings by post as I can and have the rest on display at an exhibition in Kendal in December.

I note with some dismay that you have still not completed the Countryside book. It is becoming a life's work!

Sincerely,

AW

LETTER 253: TO RON SCHOLES, 8 DECEMBER 1985

38 Kendal Green, KENDAL
8th December 1985

Dear Ron,

Thanks for your letter and kind donation.

I hope your book is selling well. I am working on my penultimate effort 'Lakeland Mountain Passes' for Michael Joseph, but with difficulty. I am obviously nearing the end of the road. I cannot now see what I am typing and must ask you to excuse errors. The TV programmes are having a great success in the Northeast, according to the producer. I have seen videos of the first two and am not at all enthusiastic about my performance. He is bringing Nos. 3 and 4 over this week for a preview.

I am having a car park made at Kapellen following police complaints about cars parking on the roadside. All goes well there.

With best wishes for Christmas and a good 1986.

Sincerely,

AW

Ron Scholes's book Understanding the Countryside *was published by Moorland in 1985. The book about Wales he was working on with AW never got completed, leaving Ron with ten AW drawings, which he always treasured. Ron retired as a headmaster in 1989. Between 1997 and 2006 he had six further countryside books published. AW's relationships with Michael Joseph produced nine handsome coffee table books which sold hundreds of thousands of copies.*

Part 21
Letters to Regular Correspondents, 1980-8

AW kept up with his regular writers – people from his past or correspondents who had been writing to him for some years – despite all the books he was doing and his eyesight and strength beginning to fade.

He didn't though keep up with many of his relations, but in 1980 he wrote to his nephew Jack Fish (son of his sister Alice who died in 1971) in Blackburn and offered him seventy-eight drawings from his latest book which could be sold to help the funds of Furthergate Congregational Church, which AW had attended as a boy, though he no longer was a church goer. The sale realised £1,000 for the church.

LETTER 254: TO JACK FISH, 20 JANUARY 1980

> 38 Kendal Green
> KENDAL, Cumbria LA9 5PP
> 20th January 1980

Dear Jack,

In a few weeks time I shall have a book published under the title of A RIBBLE SKETCHBOOK. This is a collection of 78 drawings of scenes in the Ribble Valley, and, as with all the similar books I have turned out over the past few years, the original drawings will be sold for the benefit of charities or other worthy causes.

It seems to me appropriate that in the case of the Ribble the drawings should be sold in the Blackburn area, and that, in view of your New Church Appeal, the proceeds should go to that Fund.

It you would like to have them for that purpose, and can stage an exhibition for their sale in the Memorial Hall or elsewhere in Blackburn, you can have them with pleasure. They would come to you mounted and signed ready for framing. Similar drawings from other recent books have usually sold for 12.50 each and there has been no lack of buyers. I will send a copy of the book to the Features Editor of the Blackburn Times when it is published, for review, and he might be persuaded to give it some publicity, with a note of the exhibition arrangements. You might be able to think of other ways of bringing it to notice, for example, by a circular to the other churches in the district.

I enclose a copy of a companion volume, A LUNE SKETCHBOOK, which has just been published, to give you an idea of the sort of drawings that will appear in the Ribble book. The Lune drawings are to be exhibited and sold for Animal Rescue at The Bookshop, Market Street, Kirkby Lonsdale, on Thursday to Saturday, February 14th to 16th. I mention this because if you are interested in my offer it would be a good idea for you to come over to Kirkby on the Saturday afternoon about 2 o'clock (bringing Winston and Linda if they are likely to want to help) and see for yourself how such drawings are usually exhibited and to discuss any matters that may occur to you.

I expect the book to be published and the drawings to be ready in about two months time, but would like to know whether you are willing to undertake the exhibition and sale as soon as possible so that I can notify the details on a leaflet to enclose with notices of publication that are always sent out to prospective purchasers on a mailing list who always request details of any sale of drawings.

Sincerely,

AW

George Haworth, his exact contemporary, who had been at school with him, had now moved to Arnside and wrote about all the great walks he was able to do, despite his age.

LETTER 255: TO GEORGE HAWORTH, 17 APRIL 1980

38 Kendal Green, KENDAL
17th April 1980

Dear George,

Thank you for your letter. Yes, I remember you writing some years ago, but increasing age has not improved my memory and I still cannot place you. There were so many Haworths about in those days.

I never before heard of anyone climbing Meldon Hill, or even wanting to, although obviously someone has and indeed lived there. I have often wondered about the ruins of Meldon Hall; there could be a story there. Take a photo if you ever get there. But beware the guns of Warcop. These hills are their firing targets.

Funny you should have planned a book on the Eden. The Lune book is the first of a trilogy. A companion book on the Ribble has just come out and my version of the Eden will be published in the late summer.

Yes, I keep very well, thanks, a blessing I attribute to excessive smoking. Tomorrow I am off to Blackburn for a couple of days. I rarely go there, but like to see the Rovers once every season. I shall have a look at the Furthergate area, now totally blighted.

Thank you for your invitation to call on you at Stonycroft. You make it sound like Mandalay! Fact is I am so flaming busy that I find it difficult to get away from my desk, but as you are not likely to meet me on Meldon Hill I will bear your invite in mind when next I am in Arnside.

Yours sincerely

AlfWainwright

LETTER 256: TO GEORGE HAWORTH, 7 MAY 1980

38 Kendal Green
KENDAL, Cumbria
7th May 1980

Dear George,

Thank you for the report on your successful ascent of Meldon Hill, a feat that must almost qualify for inclusion in the Guinness records. I have no doubt that the heaps of stones in fact marked the site of the Hall, which was quite near to the summit. I have never seen any references to the history of the place, but what a story it would make! Anyway, congratulations on a sterling performance.

I had a look at the Furthergate area when over in Blackburn three weeks ago to watch the Rovers. It is a most depressing scene, a wilderness. The Church still stands, but now solitary in a wasteland. And the Post Office still functions. But it is a mistake to go back to the scenes of childhood. One feels a stranger amongst strangers.

Yes, for Mandalay read Manderley. A stupid mistake. My mind must be going.

Off to North Wales in a couple of days, hoping the good weather holds. Hope to do Snowdon (by railway) and a few other summits (slowly on foot).

Be seeing you sometime.

Yours sincerely,

AlfWainwright

LETTER 257: TO GEORGE HAWORTH, 24 JANUARY 1982

38 Kendal Green
KENDAL, Cumbria
24th January 1982

Dear George,

I don't consider that you need apologize for your 1981 fellwalking exploits. Your itineraries seem pretty good, and far more ambitious than mine. In fact, the only Lakeland summits reached in that year by me were Great Carrs and Swirl How on a perfect day in November. How good it felt to be on the tops again! I came down very reluctantly. But I have not given up entirely. I have had working holidays in North Wales in the past two years and enjoyed splendid expeditions on the Glyders, Lliwedd, Snowdon, the Nantlle ridge, Cnicht, Cader Idris and a few others not forgetting the toughest of all, Tryfan, its two miles up and down taking me ten hours. I have quite fallen for North Wales. It has a greater variety of landscape than the Lakes.

I'm sorry I haven't yet fulfilled my promise to call on you, and in fact have never been to Arnside since I last wrote. Truth is, my days are so crowded, and becoming more so, that social engagements are ruled out. In spite of ten-hour working days I always seem to be behind schedule. Of course I would like to see you but it would be much more convenient to me if you were to drop in on me sometime when you are in Kendal. To preserve some measure of discipline in my life, and at the same get away from my desk and stretch my legs, I go along to Kendal Borough Museum (near the Railway Station) two mornings a week, Mondays and Thursdays, and do a two-hour stint (10–12) preparing a card index of specimens. These are my two weekly periods of relaxation, occasions when I am often visited by old colleagues and friends for a chat, and it would really suit me better than making a definite arrangement to come to see you, which would have to be subject to last minute cancellation, if you would do the same, calling around 10.30 or 11 so that I could take you out for a coffee.

In the meantime, kind regards,

Yours sincerely,

AWainwright

Frank Nash first contacted AW in 1979, offering to donate all the monies from a sponsored walk he was doing to Animal Rescue. AW and Betty were delighted – and after his first gift, invited him to visit them, which he did. He went on to do many walks, some of them enormous long distances, gathering lots of sponsors, with all the money going to Animal Rescue, especially for the creation of Kapellan, their refuge. Frank also took lots of photos on his walks and sent them to AW, who used some as research material for his various sketchbooks.

LETTER 258: TO FRANK NASH, 25 JULY 1982

38 Kendal Green, KENDAL, Cumbria
25th July 1982

Dear Frank,

Many thanks for your letter, detailing the exciting prospects of October in Lakeland. Your marathon along the High Street range seems likely to make this a memorable visit. The dates you suggest are quite convenient to us. I gather from what you say that you would really prefer to do the walk alone and have no witness to your sufferings. So be it. We will be pleased to welcome you with refreshments either on Garburn Pass or Moor Divock.

The quiz enclosed with your letter was a complete surprise and strikingly confirmed what I have suspected for some time – that I am losing my memory. I could answer only 10% of the questions, and most of the quotes I could not even remember writing.

Ghastly experiences here last Tuesday. A ten-man BBC team, complete with producer, cameraman, sound recordist, dubbing mixers and the lot, descended on us to get 'shots' and interviews for a Tyne-Tees production provisionally entitled WAINWRIGHT and due for showing in November. I am not yet recovered from the ordeal.

See you in October if not before,

Sincerely,

AW

LETTER 259: TO FRANK NASH, 7 NOVEMBER 1982

38 Kendal Green, KENDAL
7th November 1982

Dear Frank,

Thank you for your very kind letter and set of photographs, which, unfortunately, don't measure up to requirements. The viewpoints are excellent and the foregrounds good, but the background reflects the sort of weather you experienced on High Street, mist obscuring all detail. The West Wall Traverse must remain a target for 1983.

All is well here as I hope it is for you, but the weather has been pretty awful recently except for one golden day when we went up Loughrigg. There are now <u>steps</u> up the Grasmere slope!

Love from both of us and eleven cats,

AW

LETTER 260: TO FRANK NASH, 7 MAY 1983

38 Kendal Green, KENDAL
7th May 1983

Dear Frank,

Everybody seems to have enjoyed the TV programme. Actually I did myself. The agonies of apprehension soon passed when I found that the producer had mercifully cut out my bad moments in front of the camera. I couldn't recognise my own voice but I suppose the sound recorder never lies. On the whole, not bad. I could sit through it again.

The programme ended at 7.35. At 7.36 Joan Rainey was on the phone with tears streaming down her face out of sheer ecstasy – she is writing to the BBC for a repeat showing. At 7.40 another woman was on the phone, also with tears streaming down her face out of sheer ecstasy. So it went on all evening, all the callers being female (why?) and this explosion of enthusiasm for the show has been followed by a spate of letters from all over the country (most of them from unknown females) all favourable and all calling for a reply. I'm busy! Incidentally, Joan Rainey rang a few minutes ago to report that the programme had been featured on 'Pick of the week' on the radio.

I have not yet heard from Brian, but will expect to do so. I have my doubts about his publishers and the time for counting chickens is not yet.

We look forward to seeing you in the summer.

West Wall Traverse or bust.

Sincerely,

AW

LETTER 261: TO FRANK NASH, 9 JANUARY 1984

> 38 Kendal Green, KENDAL, Cumbria
> 9th January 1984

Dear Frank,

Again my great thanks for the splendid result of your magnificent marathon.

And for the portfolio of photos taken on your pilgrimage to Scafell. I have done four drawings of the W.W. Traverse from these, large enough to be included in the next volume of Lakeland Mountain Drawings but capable of reduction for Brian's proposed book. I think he is very disappointed with his publishers, who seem to be treating him very badly. I will try to get the Gazette to publish if all else fails.

I return your photos with profound thanks.

Best wishes for 1984,

Sincerely,

AW

LETTER 262: TO FRANK NASH, 22 APRIL 1984

> 38 Kendal Green, KENDAL, Cumbria
> 22nd April 1984

Dear Frank,

Good news, bad news, and no news.

The good news is that we have been granted planning permission to kennel dogs and cats at the property we have provisionally agreed to buy, despite objections from neighbouring farmers. Betty is over the moon. Now we can go ahead and complete the purchase and hope to be in operation in a couple of months. Next time you come over we will take you on a tour of the premises, in which, of course, you have every right to feel you have a stake.

The bad news is that I have been laid low over the past few weeks with an attack of bronchitis, which has left me totally disinclined for effort of any sort, even ruling out the solution of your crossword. But I have now solved six of the clues, averaging one a week, and hope to have it finished by autumn.

Yours sincerely,

AW

LETTER 263: TO FRANK NASH, 7 APRIL 1985

38 Kendal Green, KENDAL, Cumbria
7th April 1985

Dear Frank,

Many thanks for your letter and accompanying cheque, bringing <u>our</u> reward for <u>your</u> prodigious effort of last summer to an amazing total. Collecting the dues must be even harder work than the walking! We appreciate your great kindness in this matter.

When Derek called on us briefly a couple of months ago he rather gave us the impression (in between cataloguing his personal achievements) that you had rather wearied of your labours on our behalf and proposed to take a rest from marathons this year. It was something of a surprise, therefore, to learn from your letter that you seem again to be chafing at the bit. Now that the money is rolling in in great lumps from Michael Joseph and likely to continue to do so for the next two or three years the needs of Animal Rescue are being well catered for, and it would be perfectly all right if you decided not to exhaust your flesh further in the cause.

However, if your appetite for masochistic exercise continues unabated, the round of the Howgill Fells would be a perfect expedition, all the summits being neatly arranged and well defined but requiring a day of clear visibility. Your preference seems to be for the Northern Fells, a group very similar in plan to the Howgills, calling for a circular tour rather than a ridge walk, but tougher. If your choice is for the Northern Fells, I would suggest leaving your car at the Blencathra Sanatorium, and then, walking clockwise, visiting

Lonscale Pike
Skiddaw Little Man
Skiddaw
Bakestall
Great Calva
Knott
Grat Sca Fell
Meal Fell
Great Cockup
Longlands Fell
Brae Fell
High Pike
Carrock Fell
Bowscale Fell
Bannerdale Crags

Ending with a complete traverse of the main ridge of Blencathra and descending Blease Fell to the car. This itinerary visits all the fells in the group except Carl Side, Long Side, Ullock Pike, Souther Fell and Latrigg, which could only be reached by detours or a retracing of steps.

See how you feel nearer the time.

In any event I am proposing to select one of the items of capital expenditure at Kappellan of roughly equivalent cost to the total of your sponsored donations and affix a plaque bearing testimony to your efforts. This is something we can discuss when you come over and have a look round at some of the features we have introduced with Betty as Clerk of Works.

All is well here and at Kapellan, as we hope it is with you.

We send our love and grateful thanks.

Betty x AW x

LETTER 264: TO FRANK NASH, 6 OCTOBER 1986

38 Kendal Green, Kendal
6th October 1986

Dear Frank,

Many thanks for your kind letter and the accompanying parcel of cheques – a magnificent reward for your long trek over the Pennines and Cheviots. Which we appreciate greatly. Not least for the work involved in collecting the promises of your sponsors.

The letter was awaiting our return from a week in Scotland near Kyle of Lochalsh where we had a very spacious and comfortable log cabin that made tolerable six days of abysmal mist and rain. We were joined here by the BBC producer, the main purpose of the visit being to discuss a TV series on Scotland planned for next year.

I'm sorry to be so late in sending you a copy of the book, the reason for the delay being due to the publishers moving to new premises in the week of publication, their failure to send me complimentary copies being due to an oversight. I mentioned this to them a fortnight ago, and the copies have since arrived with an apology.

The Coast to Coast walk is to be published in the spring of 1987, and the Lakeland Mountain Passes in 1989, the latter having been deferred for a year because the publishers and the BBC, acting jointly, want me to do a book on Scotland to accompany the series in 1988. Ex-fellwanderer is to be published by the Gazette to coincide with my 80th birthday in January, and I will send you copy when available. So life continues hectic for me and for Betty, who spends much of her time supervising things at Kappellen.

You make a mysterious reference to Derry. I expect to be seeing him within the next fortnight to check on his final photos for the C to C walk.

Love, and again many thanks, from Betty and me.

AW

LETTER 265: TO FRANK NASH, 11 JANUARY 1987

38 Kendal Green, Kendal
11th January 1987

Dear Frank,

Betty tells me that you are considering making a flying visit next Saturday for my birthday, but please do not think of making such a long journey for so inauspicious an occasion. A nice thought though. But in any case the Gazette have invited me out on that day for a fish and chip meal, which I have accepted.

Betty also tells me that you have reported the collapse of the West Wall track out of Lords Rake. I shall be very interested to have the details next time I see you.

Good walking in 1987

AW

AW was still in contact with Chris Jesty, though he had some bad news for him in 1984 when Chris sent him a copy of the first book he had managed to get published, a guide to the Isle of Purbeck.

LETTER 266: TO CHRIS JESTY, 16 MAY 1984

38 Kendal Green, Kendal
16th May 1984

Dear Chris,

I thank you for your package and congratulate you on getting your first book in print. I recoiled in horror upon finding that the pages were stapled along the spine. This is a shocking mistake. A stapled binding means that the book cannot be opened flat, both hands being needed to consult it. The book should have been stitched down the middle so that every page would open flat on a desk or table and not need the use of hands to control it. Stapled books are infuriating and I never buy them on principle. Black mark!

Another criticism concerns the maps, which are excellently drawn but should have been given a scale in miles instead of the ridiculous 1.25000 etc. these references to size being unintelligible to everyone including myself. You have been a bit too clever here, and your device will not be appreciated by walkers.

The hand-written text is very good indeed and as clear to read as print, but the illustrations are below Mark's usual standard and a portfolio of colour photographs instead would have been more attractive.

The personal notes are poor, not well composed and largely irrelevant, and would have been better omitted. You must avoid using the word 'so'. It is no substitute for 'therefore'.

I haven't read the text, still having no wish to visit the Isle of Purbeck, but did notice that you had described it as one of the most beautiful places in Britain – a surprising statement from someone who knows Lakeland and North Wales.

I give you 5 marks out of 10, no more.

Yours sincerely,

AW

AW did try to help aspiring writers, recommending people to Bill Mitchell, editor of Dalesman magazine, though with some reservations. All the same, when Bill then sent him the manuscript of a book he was doing about Scotland, wanting AW to write an introduction, he was rather scathing about the contents.

LETTER 267: TO BILL MITCHELL, 15 SEPTEMBER 1984

38 Kendal Green, KENDAL, Cumbria
15th September 1984

Dear Bill,

I was recently given a manuscript to read written by a Mr Jack Woods, a teacher who lived near Kendal for many years and is now a verger in Westminster Abbey.

His manuscript, titled 'The North Road', is the history of the old road between Kendal and Shap with a descriptive account of the route (which can still be seen and followed for most of the way) and is supplemented by a portfolio of his own black and white photographs.

The narrative is excellent, well written and beautifully typed, but the subject is of such limited interest that he is unlikely ever to see it published, and I have told him so. Nevertheless I enquired of the Gazette about a possible paperback, but without success, and also spoke to the local Archaeological and Antiquarian Society, but the text is much longer than they can include in their annual Transactions.

Mr Woods would dearly like to see his effort published and is wondering if Dalesman would consider it for their series of paperbacks, for which it would be just about the right size. He has asked me to write to you on his behalf, to introduce him, and would like to call on you on October 19th, when he will be in this area. I hope you will agree to this. You would find his manuscript interesting, but I fear not a viable proposition because of its lack of general appeal. I have expressed this opinion to him, but it would give him a measure of satisfaction if only he could see a real live Editor with it. He is prepared for disappointment.

I hope you will grant him the favour of an interview.

Yours sincerely,

AWainwright

LETTER 268: TO BILL MITCHELL, 21 JUNE 1988

38 Kendal Green, Kendal
21st June 1988

Dear Bill,

Thank you for your letter and enclosures. Sorry to have taken so long to reply but have been run off my feet lately with one thing and another.

I have looked through your Scottish narrative with interest – and some misgivings. Your choice of title is intriguing and inventive, but I have a doubt about its impact when seen in a bookshop window. Nobody has ever heard of Muckle Flugga and people's reactions would be the same as mine, that it is another yarn about Ireland, not a popular subject, and it really needs a subtitle (journeys in Northern Scotland).

The map is awful. I cannot understand your selection of place-names nor the locations you have given them: Crianlarich in the North Sea, the Caledonian Canal apparently issuing at Aberdeen. There is no clue as to the black patches and the sprinkling of dots and no scale of miles. It is dreadful, badly-drawn, misleading and unintellible. You must omit it or substitute a much better one.

You need to check your spellings in the narrative. Bonar Bridge is not spelt Bonner Bridge and this is not the only mistake.

I am honoured by your invitation to write a foreword and am pleased to accept provided you cut out the map and any others you may think of including and correct some of the places names in the narrative, which is otherwise interesting and especially good on the natural life of the northern districts.

As I say I am very busy at present and would like to see the book in print with your illustrations, before thinking about a foreword.

Yours sincerely,

AW

As an alternative title what about 'It's a long way to Cape Wrath?' which everybody has heard about? If I were to see this title in a bookshop I would pounce on it and so would many others.

The letters to the Ainley family continued: to Margaret and daughter Catherine. AW affected to be furious, cutting her off, when Margaret announced that she was now a railway fan, rather than a fells fan.

They continued to live in Brighouse till 1984 when Richard, her husband, lost his job. They moved to Norwich – which AW warned would not be to their liking, but after two years or so, they returned to Brighouse.

LETTER 269: TO MARGARET AINLEY, 20 DECEMBER 1981

38 Kendal Green, KENDAL, Cumbria
20th December 1981

Dear Margaret,

What on earth has come over you?

Not a word about Cathy's ambition to be the first woman on Everest without oxygen. Not a word of the joys of the open countryside, of conquering savage peaks. You talk only of nasty smoky trains.

I must write you off as one once akin to me, one who thought as I did, but alas does so not more. Trains are a pre-occupation of advancing years. The fells are for the active and young in heart. You have suddenly become middle-aged.

This being so, lamentably, your next holiday must be to North Wales, where little steam trains run all over the place, not only to the top of Snowdon (which will revive memories of the days, now gone, when you loved to tread the summits) and into the depths of slate quarries, but also through the most glorious country. Enclosed is the guide to the Festiniog Railway, one of a dozen lines open to the public, which is utter joy every yard of the way and must be sheer ecstasy for an elderly train spotter.

A happy Christmas, anyway, in your new abode. Sorry I haven't a card with a train on it. Mine are all of mountains.

Sincerely,

AW

LETTER 270: TO CATHERINE AINLEY, 17 JULY 1983

38 Kendal Green, KENDAL, Cumbria
17th July 1983

Dear Catherine,

Thank you for your long and interesting letter – and congratulations on your splendid performances on the fells during your stay near Keswick. And I suppose I must congratulate your mum and dad for keeping up with you because they must be quite old now. I didn't fall out with your mum. What happened was that she went a big strange and started to love nasty steam engines instead of mountains. And she began to be frightened of lovely caterpillars. She must have been very difficult to live with. But I am glad to learn from your letter that she seems to be normal again, and it is good news that you are going back to Keswick next year.

I notice that you have a new address and I hope you like it and have a nice school. I don't like Brighouse. It makes me think of nasty steam engines.

Thank you for your photograph. You are getting to look like your mum but I hope you never suffer from the same strange ailments she has had to endure recently.

Do you remember the first hill you ever climbed? I do. It was Smearsett Scar in Ribblesdale. In those days your mum used to like me.

I must say you do write well! Not a single spelling mistake. Now that your mum has stopped writing to me, perhaps you will kindly send me a letter again after your next visit to Keswick and tell me about the lovely mountains you climb while you are there.

With love, just for you.

AW

LETTER 271: TO MARGARET AINLEY, 29 JULY 1983

38 Kendal Green, KENDAL, Cumbria
29th July 1983

Dear Margaret,

Doesn't it say somewhere in the Scriptures that a little child shall lead them? Your Catherine seems to have done the trick. She has restored your soul.

It was nice to hear from you again and find your news all of happy days on the mountains. I am reassured. You still love me despite your recent wayward behaviour. I am prepared to forgive and regard your lapse from rational thought as merely temporary, probably something to do with change of life, and accept that you are now back to normal. I was right all the time. Mountains are so much nicer that mucky steam engines. I must say I was astonished, even outraged, by your desertion of mountain tracks for railway tracks. However, this phase is past. You have returned to the fold and will not stray again. Days spent on the tops are the best days of all, and your enthusiastic account of your adventures during your stay at Keswick and eager anticipation of the next convinces me that you have seen the light. May it never grow dim again. No more gaping at nasty steam locos on the Worth Railway!

I am glad you like your new house so much, but what a tragedy that it should coincide with Richard's loss of his job. However, a man who can climb

Easy Gully has obviously enough fortitude to overcome setbacks, and I am sure things will turn out all right for you.

Catherine has promised to write to me again after her next visit to Long Close and tell me about talking her old mum and dad up the hills. Yes, OK, you can too.

AW

X (for Catherine)

LETTER 272: TO MARGARET AINLEY, 7 JULY 1984

38 Kendal Green, KENDAL, Cumbria
7th July 1984

Dear Margaret,

I received your fat parcel of goodies with anticipatory pleasure and for the most part the contents bore glad tidings of another week of high adventure amongst the Lakeland peaks, with some splendid performances, notably the direct ascent of Grasmoor End. You surprise me by reporting that a clear track has formed up this formidable buttress. When I did it all was virgin ground and I didn't expect any followers. Great Gable, too, provided another expedition, as it always does.

I can well understand that your elation at these successes was disturbed by doubts about your proposed move to Norwich. This is a lovely city by all accounts, but the contours are dismaying; in fact there aren't any. Norwich is 50 feet above the sea, according to my map, and a journey of 20 miles is necessary to reach a height of 100 feet. Good country for cycling, but not the sort of landscape that suits me. I would rather stand and look at Great Gable than Norwich Cathedral. If I were you I would delay moving house until Richard is absolutely settled in the new environment with a congenial job and a guarantee of permanency, and in the meantime commute once a fortnight. Brighouse has its faults but you are

349

amongst your ain folk there and within reach of moors and mountains. Norwich is foreign country. And is even without steam locos.

In May I had my first ever holiday in Galloway, and found it delightful, the scenery good, the people friendly and the roads very quiet. I've got a good farmhouse cottage address if you ever want it.

I hope your doubts will soon be resolved. Let me know what happens. Sincerely,

AW

LETTER 273: TO CATHERINE AINLEY, 7 JULY 1984

7/7/84

Dear Catherine,

Thank you for a splendid letter, well written and without spelling mistakes, and telling me of the exciting adventures you had on your holiday. Clearly you are now an accomplished climber. Not many people can claim to have stood on Grasmoor Pinnacle! And I am glad to know you have been on Great Gable and seen the wonderful view.

You are right in thinking that I have some cats. Seven – Totty, Tina, Pixie, Daniel, Dillon, Ginger and Jeffrey – plus two just brought in as strays – one of them, found injured, is just like the one in your photo.

AW

LETTER 274: TO MARGARET AINLEY, 18 OCTOBER 1984

38 Kendal Green, Kendal
18th October 1984

Dear Margaret,

Thank you for a very kind letter and effusive praise for the new book. Some of the pictures don't deserve it, a few (notably the Helvellyn and Blencathra frontispieces) being much too green (a fault of the printer).

As for your Mosedale Horseshoe article, I think 'Cumbria' is the best vehicle for it. The Gazette wouldn't be interested. It must, however, be typed. Send it to Mr Bill Mitchell, Editor. I found it so entertaining that I am very hopeful he would publish it. Just to show that the subject is currently topical you might preface it by saying 'having read the chapter on the Mosedale

Horseshoe in "fellwalking with W" I have written of my own experiences on this magnificent walk' lay off the personal idiosynchracies of your companions a bit and enlarge on the descriptions and emotive effects.

Hope you have now settled down well in the flatlands of Norfolk. Sincerely,

AW

X (for Catherine)

LETTER 275: TO MARGARET AINLEY, 24 MARCH 1985

38 Kendal Green, KENDAL, Cumbria
24th March 1985

Dear Margaret,

I don't want to say I told you so, but events in your new environment seem to be turning out as I expected. Norfolk is not the place to fritter away your life. You are a creature of the hills and should be among them. Norfolk is a foreign country and you are in exile. Nor are the people the same. I only once ventured into East Anglia, by train, and it was significant that none of the other passengers were looking out of the windows: there was nothing to see. I felt suicidal. Not a hill in sight.

Come back <u>home</u>, to where you <u>belong</u>.

I hope you will soon be able to tell me you are doing just that. Yours sincerely,

AW

LETTER 276: TO MARGARET AINLEY, 26 JANUARY 1986

38 Kendal Green, Kendal
26th January 1986

Dear Margaret,

Great news!!

Back to the hills and moors and steam engines.

Now you can start living again

AW

LETTER 277: TO MARGARET AINLEY, 15 JUNE 1986

38 Kendal Green, Kendal
15th June 1986

Dear Margaret,

Thank you for a long and entertaining letter from beautiful Brighouse.

We made a flying visit to Norwich a month ago to see the cathedral and the environment from which you escaped. I can appreciate your feelings, although, to be fair, it is better than Lincolnshire, which is deadly.

Glad you enjoyed the TV series. Everybody seems to have done, but it has had serious side effects. To get away from pressures we went to the north of Scotland last week and I was recognised and accosted five times, at Achiltibuie, Poolwe, Torridon, Spean Bridge and Abingdon – and found 100 letters waiting for me when we got back home. BBC now want me to do a series of five programmes on Scotland next year.

AW

X (for Alfred, not Cath, I've gone off girls who weigh 8 and a half stone)

Thank you too for the catmint bag. Our six cats pounced on it in ecstasy, and, alas tore it to shreds. It was their highlight of 1986.

LETTER 278: TO MARGARET AINLEY, 31 AUGUST 1988

38 Kendal Green, Kendal
31 August 1988

Dear Margaret,

Thank you for your graphic account of a wet week in Lakeland. The weather really has been dreadful lately. We were lucky to get a beautiful week in May near Kyle of Lochalsh. The old magic is still there.

I was interested to learn of the new path to the Pike from the Corridor Route, and particularly of the state of the West Wall Traverse as described by Richard, his report confirming others I had had.

Catherine's kindness in nominating Animal Rescue to receive her sponsorship donations is appreciated. Our thirty cats and kittens and eight dogs now in care wish me to say a big thank you to her.

Next Sunday, the 4th, I shall be on Desert Island Discs. The BBC are to do a television documentary on the Coast to Coast walk. So life goes on.

Yours sincerely,

AWainwright

AW had turned down Desert Island Discs on BBC Radio 4 several times in the past but in 1988 agreed to take part. He wanted to see if Sue Lawley's legs were as good as everyone said, but he refused to go to London to record it. Instead, Sue Lawley came to Manchester. He was driven there by Andrew Nichol of the Westmorland Gazette and afterwards they went to Harry Ramsdens for a slap-up fish and chip supper. The programme was broadcast on 4 September 1988.

Part 22
Readers' Letters, 1979–88

Even in his late seventies, AW was acquiring new correspondents, though with his eyesight getting weak and his body frail, and still doing so many books and TV programmes, he was not keen on long correspondences as he had been in the old days.

Judy Naylor, however, received a regular stream of letters starting in 1981 when she wrote to him with what he said was an unusual request. Mrs Naylor, of Appleby, was a member of a conservation group called Eden Field Club. It was the Year of the Disabled, so she decided to take a group of disabled people on a field trip – but where?

LETTER 279: TO JUDY NAYLOR, 15 JULY 1981

38 Kendal Green, Kendal, Cumbria
15th July 1981

Dear Mrs Naylor,

Thank you for your interesting letter of July 6th.

Your enquiry is so different from others I receive! And it poses a problem I must confess I have never even thought about – until now. I do so applaud your kind intention to give a party of the disabled a day in the country – a splendid gesture – and your choices of venue are excellent.

The Westmorland Borrowdale: from the gate at the Tebay end the road into the valley is narrow and tarred for a mile, and if you wished to start the walk here you would find it almost traffic-free and easy going for wheel-chairs. It leads gently uphill between mature trees with glimpses of Borrowdale Beck down on the right. At the end of the tarmac, just beyond a little bridge over a stream, the open fell on the left is the habitat of many flowers, including birds-eye primrose (not in flower in August) and marsh

354

orchid. The road continues as a rough farm track and soon descends to a bridge over the main beck where there is a delightful bathing pool. As far as the end of the tarmac the road is public and cars used to be parked on the verges there, but the farmer protested and the County Council planned to make a small car park there – whether his has been done I cannot say, not having been in the valley for some years. If it has you could take cars along instead of leaving them by the gate (there will be a notice there stating whether you can proceed further).

Bretherdale: similarly unfrequented. The tarmac road ends beyond the last farm at a couple of barns where cars can be parked. From this point a rough track continues upstream, probably too rough for wheel-chairs.

Neither valley has any history of note. It is thought that the Roman road from the camp at Low Borrow Bridge entered Borrowdale for a short distance before climbing over the fells. And Borrowdale is the valley where a huge dam and reservoir was proposed a short time ago, a plan that has happily been abandoned or at least postponed. Bretherdale is the place where a golden eagle was first sighted on its return to Lakeland about 15 years ago.

Another outing to suit your requirements would be to Shap Abbey, in a lovely quiet hollow alongside the River Lowther, where the party could perambulate or sit by the river, and of course inspect the ruins. If the Abbey has not been seen by the party before, this is the outing I would most recommend as the one least likely to lead to difficulties.

Let me say again that it is most kind of you to plan this little treat for others less fortunate. I should be interested to learn in due course how you fared.

Yours sincerely,

AWainwright

LETTER 280: TO JUDY NAYLOR, 19 AUGUST 1981

38 Kendal Green, Kendal
19th August 1981

Dear Mrs Naylor,

Thank you for your report on the outing to Borrowdale. I was so glad to learn that the event, blessed by a nice day, was such a success.

Many of your disabled friends must be very restricted in their activities, and you have earned their gratitude by giving them a day to remember. Their smiles of pleasure are your reward.

Yours sincerely,

AWainwright

LETTER 281: TO JUDY NAYLOR, 27 JUNE 1983

38 Kendal Green, Kendal
27th June 1983

Dear Mrs Naylor,

Thank you for your card and syllabus. I would have been glad to attend your outing on June 19th but was away from home. However, I hope to be present on some future occasion. Indeed, I am myself getting to a stage of infirmity that might qualify me for inclusion in the party. Old age, you know!

Best wishes. It is jolly nice of you to give pleasure to others less fortunate. Yours sincerely,

AWainwright

Mrs Naylor had written to him after their annual expedition each year, inviting him along, but he never came. In the summer of 1985, she got a call from a woman asking if she could join the walk with her husband. 'Can he walk?' asked Judy. 'Oh yes,' said the voice. Judy did not at first recognize Betty and AW when they turned up, as no names had been given. They went on the walk and enjoyed it, though AW didn't manage the walk the following year.

LETTER 282: TO JUDY NAYLOR, 27 NOVEMBER 1985

38 Kendal Green, Kendal
27th November 1985

Dear Mrs Naylor,

Thank you for a very kind letter.

I remember with pleasure our visit to Borrow Beck last summer and your generous hospitality. I hope we shall meet again on a similar occasion next year, and again be favoured with a sunny day.

Yours sincerely,

AWainwright

But they did become friends and over the next few years, Judy visited him at home, taking him some Three Nuns tobacco, his favourite. Later, when AW was ill, Judy sat with AW while Betty went shopping.

In 2010, Mrs Naylor, aged ninety-one, had moved to a home on the South Coast. 'I still feel so stupid that I never recognized him that time.'

Another woman who received quite a few letters was a Mary Reinbeck of Carlisle, who shared her memories of the good old days with AW. She died in 2003.

LETTER 283: TO MARY REINBECK, 24 SEPTEMBER 1979

c/o Westmorland Gazette,
KENDAL, Cumbria
24th September 1979

Dear Mary,

Thank you so much for one of the sweetest letters I have ever received.

It was extremely kind of you to write to me in such complimentary terms. I felt better after reading it. All warm inside, you know. It's nice to be told your work is appreciated. People these days take everything for granted.

Your story of your youthful wanderings on the fells was most interesting. With so few walkers around in those early days you certainly didn't lack courage in visiting the wild places you mention, but I am sure you must have enjoyed every step of the way. Sometimes I wish the old days would come back. There was a romance about the Lakes in those days that, sadly, seems to be vanishing. It must be the crowds and the coaches, which we never knew then. Keswick was quiet, and I remember when the only place for a meal at the end of a walk was Dalzell's chip shop – 2s 6d for a full tea.

It is good to know that you can still manage the lesser fells. Don't give up. And when you can no longer climb, just sit outside the caravan and look at them. The mountains are the best friends of all.

Thank you for taking the trouble to write, and for doing it so very nicely.

Yours sincerely,

AWainwright

LETTER 284: TO MR KENYON, I MARCH 1982

38 Kendal Green, Kendal, Cumbria
1st March 1982

Dear Mr Kenyon

Thank you for your letter. I am in a quandary about the drawings you want. I have none of the Lake District at present, but there will be some later in the year, about November, and you may prefer to wait. I have a few of North Wales and Bowland at 12.50 and a number of Scottish mountains at 8 pounds. Would you like me to send you three Scottish ones on approval, that is, you can return them if not to your liking. Or would you rather wait?

Yours sincerely,

AWainwright

LETTER 285: TO MARY REINBECK, 4 MARCH 1983

38 Kendal Green, Kendal
4th March 1983

Dear Mary,

Bless you for an extremely kind and interesting letter.

I share your sentiments about the Eden, most beautiful of all rivers, and really enjoyed exploring its surroundings. I am glad it has given you pleasure.

I was interested to read of your early years in the district especially about your journeys on the now-finished railway over the Solway, which in fact I didn't know even existed until I noticed it on an old map. Don't you think the old days were the best? I do. The romance has gone out of life. As I grow older I am [illegible] by fond memories that never seem to fade.

Thank you again for writing. And may 1983 be a good year for you.

Yours sincerely,

AWainwright

LETTER 286: TO MARY REINBECK, 30 MAY 1988

38 Kendal Green, Kendal
30th May 1988

Dear Mary,

It was nice to hear from you again. Thank you for your kind remarks about the television programmes on Scotland. Can't say I enjoyed doing this much, and I didn't like the background music in places where the silence should have been respected, but on the whole the experience was enjoyable and Carlisle-born Eric Robson was a good companion and always helpful.

Well, time passes and there is no stopping it. Let's count our many blessings and give thank for a good life.

Love to Muffin. We now have eight resident cats, all strays and all much loved.

Yours sincerely,

AW

One lucky correspondent who managed to get two letters from him, neither of any consequence, was Mr H. Davies of North London, who was, at that time, living part of the year at a cottage on the Caldbeck fells. Later he sent AW one of his own books.

LETTER 287: TO HUNTER DAVIES, 31 MAY 1983

38 Kendal Green, Kendal

Dear Mr Davies,

It's a pleasure.

But why a London address when Lakeland is at its enchanting best?

Sincerely,

AWainwright

LETTER 288: TO HUNTER DAVIES, 14 FEBRUARY 1986

38 Kendal Green, Kendal
14th February 1986

Dear Mr Davies,

Thank you for sending me an advance copy of your latest epic publication.

Unfortunately I cannot see to read the blessed thing, my eyes being too bad, and therefore cannot attempt a review.

Looking through it dimly I imagine you have had a lot of fun compiling the book and I hope a sufficient number of readers enjoy it and make the venture worth while.

Yours sincerely,

AWainwright

Other correspondents rarely managed a sequence of letters, but as ever he replied to each reader – whether they were about purchasing one of his drawings – and he sold almost all the originals from his sketchbooks and others, except his guidebooks, for around £10–£12 each, all monies going to Animal Rescue – or boasting how they had climbed al 214 of what were now being called the Wainwrights.

LETTER 289: TO MR SMITH, 30 JULY 1980

38 Kendal Green, Kendal, Cumbria
30th July 1980

Dear Mr Smith,

Many thanks for your letter. The recital of some of your Lakeland adventures struck a chord with more, I also having suffered many agonising races against the clock in the years when I had no car and had to rely on bus services.

The original drawings are always sold for charity. The next batch will be of the Eden Valley and may not be of much interest to you, but these will be followed in the late autumn by a set of 100 from a book, Lakeland Mountain Drawings, amongst them being a nice one of Harrison Stickle.

The Westmorland Gazette maintain a mailing list for out-of-town readers and advise them of each new publication, with details of the sale of the drawings. I have asked the Gazette to add your name to the list, so that you will get advance notice.

Best wishes,
Yours sincerely,

AWainwright

LETTER 290: TO GRAHAM WILKINSON, 9 SEPTEMBER 1982

c/o Westmorland Gazette, KENDAL
9th September 1982

Dear Mr Wilkinson,

It was a joy to receive and read your account of adventures in the Howgills and Lakeland and to browse through your fine accompanying photographs. What memories you revived for me! Not for years have I seen most of the scenes you depict so well and recollections were fading. It's so nice to be reminded!

Yes, as a wearer of glasses for the past 60 years I met the same problems as yourself in rain and wet mist. I used to wonder if I could devise wind-screen wipers with matches, but, being an innocent in technical matters, made no progress with the idea.

Thanks again for the pleasure your letter gave me, and for the time and trouble of writing. And of course for the photos.

May you enjoy many more happy seasons of fell wandering – in dry conditions.

Yours sincerely,

AWainwright

LETTER 291: TO GRAHAM WILKINSON, 3 DECEMBER 1985

c/o Westmorland Gazette, KENDAL
3rd December 1985

Dear Mr Wilkinson,

Thank you for your kind letter and enclosure. Yes I remember your earlier letter about the Howgills – still a very favourite area for me. I often return to them.

You ought to be ashamed to associate your name with Burness F.C.

how are the mighty fallen! Their decline over the past ten years has been amazing. Perhaps Blackburn Rovers will take them over. I still watch the Rovers twice a year, but football is not as entertaining and exciting as it used to be. There are sweepers and strikers today and nobody keeps to his allotted position. There are no wingers like Jack Bruton today, more's the pity. Anyway, there are always the hills.

Yours,

AW

LETTER 292: TO MARTYN, 19 JANUARY 1983

c/o Westmorland Gazette, KENDAL
19th January 1983

Dear Martyn,

Thank you for your interesting letter. I add my congratulations to the many you must have had on climbing all the 214 fells in Lakeland. I wish I could say you have broken a record, but in fact over the past few years I have had many letters from others who have done the same.

I envy your ambition to get to the top of all the Munros – a formidable enterprise indeed. Don't judge the Scottish mountains by the Cairngorms. Wait until you have been to Glencoe and Wester Ross and Torridon and Sutherland – these are the areas where the most magnificent mountains are to be found they put the Lakeland fells to shame. I wish you well.

I know Lammack quite well. My early years in Blackburn were spent in the Audley and Shadworth areas.

Thank you again for writing to me.

Yours sincerely,

AWainwright

LETTER 293: TO TREVOR DAVYS, 10 AUGUST 1983

38 Kendal Green, Kendal, Cumbria
10th August 1983

Dear Mr Davys,

Thank you for a very kind letter and a most interesting account of your recent holiday in Lakeland. How fortunate you were with the weather! About Knock Murton: it does seem a surprising omission, but the reason for leaving it out of the Overlying Fells was the reference I made to it on page Blake Fell 4 in the Western Fells book – that the summit had been sealed off by a Forestry Commission fence and was therefore out of bounds for walkers. I call it 'the forbidden peak'. At the time, I climbed the fence and went to the summit, finding it delightful (as were the bilberries!) but I really couldn't recommend a trespass, especially by OAPs.

I greatly appreciate your generous comments and thank you again for taking the trouble to write, and for doing is so nicely.

Yours sincerely,

AWainwright

LETTER 294: TO MRS HARGREAVES, 15 JULY 1984

38 Kendal Green, Kendal
15th July 1984

Dear Mrs Hargreaves,

Thank you for your very kind letter.

I am so glad you now have a photograph of Innominate Tarn. This will seem to bring your husband closer, and I am sure it will be a source of comfort and that it will have pride of place in your home. It was extremely thoughtful of Mr Boucher to provide it for you. As you say there are still people who go out of their way to show consideration for others. Well done, Mr Boucher.

With all good wishes,

Yours sincerely,

AWainwright

LETTER 295: TO BOB, 1 MAY 1985

38 Kendal Green, Kendal, Cumbria
1st May 1985

Dear Bob,

Thank you for your letter, copy of magazine and photos. The Litt memorial photo is excellent, and I am glad to know it is surviving the years. The one of the shelter of Great Borne does not revive any recollections: I must have missed it. Remarkable to find it in so unfrequented a spot: I think it must have been erected by the local shepherd for his own use. Don't mention Black Hill to me! I hope your campaign for loans (and new prints) is doing well enough to justify your optimism.

Yours sincerely,

AWainwright

In 1986 AW got a letter from a Mrs Patricia Brooks of Ipswich, who asked him if he remembered a relation of hers, a noted Kendal doctor called Dr Cockill. He did his rounds on a pony and trap, and during the war took it upon himself to destroy peregrine falcon's eggs as he believed falcons were killing off pigeons which were being used by the RAF to carry messages.

LETTER 296: TO MRS BROOKS, 14 DECEMBER 1985

c/o Westmorland Gazette, KENDAL
14 December 1985

Dear Mrs Brooks,

Thank you for a most interesting letter that carried my mind back to my early years in Kendal: they were the wartime years when the area was a reception centre for evacuees. I knew Dr Cockill; he was given the Freedom of the Borough for his services. You were probably fortunate with the weather on your recent visit to the Lakes at the end of the wettest summer I can remember.

Best wishes,
Yours sincerely,

AWainwright

AW kept copies of many of his letters – either a carbon if they were typed or an exact handwritten copy if they were not. At the end of the following letter to someone called Julian in 1986, Betty has written on the copy 'Forthright as always!'

LETTER 297: TO JULIAN, 2 MARCH 1986

c/o Westmorland Gazette, KENDAL
2nd March 1986

Dear Julian,

I have received your letter and enclosures, but cannot help you on principle. In my young days if I wanted to do something special, I had to save my own money until I could afford it, or do without. The idea of begging money from strangers to further my own purposes was unheard of. This is a principle that should be followed today.

Sincerely,

AWainwright

LETTER 297: TO MRS AUSTEN, 2 SEPTEMBER 1986

c/o Westmorland Gazette, KENDAL
2nd September 1986

Dear Mrs Austen,

Thank you for your interesting letter. It was certainly a splendid performance by your son (and his father!) to complete the Coast to Coast walk in such fine style and I hope they both enjoyed the adventure.

I get many reports of family parties who have done this walk but I have never heard of an 11year old (or less) having done it. Perhaps your son has broken a record! In any case he has every reason to be proud of his fine achievement.

Your sincerely,

AWainwright

LETTER 299: TO MR SAGER, 21 OCTOBER 1986

c/o Westmorland Gazette, KENDAL
21st October 1986

Dear Mr Sager,

Thank you for your kind letter. It is always a pleasure to hear from others who share my love of the Lakeland fells, as you so obviously do.

Your climbing of all the 214 fells, especially as you live so far from the district, was a splendid performance for which you have my congratulations. I was not aware of the omission of mile 214 from page 83, and was amazed when I looked it up to confirm what you say. I don't think I can blame the printer. It was an aberration on my part which I find very difficult to understand.

Yours sincerely,

AWainwright

LETTER 300: TO MR SAGER, 17 OCTOBER 1987

c/o Westmorland Gazette, KENDAL
17th October 1987

Dear Mr Sager,

Thank you for a kind and interesting letter.

Let me satisfy your curiosity on the matter you raise. True I was born and brought up in Lancashire but both my parents came from Penistone near Sheffield, so that I am never sure whether to call myself a Lancastrian of a Yorkshireman. I have always felt an allegiance to both counties.

Glad you enjoyed the book, and thanks again for writing to tell me so.

Yours sincerely,

AWainwright

A lady called Marjorie – no surname or details are known, as the letters were bought from a dealer by a Wainwright fan – got two letters, in which AW is saying that at his age, he feels it is time to retire.

LETTER 301: TO MARJORIE, 9 FEBRUARY 1986

38 Kendal Green, Kendal, Cumbria
9th February 1986

Dear Marjorie,

It was a pleasure to read your delightful account of recent wanderings on the Lakeland fells. What memories your words bring back to me! And memories are all that is left to me. I am now in my 80th year and no longer able to get up to the tops and ridges as I used to. Now I have to be content with writing about them. But I still regard days spent on the fells as the best days of all. Today, from my window, I can see them arrayed in mantels of pure white, but for me they are out of bounds. I don't complain. Instead I count the blessings of a very long innings of infinite delight. So I think you should take every opportunity to return to the beauty of the Lakes while you are still able to enjoy walking on the hills.

Thank you for troubling to write, and please do so again when you have further adventures to relate. I hope you have a splendid summer and many happy expeditions.

Yours sincerely,

AWainwright

LETTER 302: TO MARJORIE, 11 MAY 1987

38 Kendal Green, Kendal, Cumbria
11 May 1987

Dear Marjorie,

Thank you for another kind and delightful letter, as usual a joy to read.

It is good to know that you have enjoyed further expeditions on the fells since you last wrote, and in particular I am glad you have successfully accomplished the Gable Girdle despite unfavourable weather. But, as you say, this walk is a memorable experience in any conditions.

This summer I shall be busily engaged in Scotland, filming a series of five TV programmes with the BBC, recalling the highlights of my travels in the Highlands over the past forty years. My swan song, surely. It really is time I retired. But for you I wish many more happy expeditions on the fells in the years ahead.

Yours sincerely,

AWainwright

LETTER 303: TO ALYN BARNES, 3 FEBRUARY 1987

c/o Westmorland Gazette, KENDAL
3rd February 1987

Dear Mr Barnes,

Thank you for your kind letter and birthday wishes.

Your question rather surprised me because I never regarded a camera as essential. I did carry one, though, but only to record features of interest, not with any thought of picturing superb landscapes. My first, 45 years ago, was an Ensign (?), and later I used a secondhand Baldur (German). They would seem antiquated by comparison with today's cameras!

Yours sincerely,

AWainwright

LETTER 304: TO ROBERT HARDCASTLE, 23 FEBRUARY 1987

c/o Westmorland Gazette, KENDAL
23rd February 1987

Dear Mr Hardcastle (I think; sorry I could not decipher your name)

Thank you for your letter. It is always a pleasure to hear from others who share my love of the Lake District, as you so obviously do.

You point out an error in 'Ex-fellwanderer' with such conviction that I am sure you are right. I remember the year as 1963 and wrongly assumed that it was the end of that year when Lakeland was transformed into a fairyland by a three-months frost. I remember the conditions so well: it was a glorious winter. Thank you for putting me right and taking the trouble to do so.

Yours sincerely,

AWainwright

LETTER 305: TO ROBERT CHESTER: 3 APRIL 1987

c/o Westmorland Gazette, KENDAL
3rd April 1987

Dear Mr Chester,

Thank you for a very kind letter.

I can sympathise with you about miseries inflicted by Scottish midges. To avoid their attention make your visits to Scotland before the end of May or after the end of September. They don't trouble me as I am usually in a halo of tobacco smoke. They never bother people who chain-smoke cigarettes. They are afraid of getting lung cancer.

I have had dozens of letters and photographs of the rowan tree at

Buttermere over the years and am confident that this is the subject of your picture, its stunted growth due to a lack of nourishment for its restricted root system.

Yours sincerely,

AWainwright

LETTER 306: TO IAN SAGER, 19 APRIL 1987

c/o Westmorland Gazette, KENDAL
19th April 1987

Dear Ian,

Thank you for your kind letter.

In reply to your enquiry, all my hand-written books are reproduced from original manuscripts of exactly the same size, nothing being reduced or enlarged.

Yours sincerely,

AWainwright

LETTER 307: TO KEN PROCTER, 20 JANUARY 1988

38 Kendal Green, Kendal, Cumbria
20th January 1988

Dear Mr Procter,

Thank you for a kind and very interesting letter.

It is always a great pleasure to hear from others who share my love of the Lake District, as you so obviously do, and it was an added delight to read of your earlier life in Blackburn in circumstances akin to mine. I agree with you that those early times were happy in spite of the many disadvantages of life in those days. Blackburn's town centre today has lost all its former interest. I go back there only twice a year to watch the Rovers and am always glad to get away.

Your apprenticeship on the Lakeland fells was also similar to mine. Early visits were like magic, and the beauty of the scenery has never palled even after nearly fifty eyars of living amongst it.

I hope you are able to continue your visits and enjoy many more happy expeditions in the years ahead.

Yours sincerely,

AWainwright

The Milton Mountaineers, referred to in a letter by George Male in January 1988, were a group of blind climbers.

LETTER 308: TO GEORGE MALE, 24 JANUARY 1988

24th January 1988

Dear Mr Male,

Thank you for your letter and its kind invitation to me to become President of the Milton Mountaineers, which I count as a great honour, having admired their performances over many years.

My own failing eyesight would seem to be a fitting qualification for the position but after much thought I am forced to the conclusion that old age would not, and must gratefully decline. I am now in my eighties and unable to get around as I used to. I am much too ancient to take on commitments I could not fill properly.

However, I am still capable of standing treat for you all on the occasion of your assault of Blencathera and enclose a cheque to pay for the dinner etc. We shall not be able to join you. For the week commencing May 14th we are already booked for a log cabin near Plocton.

Yours sincerely,

AWainwright

LETTER 309: TO VALERIE AND JOHN MALLAM, 30 DECEMBER 1986

c/o Westmorland Gazette, KENDAL
30th December 1986

Dear Mr and Mrs Mallam,

Thank you for a very kind and most delightful letter.

Your experience in Yordas Cave was extraordinary. In several visits I have never seen lighted candles there and I am curious about their origin. So far as I know the cave has no religious associations.

Your letter was both interesting and enjoyable, and a joy to read.

Thank you for taking the trouble to tell me of your adventures. I hope you continue to have many more happy expeditions in the year ahead.

With best wishes for 1987,

Yours sincerely,

AWainwright

LETTER 310: TO VALERIE AND JOHN MALLAM, 15 AUGUST 1987

38 Kendal Green, Kendal, Cumbria
15th August 1987

Dear Valerie and John,

It was a pleasure to hear from you again and to learn more of your adventures in Limestone Country (and around Kendal Green!). You are the first to report completing all the walks in my book, and I can well appreciate your regret at coming to the end. I felt exactly the same: it is an area of which I am particularly fond and I thoroughly enjoyed every expedition I made there. All had their delights and surprises and excitements, Ingleborough perhaps most of all. Hunting all the named potholes and caves was my particular joy.

I have long given up hope of having my lost pipe returned to me. Countless searches have been undertaken according to correspondents. It is still there somewhere.

I hope Ingleton lives up to expectations and that you find more of the delights of limestone country.

Yours sincerely,

AWainwright

The Mallams of Shrewsbury wrote to AW several times, and received several letters back. At first, he gave his address as c/o the Westmorland Gazette, as he usually did with fans, but when he moved on to revealing his home address and calling them Valerie and John, they became emboldened enough to try to doorstep him. He wasn't in. However, they did a lap of honour around the Green and then pinched a pebble from his drive. They confessed this in a letter to him, hence AW's reference to 'around Kendal Green!', complete with exclamation mark. It was a warning to him that he should not become too familiar or reveal his real address to often, just in case the hordes descended.

Part 23
Tax Dramas and Official Business, 1988-90

On 21 March 1988 AW got a letter from the Inland Revenue saying that his affairs were being investigated. He was by now a well known TV presenter and author, his latest handsomely illustrated book from Michael Joseph always on the bestseller list. In all, going back to his early guides first produced by the Westmorland Gazette, and still selling well, almost 2 million copies of his books had been sold. Some tax official had clearly been puzzled by the fact that in his tax returns, his income appeared so relatively low. Was some sort of fiddle going on?

LETTER 311: TO INLAND REVENUE, 27 APRIL 1988

38 Kendal Green, Kendal
27th April 1988

Dear Sir,

I have your letter of the 25th Inst.

In reply to your enquiry, I submitted my tax return of income for 1987/8 to your office at Bootle, whence it originated, a week ago. This return included the following statement of my income from royalties received in that year:

Royalties received from Westmorland Gazette: 19, 173

Royalties received from Michael Joseph, Ltd: 8, 427

An amount of 576 was also included from Public Lending Rights.

My payments to charities out of this income amounted to 577 and is included under the heading of Covenants.

I would remind you that I have signed the Declaration that the above statements are correct, and frankly I resent the continuing inference that I am evading or avoiding tax. On the contrary I would point out that in more than thirty years of writing for various publishers I have never submitted any claim for legitimate expenses such as postages, films and film processing, stationary, travelling expenses and so on, all necessary in the compilation of my books and which must over the period amount to around 10,000.

Please let me hear from you soon that you have completed your enquiries to your satisfaction and that the matter is closed.

Yours faithfully,

AWainwright

The matter was not closed, and more letters and requests arrived from the Inland Revenue. What had made AW furious was the inference that he was avoiding payments in some way, which he knew he was not, so he was determined to fight back – even though he had so much proper work to do, in the way of books and films, and at the age of eighty-one, his physical health, if not his mental health, was declining.

A year later, in March 1989, he finally had a face to face meeting with the Inspector – and AW wrote a letter to himself, describing what happened.

LETTER 312: TO HIMSELF, 21 MARCH 1989

On March 14 1989 the Inspector wrote suggesting a meeting, and this duly took place at 38 Kendal Green, Kendal, on 20th March.

I had formed an image of him as a little bald-headed man with pince-nez but he turned out to be a strapping young fellow with a beard and a friendly disposition. He introduced himself as Mr Ibbs and said he was an Investigations Officer based in the Kendal Office.

First I asked him what had prompted this investigation, which I felt to be entirely without justification as I had always declared my income fully and paid all tax due; further, I had letters from his office every year agreeing my computations of the tax due. So why this investigation? Well, he said, it was known to the Inland Revenue that some of my books had appeared in best-selling lists and were very widely distributed: it seemed to them that possibly I was not declaring all my earnings from royalties.

He agreed that I had paid tax over the years on all royalties I had actually received. This was not the point at issue. His concern was that I had renounced some of my royalties in my contracts with publishers by signing a clause in the following terms:

'I hereby renounce all legal rights to the royalties from this book and leave their distribution to the discretion of the publishers'.

He had serious doubts about the wording of the clause. He admitted he was not an expert on contracts but felt that such a clause may not be considered to be legally effective. If such was the case I would be required to pay tax on all the royalties I had renounced (involving arrears of probably over 100,000); in other words if the clause was proved not be watertight my liability to tax would be the same as if not renunciations of royalties had taken place.

This was the main object of his investigation. I disagreed, pointing out that income tax was a tax on income received and could never be a tax on no income against which he argued that the renounced royalties were nevertheless earned by me and therefore my income which I had diverted elsewhere.

My Ibbs said that in the event of his doubts about the validity of the renunciation clauses being confirmed when his investigations were completed and I was held responsible for tax on the renounced royalties, it would now be necessary for him to make 'protective assessments to keep my file open and subject to review over the six years allowed by law for the recovery of debts. He would therefore be sending additional assessments going back to 1982/3.

The meeting ended without Mr Ibbs being offered a cup of tea.

– – –

The protective assessments arrived a few days later, requiring me to pay 20,000 for 1982/3 and 45,000 for 1983/4.

By imposing these assessments the Inspector made his greatest blunder. It was clear that he had not done his homework properly and had assumed that in both years there had been renounced royalties. But in neither year had I signed contracts with renunciation clauses. The renouncing of royalties did not commence until 1984/5. For the two years 82/3 and 83/4 I had declared and paid tax on all royalties received and no further tax could possibly be due. From then on the Inspector was on the defensive. His mistake was made clear to him but he never admitted it, nor did he countermand his instruction to the Collector to demand payment in accordance with his assessments. This was the start of an uncomfortable time for Mr Ibbs. I had him on the run, as the ensuing correspondence shows.

AW might have thought he had the Inspector on the run, but the letters and demands continued. One thing which had made them suspicious was their discovery that the Treasurer of Animal Rescue, to which so many of his royalties were going, was a Mrs Betty Wainwright.

LETTER 313: TO INLAND REVENUE, 29 MARCH 1989

38 Kendal Green, Kendal
29th March 1989

Dear Sir,

I return herewith your additional assessments for 1982/3 and 1983/4 for cancellation. They should not have been sent to me.

I already have your assurance, both in writing and verbally, that you are satisfied that I have paid tax on all taxable income received in those years, and your researches will have proved that I had no contracts carrying a renunciation clause in either year.

I must say that my hackles are rising at this continuing and unwarranted harassment, and although I know from experience that it is not the practice of the Inland Revenue to say sorry for their mistakes I do feel that a profound apology is called for in this instance.

LETTER 314: TO INLAND REVENUE, 6 APRIL 1989

38 Kendal Green, Kendal
6th April 1989

Dear Sir,

My wife has told me of your telephone call of two days ago.

You are demanding from me an additional payment of 65,000 in tax for the years 1982/3 and 1983/4 over and above the tax paid for those years, and agreed between us. You must now justify the additional assessment, if you can, by stating the dates and amounts of royalties alleged by you to have been received by me in those two years. If you cannot give substance to the additional assessments they should be cancelled. If, as you have suggested, the 65,000 is merely a fiction designed to keep my tax affairs open for those years you should not put me to the trouble of taking part in a paper chase of your own making by requiring me to complete more forms to let you off the hook.

I find it incredible that your tactics require you to make a charge and investigate later, when surely common sense dictates that you should first make your investigations and then charge only if necessary. Professor Parkinson must be writhing in his grave.

You say that you are acting in accordance with income tax law. Quote me chapter and verse where the law imposes on you a duty to charge tax on income that has not been received and that you know jolly well has not been received.

Please reply in writing and not by telephone or interview.

AW

LETTER 315: TO INLAND REVENUE, 19 APRIL 1989

38 Kendal Green, Kendal
19th April 1989

Dear Sir,

I am not in the least surprised that your letter of the 11th avoids my request for details of the royalties forming the basis of your demand for a further payment of 65,000 for the years 82/3 and 83/4. I am entitled to this information and repeat my request.

It is now almost a year since you started an investigation into my tax affairs and if you had spent a little of this time checking my file for the two years in question you would have found that I declared all my earnings, that your office wrote to me agreeing to my figures, that I had no contracts containing renunciation clauses and that I paid all tax due in full. I do not owe a penny more in tax for these two years and in demanding a further 65,000 you have scored a spectacular own goal.

I enclose a letter received from the BBC, which states that renunciation clauses have been in common use in their contracts for many years in cases where contributors to their programmes have waived their rights to fees, preferring them to be donated elsewhere, and that in all cases the renunciation has been accepted without question as absolving the signatories from any liability to tax on such fees. I am sending copies of this letter to all the parties you have involved in your enquiries, and I trust that its terms will resolve your doubts as to the validity of such clauses.

I am still awaiting an explanation of the reason why you have demanded tax at 40p on the whole of my royalties for 1987/8 after Mr

Lawson had promised me the basic rate of 25p. There has clearly been a considerable overcharge and overpayment and I hereby apply for a refund of the amount overpaid with interest at the rate charged by the Inland Revenue on overdue demands, and shall expect a corrected demand for the second instalment falling due in July.

Please reply in writing.

AWainwright

LETTER 316: TO INLAND REVENUE, 11 MAY 1989

38 Kendal Green, Kendal, 11th May 1989

Dear Sir,

The salient facts for 1982/3 and 1983/4 are as follows:

I have paid all the tax due from me.

Your records show that I have paid all the tax due from me

Your office has written to me agreeing my computations

You have demanded a further 65,000 by additional assessments

You admit that there is no substance in these assessments and still do not explain how you arrived at your estimates.

You have proved that, contrary to popular belief, fiction can be stranger than the truth. You should kill the additional assessments stone dead, not give them a lingering death by appeal or postponement. Or, if you prefer, try to prove to the Court that I owe and refuse to pay 65,000. Either way you get egg on your face and it is self-inflicted.

I am told by Michael Joseph that you have now changed tack and are not questioning the renunciation clause but instead seeking evidence that I nullified the discretion given to them by instructing them, in writing or verbally, to whom the renounced royalties should be distributed. You have again landed yourself in a dead end. I have never given such an instruction, in writing, or verbally, nor sought to do so. In any case you are out of date: it has been permissible for some years for the signatory to a renunciation clause to state the name of the Charity he wishes to benefit.

I too have gone on a different tack. I told you at our meeting that although I had been writing books for publication for almost 40 years I had never claimed my full business expenses. This benefaction to the Inland Revenue has now ceased. Take notice that in my current tax return for 1989/90 I have included 1,000 for office accommodation and 10,000 for secretarial and chauffeuring services.

You mentioned in one of your letters that I had never declared the royalties I had renounced. Of course I did not. The tax return requires to know all income received, not income that might have been received if circumstances had been different.

I note that you agree I have been overcharged on my royalties for 1988/9 but cannot understand why the overpayment cannot be adjusted for many months. I intend to withhold payment of the second instalment until I receive a corrected assessment.

I applaud your intention to get a ruling on renunciations from the Board of Inland Revenue. If you had done this in the first place such wasted time might have been saved.

At our interview you gave me certain assurances that I would now like to see in writing:

Are you satisfied that I have in every year paid tax on all royalties actually received by me?

Do you confirm that in all the years under review your office has written to me confirming their agreement with my computations?

You have been provided with the audited accounts of the Charities that have received donations from publishers equivalent to the renounced royalties. Are you satisfied that all such donations have been fully accounted for? In this connection you made a snide remark that, even so, I could have appropriated some of the money for personal use, a suggestion I found extremely offensive and ask you to withdraw; if you had studied the accounts intelligently you would know that this has not happened. On the contrary I have contributed generously to Animal Rescue out of taxed income.

You were insensitive enough to send me a leaflet on income tax fraud default or neglect. Am I suspected of fraud? Or default? Or neglect?

Please let me have your answers in full, as statements of fact and not merely as a Yes or No. I am compiling a dossier on the antics of the Kendal Tax Office, including our correspondence, and have a publisher eager to give it national coverage by a press release. I intend to call it A Black Comedy but doubt whether you would find it amusing.

In May 1989, AW sent a postcard to Mr Ibbs, Tax Inspector, from Wester Ross, where he and Betty were on holiday.

LETTER 317: TO INLAND REVENUE, 23 MAY 1989

Dear Mr Ibbs,
    Even on holiday
    In faraway Scotland
    I am thinking of you.
    Wish you were here.

In June, 1989 at long last, the Inland Revenue agreed that AW had not been guilty of income tax evasion.

LETTER 318: TO INLAND REVENUE, 21 JUNE 1989

38 Kendal Green, Kendal
21st June 1989

Dear Sir,

Thank you for your letter of the 15th informing me that the Board of Inland Revenue had confirmed that the renunciation clauses in my contracts with publishers were valid and absolved me from any tax liability on the royalties thereby renounced.

The outcome was as I expected and never really in doubt. It is nice of you to express pleasure at the decision when you must have felt some disappointment at drawing a blank after spending a year of your life barking up the wrong trees and exploring blind alleys that led nowhere. You will surely realise now that it would have been far better to have obtained the Board's opinion before starting an exercise that wasted so much of your time and the time of others. For my part I must say I found it galling to reflect that I was contributing to your salary while you were seeking to prove or disprove that I was a villain.

Your difficulty was in failing to interpret correctly the word 'renounce'. The word has no hidden or double meaning: It is exact, absolute and conclusive. When King Edward VIII renounced the throne there was no investigation into his intention, no doubt about his meaning. To renounce a thing is to give up all rights and entitlement to it.

Of course I appreciate that you were doing your duty as you saw it. In two respects, however, you exceeded your authority. You had no right to enquire how the publishers had distributed the renounced royalties, their discretion in this matter being absolute, and it was no business of yours to ascertain how the charities benefiting had spent the money they received.

You must now call off your Cumbernauld dogs, who are pursuing me with the ferocity of Rottweilers and threatening distraint or Court proceedings if I do not pay promptly the sums raised by your additional assessment. I have warned the Collector that unless he desists he will face a Court hearing for unlawfully demanding money with threats. I will spare you the discomfiture of replying to my letter of 11th May.

Nor will I embarrass you further by sending a presentation copy of the dossier I am compiling to the Board of Inland Revenue as I intended and will content myself by circulating it only amongst the people you have involved by your enquiries.

Now that this sorry saga has come to an abortive end I believe I can claim compensation for the disruption caused to my life over the past twelve months by your investigations, for the distress to my wife, for the harassment resulting from your Collector's unlawful demands and threats, and for the costs incurred by the solicitor in carrying out your instructions. I am prepared to settle this claim for a modest single payment of 5,000. Please make your cheque payable to Animal Rescue, Cumbria.

AW

AW never got his compensation, and probably didn't expect it, but he had won. He then carefully bundled up all the correspondence, having kept exact carbon copies of all his letters, and those from the Inland Revenue, plus copies of documents from the BBC and Michael Joseph which he had been obliged to seek. He tied the bundle with a pink ribbon, in best legal style, and wrote a covering note on the front which he entitled 'A Dossier of the Antics of the Tax Office – a Black Comedy.'

As a postscript, as he waited for any reply from the Inland Revenue to his last letter, he added: 'No replies have been received from the Inspector or the Collector to my letters of 20 and 21 June, nor have these gentlemen been heard of since. It is perhaps premature to assume they have fled the country. They may, of course, simply be hiding under their desks.'

AW had expended a great deal of energy on the correspondence, but there was clearly part of him which enjoyed it, knowing he was in the right, and also knowing from his own long experience in local government the bureaucratic mentality and how to play them at their own game.

While this Inland Revenue battle was going on, AW got taken round Kendal's new shopping centre and heard of the Council plans to erect, oh horrors, a statue in his honour. His letter to the Council Leisure Department is another example of his mastery of the bureaucratic prose and argument, when the need ever arose.

LETTER 319: TO MR GOODALL, KENDAL COUNCIL LEISURE DEPARTMENT, 19 JANUARY 1989

38 Kendal Green, Kendal
19 January 1989

Dear Mr Goodall,

Thank you for your letter of the 14th December and for showing me around the new shopping centre and the site of the proposed exhibition centre last Tuesday.

I found the whole development rather more pleasing than I had been led to expect, apart from the Market Hall, which is a disgrace and a sad misuse of a fine old building. The area has been cleverly planned and the links with the car parks and the Market Hall quite ingenious. My great regret, shared by many other people, is that the design and layout is entirely alien to the old traditions and characteristics of the town and yet another example of the disregard of its unique features shown over the past fifty years by planners, architects and administrators, many of them offcomers who have no feeling for the old town and apparently no knowledge of its ancient history. During the past five decades I have witnessed the draining away of Kendal's former charm and the erosion of its character. The heart has been torn out of the old town and many of its distinctive features destroyed. Most of the quaint buildings and yards have been sacrificed to make way for car parks and modern structures that are totally lacking in visual appeal. It was once a pleasure to walk around the town, but that pleasure has gone.

Bringing Kendal into the twentieth century has been a painful process and inflicted unnecessary wounds. Kendal was a town unlike any other and it has been made ordinary.

This preamble leads to a suggested compromise about the proposed Centre. Had I known of the Council's plans when they were first mooted I would have given them the thumbs down, although of course, deeply aware of and grateful for the honour they were extending to me. I have never sought the limelight, and much of the publicity I have suffered recently has been thrust upon me and is not to my liking. Friends who know me best have expressed to me the opinion that a display such as your Council has in mind would destroy my image, not preserve it. I am therefore not enthusiastic about the proposal, but am aware that a great deal of advance planning has obviously been given to it, which I would not like to be entirely abortive, and after much thought would like to make a suggestion for your consideration to redeem the situation. My suggestion is that the Centre should be made into a true Heritage Centre by staging a permanent exhibition of Bygone Kendal, the main gallery being adapted for this purpose with me coming in round the corner merely as an incident. There is, in any case, far too much space for any memorabilia of mine. I can visualise the entrance gallery used for a descriptive display of Kendal from the earliest times, with a blown-up running commentary by John Marsh illustrated by old prints and maps, with particular reference to the development of Kirkland around the Saxon Church, the Castle, and of course the growth of the woollen industry (for which the Museum has an abundance of artefacts and would doubtless be glad to release some). Then, coming to the 19th century there is ample material for display. Percy Duff has in his keeping the O'Connor collection of photographs taken around 1870–1880 and many he has himself collected: some of these could be blown up to cover the walls: I am thinking particularly of the old Pump Inn and the stage coach in Stricklangate. The drawings and maps in my 'Kendal in the Nineteeth Century' could also be used. Then, around the corner, and leading up to me, the Westmorland Gazette could be let loose to make up a display of the old printing press first used for the Pictorial Guides with the wooden blocks first used, and, under cover, a selection of the original pages of the books they have published, including my original maps of Westmorland and the Antiquities of Cumbria. Then, at the end of the room, there could be a bust of me (not a statue) with photographs of the cottage where I lived, the Town Hall and school and of the dark satanic mills of Blackburn and of the Rovers' ground, together with the few mementos of fellwalking I still have. Upstairs the video room could remain as planned.

The sale of books on the premises would probably be opposed by the local booksellers, but if this is to be permitted the London publishers, Michael Joseph, Ltd. Have made it known to me that they would like a small section for their own display of the cut-out cardboard models and photos they have used in advertising their Wainwright publications.

These are my thoughts on 19th January 1989.

Yours sincerely,

AW

Despite all his fame, nationally and locally, AW received a rather hurtful personal blow in January 1990 from his old publishers, the Westmorland Gazette. He wrote them a furious letter, telling them just what he thought of them.

LETTER 320: TO MR ORR, 18 FEBRUARY 1990

38 Kendal Green, Kendal, 18th February 1990

Dear Sir,

I understand that you have decided not to proceed further with the publication of the book LIMESTONE COUNTRY although the outlay has been approved by your Head Office.

The work of compiling the text of the book, which is now completed, has occupied my time for the past six months, and the photographer you commissioned to supply the illustrations has been engaged on the work for an even longer period and has additionally incurred considerable expenses on films, processing and transport. I am appalled by your callous disregard of our arrangement in abandoning the project without explanation or apology, especially as it follows so closely upon your betrayal of our long-standing agreement that the guidebooks should always be printed in Kendal.

I am sorry to end my long association with the Gazette on a sour note but cannot possibly continue to have a relationship with a firm whose word cannot be trusted.

I must ask you to confirm your decision <u>in writing</u> and <u>immediately</u>, and state, <u>also in writing</u>, your proposals for compensating the photographer, Mr Geldard, and myself for the work we have done for you and which you have now declared abortive.

A copy of this letter has been sent to Mr Stevenson at Westminster Press.

Yours faithfully,

AWainwright

The book Wainwright in the Limestone Dales, with photographs by Ed Geldard, was published by Michael Joseph in March 1991, two months after AW had died.

Part 24
Last Letters to Old Friends and
Old Correspondents, 1985–90

AW kept corresponding to the end, always replying to old friends from the past, even if he had not seen them for decades, and some he could hardly remember, and to his regular writers, fans who had grown into pen friends.

He didn't write a lot to Doris Snape, but then since he had left Blackburn, he usually saw her twice a season, when he went to watch Blackburn Rovers and stayed with her. Her husband Tom Snape, who ran a radio shop in Blackburn, had been one of AW's oldest friends, and together they had begun the Rovers Supporters' Club, but he had died young, in his forties. Even before that, AW often suggested that he and Doris were more than good friends, that she fancied him. Doris, when her husband was still alive, kept a diary and referred to her meetings with AW in code. What happened later, when she was a widow and AW stayed with her? It is hard to tell, though Ruth, AW's wife, was always jealous. Did he think of marrying her when his marriage to Ruth had collapsed – and before Betty came along? Doris's family believe he did suggest it, but there is no evidence. Betty was sensible and mature about his friendship with Doris and never felt threatened. She encouraged him to see Doris, and keep up their friendship which had lasted for so many decades

LETTER 321: TO DORIS SNAPE, 19 MAY 1985

38 Kendal Green, Kendal
19 May 1985

Dear Doris,

First of all, thank you for having me last month, it was a welcome change for me, and greatly enjoyed.

The day after my return was the day fixed for the ascent of Penyghent with the BBC team, and fortunately we were favoured with a brilliantly sunny day. I managed to get to the top, very slowly, in spite of a strong and cold east wind and I think everything went off all right. The BBC team, eight of them, are all very young, in their teens and twenties, even the producer being only in his mid thirties. I get on well with all of them and Betty enjoys their company.

Since then I have been kept fully occupied. The Managing Director of Michael Joseph has been over to see me with a request that I do more books for them, but it seems unlikely that I will be able to. My eyes are getting worse.

There is also a proposal afoot by the Cumbria Tourist Association to set aside a room in Brantwood (John Ruskin's house at Coniston, open to the public) as a Wainwright Memorial Room with a permanent display of my original manuscripts, drawings and so on. I am lukewarm about the idea, especially their intention to have a bust made of me, but the Gazette are very enthusiastic and I think the scheme will develop.

There is also a great deal of publicity going on by the Gazette to find the purchaser of the millionth book which has just been published secretly but specially marked. When the purchaser has been found he is to be given a free week's holiday in a hotel in the Lake District and I have to present him at a dinner with a set of table mats made from my drawings. These sets are selling at 170!

Last week I was with the BBC team again, this time at Haweswater. On the day arranged for filming the weather was awful, with continuous rain, and nothing could be done. But we went there again on the following day and enjoyed a simply glorious walk with the cameras. I almost enjoyed the experience! Next month we area due in Teesdale.

The Pennine way book is to be published on June 12th with a fanfare of publicity. The demand is so great that the publishers have had to order a reprint before publication. I have declined an invitation to be a guest of honour at a celebration at Malham in June, when my fellow guests were to be Mike Harding and Barbara Castle. No thanks!

The football season ended with disappointment for the Rovers, but I have no regrets. They are not good enough for promotion. No need to send any more cuttings, thanks. Cousin Eric at Penistone has been in hospital for ten weeks and is back home but bedfast. I must try to get over to see him later in the summer.

I think that's all my news. I was sorry to learn that you had suffered another fall and hope it had no serious effects and that you and Cindy are both well.

Hope to see you here soon.

Love from Betty and myself to you both

Alf x

Fred Sellers (1906–90) was another old friend from Blackburn, with whom he had worked in the Treasurer's office – where Fred remained all his working life, retiring as Chief Internal Auditor. AW had written to him in 1985 asking if he had any drawings or photographs from their office days as AW wanted to use some in his book Ex-fellwander, published in 1987.

Fred Sellers's daughter Stephanie remembers going with her father as a little girl to visit AW in Kendal in the 1950s – but made to sit outside in the car while her father and AW talked. She thinks now that AW was moaning about his unhappy marriage, an unsuitable topic for a young girl.

In this letter, one line has been blanked out by Fred Sellers himself – and in the margin he has written 'Mistaken – not my story.'

LETTER 322: TO FRED SELLERS, 2 DECEMBER 1985

38 Kendal Green, Kendal
2nd December 1985

Dear Fred,

Kendal's postmaster did what he was requested to do, and it was an unexpected pleasure to receive and read your letter and enclosures. Through the mists of time I recognised your handwriting on the envelope.

I cannot match your activities during the years that have passed. Foreign travel, music and gardening mean nothing to me. You have many wonderful experiences to recall; in comparison my own life has been unexciting and uneventful. I have never been out of the UK, or even south of Lancashire except for an exploration of North Wales. The highlands and islands of Scotland have been my favourite stamping ground for the past 40 years and I have explored all parts of the north of England, writing over 50 books in the process. Twice a year I go to Blackburn to watch the Rovers.

Bob Alker, living in Garslang, provides an obituary service for me, keeping me informed of members of staff who pass on – and there have been many. I had letters from Harold Hirst and Norman Tennant recently; otherwise I have lost touch. It is good to know that Lawrence is still around. I have bee exceptionally fortunate in steering clear of illness. I completed 47 years in local government without missing a day, or even an hour, through sickness, and this good fortune has persisted since retiring from work. Some memories of the old days persist. Concerning yourself I remember the horrendous moment when you opened a bottle of red ink with disastrous results. Blackburn is now almost unrecognisable. Charnleys has disappeared, Penks is a furniture store. Furthergate Church has been dismantled, the town centre has become a maze with many of the old features gone for ever. I liked it better as it was before the planners moved in.

I return the drawings to your custodianship. I am surprised they have survived. Arnold Haworth supplied a few before his death.

I see you have changed your address. You were living in Buncer Lane when last I heard of you.

I hope you keep well, and keep on keeping well for many more years. But there is no hiding the fact that we are both getting bloody old.

Sincerely,

AlfW

Len Chadwick was one of his main researchers on the Pennine Way, to whom he wrote many letters. They never met, and AW never quite knew the extent of his poverty and misfortunes. In 1986, Len had a stroke and was put into a home where he died, alone, in 1987.

LETTER 323: TO LEN CHADWICK, 15 JUNE 1986

c/o Westmorland Gazette
Kendal
12th June 1986

Dear Len,

I was saddened today by a letter from your friend Joan Birchenough telling me that your walking days are over and that you are now confined to a home. I have not heard from you for many years and often wondered if you were alright.

Now you must be content with memories of many happy wanderings on the fells and especially on the Pennines. I know how much you enjoyed those days of freedom on the hills. I hope you can still see the old familiar and well-loved places in your mind's eye, and that recollections of them are source of comfort in your present circumstances.

Yours sincerely,

AWainwright

John and Mary Helps were not regular correspondents – but AW always remembered how they had met – back in June 1954 in Scotland when they were on their honeymoon and he and Henry Marshall were in the first flush of excitement with plans for the Pictorial Guides.

LETTER 324: TO JOHN AND MARY HELPS, 17 JUNE 1986

38 Kendal Green, Kendal
17 June 1986

Dear John and Mary,

Your letter came as an unexpected and very pleasant surprise. Yes, I remember the day well: it was one of the highlights of my life. In fact, only the day before your letter arrived I was looking through my Scottish photographs and looked long and earnestly at the one I took of the three of you at the summit cairn, and wondered what had happened to you. It is good to know that you are well, and share my love of the Lake District. Mr Marshall died in 1964. I have continued my annual pilgrimages to Scotland, and after retiring in 1967 settled down to writing books, having churned out 50 since then.

It was nice to hear from you again. Thank you for a very kind letter and generous donation for the animals.

Sincerely,

AWainwright

Weaver Owen was another voice from the past who suddenly wrote to him – the Kendal bank manger who spent a night on the fells with him around 1949.

LETTER 325: TO WEAVER OWEN, 21 JUNE 1986

38 Kendal Green, Kendal
21st June 1986

Dear Mr Owen,

What a pleasure to hear from you again and to be reminded of happy days spent on the fells in your company. I am living on memories nowadays, my fellwalking days being virtually at an end, and what a blessing they are! Those were happy days!

Kendal was better in those days, too, before its character was destroyed by modernisation. Remember Archie? I still see him quite a lot. I hope you keep in good health, as I do except that my eyesight is failing. But no complaints; I've had a long innings and enjoyed it all.

Sincerely,

AWainwright

During the 1980s, George Howarth, who had been at school with AW and now lived in Arnside, wrote to AW on his birthday every January – and always got a letter back, saying much the same things. But the handwriting and the typing got worse as AW grew unable to see the mistakes he was now making.

LETTER 326: TO GEORGE HOWARTH, 4 FEBRUARY 1987

38 Kendal Green, Kendal
4th February 1987

Dear George and Elsie,

Thank you for your birthday wishes and an interesting letter. I'm glad to learn that you have resumed fell walking, and have some splendid performances to report. I myself am having to be content with memories.

There aren't many Blackburn contemparies of mine left. Almost every week I get word of someone popping off who I knew well. I'm beginning to feel lonely and overlooked!

I still go past Furthergate P.O twice a year on my way to the Rovers.

Thanks for inviting me over to see you. We'll come when the pressures ease.

AW

I hope you can read my scribble. I can't see what my pen is doing these days.

LETTER 327: TO GEORGE HAWORTH, 23 JANUARY 1988

38 Kendal Green, Kendal
23rd January 1988

Dear George,

Thank you for your letter of the 16th and birthday wishes. You got it just right. I was 81 on the 17th, and so far I feel just as I did when 80. I have no complaints either but am rather envious of your recent fellwalking exploits. Crinkle Crags was quite an achievement, one of which to be proud. As for myself I have had to put my boots away for good. I cannot see where I am putting my feet on rough ground and in any case am assailed by breathlessness after effort, so am having to subsist on memories, brought back to mind while sitting in a comfortable rocking chair. Still, as I say, no complaints. Life is good. I still go to Ewood twice a year to watch the Rovers and recapture the old atmosphere although actually I can only glimpse the ball occasionally and cannot recognise the players. Blackburn town centre is a jungle of concrete. Now they are pulling down the railways station.

It's years since I was in Arnside, but will call on you when next we are there.

Yours sincerely,

AW

LETTER 328: TO GEORGE HAWORTH, 19 JANUARY 1989

38 Kendal Green, Kendal
19th January 1989

Dear George,

Thank you for your letter and interesting news of bygone days.

I fell pretty awful for not getting in touch earlier, but life really has been hectic lately and with Betty spending almost every day at our animal shelter, we have simply not been able to go anywhere since last May (the week you were in Skye) when we had a short break at Plockton, where I have booked again for May 20–27 this year.

Yes I remember most of the names you mention: Boddy, street, and Co. There was a Harry Riding, too, and a Miss Haydock, Arts Teacher, who died last year. The Harwood Street area, cleared to make way for a new road that never came, is now a desert and a big Tescos stands on the site of the greyhound track. A friend writes to tell me that the Palace has been demolished. Acrrington Road School has gone completely. Happy Birthday, and I'll try to see you in 1989.

Excuse the typing – I can't see the printout.

Sincerely,

AWainwright

LETTER 329: TO GEORGE HAWORTH, 21 JANUARY 1990

38 Kendal Green, Kendal
21st January 1990

Dear George,

Thank you for your letter and birthday greetings. Time marches on and there is nothing we can do to stop it. Life is ebbing away whether we like it or not.

Failing eyesight has put an end to all outdoor activity for me although otherwise I keep fairly well. I can just see the keys of the typewriter (but not the printout) and keep on writing, but can no longer read. Fortunately I have a wealth of happy memories to occupy my thoughts.

I was in Blackburn a few months ago and don't like the changes there. Now there is talk of demolishing the railway station (sold to Booths). The Palace has been pulled down and the greyhound track in Hill Street has given place to a huge Tesco supermarket . . . only Ewood Park remains as it was although even here the Riverside stand has gone.

Yes we will give you a call in the near future.

Yours sincerely,

AW

Roderick Hamm had written to him in the past. He was the son of an old colleague of AW's, Norman Hamm, who became Borough Treasurer of Blackburn. The book which AW said had inspired him appears to have been Swiss Pictures Drawn with Pen and Ink originally published in 1866 by the

Religious Tract Society. It later appeared in different editions and versions and it is not clear which edition AW was given.

LETTER 330: TO RODERICK HAMM, 1 MARCH 1987

c/o Westmorland Gazette, Kendal
1st March 1987

Dear Roderick,

Thank you so much for your kind letter and good wishes. It was, of course, a surprise to hear from you, but a nice thought on your part to write.

Your letter evoked many memories of half a century ago. I remember your father well and was distressed to learn of his early death soon after I left Blackburn. I remember him giving me a book on the day of my departure: he had bought it for tuppence at a secondhand book shop: it was an illustrated volume on Switzerland containing many pen and ink drawings; he thought I would like it. I did, and in fact it sparked off in me an ambition to do mountain drawings that was to be a dominant interest in later years.

It was nice, too, to see how well you have prospered in your chosen profession. You have done jolly well. Your father would have been proud of your achievements.

Yours sincerely,

AWainwright

LETTER 331: TO RODERICK HAMM, 13 AUGUST 1987

c/o Westmorland Gazette, Kendal
13th August 1987

Dear Roderick,

Thank you for your exceedingly kind letter and invitation to join you and your colleagues at your meeting in January. I count this a great honour.

I am afraid, however, that I am now too old and decrepit to find enjoyment in occasions of this nature and have settled into a senile stupor that rather resents interruption and disturbance. Twice a year I make the effort to attend Ewood Park although my eyes are now so bad that I cannot follow the play. Nor do I take lunch these days.

It seems churlish to decline so kind an invitation. But I am afraid I

must. I am a back number, not obsolete as yet but very nearly so.
Sorry, please forgive.
Yours sincerely,

AWainwright

LETTER 332: TO RODERICK HAMM, 1 SEPTEMBER 1987

c/o Westmorland Gazette, Kendal
1 September 1987

Dear Roderick,

Thank you for your further kind letter.

Our brief correspondence has led to my recalling many half-forgotten incidents of my years at Blackburn with your father. I remember his appointment as Chief Accountant very well and his distressing accident at home that caused a long convalescence during which he developed a strong affection for the works of Charles Dickens. It was his final gesture on my last day at Blackburn when he gave me a book of Alpine drawings he had bought for tuppence at a second-hand bookshop that led to my attempting mountain drawing as a pastime that was to prove so very rewarding. I was later deeply sorry to learn of his passing. He was a good man.

Yours sincerely,

AWainwright

Ken Shepherd was the local photographer in Kendal, to whom AW first started taking his snaps around 1950 for him to develop, print and improve, if he could, for AW was a poor photographer. Ken also did official photos for the Borough Treasurer's office and in 1983, in AW's early TV programme, one of these staff photos was used.

LETTER 333: TO KEN SHEPHERD, 7 MAY 1983

38 Kendal Green, Kendal
7th May 1983

Dear Ken,

So nice of you to write! I was rather apprehensive about appearing on the TV show but mercifully the producer cut out many of my bad moments in front of the camera and I was pleased with the final result.

Yes, those staff photos were yours. I wasn't expecting them – Percy must have supplied them.

With best wishes, and thanks to you both.

AWainwright

LETTER 334: TO KEN SHEPHERD, I MAY 1988

38 Kendal Green, Kendal
1st May 1988

Dear Ken,

Thank you so much for your very kind letter. It was good of you to trouble to write.

Age is telling on me. My pedestrian activities are severely curtailed at present by failing eyesight and a shortage of breath, although otherwise I keep well. But in any case my trips to the Lakes have not the pleasure they formerly had because of the crowds of visitors of the wrong type that now infest the villages and valleys.

I am currently sorting through the enlargements you did for me, the Gazette having suggested publishing a book of my photographs of Lakeland and another of Scotland.

I should of course always be delighted to see you if you cared to walk across sometime.

We are going on a nostalgic return to Plockton on May 13th to see once again some of the places with happy memories for us.

With best wishes,

Sincerely,

AW

W.A. Poucher, the well-known Lake District author and photographer (whose main job was chief perfumer for Yardley) had always been admired by AW since his first book appeared in 1940. When Walter Poucher died in 1988, AW wrote to his son John.

LETTER 335: TO JOHN POUCHER, AUGUST 1988

Dear Mr Poucher,

Your father has been a hero of mine since his *Lakeland Through the Lens* was published. He was a perfectionist with the camera and I greatly admired all his work in the last fifty years. I met him only once as he was returning from three weeks in Scotland when he had never taken a single picture because conditions were never right.

His great love, as mine is, was the Lake District. He will be greatly missed. He had a wonderful innings and I am sure he enjoyed all of it, but a future without a new Poucher is a bleak prospect for me and countless others.

Yours sincerely,

AW

Chris Jesty, who had helped him with maps for some years, received some good news in May 1989. AW had always been against the notion of any revisions being needed for his Pictorial Guides, but now he was thinking of the future life of his guides. He also went on to offer Chris more work on another book he was currently working on, doing a map for what became the Limestone Dales book (the one turned down by Westmorland Gazette, but published later by Michael Joseph).

LETTER 336: TO CHRIS JESTY, 11 MAY 1989

38 Kendal Green, Kendal
11 May 1989

Dear Chris,

Thank you for your letter.

The Gazette and I are in agreement that you area the best person (and indeed the only one we know) capable of revising the Pictorial Guides to the Lakeland Fells and maintaining the neatness of the originals. But we are also agreed that no revision should take place during my lifetime.

If you wish to make a start on this project do so by all means, but bear in mind that I am only 82 and may live for another 20 years, during which time your revisions may themselves need revising.

I may be able to offer you a commission later this year. I am just starting a book on the limestone country around the Three Peaks and will require a quarto-size map of the area between Kirkby Stephen and Malham. I cannot now draw maps myself because of failing eyesight. More about this later.

Yours sincerely,

AWainwright

LETTER 337: TO CHRIS JESTY, 3 JUNE 1989

38 Kendal Green, Kendal
3rd June 1989

Dear Chris,

Thank you for your letter and offer of help.

When the time comes I will give you the place names I need on the map, but am at present so overwhelmed by correspondence and commitments that I haven't found time to put pen to paper for the past two months. I think it may be next spring before I call on your excellent services.

With best wishes,
Yours sincerely,

AWainwright

LETTER 338: TO CHRIS JESTY, 5 NOVEMBER 1989

38 Kendal Green, Kendal
5 November 1989

Dear Chris,

I think I may have a commission for you that would serve to introduce you to the London publishing empire.

I have done a book on the mountains of Lakeland for Michael Joseph Ltd, and a full-page (quarto) map of the district is needed for the frontispiece. I can no longer see to do this myself, much though I would have liked to, and the cartographer Josephs have employed for earlier publications is no longer available through illness.

What is wanted is a very simple map covering the area from Caldbeck in the north to Kendal in the south, and from Ennerdale Bridge to the M6 in the east. A scale of four miles to the inch would probably be needed.

The lakes, major tarns, villages and valleys need including and the principal roads, but all these features must be incidental to the selected summits, which will have to be indicated and named prominently, all else being incidental and relatively faint. A list of the mountains to be named is enclosed: no others need be shown.

If you feel able to tackle this perhaps you would first submit a rough map so that I can include or omit items as necessary. If, however, you do no want to do it or lack the time, please let me know. . . .

Yours sincerely,

AWainwright

LETTER 339: TO CHRIS JESTY, 16 NOVEMBER 1989

38 Kendal Green, Kendal
16th November 1989

Dear Chris,

Thanks for dealing with matters so promptly.

I myself have never sought the permission of the Ordnance Survey for any of their maps I have copied and have never had any trouble, but I understand they have recently been charging royalties for copies as well as reproductions of their maps. It may be as well to get their permission. If you can find the time it might be an idea for you to take the finished map to their office in Southampton and get their OK. If they demand a royalty that is a matter for the publisher to settle.

Yours sincerely,

AWainwright

Forgive the poor typing. I can now barely see to hit the right keys.

LETTER 340: TO CHRIS JESTY, 20 DECEMBER 1989

38 Kendal Green, Kendal
20th December 1989

Dear Chris,

I have now finished the narrative of my book on the Three Peaks area and should be grateful if you would prepare a map for the frontispiece on the scale of one inch = 4 miles. I enclose an old map I have cut out to show the area to be covered. It is OK for roads except for a new Settle bypass but most of the railways have gone.

I enclose a list of the places I would like named. There is no hurry for a few weeks. Please submit a draft for approval.

Jenny Dereham tells me you have been in touch and confirmed no royalty is payable for a copy.

Publishers of the Three Peaks book will be Westmorland Gazette.

Many thanks,

AW

LETTER 341: TO CHRIS JESTY, 28 JANUARY 1990

38 Kendal Green, Kendal
28th January 1990

Dear Chris,

The map has been safely received and is excellent. The publishers, Westmorland Gazette, are also delighted.

It is good of you to suggest no charge but I know the amount of work involved and must ask you to accept the token cheque enclosed.

Yours sincerely,

AWainwright

Christ Jesty went on to be commissioned to revise the Pictorial Guides afer AW's death.

One of AW's last letters was to the Ainleys, with whom he had been corresponding for decades. They had returned to Brighouse – where today, Margaret and Richard, now retired, are still living. Catherine, their daughter, is now thirty-nine, working as a verger at Lichfield Cathedral, married to a priest, still walking in the Lakes and still has the rucksack which AW gave her as a baby.

LETTER 342: TO MARGARET AINLEY, 20 FEBRUARY 1990

38 Kendal Green, Kendal
20th February 1990

Dear Margaret and family,

It was nice to hear from you after a rather long silence, and good to know that all is well and that Brighouse is still the loveliest place in the country. I'm glad you enjoyed the Coast to Coast TV series. It is always fun making these films but the aftermath is less welcome – a flood of letters, all nice but far more than I can cope with. Some have to go unanswered, which grieves me. However it is good to know that you maintain your interest in the great outdoors and faraway places. My walking days are over, I am sorry to have to admit, but can no longer see where I cam putting my feet and that is the signal to quit and sustain myself on memories. Let me know when you have all done the Coast to Coast Walk, and until then keep well and enjoy this wonderful life we have. But take my advice – keep away from Norfolk.

Yours sincerely,

AWainwright

The last known surviving letter from AW was written in October 1990 to his old friend from the Blackburn office days, Bob Alker

LETTER 343: TO BOB ALKER, 16 OCTOBER 1990

38 Kendal Green, Kendal
16th October 1990

Dear Bob,

I cannot possibly make any advance arrangements. I find myself hounded by the media, callers, correspondents, beggars, tax snoopers, animal problems, religious fanatics who since D.I Discs, flood my mail with tracts and implore me to give myself to God. Tomorrow, Monday, I start filming a four-programme TV series on the Coast to Coast Walk which will take me out on location quite a lot shortly. Life is interesting but hectic.

I shall be retiring next spring after completing two more books for Michael Joseph, and not until then will I have free time.

So tell Eric to keep on breathing a while longer and I will see you both next year.

AW

AW never completed that Coast to Coast TV series. He fell ill after three days of filming. He returned home to Kendal and went into hospital. Three weeks later he was allowed home and began to do some gentle typing, but after Christmas he fell ill again and was back in hospital. His heart failed and he died on 20 January 1991, three days after his 84th birthday.

Wainwright's Books and Maps

Pictorial Guides to the Lakeland Fells
1. *Book One:* The Eastern Fells 1955*
2. *Book Two:* The Far Eastern Fells 1957*
3. *Book Three:* The Central Fells 1958*
4. *Book Four:* The Southern Fells 1960*
5. *Book Five:* The Northen Fells 1962*
6. *Book Six:* The North Western Fells 1964*
7. *Book Seven:* The Western Fells 1966*
8. Fellwanderer: *The Story behind the Guidebooks* 1966
9. The Pennine Way Companion 1968*
10. A Lakeland Sketchbook 1969*
11. Walks in Limestone Country 1970*
12. A Second Lakeland Sketchbook 1970*
13. A Third Lakeland Sketchbook 1971*
14. Walks on the Howgill Fells 1972*
15. A Fourth Lakeland Sketchbook 1972*
16. A Coast to Coast Walk: *St Bees Head to Robin Hood's Bay* 1973*
17. A Fifth Lakeland Sketchbook 1973*
18. The Outyling Fells of Lakeland 1974*

Scottish Mountain Drawings
19. *Volume One:* The Northern Highlands 1974
20. *Volume Two:* The North-Western Highlands 1976
21. *Volume Three:* The Western Highlands 1976*
22. *Volume Four:* The Central Highlands 1977
23. *Volume Five:* The Eastern Highlands 1978
24. *Volume Six:* The Islands 1979*

25. Westermorland Heritage 1974*
26. A Dales Sketchbook 1976
27. Kendal in the Nineteenth Century 1977
28. A Second Dales Sketchbook 1978
29. A Furnesss Sketchbook 1978
30. Walks from Ratty 1978

31. A Second Furness Sketchbook 1979
32. Three Westmorland Rivers 1979
33. A Lune Sketchbook 1980
34. A Ribble Sketchbook 1980
35. An Eden Sketchbook 1980

Lakeland Mountain Drawings

36. *Volume One* 1980
37. *Volume Two* 1981
38. *Volume Three* 1981
39. *Volume Four* 1983
40. *Volume Five* 1984

41. Welsh Mountain Drawings 1981
42. A Bowland Sketchbook 1981
43. A North Wales Sketchbook 1982
44. A Wyre Sketchbook 1982
45. A South Walkes Sketchbook 1983
46. A Peak District Sketchbook 1984
47. Wainwright in Lakeland 1983
48. Old Roads of Eastern Lakeland 1985
49. Ex-Fellwanderer 1987
50. Fellwalking with a Camera 1988
51. Fellwalking with Wainwright *with photographs by Derry Brabbs* 1984
52. Wainwright on the Pennine Way *with photographs by Derry Brabbs* 1985
53. A Pennine Journey 1986*
54. Wainwright's Coast to Coast Walk *with photographs by Derry Brabbs* 1987
55. Wainwright in Scotland *with photographs by Derry Brabbs* 1988
56. Wainwright on the Lakeland Mountain Passes *with photographs by Derry Brabbs* 1989
57. Wainwright in the Limestone Dales *with photographs by Ed Geldard* 1991
58. Wainwright's Favourite Lakeland Mountains *with photographs by Derry Brabbs* 1991
59. Wainwright in the Valleys of Lakeland *with photographs by Derry Brabbs* 1992
60. Ordnance Survey Outdoor Leisure Series 1:25 000, Map 33 – Coast to Coast Walk: St Bees Head to Keld 1994
61. Ordnance Survey Outdoor Leisure Series 1:25 000, Map 34 – Coast to Coast Walk: Keld to Robin Hood's Bay 1994

* Books marked with an asterisk have been reissued by Frances Lincoln.

The first fifty books (1–50) were originally published by the Westmorland Gazette, except for: Books 1–5 which had the name Henry Marshall as publisher until 1963 when Westmorland Gazette took them over; No. 30 published by the Ravenglass and Eskdale Railway Co.; No. 47 published by Abbot Hall. Books 51–9 were first published by Michael Joseph; maps 60 and 61 published by the Ordnance Survey in conjunction with Michael Joseph.

Other Wainwright works
Map of Westmorland 1974
Map of Cumbria 1980

Wainwright illustrations in others' publications
Inside the Real Lakeland by A.H. Griffin, Guardian Press, Preston, 1961
Annual Accounts of Southern Lakes and Lune Water Board, 1963–73
Scratch and Co. by Molly Lefebure, Gollancz, 1968
The Hunting of Wilberforce Pike by Molly Lefebure, Gollancz, 1970
The Plague Dogs by Richard Adams, Allen Lane, 1977
Guide to the View from Scafell Pike, Chris Jesty Panoramas, 1978
Climbing at Wasdale Before the First World War by George Sansom,
    Castle Cary Press, 1982

Index